AMERICAN MACCABEE

American Maccabee

THEODORE ROOSEVELT
AND THE JEWS

Andrew Porwancher

PRINCETON UNIVERSITY PRESS
PRINCETON & OXFORD

Copyright © 2025 by Princeton University Press

Princeton University Press is committed to the protection of copyright and the intellectual property our authors entrust to us. Copyright promotes the progress and integrity of knowledge created by humans. Thank you for supporting free speech and the global exchange of ideas by purchasing an authorized edition of this book. If you wish to reproduce or distribute any part of it in any form, please obtain permission.

Requests for permission to reproduce material from this work should be sent to permissions@press.princeton.edu

Published by Princeton University Press
41 William Street, Princeton, New Jersey 08540
99 Banbury Road, Oxford OX2 6JX

press.princeton.edu

All Rights Reserved

ISBN 978-0-691-20366-9
ISBN (e-book) 978-0-691-27163-7

British Library Cataloging-in-Publication Data is available

Editorial: Fred Appel and James Collier
Production Editorial: Kathleen Cioffi
Text and Jacket Design: Katie Osborne
Production: Erin Suydam
Publicity: Kate Hensley and Kathryn Stevens
Copyeditor: Hank Southgate

Jacket image: Glasshouse Images / Alamy Stock Photo

This book has been composed in Arno Pro with Etna

Printed in the United States of America

10 9 8 7 6 5 4 3 2 1

To Kristen

Do not be afraid, for I am with you;
I will bring your children from the east.

—ISAIAH 43:5

CONTENTS

List of Figures xi
Acknowledgments xiii

	Introduction	1
1	Ascent	16
2	Romanian Note	67
3	Kishinev Petition	89
4	Passport Question	126
5	Peace at Portsmouth	155
6	Pogroms	179
7	Appointments & Immigrants	222
8	Election Year	255
	Epilogue	281

Author's Note 289
Abbreviations 291
Notes 293
Index 343

FIGURES

1.1	Lower East Side	17
1.2	Peddler	21
1.3	Theodore Roosevelt, circa 1895	29
1.4	Jacob Riis	36
1.5	Colonel Roosevelt	53
2.1	Oscar Straus	69
2.2	Jacob Schiff	70
2.3	John Hay	73
3.1	"A Skeleton of His Own"	95
3.2	Alice Roosevelt	100
3.3	"One Little Match May Fire the Whole Bunch"	111
3.4	"Stop Your Cruel Oppression of the Jews"	119
3.5	"Excuse Me, I'm Too Busy Weeping over This Delaware Affair"	123
4.1	"All in Favor of the Nomination Will Say Aye!"	133
5.1	Sergei Witte outside the Wentworth Hotel	164
5.2	"Kishineff Must Be Paid For—with Interest"	172
6.1	"The Russian Idea of Freedom"	181
6.2	"Hands across the Sea"	188
7.1	Ellis Island	245
9.1	Theodore Roosevelt, post-presidency	282

ACKNOWLEDGMENTS

My debts are many; my gratitude runs deep. Numerous people and institutions helped make this book possible. I was the beneficiary of an Ernest May Fellowship at Harvard University, which afforded me unobstructed time to research and write. Many thanks to Professors Logevall and Ferguson for the opportunity and to the other fellows in my cohort who provided good cheer and good feedback. Yet another fellowship brought me to the University of Texas where the Clements Center hosted me in the early days of this project. I am grateful to its director at the time, William Inboden, who needed little convincing that religion has played a vital, if often overlooked, role in American foreign policy. Throughout the project, Professor Jonathan Sarna of Brandeis University generously offered his advice.

Princeton University Press has been a wonderful publisher. My editor, Fred Appel, is always encouraging and exceedingly patient. I am grateful to his colleagues at the press in their various domains who do so much behind the scenes to help authors like me. Thanks as well to the anonymous readers whose reports on my manuscript were full of thoughtful suggestions; this book is better for their insights.

I am honored to publish this book in the Library of Jewish Ideas series, cosponsored by the Tikvah Fund. Many thanks to Tikvah for its considerable support. My series editor at Tikvah, the legendary Neal Kozodoy, warrants special acknowledgment. His encyclopedic knowledge of Jewish history and relentless dedication to wordsmithing have immeasurably enriched this book.

Numerous archivists and librarians at the Library of Congress, Massachusetts Historical Society, and Houghton Library made feasible the otherwise forbidding task of sorting through the countless letters that provided much of the grist for this study. The Lucius Littauer Foundation kindly subsidized my archival research.

My work on this book spanned a move from the faculty at the University of Oklahoma to that at Arizona State University. I am appreciative of colleagues in both institutions for their collegiality. In Norman, I belonged to the Department of Classics and Letters under the leadership of Scott Fitzgerald Johnson and the Judaic Studies program under Alan Levenson. Both scholars have earned my gratitude many times over. In Tempe, colleagues at the School of Civic and Economic Thought and Leadership provided an ideal home to pursue questions of faith and freedom in American statecraft. I was also fortunate to have a succession of highly diligent research assistants—Carly Kirkland, Allie Schwartz, and Maria Buscemi.

Any merit to this book belongs in no small part to the foregoing people and institutions; any faults are my own.

If writing a book can be a lonely endeavor, it has been far less so for the support of my family. My parents, Donna and Rick, have always encouraged my curiosity wherever it led me since childhood; this book has been no exception. Much of what follows in the pages ahead—the story of Jewish immigrants fleeing Old World hate for New World hope—will be familiar to them already. They heard such testimony firsthand from their own relatives.

I am indebted to the professor whose impact on me has been the greatest: my sister, Kara. Thanks as well to other penman in the family, Jonathan, and their three lively children.

And then there's Kristen. When I began this project, she was a stranger. As I finish it, she is my wife. Whether happenstance or kismet, we met in a small New England town of particular relevance to this book. In the years that followed, she became my confidante, my companion, and my champion. She has given me so very much. If I spend the rest of my life repaying my debt to her, it would not suffice. But I hope this book's dedication to her may be a humble start.

Andrew Porwancher
Tempe, AZ

AMERICAN MACCABEE

INTRODUCTION

"I wish I had a little Jew in me," Theodore Roosevelt once mused to a friend. Mere wishing would indeed mark the limits of Roosevelt's claim to Jewish ancestry—not a drop of Jewish blood coursed through his veins. If anything, he was the ultimate insider of the Protestant elite that had long dominated American life. His father descended from a wealthy family whose eminence in Manhattan dated back generations. His mother was a Southern belle from Georgia whose lineage included a delegate to the Continental Congress. Theodore lived a life consistent with his patrician pedigree, enrolling at Harvard, serving as a military officer, and seizing the grandest prize of all: the Oval Office.[1]

This silver-spooned statesman who had grown up in the fashionable neighborhood of Gramercy Park in New York had little in common with the Yiddish-speaking immigrants moistening their brows in the sweatshops of the Lower East Side just a short walk away. Roosevelt's privileged path was even further removed from the dreadful subsistence of Jews struggling to survive in Eastern Europe. And yet, for all the differences between Roosevelt and embattled Jews on both sides of the Atlantic, their causes became pivotal to his presidency. He would help shape their lives—and they, in turn, his legacy.

When an assassin's bullet felled William McKinley and catapulted Vice President Roosevelt to the White House in 1901, few could have imagined the central role that Jewish issues would play in TR's administration. But those issues would make front-page headlines, feature in State of the Union messages, and become rallying cries in political campaigns. It is striking, then, how little ink historians have spilled on the Jewish dimensions of his presidential tenure. Many excellent volumes do comprehensively cover other aspects of Roosevelt's statecraft. Yet his Jewish affairs—diplomatic and domestic—have never before received book-length treatment. This study offers the first, surfacing numerous historical sources that were previously unexplored in the vast canon of Roosevelt scholarship.

Notwithstanding Roosevelt's blue-blooded background, arguably no predecessor of his would have arrived at the White House better prepared to address antisemitism abroad and its ripple effects at home. He served as New York's enterprising police commissioner in the mid-1890s, becoming a conspicuous presence on the Lower East Side. Nowhere else in America did Eastern European Jewish immigrants concentrate in such immense numbers. To New Yorkers, it was simply "the East Side." Jewish crowds crammed into local venues to hear Commissioner Roosevelt espouse his egalitarian ethos. He also sought to undermine antisemitic tropes about Jewish frailty by encouraging the neighborhood's brawny Jews to join his police force. And at East Side nuptials, Roosevelt even escorted Jewish brides to their wedding receptions.[2]

Soon TR was famously leading the Rough Riders into battle, where Jewish volunteers joined their mustachioed colonel in facing down Spanish snipers amid the Cuban hills. He took great pride in those Jewish soldiers, especially one nicknamed "Pork Chop." Roosevelt quickly translated his military renown into a successful gubernatorial race in New York. From the governor's mansion, he descended into the bowels of the East Side tenements to see for himself the Jewish garment workers slaving over sewing machines in hazardous conditions for paltry wages. TR consequently rallied the state legislature to implement major reforms.[3]

Roosevelt's deep history with the Jewish community would lend him insight and credibility when he seized the reins of presidential power at the record age of forty-two and confronted a vexing series of Jewish issues. Yet his past experiences with Jewry only took him so far in forging a better future for Jews. With each challenge, he found himself navigating dueling demands. The opposing forces acting on Roosevelt at any given moment were often impossible to reconcile. This book argues that the combustion of those forces resulted in two Theodore Roosevelts. One inspired his Jewish constituents; the other disappointed them. One spoke up for persecuted Jews overseas; the other kept a studied silence. One roundly repudiated Jew-hatred; the other indulged in antisemitic tropes. One warmly embraced Jewish immigrants; the other sought to limit their admission. One called on Jewish newcomers to honor their heritage; the other expected their homogenized assimilation. One advanced Jewish causes selflessly for humane principles; the other did so self-servingly for electoral politics. In short, Roosevelt personified the contradictions and complexities of the nation that elected him.

The thorniest dilemma involved crafting an American response to Russia's barbarous breed of Jew-baiting. From the czar's throne in the capital of St. Petersburg, Nicholas II ruled over half the world's Jews. They endured debilitating restrictions: schools instituted quotas on Jewish students, professional guilds curbed Jewish membership, and huge swaths of Russian territory excluded Jewish residents. As severe as these strictures were, no one yet knew when the twentieth century dawned that Russian Jewry was on the eve of its greatest crisis yet.[4]

Roosevelt's tenure in office happened to coincide with an appalling wave of mob attacks against Russia's Jews known as pogroms—a Russian term meaning "devastation." For three horrifying years, marauding gangs of ordinary Russians routinely slaughtered their Jewish neighbors. Sometimes Russian authorities passively watched the butchery; other times they actively encouraged it. Never before in the dark history of that empire had Jewish blood flowed so freely. Most Russian Jews lacked the means to flee the corpse-strewn rubble of their communities, where they lived under the omnipresent threat of the next massacre. These catastrophic circumstances prompted Roosevelt to engage in an ongoing calculus about how to stanch the Jewish bloodbath.[5]

Certainly, Russia wasn't the only country whose antisemitism begged Roosevelt's attention. So did Romania and Morocco. Roosevelt felt relatively emboldened in confronting those weaker states over their anti-Jewish bigotry. But Russia had far more power than these other nations. It also had far more Jews. Nowhere else were the risks—and the stakes—of Roosevelt's Jewish diplomacy so high. America was just then emerging as a major player in the global arena, and Jews the world over anxiously waited to see whether Roosevelt would use his nation's newfound stature to advance a humanitarian vision in the czar's dominions.[6]

As Roosevelt contemplated his options, several variables weighed in favor of a diplomatic intervention on behalf of Russian Jewry. TR harbored a longstanding affinity for the Jewish people and genuinely abhorred the atrocities visited upon them. He was also drawn to the idea of America as a moral lodestar in the world. Many of his constituents felt the same way. They were aghast at the gruesome details of Russian-Jewish life—men savagely beaten, women serially violated, children tragically orphaned. Across the United States, mass protests of Jews and Gentiles pleaded for their president to intercede. They imagined that if Roosevelt forcefully spoke out, his words would affirm America's high-minded ideals and shame Russia into reversing its repression.[7]

But countervailing considerations advised against a rebuke of Russia. European officials were unnerved that Roosevelt would potentially flout a strong diplomatic norm that forbade one country from meddling in another's domestic affairs. Roosevelt's own State Department was similarly alarmed at that prospect. Rumors flew—with more validity than the president realized—that his secretary of state might resign over TR's possible intervention.[8] And any American remonstrance of Russia would carry substantial risks. It could alienate the czarist regime, which would resist the perception that St. Petersburg took orders from Washington. The Russians could retaliate by closing prized ports to U.S. trade or, even worse, severing diplomatic ties entirely. Roosevelt also fretted that issuing public denunciations of pogroms might actually exacerbate problems for Russia's Jews. Although he didn't specify what problems he foresaw, undoubtedly his fear was that Russian Gentiles who resented America's bid to shame them might reassert their pride by further lashing out at their Jewish neighbors. Complicating matters was America's own scourge of mob violence directed at a marginalized minority—if Roosevelt admonished Russia over its Jewish carnage, he risked provoking an embarrassing censure from St. Petersburg about the ruthless lynching of Blacks in the United States. Perhaps most significantly, no other head of state in the world had dared to confront Russia over the pogroms. Roosevelt would be going it alone.[9] These fraught factors underscore an exasperating truth about international affairs: evil in the world may be unambiguous, but determining the optimal diplomatic response is rarely straightforward. Amid profound uncertainties and competing exigencies, Roosevelt pursued an ever-changing foreign policy with Russia.

At times, Roosevelt defied both the czar and international custom by emphatically championing the cause of Russia's Jews. He insisted the United States had a "manifest duty" to condemn the brutality that pogromists inflicted on Jewish victims. Grateful Jews in America celebrated him for his rhetorical defense of their coreligionists abroad. Roosevelt's approach at such moments should suggest a reappraisal of his famous maxim, "Speak softly and carry a big stick," by which he meant backstopping diplomacy with armed force. That aphorism did fairly describe Roosevelt's imperial disposition toward Latin America. But in his willingness to challenge Russia absent any military threat, we see a striking illustration of the reverse: Roosevelt spoke loudly with no stick at all.[10]

In other instances, however, he opted for public silence. Conditions periodically required him to promote Russian-Jewish interests covertly and thereby forgo popular credit. Sometimes he deemed it prudent to abstain from even private entreaties to St. Petersburg, especially when Russian society at large began to spiral into a violent abyss. Despite his compassion for oppressed Jews, Roosevelt harbored significant doubts about America's ability to police the world. His calculated reserve at such times frustrated his Jewish supporters at home. But it should also serve to complicate accusations of "cowboy diplomacy" that his critics leveled against him in his day and thereafter. Roosevelt has often been derided for applying a Wild West approach to global affairs and violently thrashing about the world stage.[11] To be sure, he oversaw an aggressive expansion of American influence in the Western Hemisphere. But declassified records from Roosevelt's Jewish diplomacy reveal his keen sensitivity to shifting context. We find in that version of Roosevelt not so much cowboy bravado as careful calibration.[12]

Another noteworthy feature of Roosevelt's foreign relations was his tendency to relocate decision-making on Jewish matters away from the State Department and toward an inner circle of Jewish allies. Only one of his Jewish confidants even worked for his administration. Roosevelt was perfectly content to resolve key questions of Jewish diplomacy through, say, a freewheeling conversation over lunch at his summer house with a handful of informal Jewish advisors. The State Department often found itself reduced to executing orders instead of driving policy. And Roosevelt's Jewish associates didn't merely guide his thinking on Jewish issues. They also pursued their own shadow diplomacy, directly beseeching foreign officials to alleviate Jewish suffering. In Roosevelt, these Jewish leaders found a partner willing to discreetly augment their efforts through his own channels.[13]

The composition of Roosevelt's Jewish brain trust reflects a schism in Jewish life in that era. His Jewish foreign policy concerned the great mass of Eastern European Jews who subsisted on meager earnings and Orthodox pieties. Yet Roosevelt didn't consult immigrants who had freshly fled that benighted world. Instead, he relied on the counsel of elite American Jews whose profiles were very different from their persecuted coreligionists overseas—his advisors were Central European in their origin, rich in their resources, and Reform in their Judaism. They lived in Upper East Side townhomes, not Lower East Side tenements. For all Roosevelt's handshaking and speechifying in Jewish slums, behind closed doors he depended on the kind of assimilated Jew he might have once met amid the verdant quads of Harvard Yard or at a posh party in an uptown brownstone.[14]

★ ★ ★

Antisemitism posed problems not just beyond America's borders but also within them. Roosevelt well knew that Jew-hatred had significant purchase on his own country. After all, many of his best friends were antisemites. The elites who populated his social stratum were often aghast at the specter of their summer resorts and prep schools becoming overrun with affluent Jews. Nor did these genteel Anglo-Saxons thrill to the immiserated Jewish immigrants flooding their city streets.[15]

Roosevelt may have hobnobbed with bigots, but that didn't mean he let their prejudice stand unanswered. Shortly after his college graduation, Roosevelt castigated fellow members of a Republican club who wanted to reject a Jewish applicant on religious grounds.[16] Likewise, a Roosevelt companion once claimed in print that no Jew should become a military officer, prompting TR to press him, "Don't you think this criticism was unjust?"[17] And after hosting a novelist for an afternoon at the Harvard Club, Roosevelt noticed that the writer's newest short story featured a Jewish antagonist but exclusively Gentile protagonists. "There ought also to be a Jew among them!" urged Roosevelt.[18] The best indicator of TR's goodwill toward Jews wasn't his vocal defense of Jews in public, where he stood to score points with Jewish constituencies. It was, rather, his willingness in private moments to risk alienating friends over their intolerance of Jews when he had nothing to gain.

American antisemitism was hardly limited to Anglo-Saxon aristocrats who knocked back champagne flutes at Newport parties while scoffing about Jewish bankers. Heartland farmers and urban slum-dwellers also engaged in their share of Judeophobia. All manner of stereotypes gained traction across these varied segments of society: Jews were puppet masters manipulating Gentiles; Jews were perverted seducers of Christian girls; Jews were rapacious capitalists bamboozling the common people. But America wasn't uniformly prejudiced toward Jewry. The nation had a philosemitic streak that cherished the Jewish community. Many Gentiles extended a helpful hand to Jewish immigrants and denounced Jew-hatred in its many forms.[19]

Roosevelt embodied that very contradiction. He repeatedly repudiated antisemitism, and yet Roosevelt himself periodically peddled the kind of prejudice he condemned from others. TR once derided a Jewish journalist as a "circumcised skunk." And in a letter to a friend, Roosevelt employed the antisemitic epithet "sheeny" to describe a Jewish politician. The word "sheeny" was sufficiently offensive by the standards of TR's own era that his friend doctored Roosevelt's letter before it appeared in a published collection of their correspondence. Roosevelt also occasionally suffered from delusions that furtive Jewish machinations lay behind troubling global developments.[20]

His antisemitism and philosemitism didn't always sit in tension; they sometimes fused together in unexpected ways. As police commissioner, he wanted to gather Jewish officers for an important opportunity, but Roosevelt engaged in stereotyping by instructing a subordinate to identify Jewish policemen based solely on their facial features: "the stronger their ancestral marking, the better," Roosevelt insisted. During his presidency, he made a historic appointment of a Jew to a major office; however, TR indelicately suggested that younger Jews should look up to that appointee as the "ideal of the successful man rather than some crooked Jew money-maker." And after his administration, Roosevelt praised Jewish children for outpacing their Gentile counterparts in school, yet by asserting that "the Jewish children are very much brighter than the American," he implied that Jewish students were somehow not quite American.[21]

In paradoxically melding philosemitic and antisemitic sentiments, Roosevelt was actually typical of innumerable American Gentiles. One historian of Jew-hatred has perceptively observed, "A stereotype may express ambivalent emotions. It may blend affection and contempt. . . . Many Americans were both pro- and anti-Jewish at the same time."[22] Roosevelt's own mixture of benevolence and bias toward Jews does not appear to have damaged his standing with his Jewish constituents—perhaps because Jews themselves sometimes advanced Jewish interests by relying on antisemitic stereotypes. For example, the czar's regime genuinely believed that Jews manufactured public opinion in the United States, and Roosevelt's Jewish-American allies were more than happy to leverage that unfounded paranoia in their shadow diplomacy with Russian officials.[23]

Roosevelt's views about Jewish immigration were similarly conflicted. From colonial times until McKinley's death—a period stretching a quarter-millennium—America had amassed a Jewish population of one million. It took only the seven-and-a-half years of Roosevelt's presidency to nearly double that figure, as Jewish survivors of persecution packed the docks at American ports. This unprecedented crush of Jewish refugees raised hard questions for the nation, both practical and moral. Indigent Jews overwhelmed city slums and saturated the labor market. Whether to receive these desperate souls in unlimited numbers was a difficult quandary. Certainly, Jews weren't the only immigrant group whose inflow generated controversy. But American antisemitism made Jewish migration especially charged.[24] Rival imperatives over immigration led to two Theodore Roosevelts: one who earned the devotion of his Jewish constituents and another who elicited their distress.

The first Roosevelt spoke movingly of Jewish immigrant contributions to American life. His administration openly celebrated the idea of the United States as an asylum for the world's downtrodden. Acutely aware that turning back Jewish arrivals often meant consigning them to a grim fate in their lands of origin, TR chastised the Ellis Island commissioner over his questionable deportation of Jews. Roosevelt even made a dramatic visit to that symbolic speck of land in New York harbor to announce a special committee—with Jewish representation—that would expose prejudicial practices. Most strikingly of all, Roosevelt entrusted the oversight of immigration law to a foreign-born Jew, an audacious move in an era when many "old stock" Americans were in thrall to xenophobia.[25]

But Roosevelt aggrieved his Jewish friends by backing a congressional bill that threatened to close the gates to the most marginal Jewish immigrants. The bill sought to make literacy in any language a prerequisite for admission into the country. Although neutral on its face, the bill would disproportionately reject Eastern European Jews, whose literacy rates were much lower than newcomers from the likes of England or Denmark. Roosevelt's intentions weren't sinister in endorsing the bill. He worried that immigrants who had already settled stateside would struggle to overcome poverty if their wages and living conditions were perpetually suppressed by an unrestricted deluge of foreign labor. A literacy test, Roosevelt maintained, could check industries that were taking unfair advantage of mass migration.[26]

Even so, Roosevelt's position alienated his Jewish allies. They rightly fretted that a literacy test would pose an existential threat for countless Jews seeking to escape habitual bouts of butchery overseas. And Roosevelt's support for the bill placed him on the same side as prominent xenophobes—or "nativists"—who wanted to attenuate Jewish immigration for fear it was corrupting the nation's racial purity. The bill ultimately failed to pass, but no thanks to the president.[27]

His odd confluence with nativists on the literacy test wasn't the only strange dynamic that immigration engendered in American political life. Recent Jewish arrivals, who favored an open door on immigration, found themselves aligned with the very industrial interests that exploited them. Meanwhile, some antisemitic nativists joined American Jewry in demanding pro-Jewish reforms in Russia. These nativists hoped that improved circumstances for the czar's Jewish subjects would stem the succession of steamships filled with Russian Jews clutching one-way tickets to Ellis Island.[28]

In perhaps the most counterintuitive development, Roosevelt's closest Jewish advisor—who usually embraced Jewish immigration—encouraged TR to officially lament the Jewish influx from Romania. The origins of this peculiar tactic resulted from the diplomatic protocol that discouraged a given country from criticizing another's internal affairs, even on humanitarian grounds. Roosevelt's Jewish aide prevailed upon him to adopt the following pretextual argument: because Romanian antisemitism prompted a Jewish exodus to American shores that purportedly burdened the United States, Romania's Jew-hatred was an *international* issue and thus susceptible to American reproach.[29]

In truth, Roosevelt had no qualms about admitting Romanian-Jewish refugees—they then numbered fewer than seven thousand annually—but he understood the merit of posturing as if he did. By citing America's self-interest in reducing immigration, the Roosevelt administration was able to issue a rebuke of Romanian bigotry while paying heed to diplomatic norms. This episode runs counter to the commonplace judgment that America's foreign policy has repeatedly used the language of altruism to camouflage a self-serving agenda. To be sure, that critique does fairly describe numerous incidents in the nation's history. But the Roosevelt administration's censure of Romania offers a stunning example of the opposite: America's disingenuous invocation of its self-interest to justify what was actually a humanitarian endeavor.[30]

It doesn't follow, however, that Roosevelt's intentions in his Jewish diplomacy were purely magnanimous. His international statecraft bore an intimate relationship to his pursuit of the Jewish vote at home. Roosevelt was a political animal whose ascent began in New York City, where the booming Jewish population enjoyed increasing clout with each new campaign season. Even as Roosevelt reached the national stage, he remained ever mindful of newly naturalized Jews who flocked to polling stations on election days. His Jewish diplomacy became his central pitch to these voters.

Roosevelt made sure that his resistance to antisemitism abroad featured in his party platform, his nomination acceptance, and surrogate speeches. So attuned was Roosevelt to the Jewish vote that he even let his electoral ambitions dictate certain foreign policy decisions. Amid the height of his reelection bid in 1904, for instance, Roosevelt empowered the chairman of the Republican National Committee to opportunistically declassify State Department records that would reveal a recent clandestine effort by TR on behalf of Jews. And during another election cycle, Roosevelt appeased Jewish voters by placing incessant pressure on his secretary of state to reverse an extradition ruling that would have returned a Russian émigré to the bear's claws. It would go too far to suggest that Roosevelt's Jewish diplomacy was exclusively a tool of his electioneering—after all, he sometimes secretly advanced Jewish causes overseas without any intent or attempt to later garner public credit. But it would be obtuse to ignore his willingness, whenever November grew near in even-numbered years, to make foreign policy the handmaiden of domestic politics.³¹

Given his vast remit as president, Roosevelt's granular attention to the Jewish vote is rather remarkable. One might think that a sitting head of state—responsible for a breathtaking array of challenges—wouldn't have time to peruse obscure Jewish periodicals. But when a Jewish college student published an article endorsing Roosevelt's reelection in a monthly magazine called *Menorah*, TR gushed about the piece to a friend. Nor did Roosevelt's presidential duties preclude him from keeping a close eye on municipal Jewish politics back in New York City. He was indignant when the local Republican Party put forward a slate of judicial nominees for the city bench that featured merely a secular Jew and not also an Orthodox candidate. Indeed, Roosevelt personally intervened to remedy the omission.³²

Roosevelt's consistent focus on the Jewish electorate paid dividends at the ballot box. Naturally, he found favor with assimilated Jews who conventionally voted Republican; the genuinely striking feature of Roosevelt's electoral success is that he fared so well with Democratic-leaning Jewish immigrants. It is a testament to his popularity with the latter set of Jews that Roosevelt pulled off an extraordinary coup for a Republican presidential nominee: he actually won the Lower East Side. In another measure of his Jewish support, Roosevelt outran every last down-ballot Republican at East Side polling stations. TR's astounding performance with Jewish constituents demonstrates that their appreciation of his boldest actions in Jewish diplomacy far outweighed their frustration with his more cautious moments.

Roosevelt's pitch to Jewish voters was, like nearly all else, riddled with contradiction. He often decried identity politics, insisting that he paid Jews in the United States the respect of treating them as simply Americans. Roosevelt esteemed the notion of civic life as a realm where common citizenship, not ethnic identity, mattered. But that was a pleasing fiction. Ethnic issues resonated with ethnic voters, Jews among them;

politicians responded accordingly, Roosevelt among them. Whether touting his defiance of the czar or lining up Jewish surrogates to barnstorm the East Side, the reality is that Roosevelt routinely courted Jews *as* Jews.[33]

This tension between identity-neutral and identity-centric politics frequently surfaced when Roosevelt exercised his power of appointment. He regularly espoused the importance of religious diversity in his hiring. But Roosevelt was equally attracted to a competing conceit: the government workforce as an identity-agnostic sphere where talent alone counted. These dueling strains in his thought led to a fair degree of incoherence—in one breath he would remark on the need to deliberately include Jews in American governance, and in the next he would deny that religion played any factor in his selection of Jewish appointees. Roosevelt never was able to resolve the conflict between the identity-driven ideal of inclusivity and the identity-free ideal of meritocracy.[34]

Ambivalence about the pertinence of Jewish identity also characterized his checkered approach to Jewish assimilation. Sometimes Roosevelt emphasized a kind of uniform Americanism that called on Jewish immigrants to leave behind their Old Country ways. The version of Roosevelt who preferred homogenizing assimilation was most pronounced in his enthusiasm for the controversial play *The Melting Pot*. It tells the improbable love story of two young Russian immigrants in New York: a Jewish man whose family was slaughtered in a pogrom, and a Gentile woman whose father perpetrated that very pogrom. Across the United States, Jews panned *The Melting Pot* for effectively expecting them to abandon their heritage and intermarry their way into self-erasure. But Roosevelt saw in the play's storyline the promise of a unified America freed from Old World enmities. He considered *The Melting Pot* one of the greatest influences on his life.[35]

There was, however, a pluralistic Roosevelt who believed that Jews could integrate into the United States by honoring, not disowning, their culture. He praised Jewish Americans for remaining admirably "loyal to their faith and their race traditions." And the Jewish tradition that Roosevelt most venerated was the heroism of the Maccabee warriors. He upheld those ancient Jewish rebels as a model for American men of

Jewish faith. TR saw Maccabee lore as a useful antidote to the antisemitic trope that male Jews were feckless cowards. In Roosevelt's estimation, Jewish men needn't shed their heritage to shed that stereotype—to the contrary, they should embrace their own proud legacy of Maccabean valor.[36] When Roosevelt once said he wished he had a little Jewish blood in him, he surely meant this archetype of the American Maccabee.

★ ★ ★

Writing presidential history is often a fraught exercise, Jewish history even more so. The nexus might well be combustible. Some caveats here will hopefully mitigate the risk of readers misinterpreting the book's goals.

In recovering the underappreciated role of Jewish people and Jewish issues to Roosevelt's life, this study doesn't intend to imply that his days comprised an endless succession of Jewish matters. His attention was divided across many other concerns, which have received ample treatment from other scholars. In other words, I seek to enrich our already robust understanding of a multifaceted leader. Precisely because Roosevelt's presidential portfolio was so extensive, he regularly entrusted Jewish allies with the daily management of his Jewish affairs, and he would weigh in at crucial moments—accordingly, some chapters that follow tell their story even more than his. This investigation, moreover, circumscribes its scope to Jewish causes, so it could give the misimpression that Roosevelt engaged those Jewish allies exclusively on Jewish topics; the reality is that he leaned on them for all manner of advice. Another important disclaimer: this volume does refer passingly to other ethnic groups for context, but as every work of scholarship must mark its limits somewhere, a comprehensive discussion of non-Jewish communities lies beyond my ambit here.

When a new book appears on an American president, it is a natural instinct for many readers to reassess that president's reputation—for better or worse—in light of fresh findings. The ensuing chapters may burnish Roosevelt's reputation in some eyes and tarnish it in others. Whether readers close the covers of this book thinking better or worse of the twenty-sixth president is their prerogative. But neither outcome is the author's aim. The sole ambition of this study is to reckon with the historical record in its full complexity.

The Jewish issues that preoccupied Roosevelt were significant—making front-page headlines, featuring in State of the Union messages, turning up in campaign speeches—because they weren't of consequence to Jews alone. Indeed, they implicated paramount questions of American life. Would the United States become an ascendant voice for moral clarity on the global stage? Would the country serve as a refuge for huddled masses from foreign lands? Would recent arrivals to American shores find that abandoning their heritage was the cost of acceptance? At stake in all these questions was nothing less than America's self-definition. That Roosevelt's answers were so conflicted reflected a nation struggling to know its own soul; that these questions remain contentious still today lends the story of Theodore Roosevelt and the Jews a timeless urgency.

1

ASCENT

When the novelist Henry James visited the Lower East Side at the dawn of the twentieth century, he encountered "a Jewry that had burst all bounds."[1] A guidebook for tourists more flatteringly portrayed the neighborhood as home to a "wondrously preserved Semitic people."[2] In his famous exposé of New York's slums in the 1890s, *How the Other Half Lives*, the Danish-American reformer Jacob Riis described entering the Lower East Side from Bayard Street. "No need of asking here where we are," he reflected. Yiddish signs, Eastern European kaftans, and bearded men with yarmulkes all gave the unmistakable indication that Riis was now in "Jewtown."[3]

The sheer density of "the East Side" was arresting. "Nowhere in the world are so many people crowded together on a square mile as here," Riis reported.[4] The concentration of these people far exceeded the infrastructure, rendering filth and odor all but inevitable. One journalist recounted how residents venturing into the streets encountered "a thousand stenches of their own and others' making."[5] Amid the cramped blocks and side alleys was a chaotic mix of pushcarts, horses, and human beings. Traffic lights and stop signs were nowhere to be found—carriages and wagons moved in all directions at once.[6]

Six days of the week, commerce was the lifeblood of the Lower East Side. Along the sidewalks were storefronts of bakers, grocers, and clothiers.[7] And the streets were open-air markets where most of life's necessaries could be procured for pennies from peddlers. For centuries, European Jews had sold their wares from pushcarts—the time-trusted

FIGURE 1.1. "How the other half lives" in a crowded Hebrew district, Lower East Side, New York City. *Source:* Library of Congress, Prints and Photographs Division.

trade of the peddler was thus a natural default for many Jewish immigrants in the New World. Renting a pushcart on the East Side cost ten cents daily (almost four dollars today); some enterprising peddlers simply refashioned baby strollers.[8]

The weekly heyday for peddlers took place on Fridays on Hester Street at the ironically named "Pig Market," where everything *but* pork was for sale. "There is scarcely anything else that can be hawked from a wagon that is not to be found," Jacob Riis noted, "and at ridiculously low prices." Vendors and buyers haggled loudly over all imaginable goods—spectacles and suspenders, cups and candlesticks, pants and pickles.

Fowl on offer for Shabbat dinner had, of course, been slaughtered according to kosher law. Five peaches cost a penny; broken eggs might be given away for a song. Even by the standards of the East Side, the Pig Market was congested. Riis marveled at "the crowds that jostle each other at the wagons and about the sidewalk shops.... Pushing, struggling, babbling, and shouting in foreign tongues, a veritable Babel of confusion."[9]

Two short blocks from the heart of the Pig Market, Hester Street intersected with Allen Street, home to a notorious red-light district. Jewish prostitutes placed red lamps in their windows to signal their trade. One renowned prostitute always took leave from work on the High Holy Days, explaining to a journalist matter-of-factly, "I go to shul."[10] On nearby Forsyth Street, Synagogue Beth Israel shared a wall with a brothel; praying congregants competed with paying customers for vocal supremacy.[11] It was hardly atypical to find sanctity and sin comingling in turn-of-the-century New York.

Forsyth Street ran parallel to Orchard Street with its many restaurants. Diners willing to part with thirteen cents (about five dollars today) could enjoy a veritable feast: stew, pie, bread, soup, pickles, and a beer.[12] Or they could turn right onto Houston Street and try the salami at a beloved deli—known today as Katz's—that was a well-known haunt for performers in the Yiddish theaters.[13] Sometimes those theaters staged original content; other times they would adapt a Shakespearean classic with a Jewish twist. Lower East Side audiences were probably unaware that the original version of *Hamlet* did not involve a subplot where the titular character trains to become a rabbi.[14]

A six-minute stroll west on Houston Street landed you at the base of Second Avenue. That street featured so many cafés serving knishes—a hot doughy snack favored by Ashkenazi Jews—that it became known as "Knish Alley." These cafés formed the intellectual nexus of the Lower East Side, as patrons engaged in boisterous debates or otherwise channeled their competitive instincts into chess matches. Turning right from Second Avenue, East Siders took refuge from the neighborhood's grime at the Tenth Street Baths (still open today). Here was one of dozens of Jewish bathhouses that offered a hot *shvitz*—or sweat bath—followed by a cold shower. Bathhouses were essential because in-home tubs were rare and washing before Shabbat was a sacred obligation. Reprieve from the street might also be sought in the barbershops, where locals forgot their workaday troubles amid conversation and card games. Candy stores, too, were popular gathering places. Many customers came for the "egg creams," a flavored fizzy drink made with neither egg nor cream. Other candy store regulars discreetly gambled; illicit betting was curiously commonplace at the confectionaries dotting the neighborhood.[15]

Roaring above Allen Street was the elevated train. The pandemonium that prevailed in the train was every bit as frenetic as life below. Price Collier, a Midwesterner visiting New York in the 1890s, described the train cars as "gymnasiums on wheels." Merely sitting down could be a Herculean feat. As an exasperated Collier explained, "People bending to sit down, as the car starts, place their posteriors anywhere but where they intended, and not infrequently in a space already occupied by another." Standing passengers firmly gripped the leather straps suspended from the ceiling, a necessary precaution when the train rounded bends at a New York pace. Enduring the ride required not just physical dexterity but mental focus. "A second's inattention, a moment's respite from the dangling leather which hangs from the roof, and you are shot into somebody's back, bosom, or belly," warned Collier. He was impressed by New Yorkers' equanimity amid the anarchy, for "no one seems disturbed or greatly put out by this involuntary riot which takes place every few seconds."[16]

The elevated train afforded a grisly view into the dark heart of the Lower East Side: the tenements.[17] At all hours, passengers could glimpse into the open windows of these brick buildings—ordinarily five to eight stories tall—crammed with impoverished Jewish families.[18] "The architecture seemed to sweat humanity at every window and door," a British writer remarked. "The thought of the hidden interiors was terrifying."[19] This particular Englishman may not have summoned the nerve to venture inside these hellish buildings, but those who did would first brave narrow stairwells in the dark. From the kitchens wafted the scent of fish, cabbage, and onions. Yet neither smell nor taste was the dominant sensation of the tenements; it was sound. Because tenement units often doubled as living spaces and sweatshops, the buildings radiated with "the whir of a thousand sewing-machines," Riis recounted, "worked at high pressure from earliest dawn, till mind and muscle give out together."[20] More East Side Jews worked in the garment industry than in all other occupations combined.[21]

Today the term "sweatshop" generally denotes a factory—and indeed some East Siders did labor in garment factories—but most Jews in the "rag business" toiled in the cramped confines of the tenements. They took fabric cuts from manufacturers and turned them into whatever article of clothing they specialized in, perhaps trousers or coats.[22] The daily drudgery of work could stretch to eighteen hours in unfathomably tight quarters.[23] "It is not unusual to find a dozen persons—men, women, and children—at work in a single small room," Riis detailed.[24] Close proximity and poor ventilation made the tenement stifling, especially amid the humidity of the summer.[25]

Overcrowding in the buildings meant that residents were forced to take turns sleeping. People commonly stole to the roofs for their evening slumber in the warmer months, hoping to escape the congestion, the heat, and the bedbugs in the apartments below. To offset living expenses, a family could further compress its limited space by taking in Jewish boarders. Some boarders were single, having made the trip to America solo, while others had wives and children back in the Old Country. Individual apartments lacked running water; at best, a building might have a communal faucet in the hallway. Tenement life was gloomy—literally. Most rooms were deprived of natural light, and the gas employed to illuminate them was used sparingly to reduce costs. Dim lighting made it all the easier for vermin to scurry undetected, especially if the rats took cover under the piles of fabric typically blanketing the sweatshop floors.[26]

The bleakest units in a given tenement were in the basement. Riis recalled meeting a trio of peddlers who shared a cellar apartment where "the feeblest ray of daylight never found its way." Standing on their

FIGURE 1.2. A peddler next to his bedroll in an East Side cellar on Ludlow Street. *Credit*: Jacob Riis. *Source*: Smithsonian American Art Museum, Museum purchase through the Luisita L. and Franz H. Denghausen Endowment.

muddied floor, he held up his candlelight to find three "sallow faces look[ing] more like hideous ghosts than living men."[27] For many tenement residents, the only hiatus from their crowded quarters was a half-hour's leisure separating a long day from a short sleep. These buildings seemed to embody the muted despair of their inhabitants. In Riis's elegiac words, "The thousands of lighted windows in the tenements glow like dull red eyes."[28]

Befouled conditions on the Lower East Side facilitated the spread of disease. Epidemics were tragically common.[29] New York health officials gruesomely dubbed one subsection of the East Side the "suicide ward" owing to rampant deaths from typhus. Exacerbating matters, many sick Jews avoided the hospitals for fear they would be butchered there—surely a residual trauma from the Old World where Jewish lives counted for little.[30]

Although some Jewish immigrants managed to secure an education stateside and join the learned professions, the great majority remained laborers.[31] Many did not have time to learn English, much less become doctors or lawyers in their new Anglophone homeland.[32] Their hopes thus rested with their children's future. Jewish youths typically attended local public schools during the day and then, before supper, received some supplemental Jewish instruction in tenement schools.[33] The public schools were nearly as Jewish in composition as the religious ones; for every twenty pupils in an East Side public school, nineteen were Jews. Public schools emphasized American civics, U.S. history, and above all the English language. The availability of free schooling and the Jewish premium on education proved a powerful combination. Jewish families enjoyed remarkable upward mobility, with the children of immigrants achieving a degree of success that their parents rarely imagined for themselves. "America is a land of gold," one mother told her son. "There is no gold in the streets. The gold is in your head." And yet many other desperate families opted to use their children in sweatshops rather than send them to school; child labor mitigated today's burdens, even as it minimized tomorrow's opportunities.[34]

School hours aside, children were a ubiquitous sight on the East Side. An observer remarked, "The sidewalks swarm with children, and the air rings with their clamor, as they fly back and forth at play."[35] The most scholastic among them could be found at the Chatham Square Library, waiting to check out books in a long line that often wound its way down two stories and spilled onto the street. Other youths found less educational ways of passing time, like putting an infant sibling in a basket and letting her float along the grungy waters that lined the gutters. Still other children might pet horses in the street, sharing lollipop licks with the grateful animals.[36]

A Yiddish newspaper described the Lower East Side as a "city within a city." But even that description glossed over its multiplicity of Jewish subcultures.[37] Russian, Hungarian, Romanian, and Galician Jews all had their own enclaves within the neighborhood. And those enclaves were divided even further, with a given synagogue designated for immigrants hailing from the same town in the Old Country.[38] "Hometown societies" sprang up that helped organize life for newcomers, who could fraternize with and lean on fellow Jews from their specific place of origin.³⁹

If a brief stroll through the Lower East Side was a tour of Eastern Europe, then a marginally longer stroll just beyond "Jewtown" was a tour of the world. A few blocks in any given direction might mean broaching the Irish neighborhood with its tough-minded gangs, or Chinatown where a penny would fetch a sugarcane stick, or Little Italy, which felt indistinguishable from Naples.⁴⁰ These ethnic districts served as reminders that Jews weren't the only ones enduring hardscrabble lives in urban slums.

Despite the challenges facing Jewish immigrants, the New World still marked a meaningful improvement over the perilous conditions they had fled in Eastern Europe. On the eve of the great Jewish migration to America, which began in the 1880s, about half the world's Jews lived in a region known as the "Pale of Settlement" within the Russian Empire. "Pale" refers to a stake in the ground that denotes the boundaries of a territory. The Pale of Settlement extended well beyond modern Russian borders, including parts of present-day Ukraine, Poland, Lithuania, and Latvia, and all of Moldova and Belarus.⁴¹ (This book uses the term "Russian Jews" broadly as a referent to all Jews within the Russian Empire.) Russian law required that Jews, with few exceptions, reside in the Pale.

After the assassination of Czar Alexander II in 1881, conditions for Russia's Jews worsened. They became scapegoated by the masses and the state alike for the czar's murder even though all four assassins were Gentiles. Between 1881 and 1882, over two hundred Jewish communities were subjected to pogroms that claimed Jewish lives and destroyed Jewish property. Extralegal violence was compounded by official action. The so-called May Laws imposed harsh constraints on Jews. Their right to settle in various locales grew limited, even within the Pale, as was their ability to travel between communities. Jewish artisans who had been granted exceptions to live outside the Pale suddenly found themselves obligated to relocate within it. Jews faced quotas in high schools, at universities, and amid the professions.[42]

As antisemitism in its sundry cultural and legal forms made life ever more intolerable, many Jews began to cast their eyes westward toward America. They thrilled to the prospect of religious liberty and economic opportunity in the United States. A reprieve from prejudice and poverty seemed to await them just across the Atlantic. And thanks to steamships, an overseas journey that had once spanned three months now only took a week or two.[43]

The Pale wasn't the only place in Europe prompting a Jewish exodus to America in the latter years of the nineteenth century. Many Jews left their homes in Romania and Austria-Hungary, with a smaller stream coming from Western European nations. Sephardic Jews from Greece and Turkey also found their way to the United States.[44] The diversity of Jewish immigrants notwithstanding, it was Ashkenazi Jews from the Pale of Settlement who would increasingly predominate in American Jewish life.[45]

Even as unprecedented legions of Jews depleted their meager savings on one-way tickets to the New World, more stayed in the Pale than left during the latter decades of the nineteenth century. Their reasons for remaining were partly financial. Pricey bribes were required to secure the necessary paperwork to leave Russia. And the trip itself was expensive, costing more than the typical Jew's yearly income. Devout Jews often preferred to suffer the indignities of life in the Pale rather than expose their sacred faith to the irreligious materialism that was supposedly corrupting the United States.[46] Ultimately, circumstances for Jews of the Pale would worsen so severely that even the reluctant among them took their chances on America in growing numbers.

For those who decided to cast their lot on the Lower East Side—and in similar Jewish enclaves in Chicago, Baltimore, Boston, and Philadelphia—they found that the anxieties of the pious souls back home weren't wholly unfounded. The religious strictures of the Eastern European shtetl, or Jewish village, gave way to that most quintessential of American values: choice. Some Jewish immigrants flocked to socialism and its skepticism of religion. Others fell in with the anarchists, who flouted Yom Kippur by hosting dances. Individual Jews were free to engage with their heritage on their own terms, if at all. For most East Side Jews, that meant choosing to sustain the faith of their ancestors. They kept kosher and maintained Shabbat as natural extensions of their observant upbringings in the Old Country. New York was home to hundreds of synagogues that formed the backbone of communal life.[47] The ancient sanctity that infused the East Side was perhaps most evident in a shiva house, where the recently buried were grieved. "A visit to a Jewish house of mourning is like bridging the gap of two thousand years," Jacob Riis memorably wrote. "The inexpressibly sad and sorrowful wail for the dead . . . comes back from the ages like a mournful echo."[48]

Here, then, was America's largest Jewish neighborhood. Old World traditions and New World temptations, grinding poverty and novel opportunity, collective belonging and individual freedom, Yiddish and English, piety and vice—all condensed into a couple square miles of teeming humanity. Slum life on the East Side may have been rife with hazard, but it was also rich with hope. No quota limited the number of Jews who could join a given profession. No edict precluded Jewish children from attending school. No pogrom ransacked Jewish businesses or shed Jewish blood. Rather than relegated to second-class citizenship, an impoverished Jew could cast a ballot that tallied just the same as the wealthiest Gentile's. But the Lower East Side wasn't only the starting point for so many Jews grasping at the American Dream. Amid its swarming streets, in the summer of 1895, a young police commissioner began chasing a dream of his own.

Theodore Roosevelt's ascension to the head of the New York Police Department was of great consequence—for him and for the city alike. He had spent the better part of a decade in a substantive but obscure role as leader of the Civil Service Commission in Washington.[49] During those years, his hometown would have offered limited opportunities for a Republican such as himself. New York City was dominated by Tammany Hall, a Democratic organization that had perfected the art of machine politics. The Tammany bosses knew how to manufacture votes from impoverished immigrants but did not fundamentally improve their lives. Little was done by the machine to meaningfully address the perilous conditions in ethnic slums—the long hours, the unhygienic apartments, the scant municipal services. However, Tammany did welcome foreigners bewildered by their adopted homeland, furnishing them with some basic necessities like food and clothing. Tammany district captains surfaced at important events on their assigned turf; in the Jewish neighborhoods, that could mean attending a constituent's bar mitzvah, gift in hand. Some immigrants who displayed their loyalty and value to the machine might even get rewarded with a low-level post in municipal government. Come election day, Tammany reaped the benefits of these efforts.[50]

If Tammany was effective at engineering ethnic votes, it was also corrupt. The police department under Tammany rule was particularly unscrupulous. From furtive kickbacks to gratuitous violence, many officers exacerbated rather than mitigated the rampant crime prevailing in the city. The shortcomings of crooked governance became particularly pronounced amid the alarming economic conditions of 1894. New York City suffered from the same high unemployment and labor strikes that were plaguing the country at large. Voters were finally ready to loosen Tammany's grip on power.[51]

A wave election that year ushered reform-minded Republicans into office nationwide, including the mayor's office in New York.[52] And the thirty-six-year-old Theodore Roosevelt was just the kind of zealot that the new mayor needed to clean up the police department—and, in turn, the city itself. Roosevelt became police commissioner in May of 1895, serving as president of the four-member Police Board.[53] He embodied the ethos of the inchoate progressive movement that would redefine American politics for the next twenty years and give this period its name: the Progressive Era.

Although progressivism was not a monolith, its adherents tended to coalesce around some broadly shared goals. For one, they sought to uproot the spoils system that doled out government jobs to unqualified lackeys. Progressives wanted power entrusted to highly trained professionals whose management of public affairs was apolitical and efficient. Roosevelt had already stood at the forefront of demanding greater accountability from municipal government—as a young state legislator in 1884, he had chaired an investigatory committee that exposed widespread graft under the Tammany regime.[54] He would later laud the 1894 election as a triumph not for Republicans per se but for integrity in civic life. "The victory had been won, not on party lines," he insisted, "but as a fight for decent government, and for the non-partisan administration of municipal affairs."[55] In his new role as police commissioner, he could personally remake the force to better reflect his own premium on professionalism and probity.[56]

Progressives like Roosevelt didn't merely aim to address corruption in civic life—they wanted to remake a society in the throes of an ever-accelerating industrial revolution. To be sure, a modern economy had brought a host of benefits, from technological wonders to affordable goods. But it also led to overpopulated cities whose immigrant workers spent interminable days in dangerous factories for pitiful wages. Progressives did not wish to dismantle industrial capitalism so much as attenuate its excesses through labor reforms.[57] "We must protect the crushable elements at the base of our present industrial structure," Roosevelt once declared in a speech.[58]

Alongside their economic agenda, many progressives nurtured a strong moralistic ethic. The movement's leaders hoped to eradicate behavior they deemed sinful—prostitution, drinking, and gambling. Theirs was a vision rooted in the Social Gospel, a mode of Protestantism that created a religious justification for reformers to impose, in top-down fashion, their own middle-class values on others, including recent immigrants. Social Gospel enthusiasts felt a benevolent obligation to help these newcomers and a paternalistic obligation to mold them.[59]

Roosevelt emerged from this action-oriented strain of American Christianity. In his boyhood, the family's pastor was a renowned Social Gospel clergyman.[60] Then, as a teenager, Roosevelt told a minister that he wanted to be a "doer," to operationalize his faith through deeds.[61] As he brought his moralizing instincts into his police duties, his admirers saw Roosevelt as a principled change agent. Yet others, even in his own party, grew concerned that his righteousness was making him problematically inflexible. Roosevelt insisted, for instance, on stringently enforcing a previously moribund blue law that empowered him to shut down saloons on Sundays; some Republican leaders feared a backlash by a hard-drinking electorate.⁶²

The progressive movement had a complicated relationship with the political party system. In New York City at this time, where Democrats had long practiced machine politics, progressives unsurprisingly leaned Republican. But nationally the major parties found within their ranks both proponents and critics of progressivism. The progressives on both sides of the aisle would gain in strength over the course of Roosevelt's lifetime.

As Roosevelt waged his two-front war—reforming the police on the one hand, policing the city on the other—he was hardly content to remain behind a desk at his headquarters. TR took to the streets. Block by block, he barnstormed the city, giving speeches about his meritocratic approach to municipal affairs. Roosevelt became a fixture in "Jewtown" that summer, as East Side audiences squeezed into various venues to hear from the new police commissioner. His barrel-chested build gestured toward his physicality, his thick spectacles toward his intellectuality, and his dapper attire toward his gentility.⁶³

Roosevelt proudly told the East Side crowds that an immigrant Jew who was poorly connected but richly talented would confront no obstacle to gainful employment in the police department. In one speech, he recounted weighing two candidates for a health inspector post, which fell under the police department's purview. One applicant had a profile that would have all but ensured his appointment under Tammany reign: born in America, educated at Columbia University, and backed by an alderman. He was the type of person readily recognized as a "good fellow," Roosevelt explained. The other contender for the job was a Russian-Jewish immigrant who "certainly hadn't an influential friend." But that Jewish candidate impressed Roosevelt by having "worked his way by the hardest kind of study" to earn a position on the

FIGURE 1.3. Theodore Roosevelt, circa 1895. *Source*: The Miriam and Ira D. Wallach Division of Art, Prints and Photographs: Print Collection, The New York Public Library.

Tenement House Commission, which the state legislature had formed the year before to investigate those buildings' bleak conditions. "Under the old system, that Russian Jew wouldn't have had a show," Roosevelt declared. "Nobody would have attempted to have appointed him under the system of practical politics; the man with social standing, the man who was a good fellow, who had the alderman back of him . . . should have gotten it as a matter of course." Then came the punch line: "We appointed the Russian Jew."[64]

TR relished the opportunity to carry his meritocratic message directly to these people. "The crowded East Side audiences of Second Avenue and Avenue 'A' greet me with an enthusiasm I never anticipated," he marveled in a letter to his friend, U.S. Senator Henry Cabot Lodge. Roosevelt then hedged, "Of course there is much hostility shown too"—to be expected, given that this was conventionally Democratic terrain—"but the wonder is that I should have so strong a following among them." The atmosphere at his speeches was boisterous. As Roosevelt elaborated, "I have spoken again and again in packed halls on the East Side during the summer with the temperature at [the] boiling point, both as regards the weather and the audience." Sometimes a contrarian spectator would heckle Roosevelt, who would then invite the heckler to take the stage alongside him for a debate. At such moments, "I have never failed to carry the house with me at the end," Roosevelt boasted to Lodge, observing, "It has been in some respects like a campaign."[65]

In light of Democratic strength on the East Side, the police commissioner's growing popularity there was striking indeed. Two Republican figures affiliated with the Excise Board—which granted and revoked liquor licenses—were overjoyed by Roosevelt's inroads on the neighborhood: one was Joe Murray, the board's Irish Catholic president; the other was Julius Mayer, the board's Jewish lawyer.[66] As Roosevelt relayed to Lodge, "Joe Murray and the counsel of the Excise Board (a very honest little East Side Jew) are in ecstasies, and insist that my course is making a big gain for the Republican Party."[67] TR may have felt compelled to stress the Jewish lawyer's integrity given that Lodge had a dim view of Jewish immigrants and might have otherwise assumed the worst.[68] Roosevelt's insistence on sober Sundays, which chafed many New Yorkers, wasn't a liability with Jewish voters, as Jews tended to abstain from saloons.[69] "I cannot now recall ever having known a Jewish drunkard," mused Jacob Riis.[70]

Elections for the New York state legislature were pending that November. Although Roosevelt was preaching nonpartisanship to these crowds, that very message was itself partisan—after all, Republicans had employed it to great effect against Tammany the prior fall. Roosevelt's law-and-order commitment to shutting down saloons on Sundays also had a patina of neutrality that obscured a partisan bite: many saloons were de facto clubhouses for the Tammany faithful.[71] For the remainder of Roosevelt's career in public life, lofty principles and electoral considerations would often bleed into one another.

ASCENT 31

TR was too shrewd a politician to be naïve about GOP prospects in New York City that November. After the prior year's wave, in which Republicans vastly outperformed their typical showing, a regression to the city's Democratic mean seemed all but inevitable. But Republicans still enjoyed an advantage among upstate voters, and Roosevelt held out hope that GOP victories there would ensure the statehouse stayed in Republican hands. "If we keep the legislature, even though Tammany gets the City, we shall have held our own," he wrote Lodge.[72] On election day, the results accorded with Roosevelt's clear-eyed expectations: Tammany candidates did well in New York City, but Republicans, thanks to upstate support, retained control of both legislative chambers in Albany.[73]

Roosevelt was proud of the Jewish representation on the New York Police Department. Writing in *Munsey Magazine*, he observed that "few people have any idea" of the "large number of Jewish policemen on the New York force." Not all Jews, however, were fit for police work. Roosevelt thought that the majority of Jewish immigrants from Eastern Europe required more time in America to overcome the malnourishment of their Old World lives. As his *Munsey* article put it, "The great bulk of the Jewish population, especially the immigrants from Russia and Poland, are of weak physique and have not yet gotten far enough away from their centuries of oppression and degradation to make good policemen." But there were still Jews aplenty whose physical prowess made them ideal candidates. "The outdoor Jew who has been a gripman, or the driver of an express-wagon, or a guard on the Elevated [train], or the indoor Jew of fine bodily powers who has taken to boxing, wrestling and the like, offers excellent material for the force," Roosevelt assured readers.[74]

His article detailed that many Jews on the force were promoted for "conspicuous gallantry." Roosevelt stressed that Jews who ascended the career ladder did so purely on the basis of merit. "I should positively refuse to 'recognize' any creed, or any nationality, or anything else except fitness," he insisted. "If there were ten promotions, and the best ten candidates were Jews, they would secure all the prizes, but if they were not the best, then none of them would be promoted."[75] That he articulated similar sentiments in private correspondence suggests the sincerity of his views here.[76] If Roosevelt championed merit in hiring and promotion, he also wanted diversity. Years later, in his autobiography, he celebrated that "the New York police force is a body thoroughly representative of the great city itself."[77] Merit and diversity would uneasily coexist as competing ideals throughout Roosevelt's political career.[78]

For New York's Jewish newcomers, the sight of a fellow Jew sporting a police uniform was a stirring symbol of American possibility.[79] Policemen back in Russia enforced discriminatory laws against Jews, and during the outbreak of pogroms, they had passively watched as mobs mercilessly beat Jewish victims.[80] Given that grisly context, Jewish membership in the New York Police Department threw into high relief the differences between Old World hazards and New World hopes.

The archetype of the Jewish policeman challenged not only Jewish assumptions that police were crooked but also Gentile assumptions that Jews were anemic. An American health official writing in *Popular Science Monthly* reflected boilerplate attitudes about Jews in this respect. "In physique they rank below all other immigrants, and few seem capable of hard physical labor," he reported. "They seem to have no muscular development, and are prematurely old at an age when a German or a Scandinavian is still in his prime." Similarly, a retired Harvard professor sneered, "The Jew's weak point is always physical cowardice." In the face of such antisemitic stereotyping, many Jews sought to prove their manhood. Increasing numbers of Jewish men flocked to boxing gyms. And some became policemen on Roosevelt's force. In so doing, they proved that Jews were more than enfeebled survivors of the shtetl. They could become commanding figures, defenders of the people and the law.[81]

Roosevelt may have nursed a particular affinity for his Jewish officers because he had traveled a similar path from frailty to fortitude. In childhood, Roosevelt suffered from a litany of medical issues. His lungs labored under the strain of asthma, his stomach endured the discomforts of nausea, and his bowels were afflicted with nervous diarrhea. "I feel badly," the young Roosevelt once told his mother. "I have a toothache in my stomach." His father instilled in him a conviction that overcoming ailments was a matter of sheer grit, advising his ailing son, "Theodore, you have the mind but you have not the body.... You must make your body." Roosevelt developed an obsession with masculine physicality, exercising diligently in the home gym that his father had installed. In the fullness of time, Roosevelt came to master his maladies. He emerged as a decent boxer in his Harvard days, mirroring the Jewish proclivity for pugilism.[82] And in his twenties, Roosevelt roughed it as a rancher in Badlands of the Dakota Territory.[83] He carried this premium on rugged machismo into his role as police commissioner, valuing Jews and Gentiles on his force who shared his ethic of manly courage.

When Roosevelt proudly recalled the vitality of his Jewish policemen, he did so with notable reference to Jewish antiquity. Roosevelt wanted his "officers of Jewish extraction" to embody "the Maccabee type" who showed "nerve and hardihood."[84] Here, he was alluding to the ancient Jewish warriors known as the Maccabees, famous for revolting against Greek persecution and establishing Jewish control of Judea. His interest in Maccabee lore likely stemmed from personal experience. As an adolescent in 1873, Roosevelt sailed with his family to the Holy Land and alighted from their ship in Jaffa, an important site in the Maccabean rebellion. The Books of the Maccabees related how upwards of two hundred Jews were deliberately drowned in Jaffa, prompting the Maccabees to avenge those deaths by setting fire to Jaffa's harbor.[85] Roosevelt almost certainly learned something of this history during his visit.

His description of Jewish policemen as Maccabees also gestures toward a pluralistic strand in his thinking. Roosevelt rejected the commonplace notion that Jewishness and weakness were of a piece. Instead, Jews could live up to his masculine ideal by honoring, rather than effacing, their Jewish heritage. Reflecting on his time as police commissioner, he remarked in a private letter that the Jewish cultivation of Maccabean instincts would serve to blunt antisemitism by showcasing that Jews could be brawny and not just brainy. "I made up my mind it would be a particularly good thing for men of the Jewish race to develop that side of them which I might call the Maccabee or fighting Jewish type," Roosevelt shared. Gentiles would then see that Jews were not only "successful and thrifty businessmen and high-minded philanthropists, but also able to do their part in the rough manly work, which is no less necessary." In so doing, Jews could "put a stop to the unreasoning prejudice against them."[86] TR wasn't denigrating intellectual achievement but valorizing physical mettle as a complementary value. Roosevelt himself combined the cerebral and corporeal in his daily life—even as he did the gritty work of policing New York, he somehow managed to finish writing his multivolume historical study of the American West that he had begun years earlier.[87]

Of all the Maccabee types on the police force, one always stood out in Roosevelt's eyes: Otto Raphael. He was, in Roosevelt's words, a "genuine East Sider."[88] The Raphael family had emigrated from Russia and opened a struggling meat market on Allen Street, where Otto Raphael helped out. He was roused one evening in 1895 by the scent of smoke when a nearby tenement became engulfed in flames. Raphael knew firsthand how dangerous the tenements could be, even under the best of conditions; his mother had died a few years earlier when she tripped into a cellar apartment. On the fateful night of the fire, Raphael—in his mid-twenties and full of vigor—ran into the burning building multiple times to rescue people trapped inside.[89] His bravery was all the more noteworthy given that fires in overcrowded tenements could be extremely lethal. As Jacob Riis recounted in macabre terms, "A fire-panic at night in a tenement ... is a horror that has few parallels in human experience."[90]

Later that year, Raphael attended a talk by Roosevelt at a YMCA downtown. The philanthropist who had invited Roosevelt to speak insisted that TR meet the local hero who had saved numerous lives from an inferno. Roosevelt sized up Raphael as "a powerful fellow, with [a] good-humored intelligent face." The new police commissioner encouraged Raphael to take the police exam and try to earn a spot on the force.[91] Raphael made the cut, reportedly ranking tenth out of 380 applicants for mental aptitude and first for physical ability.[92] Joining the police was a source of great pride for Raphael—and of great practicality. His salary enabled him to educate his younger siblings and to send for other family members who had been left behind in Russia.[93]

As it turned out, Raphael had a skill set of keen interest to Roosevelt. The Jewish policeman had some amateur boxing titles to his name and became Roosevelt's sparring partner. Their friendship, cultivated in the ring, would last a lifetime. Roosevelt came to know Raphael's entire family, and after TR's rise to the presidency, Raphael would visit him at the White House.⁹⁴ Later, Roosevelt made a point of writing affectionately about Raphael in his autobiography. For all the differences between them, Roosevelt emphasized the similarities: "He and I were both 'straight New York' to use the vernacular of our native city."⁹⁵

Roosevelt brought to the police department a reformer's ardor, and in so doing he found common cause with many of the progressive pioneers who were engaged in humanitarian work on the East Side. Some were Jews; others were Gentiles. Most notable among the latter was Jacob Riis himself. The Danish immigrant's pathbreaking book *How the Other Half Lives* had stirred the national conscience with its searing depictions of life in "Jewtown" and other New York slums. Riis thereby helped catalyze an era of journalistic "muckraking" (a term that Roosevelt popularized). This mode of exposé reportage offered advocacy as much as description, and its practitioners were highly comfortable forging alliances with likeminded politicians.⁹⁶

Just after the 1890 debut of *How the Other Half Lives*, Roosevelt was so struck on turning its pages that he headed over to Riis's office at the *Evening Sun* newspaper to find the author. But Riis was absent, prompting Roosevelt to leave his calling card with a succinct message scribbled on the back: "I have read your book and I have come to help."⁹⁷ Roosevelt would finally make good on that promise five years later when he took over the police department. Riis became the new commissioner's personal tour guide of the city, giving Roosevelt a firsthand introduction to the onerous conditions plaguing New York's immigrant enclaves—including the Lower East Side.⁹⁸

That a native New Yorker like Roosevelt needed an outsider to show him his own city suggests much about the class divide in contemporary New York.⁹⁹ Roosevelt's rarefied upbringing in the genteel neighborhood of Gramercy Park made him a stranger to the dismal poverty mere

FIGURE 1.4. Jacob Riis. *Credit*: Frances Benjamin Johnston. *Source*: Library of Congress, Prints and Photographs Division.

blocks away. "It is a fairy-land of contrasts," one observer remarked of New York City. "One moment you are tumbled through streets full of ruts and holes; the next . . . you dine off gold plates and drink out of crystal vessels."[100] Roosevelt knew more of the gold than the ruts, but he was eager to learn from Riis about the indigent New Yorkers whose health and safety were now his responsibility.[101]

TR grew acquainted with leaders of the settlement house movement who were then training their energies on the Lower East Side. Settlement houses were iconic Progressive Era institutions, to be found in several American cities, which helped immigrants adapt to their new environment and ascend out of poverty. The term "settlement" derived from the practice of reformers personally settling in the neighborhoods they served. One such settlement on the East Side was the Educational Alliance—nicknamed the "Palace of Immigrants"—which offered classes thirteen hours a day. Instruction ranged from etiquette to English. For newcomers still limited to their mother tongue, Yiddish copies of the Declaration of Independence were made available. The Educational Alliance also sponsored performances and lectures. Literary luminaries from the novelist Mark Twain to the playwright Sholem Aleichem presented there.[102]

Among Roosevelt's closest collaborators in the settlement house movement was Lillian Wald, the twenty-eight-year-old founder of the Henry Street Settlement on the East Side. She was the daughter of an affluent German-Jewish family in Cincinnati who had opted out of her life of privilege to take up nursing in New York City.[103] At Wald's behest, Roosevelt became an honorary inductee to her settlement's American Hero Club, dedicated to the study of great figures from U.S. history. He must have been the only mustachioed member of the group; the other participants were local boys no older than twelve.[104] The club was precisely the kind of endeavor that appealed to Roosevelt, whose general approach toward immigrants was to extend a hand while also expecting them to become patriotic Americans.

Roosevelt's involvement with Wald and her settlement, which would become a lifelong connection for him, speaks to the complexity of his professional attitude toward women. On the one hand, he subscribed to a highly conventional view of gender roles. His ethic of roughhewn masculinity rested on a patriarchal worldview that would have women relegated to the domestic sphere.[105] "The greatest thing for any woman is to be a good wife and mother," he once told a female writer.[106] And yet Roosevelt increasingly developed warm working relationships with women who were active outside the home—journalists, novelists, and reformers. As one historian has astutely observed, "It is ironic that the sort of woman most deplored by Roosevelt became his natural political ally."[107] A number of these women, like Wald, were Jewish.[108]

Her settlement house was bankrolled by Jacob Schiff, a successful financier and philanthropist of Jewish faith. If the East Siders who relied on Wald's services represented one segment of New York Jewry ("downtown Jews"), her benefactor personified the other ("uptown Jews"). Uptown Jews luxuriated in expensive townhouses on fashionable streets; downtown Jews crowded into East Side tenements. Uptown Jews originated from Central Europe, often Germany; downtown Jews came from Eastern Europe, typically Russia. Uptown Jews practiced Reform Judaism; downtown Jews gravitated toward Orthodoxy. Uptown Jews had migrated to America in the middle decades of the nineteenth century; downtown Jews were fresh arrivals. Uptown Jews were Americanized; downtown Jews were still learning the ways of their adopted homeland. Uptown Jews met with success in banking and law; downtown Jews subsisted in sweatshops and hawked goods from pushcarts. Of course, exceptions abounded to the neat divisions enumerated above.[109] But the general patterns distinguishing uptown and downtown Jews were real—and could be found in other American cities that likewise had a divide between established Jews and their not-yet-assimilated coreligionists.[110]

Uptown Jews wanted to help their downtown counterparts who had fled dire circumstances abroad and who were now enduring the indignities of tenement life. After all, many established Jews weren't far removed from their own impecunious beginnings in America. They too had hustled on the Lower East Side before moving upward—in social standing and in street number. Their considerable philanthropy subsidized schools, hospitals, and settlement houses for recent Jewish immigrants. But these wealthier Jews had mixed motives for funneling their resources downtown. They feared their own stature in society might be imperiled if their coreligionists from Eastern Europe failed to better their station and quickly Americanize. As a German-born rabbi on the Upper East Side fretted, "Will the Russian or Romanian Jew—now an object of pity owing to his defective education, his lack of culture, his pauperism, his utter helplessness—drag American Judaism down from the honorable position it has attained?" The townhouse Jew and the tenement Jew shared a common faith; they were destined to also share a common reputation in Gentile eyes.[111]

Prior to Roosevelt's tenure in the police department, his exposure to Jews had been of the uptown variety, as might be expected of a patrician Gentile. Among his college friends was a Jewish boy who hailed from a wealthy family and had studied at a prestigious academy on the Upper West Side before attending Harvard with TR.[112] When Roosevelt launched his political career as a state legislator in the early 1880s, he affiliated with elite Jews in New York City's Republican circles.[113] He even appeared at an uptown Purim party in 1883.[114] But now, as police commissioner, Roosevelt was gaining his first sustained exposure to Eastern European Jewry. His entrée into their world was sufficiently well received that he became a distinguished guest at Jewish weddings, often bestowed the honor of escorting the bride or her mother to the banquet following the ceremony.[115]

TR cultivated ties to Protestant reformers who were teaming with the likes of Lillian Wald to ameliorate the dire conditions of the Lower East Side. At a supper that Wald hosted at the Henry Street Settlement, for instance, Roosevelt dined with William Dean Howells, a literary giant of the age.[116] Howells soon thereafter published an essay about the neighborhood called "An East-Side Ramble," prompting an enthusiastic response from Roosevelt. "That was a very remarkable study of the life of the East Side Jew; I enjoyed it much," the police commissioner wrote, inviting Howells to a meal at his home.[117] Roosevelt also prevailed upon the Protestant matron of the illustrious Van Rensselaer family to provide funds for a girls' library on the Lower East Side.[118] TR came to know yet another Protestant reformer named James Bronson Reynolds, who ran an East Side settlement house.[119] Reynolds made the mistake of permitting Christian missionaries to try proselytizing the Jews who frequented his settlement. These conversion attempts ceased after the intervention of Jacob Schiff, who was helping underwrite not just Wald's operation but Reynolds's as well.[120]

Roosevelt also regularly showed up at a public school on Houston Street whose students—or "scholars" as TR called them—were largely

Jewish. He was "immensely interested" in the school, which was a vital means of upward mobility for the children of Jewish immigrants.[121] Education was a battleground for church-state relations, and Roosevelt thought it vital to separate the two. For him, that meant keeping public schools nonsectarian and withholding state funds from religious schools. Roosevelt would later explain that although he was personally comfortable with Bible recitations in public schools, wherever "Jews may object to its being read" he would "openly stand against reading the Bible."[122] As Roosevelt saw firsthand on the East Side, public school classrooms full of Jews were often led by Christian teachers, and he was sensitive to the delicacy of that dynamic.

Many Gentiles may have joined Roosevelt in building bridges to the Jewish community, but others chafed at the idea. A significant faction of the patrician class—typically native-born Americans who were abundant in resources and Northern European in descent—found Jews unacceptable. In New York City and elsewhere, reactionary elites grew alarmed at the newfound prominence of uptown Jews. Old Money gentry were generally fearful of becoming displaced by the New Money crowd born of industrial capitalism. Uptown Jews, successfully riding the wave of a modern economy, seemed to exemplify this threat.[123] Anxieties about a Jewish takeover were, of course, wildly overblown; the silk-stocking Anglo-Saxons still enjoyed outsized control of American society.

Henry Adams epitomized elite paranoia about Jewish domination. He was a scion of the Adams presidential dynasty and perhaps the most virulent antisemite of the upper classes. "We are in the hands of the Jews," Adams lamented to a British politician. "They can do what they please with our values."[124] Despite Adams's immensely privileged life, he nevertheless insisted to a senator's wife, "In a society of Jews and brokers, a world made up of maniacs wild for gold, I have no place."[125] The likes of Adams helped ensure that well-heeled Jews were often blackballed from institutions—private schools, social clubs, summer resorts—that were de rigueur for blue-blooded Gentiles.[126] Roosevelt befriended Adams and his ilk, but TR himself wasn't complicit in excluding Jews. In fact, as a twenty-something beginning his involvement in New York politics, Roosevelt threatened to terminate his membership in a Republican club after some participants sought to refuse a Jewish applicant. Roosevelt's defiant stand against antisemitism resulted in that applicant's admission.[127]

A prominent Reform rabbi in New York voiced exasperation that the Jew who did assimilate was regarded as menacing but the Jew who did not was derided as clannish: "How singular that, when the Jews attempts to . . . mix freely with his neighbors, he is repelled and unceremoniously shown back to his own tribe; and if he keeps there, he is accused of hereditary and ancestral pride."[128] Such was the illogic of Jew hatred.

The antisemites of "polite society" were distressed not only by the Jewish nouveau riche.[129] Highborn hate was also directed at the impoverished Jewish immigrants then flooding American ports. Henry Adams shuddered at the "Polish Jew fresh from Warsaw or Kraków . . . a furtive Yacoob or Ysaac still reeking of the Ghetto, snarling a weird Yiddish to the officers of the customs."[130] Arguably the most institutionalized expression of genteel antisemitism was the Immigration Restriction League, founded in the mid-1890s by three young Harvard grads of Anglo-Saxon descent. They hoped to suppress the influx of Jews as well as other "undesirables" from Southern and Eastern Europe. "Shall we permit these inferior races to dilute the thrifty, capable Yankee blood?" asked one of the league's founders in the *Boston Herald*.[131]

The gentry wasn't the only social class in America giving vent to Judeophobia. Farmers in the heartland could not grasp the complex interplay of global forces that were increasing their costs and reducing their profits. Instead, they gravitated toward the simplicity of a scapegoat: the Jew. Rural populists saw Jews as shifty financiers who didn't produce goods of value but merely served as middle men, transferring funds and taking an unjust cut.[132] Many hapless agrarians were sure their misery came at the hands of Jewish bankers in coastal cities.[133] Disaffected farmers banded together to form a third party, the Populist Party, in the 1890s. During the party's national gathering in 1896, the Associated Press reported, "One of the striking things about the Populist convention . . . is the extraordinary hatred of the Jewish race. It is not possible to go into any hotel in the city without hearing the most bitter denunciation of the Jewish race as a class and of particular Jews who happen to have prospered in the world."[134] Although these bigoted soil tillers shared little in common with the moneyed patricians of the East Coast, both groups reacted to the disorientation of modernity by lashing out at Jews.[135]

Yet another demographic contributed to the age's antisemitism: urban immigrants. In several American cities, other ethnic enclaves—Irish, Italian, Polish—abutted Jewish neighborhoods. Close proximity amid dire living conditions didn't always make for warm relations between immigrant groups. Jewish peddlers were subjected to jeering, stone-throwing, and beard-pulling. At worst, street gangs beat up innocent Jews for sport. Police assistance was no guarantee in many municipalities, and so Jews took to forming their own protective associations.[136]

Even as American antisemitism was a reaction to recent developments—from industrial capitalism to global migration—it was also grounded in older prejudices. The trope of the dishonest Jewish swindler, which applied as readily to the pushcart peddler as to the Wall Street banker, had deep roots in world history. For centuries, diasporic Jews had been bereft of their own homeland. They resided in various societies as outsiders whose opportunities to earn a livelihood were often legally limited to trade and finance. Even as Jews were shunted into particular fields of commerce, they were resented for their prominence in those very fields. This paradox of prejudice endured into Roosevelt's era. The age of industrial capitalism placed a rising premium on the commercial expertise that Jews had long cultivated. In other words, Jews were well positioned to navigate a modern economy precisely because of their fraught history. Their success predictably gave fresh life to timeworn stereotypes about deceitful Hebrews.[137]

Christian teachings inflected American antisemitism as well. The Jews, after all, were culpable for Jesus's death—at least according to some interpretations of the New Testament. Many Christians were bound to feel hostility toward a people who were allegedly responsible for deicide.[138] The Christian basis for antisemitism was hardly lost on American Jews of Roosevelt's day. The *Jewish Messenger*, a New York–based paper, suggested that "the religious training of the Christian" was the principal factor in "the persistency of popular prejudice against the Jew." The paper elaborated, "As most Christians have capacity to understand only the material elements in the crucifixion, they take a grim religious pleasure—a sense of duty done—in crucifying the Jew."[139] For some Christians, the New Testament also seemed to provide a Biblical basis for stereotypes about Jewish avarice, as Jesus angrily confronted Jews who were desecrating the Temple by using it as a forum for money changing.[140]

It is unsurprising, then, that many of the era's most strident Jew-baiters were Christian clergymen. A reverend in Baltimore preached from the pulpit that the Jew is "merciless, tricky, vengeful—a veritable Shylock who loses every sentiment of humanity in his greed. Of all the creatures who have befouled the earth, the Jew is the slimiest."[141] Christianity, however, was not monolithic; mainstream clergy in America eschewed antisemitism.[142] Indeed, many of the nation's most outspoken critics of Jew-hatred were men of the cloth. But to the extent that Judeophobia did have purchase on American life, the blame lay with ancient prejudices as much as modern conditions.

Theodore Roosevelt had a conspicuous confrontation with antisemitism during Hanukkah in his first year as police commissioner. A vicious Jew-hater from Germany, Hermann Ahlwardt, was planning a trip to New York City to spread his invidious message. He was cartoonishly villainous. In the late 1880s, Ahlwardt was sacked as a school headmaster after the revelation that he had stolen funds designated for the children's Christmas party. The disgraced Ahlwardt sought public redemption through antisemitism, publishing bigoted screeds at a prolific rate. It then surfaced that he had forged documents to promote his anti-Jewish conspiracy theories, and Ahlwardt was consequently sentenced to prison. His four months behind bars did little to dampen his ardor for hate-mongering. Upon his release, Ahlwardt won a seat in the German parliament by persuading farmers in a rural district that Jews had secretly orchestrated the global downturn in crop prices. His election afforded him legal immunity from prosecution for peddling falsehoods.[143]

When Ahlwardt set his sights on an American speaking tour—including a planned lecture on the Lower East Side—anxious Jews approached Commissioner Roosevelt. They asked TR to bar Ahlwardt from speaking or at least to deny him police protection. But Roosevelt could not grant their request without violating the principle of free speech. And even absent that constitutional right, he believed that government censorship would only serve to turn Ahlwardt into a martyr. Roosevelt would later recall feeling that "the proper thing to do was to make him ridiculous." To that end, TR devised an exceedingly clever scheme: he would provide Ahlwardt a police detail comprised entirely of Jewish officers.[144]

Roosevelt summoned a subordinate on his force and instructed him, "I wish a list made of thirty good, trusty, intelligent men, all Jews." It was crucial to Roosevelt that these officers look unmistakably Jewish. As he told the subordinate, "Don't bother yourself to hunt up their religious antecedents; take those who have the most pronounced Hebrew physiognomy—the stronger their ancestral marking, the better." The Jewish policemen selected for duty were brought to the commissioner for inspection. With his blue eyes and golden glasses, Roosevelt surveyed the assemblage. One of his associates later marveled, "A more Hebraic group of Hebrews probably never were gathered in one small room."[145]

Roosevelt informed these officers of the unusual and vital duty ahead of them. "Now, I am going to assign you men to the most honorable service you have ever done—the protection of an enemy and the defense of religious liberty and free speech in the chief city of the United States," he announced. "You all know who and what Dr. Ahlwardt is. I am going to put you in charge of the hall where he lectures, and hold you responsible for perfect good order there throughout the evening." Roosevelt explained that their safeguarding Ahlwardt did not, of course, proceed from any affinity they had for his views. Rather, they would be defending the very constitutional liberties that American Jews held dear. In Roosevelt's words, "I have no more sympathy with Jew-baiting than you have. But this is a country where your people are free to think and speak and act as they choose in religious matters, as long as you do not interfere with the peace and comfort of your neighbors, and

Dr. Ahlwardt is entitled to the same privilege." He added, "It should be your pride to see that he is protected. . . . That will be the finest way of showing your appreciation of the liberty you yourselves enjoy under the American flag."[146]

On the second night of Hanukkah, around 150 people gathered at Cooper Union—an iconic venue on the Lower East Side—to hear Ahlwardt's much-anticipated speech. The press estimated that fully a third of the spectators were policemen and detectives, another third were Jews who had come in protest, and the last third consisted of Gentiles of varying nationalities who were presumably amenable to the speaker's agenda. Ahlwardt took the stage at eight that evening, met by a mix of scattered applause and shouts of disapproval. His remarks inevitably veered into antisemitism, and the Jewish civilians in the crowd taunted him in turn with "a perfect Niagara of hisses and cries," the *New York Times* reported. Despite the heckling, the galling grin plastered on Ahlwardt's face remained unbroken. The night's greatest drama unfolded when Ahlwardt denounced the Jews for their "odious peculiarities," prompting an East Sider named Louis Silverman to cock his arm, egg in hand. "A nice white egg performed a graceful parabola through the air in the direction of Herr Ahlwardt's smiling face," the *Times* recounted. "He danced aside, with a degree of agility not indicated by his [portly] form, and the egg smashed and spluttered on the chair behind him." Two more eggs were launched before officers seized Silverman and dragged him to the nearby police station on Fifth Street.[147]

The episode would become part of Roosevelt's lore with the Jewish community. With great pride he routinely recalled how "Ahlwardt delivered his violent harangues against the men of Hebrew faith, owing his safety to the fact that he was scrupulously protected by men of the very race which he was denouncing."[148] Roosevelt understood that the sight of Jewish policemen selflessly guarding the German Jew-hater did far more to undermine Ahlwardt's repugnant ideas than preemptive censorship ever could have. Reflecting on the incident years later in his autobiography, Roosevelt remarked, "It was an object-lesson to our people, whose greatest need it is to learn that there must be no division by class hatred, whether . . . of creed against creed, nationality against nationality, section against section."[149] This was merely the first of Roosevelt's confrontations with European antisemitism.

★ ★ ★

Notwithstanding TR's adroit handling of the Ahlwardt affair, Roosevelt himself sometimes traded in antisemitic tropes during these years. One such instance transpired in the wake of the 1896 presidential election, which saw Republican William McKinley wrest the White House from Democratic hands. The victory was doubly sweet for Jews working in New York's financial industry. For one, the incoming Republican president aligned with their preference for keeping the U.S. dollar on the gold standard. And the GOP win also marked a triumph over religious prejudice against Jews, given that the antisemitic Populist Party had opted to back the Democratic nominee.[150]

"The victorious Republican leaders have taken to feasting themselves," Roosevelt told his older sister, Bamie. He explained that he had attended a number of these opulent celebrations. "One was a huge lunch by the Seligmans"—one of the nation's most prominent Jewish families who enjoyed warm relations with Roosevelt—"where at least half the guests were Jew bankers." Referring to Henry Adams's brother Brooks (who shared Henry's antisemitism), Roosevelt joked, "I felt as if I was personally realizing all of Brooks Adams's gloomiest anticipations of our gold-ridden, capitalist-bestridden, usurer-mastered future."[151] TR was partly mocking Brooks Adams's paranoia but partly reinforcing tropes about the Jewish overlords of world finance.

That checkered statement aside, one of Roosevelt's private remarks from his police days stands out for the unalloyed nature of its prejudice. After a prominent Jewish Republican—fearful that the police commissioner's crusade against drinking would backfire at the polls—tried to marginalize Roosevelt politically, TR derided him as a "graceless sheeny" in a letter to Senator Lodge. "Sheeny" is an epithet for a Jew.[152] The slur was so offensive that when Lodge produced a published edition of their correspondence, the senator bowdlerized TR's letter so that it read "graceless person."[153]

★ ★ ★

The incoming McKinley regime meant new opportunities for Republicans on the make, Roosevelt among them. He was favored with a plum post: Assistant Secretary of the Navy. Roosevelt's interest in the Navy dated back to his Harvard days, when he first began writing a book entitled *The Naval War of 1812*.[154] It elicited favorable reviews upon publication in 1882; historians today still regard it as a classic in the field.[155] With this new appointment in the McKinley administration, Roosevelt would transition from chronicler of naval affairs to practitioner of them. And he took advantage of his naval office to help push America into a war in the Caribbean—one with important consequences for his relationship with Jewry.[156]

Cuban rebels were then engaged in a lethal struggle for independence against the island's European colonizer, Spain. The Spanish had subjected Cuba to autocratic rule and extracted wealth from the island for their own benefit for years. Like most Americans, Roosevelt's sympathies lay with the guerilla fighters. The United States, after all, had once been an emergent nation in the Western Hemisphere that freed itself from a European monarchy. The Cuban rebels also benefited from a successful propaganda campaign in America—they even opened a public relations office in New York—as stateside newspapers dutifully whipped up support for the Cuban independence movement. While Spain's human rights abuses against Cuban civilians during the conflict were very real, American journalists glibly exaggerated the depths of Cuban suffering.[157]

Roosevelt fervently wanted U.S. forces to help the rebels break their stalemate against the Spanish troops. He believed that military intervention in Cuba would allow the United States to project its own power in the hemisphere and thereby deter other European powers from entertaining designs on America's backyard.[158] But Roosevelt's eagerness for conflict with Spain wasn't just about his vision for an expanding sphere of American influence. He and other pro-war "jingoes" saw the battlefield as the ultimate arena for manly courage.[159] American men could find in the crucible of war an antidote to the crass consumerism that was seen as eroding national morality.[160] Roosevelt in particular had contempt for a certain kind of "effeminate" man who was "over-civilized, over-sensitive, [and] over-refined."[161] With war against Spain possibly on the horizon, he was desperate to personally serve on the front lines.

The Cuban rebels had first launched their military campaign in 1895, stirring hopes in the newly minted police commissioner that America would join the cause. Roosevelt told the New York governor that he would like to serve as a captain if the state raised a volunteer regiment. But no such regiment materialized as the United States remained on the sidelines.[162] Two years later, with Roosevelt now in the Navy and still hoping for American intervention, he conveyed to President McKinley that he would want to engage in combat in the event of war against Spain. Perhaps Roosevelt's lust for battle was rooted in a sense of shame about his father's decision to hire a substitute to fight in his place during the Civil War. Or maybe Roosevelt had a death wish, a romantic yearning to perish with honor on the field of battle.[163] By his own telling, Roosevelt felt that he would be guilty of hypocrisy should he fail to wield a weapon in wartime after spouting "jingo doctrines." He was referring here not just to his bellicose rhetoric about Spain specifically but his longstanding tendency to praise the virtues of military service generally.[164] From his perch at the Navy, Roosevelt tried to cajole McKinley into war, but the president was resistant.[165] McKinley knew too intimately the horrors of war—he had served as a private in the Union Army—and he did not wish to see "the dead piled up" once more.[166]

Roosevelt sent a strikingly candid letter to a Navy captain in the fall of 1897 accusing French-Jewish financiers of profiting off Spain's counterinsurgency against the Cuban rebels. "The Jew moneylenders in Paris, plus one or two big commercial companies in Spain, are trying to keep up the war," he alleged.[167] In reality, Roosevelt had it backwards. French investors—Jew and Gentile alike—actually wanted the conflict to end. Precisely because numerous French citizens and banks owned Spanish bonds, they didn't want to see Spain bankrupt itself in a costly struggle against the Cubans.[168] It is telling that Roosevelt felt compelled to identify the French investors as "Jew moneylenders" and to erroneously assume the worst of them; plainly, he was susceptible to defamatory tropes about Jews in finance, even as he himself cultivated warm relationships with Jewish bankers in America.

Events soon conspired to hasten the declaration of war that Roosevelt had long craved. First, in early February 1898, rebels intercepted and leaked to the press a private letter in which the Spanish ambassador in Washington ridiculed McKinley as feckless. Americans deemed the letter an outrage to national honor.[169] And then, just six days later, came a seismic development: the U.S.S. *Maine*, which had dropped anchor in Havana's harbor, suddenly exploded. The blast was so violent that it could be felt throughout the Cuban capital. While some on board the *Maine* died instantly in the blast, most either drowned or burned alive. Around 260 souls lost their lives in all.[170]

Naturally, an American public already primed for war presumed that Spain was culpable for the disaster.[171] The Spanish disclaimed any responsibility.[172] A few lone voices at the time suggested that the explosion was likely the result of an accidental fire, a view that would gain some traction among later generations of experts.[173] Whatever the truth, the American press seized on the *Maine* tragedy to rally the people behind military action in Cuba. "Remember the *Maine*, to Hell with Spain" became a ubiquitous slogan.[174] McKinley still wanted to find a peaceful path forward. It would take two months for the reluctant president to acquiesce to the war fervor sweeping the country—in April, he finally solicited and received congressional approval to dispatch troops.[175]

To be sure, America was home to prominent anti-imperialists who decried the imminent war. They cringed as the United States prepared to flex its muscle abroad. Even as they recognized that Spain maltreated the Cuban people, the anti-imperialists marshaled an array of arguments against intervention. For one, they feared that a new generation of American leaders—who had come of age after the Civil War and thus were untouched by its blood-tinged lessons—were recklessly plunging the country into a violent confrontation. The anti-imperialists also observed that repression in Cuba, while regrettable, wasn't unique globally and thus did not warrant exceptional involvement from the United States. They further counseled their fellow citizens to address humanitarian challenges at home—such as anti-Black lynching and rampant poverty—before seeking out crises abroad.[176] And although pro-war Americans viewed their impending incursion into Cuba as a natural extension of George Washington's fight against an Old World empire, the anti-imperialists offered a very different interpretation: an American nation founded in defiance of European colonialism was now ready to join the European scramble for control of foreign territories or at least outsized influence over them.[177]

A renowned Harvard professor, Charles Eliot Norton, pithily captured the anti-imperialist mood in an iconic speech in Cambridge. "A generation has grown up that has known nothing of war.... And now [all] of a sudden, without cool deliberation, without prudent preparation, the nation is hurried into war, and America—she who more than any other land was pledged to peace and goodwill on earth—unsheathes her sword," Norton lamented. "She has been forced to turn back from the way of civilization to the way of barbarism, to renounce for the time her own ideals."[178] Those who shared Norton's fears would become increasingly alarmed as America soon set its sights not just on Cuba but also Hawaii, Guam, Puerto Rico, and the Philippines. From the anti-imperialist perspective, the United States seemed less of a liberator than a colonizer.[179]

TR had no such qualms at the prospect of an American empire stretching beyond its shores. He imagined the United States as a benevolent influence on other lands.[180] So did most of his fellow citizens, as the anti-imperialists found themselves decidedly in the minority.[181] Despite the profound differences between the interventionists and the anti-imperialists, each camp touted itself as standing up for humanity abroad.

★ ★ ★

Having long fantasized about martial glory, Roosevelt finally had his chance. He was named lieutenant colonel of the First Volunteer Cavalry, better known as the "Rough Riders" and led by Colonel Leonard Wood. TR's first task was helping select from some twenty-three thousand applicants the one thousand men who would brave Spanish bullets alongside him.[182] Roosevelt took satisfaction in assembling a heterogenous group, from Princeton alums and rugged cowboys to polo players and Cherokee Indians. He would proudly reminisce, "All—Easterners and Westerners, Northerners and Southerners, officers and men, cowboys and college graduates, wherever they came from, and whatever their social position—possessed in common the traits of hardihood and a thirst for adventure."[183] Given the life-and-death circumstances, the composition of the Rough Riders offers perhaps the best evidence that Roosevelt's long insistence on the benefits of diversity wasn't merely optical.

Among his recruits were Jews. Many Jews were ineligible, despite their physical prowess, because they lacked experience on horseback. When his old friend from the police force Otto Raphael offered his services, Roosevelt responded with disappointing news. "My dear Officer Raphael: I should like to take you with me, but I am very much afraid I won't be able to," Roosevelt informed him. "You see, we only want men who ride well, and I don't think you have ever done any riding."[184] Even though a champion boxer like Raphael did not fit the profile of a Rough Rider, about eight Jews did make the cut, many from the West.[185]

Their reasons for enlisting are not difficult to imagine. As with non-Jewish volunteers, they surely felt a sense of civic duty at a moment when patriotic zeal was galvanizing the nation. They were also undoubtedly aware that fellow Jews had counted among those servicemen lost in the U.S.S. *Maine* explosion.[186] And the opportunity to fight Spain would have held special appeal for Jews—the Spanish Inquisition was a relatively fresh memory, having officially ended only sixty years earlier. Rabbis around the country reminded their congregants that America's enemy was the self-same that had perpetrated a historic genocide of the Jewish people. At Sinai Temple in Chicago, a sermonizer juxtaposed Spain's tradition of persecution with America's commitment to freedom. "The civilization of the inquisition and the civilization of religious tolerance stand at opposite poles," he asserted.[187] Meanwhile, the Jewish press depicted the war in Biblical terms by analogizing the Spanish king to Pharaoh, the Caribbean Sea to the Red Sea, and the American troops to the Chosen People.[188]

As the Rough Riders began their training in San Antonio, the men gave each other ironic nicknames. An unworldly cowpuncher became "Metropolitan Bill," a soldier of tender heart and few words was called "Hell Roarer," and an especially strident recruit picked up the sobriquet "Prayerful James." Two of the nicknames had Jewish inflections. A decidedly non-Jewish Irishman was designated "Sheeny Solomon." And, as Roosevelt recalled, "A young Jew who developed into one of the best fighters in the regiment accepted, with entire equanimity, the name of 'Pork Chop.'"[189] Soon this hodgepodge of volunteers would follow Roosevelt into mortal danger.

When the Rough Riders landed on Cuban shores in late June, they were beset with hazards: scorching sun, torrential downpours, punishing marches, muddy terrain, and mosquito swarms. Some of those insects carried a deadly virus known as "the black vomit," which induced its human victims to puke up their own intestines. And Mother Nature's perils were compounded by the lethal threat of Spanish snipers hiding amid the thick jungle foliage.[190] Naturally, Roosevelt endured these fraught conditions in a custom uniform he had ordered for himself from Brooks Brothers.[191]

The ultimate goal was the capture of a key city, Santiago. But the Rough Riders, alongside other American regiments, would first have to fight their way through the San Juan Heights—a series of hills manned by Spanish infantry. Just before the Americans launched their offensive, Rough Rider commander Leonard Wood was suddenly reassigned to fill in for a general who had taken ill. Roosevelt accordingly was promoted to colonel and given full command of the Rough Riders. On the morning of July 1, they began their assault. TR was fearless in the face of the death. "He's a perfect devil in action," one of his men remarked. "He's always ahead, waving on the men with his sword in one hand and a big revolver in the other, and yelling all the while like a garret full of cats let loose."[192]

A Jewish Rough Rider named Sam Greenwald sent a letter from the front to his father. "We have been since the 1st fighting our way into Santiago and some of it was pretty hot fighting," Greenwald recounted. Although he had none of Roosevelt's romanticism about military conflict—"I tell you war is a terrible thing"—Greenwald showed courage

FIGURE 1.5. Colonel Roosevelt. *Source*: Library of Congress, Prints and Photographs Division.

under fire. As he pridefully relayed in his letter, "I have been made a lieutenant and, the beauty of it, I won it on the field."[193] Roosevelt himself had personally promoted Greenwald for "gallantry" in battle.[194] Yet another Jew, Sam Goldberg, caught a bullet in the hip and still soldiered onward.[195] These efforts were not in vain—the Rough Riders together with other American regiments seized the hills, and within a matter of days, Santiago itself was theirs. A defeated Spain quickly signaled to Washington it was prepared to broker terms, and a peace conference was scheduled for Paris that fall.[196]

★ ★ ★

The Jewish press gloried all summer in stories about the heroism of Roosevelt's Jewish troops. These tales of Jewish bravery challenged various stereotypes about Jewish men as weak in body, disloyal to the country, and more likely to profit off a war than to fight in one.[197] San Francisco's Jewish newspaper *Emanu-El* declared, "The Jewish volunteers fight not as Jews, but as Americans who love and honor the flag that rouses the Maccabean blood in them." This comment reflected a certain tension within American Jewry. On the one hand, *Emanu-El* wanted these Jewish soldiers to be seen as purely American, "not as Jews"—the paper liked to imagine the Rough Riders as a faith-neutral body whose Jews and Gentiles stood upon an equality precisely because religious identity was immaterial. On the other hand, the reference to "Maccabean blood" betokened a desire to emphasize a specifically Jewish heritage.[198]

As the victorious American troops in Santiago waited for the military to orchestrate their return home, they were visited by Joseph Krauskopf, a prominent rabbi from Philadelphia. He journeyed to Cuba in his capacity as a leader of the National Relief Commission, an interfaith charitable organization that tended to wounded and ill soldiers. When Krauskopf arrived in Santiago, the presiding officer sent orders to have Jewish soldiers from the various regiments summoned so that the rabbi could greet them. Never one to miss out on anything, Roosevelt insisted on joining his Jewish troops. He had met Krauskopf once before and now boasted to the rabbi about the exploits of his Jewish Rough Riders. Krauskopf reconstructed his conversation with Roosevelt in a report that was widely reprinted in the Jewish and mainstream press alike.[199]

In mid-August, the Rough Riders were transported to Montauk, Long Island, where they would spend the next month convalescing before mustering out. The troops were welcomed in Montauk with an enthusiastic reception from grateful citizens. Upon arrival, Roosevelt spoke to the press and touted his regiment's religious diversity: "Of the last five promotions I recommended from the ranks to the grade of Second Lieutenant, one was a Jew, one a Catholic, and two Protestants."[200]

The Rough Riders' demography was less representative when it came to race. Military policy segregated Black servicemen into their own regiments. These so-called Buffalo Soldiers served valiantly in the Spanish-American War, fighting side-by-side with Roosevelt's men in taking the San Juan Heights. The Buffalo Soldiers earned high praise for their valor. As a private under Roosevelt's command remarked, "There is not a man in the Rough Riders but takes off his hat to the negroes."[201] Roosevelt himself was less gracious. In both public statements and private letters, he minimized the contributions of the Buffalo Soldiers and thereby amplified the role his own regiment played.[202]

Indeed, Roosevelt's instinct for inclusivity would often extend to Jews far more than to Blacks throughout his career, especially in military matters. The "Brownsville affair" during his presidency stands out as an especially notorious moment in Roosevelt's attitude toward Blacks. In the Texas border town of Brownsville, mysterious men arbitrarily fired shots into houses and shops one evening. White townsfolk were quick to cast blame on a battalion of Black soldiers stationed at a nearby fort. But no evidence linked the shootings to anyone in the battalion. Instead of exonerating the Black troops accordingly, military investigators chose to assume that the battalion was engaged in a "conspiracy of silence" wherein innocent soldiers were supposedly covering up for whoever was guilty among them. Those investigators advised TR to summarily discharge the entire battalion "without honor," and Roosevelt obliged. One scholar notes, "This remains the only instance of mass punishment without trial in the history of the U.S. military." Generations later, the military would reopen its inquiry and posthumously absolve the discharged troops.[203]

To be sure, Roosevelt wasn't uniformly hostile toward Blacks. He famously took political heat, for instance, after hosting the Black leader Booker T. Washington at the White House.[204] But with respect to Brownsville, it is hard to imagine TR having a comparably unfair reaction had the episode involved accusations against Jewish servicemen.

Roosevelt's feats in Cuba earned him a cover story in *Harper's Weekly* and favorable headlines nationwide. He was, arguably, the most popular person in America. His overnight celebrity came at a particularly auspicious moment in state politics. New York's Republican governor was embroiled in scandal; the party would need a new candidate if it hoped to keep the governor's mansion in GOP hands.[205] Merely two weeks after disbanding the Rough Riders in mid-September, Roosevelt claimed the Republican nomination for the state's top office.[206]

He kept a keen eye on Jewish voters as election season kicked off. His premium on religious equality among the Rough Riders promised to redound to his benefit in Jewish enclaves. In Roosevelt's very first stump speech of the campaign, he highlighted the egalitarian culture of his regiment, wherein every soldier, "whether Protestant or Catholic, Jew or Gentile . . . was treated on his merits as a man." He saw fit in this opening address to mention by name one of the Jewish war heroes he had promoted, Sam Greenwald.[207] Some supporters at his events dressed as Rough Riders, not to be confused with actual Rough Riders who also showed up to support their colonel.[208]

Two days into his role as a gubernatorial candidate, TR wrote to Abraham Wolbarst—a young Jewish doctor and local Republican politico—to inquire about the Roosevelt campaign's prospects in the East Side's fourth district. Wolbarst was decidedly optimistic, provided that Roosevelt put in the effort. "With an honest, energetic, and aggressive campaign, the district will give you a handsome vote," replied Wolbarst. "This district is largely Jewish and can be depended upon to support you heartily. You have many friends among the downtown Jews, who have always admired an honest public official." The moment was ripe for Roosevelt to capitalize on the goodwill he had cultivated with Jewish immigrants during his tenure as police commissioner. Wolbarst advised, "As the campaign advances, it would be well to interest the East Side peddlers in a body on your behalf. They will never forget the noble treatment received at your hands while in the Police Department."[209] Given Tammany's conventional strength with immigrants, Wolbarst's remarks were overly rosy. Democrats were destined to prevail in New York City, including on the East Side. The crucial question was whether Roosevelt could narrow the Democratic margin of victory in the city and then make up the difference upstate.

An astute politician, Roosevelt took no votes for granted. He wrote to a New York City congressman, Lemuel Quigg, about the campaign's need to incorporate more grassroots figures of the Wolbarst variety. "It seems to me that there should be an immediate effort to arrange—especially in the German, Jewish, and Scandinavian communities—meetings" with "men like Dr. Wolbarst, and the local leaders in each Assembly district," Roosevelt insisted. He was growing anxious about turnout, warning Quigg, "The registration does not look as well as it should, and no stone should be left unturned."[210]

Five days later, an apprehensive Roosevelt sent Quigg a follow-up letter about two Lower East Side districts. "I am told that in both the 4th and 8th Assembly districts, very little is being done," he relayed. TR urged action and recommended they turn to an old ally: "Jacob Riis of the *Sun* wants to give all the help he can" with "the East Side people." Roosevelt also sought to ensure that Republican leaders were properly supporting the Blaine Club, an organization for Jewish Republicans on the Lower East Side. "Some financial aid should be given to the Blaine Club," Roosevelt suggested, telling Quigg that the Blaine Club members "are, I think, sincerely for me; but they are very poor, and they have to have a little aid to enable them to hold meetings or get out banners." He floated some other names with credibility on the East Side who could be leaned upon to promote the Republican cause. "Can't Meyer Isaacs be asked to speak?" Roosevelt asked, alluding to a Jewish lawyer who was well connected in GOP circles. And in case Congressman Quigg missed the letter's earlier reference to Jacob Riis, Roosevelt anxiously signed off, "Can't you see Riis?" and then added in a postscript, "Do send for Riis."[211]

Soon the Republican State Committee was inundating the Lower East Side with Yiddish flyers, which depicted the American victory over Spain as righteous vengeance against a wicked nation that had shed Jewish blood during the Inquisition. "Spain now lies punished for all her sins," the flyer proclaimed, crediting Theodore Roosevelt and President McKinley. "Every vote for the Colonel of the Rough Riders is approval of McKinley and the War. Every vote for Roosevelt's opponent is a vote for Spain.... Vote to express your approval of Spain's defeat." The Republicans plainly believed—probably correctly—that the emotional symbolism of a historic victory over Spain loomed larger than local issues for a great many Jewish constituents.[212]

An enterprising candidate like Roosevelt wouldn't leave it entirely to deputies and flyers to do his bidding; he resolved to barnstorm the East Side himself. Roosevelt took a grand tour of the neighborhood in early November, stopping at various spots to give speeches. As a horse-drawn carriage carried him through the streets, a small army of cheering boys accompanied the candidate.[213] Adults surfaced too—some standing on tenement roofs, others peering through factory windows, still more congregating on street corners—to catch a glimpse of Roosevelt. The streets were festooned with streamers and bunting for the occasion, and portraits of TR hung from fire escapes. When exuberant crowds chanted his name, it sounded like these native Yiddish speakers were saying "Meester Rosenfeldt." One journalist reported that this Judaic pronunciation was "every bit as cordially received [by Roosevelt] as though the candidate really spelled his name in the East Side way."[214]

Notwithstanding these signs of approbation, some unsavory characters who opposed Roosevelt were prepared for mischief. "It might have been called an unmixed political triumph," the *New York Times* commented, "had not the enemies of the Republican candidate been awaiting his coming with sticks and stones and the kind of dead cat known to the boys of the East Side as 'sun birds.'"[215] The term "sun bird" was presumably an allusion to the fact that these deceased animals became aerial when hurled at a given target.

In a race that attracted national attention, Roosevelt emerged victorious on election day. His popularity with upstate voters sealed his win. And although Roosevelt expectedly lost the Democratic stronghold of New York City, he notably outran the rest of the GOP ticket there. The *Boston Evening Journal* attributed "his strength among the Hebrews" as a key factor in his relative success at the polls.[216]

★ ★ ★

The newly inaugurated governor harbored grave concerns about the unsanitary sweatshops so prevalent in the tenements. Roosevelt was not far removed from his days as police commissioner, when Jacob Riis had first introduced him to the perils of slum life during late-night strolls. There was a state law on the books promulgating numerous regulations for tenements to improve health and prevent overcrowding: strictly hygienic apartments, only one family per unit, no labor performed in bedrooms. But merely passing a law is different from actually implementing it. Roosevelt doubted that state inspectors were rigorously applying the statute, and he turned once more to Riis as an advisor. "I think that perhaps if I looked through the sweatshops myself with the inspectors, as well as looked over their work," Roosevelt wrote Riis, "we might be in a condition to put things on a new basis, just as they were put on a new basis in the police department after you and I began our midnight tours."[217]

The governor tapped Riis to personally orchestrate a visit to the sweatshops. Riis vividly recalled the outing, noting that the oppressive heat barely registered with the inexhaustible Roosevelt: "It was one of the hottest days of early summer, and it wore me completely out.... Him it only gave a better appetite for dinner." They diligently examined twenty of the East Side's most squalid tenements. Roosevelt was bitterly disappointed. He minced no words in dressing down the district's inspector who had joined them. "I do not think you quite understand what I mean by enforcing a law," the governor began. "I don't want it made as easy as possible for the manufacturer. I want you to refuse to license anybody in a tenement that does not come up to the top notch of your own requirements." Roosevelt admonished the inspector to put not just manufacturers but the building proprietors on notice: profiting off lax standards would no longer be tolerated.[218]

The problem, Roosevelt believed, wasn't just enforcement but the inadequacy of the law itself. Accordingly, he called for legislation that would, in Riis's words, fight back against "the mercenary hostility of the slum landlord."[219] The governor pleaded with lawmakers in Albany to fund a special commission that would conduct a thoroughgoing investigation and recommend statutory reforms. When the statehouse failed to demonstrate a Rooseveltian sense of urgency on the matter, he sent legislators an emergency message stressing the unprecedented opportunity before them. Perhaps never before in state history—Roosevelt declared—had lawmakers contemplated "a measure of more real importance to the welfare of those who are least able to protect themselves and whom we should especially guard from . . . the rapacity of those who would prey upon them." The legislature ultimately acceded to his request, and Roosevelt stacked the new commission with reformers who shared his outlook. They proposed statutory provisions to address a host of ills in the tenements, from fire hazards to rampant filth. Unsurprisingly, the Jewish press took a keen interest in these developments given the stakes for untold Jewish immigrants. The commission's work ultimately culminated in the passage of the Tenement House Act, which would take effect shortly after Roosevelt's departure from the governor's mansion.[220]

Among the perquisites of gubernatorial office is the power of appointment, and Roosevelt placed a number of Jews in important positions. These ranged from a seat on the Court of Appeals to executive posts like the State Gas Meter Inspector.[221] Roosevelt also named a Jewish woman in Syracuse, Etta Falker, to the Board of Managers for a women's prison. According to the press, she was the first Jewish woman to receive an appointment from a New York governor.[222] Nor was it easy to find a comparable figure beyond New York's borders. The *Hebrew Standard* newspaper mused, "Probably no other Jewish lady in the United States occupies such an important social and official position."[223]

As governor, Roosevelt was dogged by a philosophical contradiction with respect to hiring and promotion: he valued Jewish participation in government, but he also espoused a meritocratic ideal that paid faith no heed. In a private letter to a Gentile, Roosevelt emphasized his deliberate efforts to ensure religious diversity in his appointments. "On the State Board of Charities," he wrote, "I thought it was right to see that the different creeds had representation, and I think that the Jews whom I appointed . . . were as fine a body of American citizens as have ever been put on such a board." And yet, in that very same letter, Roosevelt denied that the religious identity of prospective appointees informed his decisions about whom to name for various offices. "When I appointed Judge Hirschberg of Newburg on the Appellate Division of the Supreme Court, I did so not because he was a Jew but because I thought he was the best judge for promotion," TR insisted. The rest of the letter oscillated between the ideals of intentional pluralism and faith-blind merit. In one sentence, Roosevelt explained that he recruited Jews to his police force, in part, to counter negative stereotypes about Jewish weakness. But in another sentence, he celebrated that his promotion of a Jewish Rough Rider to lieutenant bore no relationship to the soldier's religious background.[224] TR would prove just as inconsistent on this issue during his presidency.

Governor Roosevelt's interest in Jewish appointees wasn't limited to his own state. When he caught wind that antisemitic forces were trying to stymie a Jewish candidate under consideration for a federal post, TR personally intervened with President McKinley. "I have seen a good deal of Mr. [Israel] Fischer and am very strongly prepossessed in his favor," Roosevelt shared. "He is a public man of high character—a man who in every way comes up to the standard of qualifications you have a right to demand." TR then confronted the question of religious bigotry directly, acknowledging, "I have been informed that some opposition has been expressed to you because of Mr. Fischer's faith, he being a Jew, but I know that it is absolutely needless for me to say anything whatsoever on this score, for I know that you are incapable of so much as considering whether a man is Jew or Gentile, Catholic or Protestant, so long as he is a good American and a good citizen, and both of these Mr. Fischer is."[225] Fischer received his appointment.

During his governorship, Roosevelt had occasion to address anti-Jewish prejudice not just at home but overseas as well. The world over was then paying close attention to France's most notorious episode of antisemitism: the Dreyfus Affair. Alfred Dreyfus was a Jewish captain in the French army who had been wrongly convicted of divulging state secrets to the Germans. Although the charges were bogus, they dovetailed with long-running stereotypes found in many countries that Jews were disloyal citizens. Now Dreyfus was serving a life sentence on Devil's Island, a French penal colony off the South American coast. French animus against Jews made it difficult for the imprisoned Dreyfus to secure a fair appeals process by which he might clear his name and regain his liberty.[226]

As France's baseless persecution of Dreyfus drew international condemnation, the inveterate antisemite Henry Adams saw the global clamor as yet more evidence that Jews were secretly pulling the strings of world affairs. Adams's paranoia earned him the ridicule of his friend John Hay, who was then serving as the American ambassador to the United Kingdom and would later become Roosevelt's secretary of state. In a personal letter to a fellow diplomat, Hay mocked Adams for becoming "clean daft over the Dreyfus affair." It seemed to Hay that Adams believed "the Jews are all the press, all the cabinets, all the gods and all weather. I was amazed to see so sensible a man so wild." In a similar vein two months later, Hay joked to a senator's wife that Adams—still exasperated by worldwide advocacy for Dreyfus—was liable to blame Jews for the eruption of Italy's most notorious volcano: "When he saw Vesuvius reddening the midnight air, he searched the horizon to find a Jew stoking the fire."[227]

The irony here is that the Jewish reaction to the Dreyfus Affair was fairly reserved. To be sure, Jews on both sides of the Atlantic earnestly called for his release, but they generally did so with a measure of moderation. French Jews feared that strident agitation could backfire. America's Jewish leadership, meanwhile, was reluctant to recognize that the Enlightenment project of religious equality might be failing in Western Europe. These uptown Jews preferred to treat the Dreyfus Affair as an anomalous miscarriage of justice against an unfortunate Frenchman, not as a symptom of structural antisemitism. To grapple with the full implications of French prejudice would have raised uncomfortable doubts about the Jewish future in supposedly civilized nations. Downtown Jews, however, proved an exception to this dynamic. With the memory of their own Old World oppression all too fresh, they drew a straight line from Russian pogroms to Dreyfus's persecution.[228]

Governor Roosevelt's views on Dreyfus stood in sharp relief to Henry Adams's, their shared social circle notwithstanding. When word reached America that Dreyfus was finally granted a retrial, Roosevelt wrote a sympathetic letter addressed to three interested parties: two Jewish philanthropists and a philosemitic preacher who had just authored a book about Jewish contributions to the world. "Gentlemen, I feel the most heartfelt joy over the action now taken in relation to Captain Dreyfus, and the attempt to partially redress the hideous wrong done to him," Roosevelt conveyed. And he praised a French colonel who had come forward with exculpatory evidence on Dreyfus's behalf despite immense pressure on that colonel to conceal it: "I trust also that we shall not forget the splendid courage and disinterested patriotism and loyalty of gallant Colonel Picquart."[229] Dreyfus would be convicted yet again in his retrial that summer, but the ensuing global outrage induced the French president to summarily pardon him.[230]

The *Idaho Daily Statesman* saw in the Rough Rider legacy an American answer to the Dreyfus Affair. The paper reprinted a quotation from Roosevelt extolling his regiment's religious diversity and then added in its own wording, "In France, that pretends to be a republic, they degrade an officer and send him into solitary confinement because he is a Jew, but in the United States there is no difference between the Jew and Gentile."[231] The *Statesman* was overselling the case—America had its own issues with religious prejudice. But even so, no antisemitic incident comparable to the Dreyfus Affair marred the records of the U.S. military. And Roosevelt's frequent plaudits about his Jewish Rough Riders did indeed offer a marked contrast to France's deplorable treatment of Captain Dreyfus.

Governor Roosevelt looked ahead to his political future with ambivalence. William McKinley was pursuing reelection but needed a running mate owing to the death of his vice president the prior fall. The president opted to stay neutral in the selection process, content to defer entirely to the discretion of the upcoming Republican National Convention.[232] Roosevelt was the odds-on favorite, but he didn't thrill to the prospect. The vice presidency of that era was an office best suited to an empty figurehead content to idle away the time. In other words, it was a terrible fit for TR.[233] He preferred to seek a second term as governor. Before the convention, Roosevelt lamented to a friend, "In the Vice-Presidency I could do nothing." But he was prepared to abide the convention vote.[234]

As the delegates were deciding the destiny of the ticket on a hot June day in Philadelphia's convention hall, Roosevelt holed up in a nearby hotel room awaiting the results. He distracted himself with the writings of Josephus, the acclaimed scholar of ancient Jewish history. So immersed was Roosevelt in Jewish antiquity that he failed to notice that his sister Corinne had knocked at his door, entered his room, and was standing over his shoulder. When she saw what Roosevelt was reading, Corinne broke the silence with laughter. She later recalled finding it irresistibly "quaint" that amid all the pomp and politicking of the convention, her brother was "quietly apart, perfectly absorbed in the history of the Jews of a long-past day."[235]

The RNC delegates enthusiastically nominated Roosevelt to serve as McKinley's running mate, with 925 votes in his favor and only one opposed. The lone dissenter: Roosevelt himself.[236] He made his peace with his fate and accepted the nomination. Roosevelt dashed off a letter to an American diplomat a few weeks later, acknowledging, "I am completely reconciled to being the candidate for vice-president now."[237] His mixed emotions aside, Roosevelt was boundlessly energetic as a campaigner, crisscrossing America at a frenetic pace on behalf of the Republican ticket. The race offered voters a rematch of the 1896 cycle when McKinley had faced off against William Jennings Bryan. On election day, McKinley and Roosevelt notched a dominant victory.[238]

Among Roosevelt's well-wishers on his electoral triumph was a friend from the police force. "Best success to you in your new office," telegrammed the Jewish police officer Otto Raphael. "May God have only happiness in store for you."[239] Roosevelt was "touched" by the gesture from his old sparring partner.[240] Meanwhile, Lucius Littauer—a Jewish congressman whose relationship with TR dated back to their Harvard days—messaged Roosevelt with words of "joyous congratulations!" But

Littauer's comment came with a caveat: "My only regret is that you must waste four years in a position unsuited to your abilities."[241] Four years would prove far off the mark.

Merely six months into his second term, McKinley was shaking hands with a crowd in Buffalo when an anarchist shot him at close range. McKinley underwent emergency surgery, and Roosevelt rushed to Buffalo. After a few days, McKinley's condition was sufficiently improved that Roosevelt set off to join his family on a planned vacation in the Adirondack Mountains of upstate New York.[242] The vice president received a gracious letter the next day from William Cohen, a Jewish jurist who was now practicing law after a stint on the bench. Roosevelt counted Cohen as a legal advisor and a friend—they had most likely first met when both were law students at Columbia in 1880.[243] "As everyone knows, you have been placed in many delicate and trying situations in your busy life; I venture to say that no one of them called upon you for more judgment and tact than when you were at the side of our wounded president," wrote Judge Cohen. "Never in your whole public career has your conduct been so perfect; silent and dignified when the outcome was uncertain, cheerful when the conditions warranted—with a sense of duty always present, reluctantly ready to act in case you should be called upon."[244] The letter made an impression on Roosevelt, who told Cohen that he would "keep it permanently."[245]

Just when it seemed that McKinley had been spared, his wound grew infected, and the once-favorable prognosis became grim.[246] A ranger hurried up the mountainside where Roosevelt was hiking to convey the urgent news.[247] Early the next day, as Roosevelt was hastening back to Buffalo, McKinley took his final breath.[248] "Now the dreadful has occurred," a somber Roosevelt relayed to Judge Cohen, "and the only thing for me to do is to take up the burden and bear it as manfully as I can."[249] After arriving in Buffalo, Roosevelt quickly took the oath of office in a friend's parlor. At age forty-two, he had become—and remains still—the youngest president in American history.[250]

★ ★ ★

Roosevelt's trajectory to the Oval Office was astounding. In four short years, he had accelerated through a dizzying succession of roles: police commissioner, navy official, Rough Rider, New York governor, vice president, and now, suddenly, he was the most powerful man in America. At every stage in this improbable journey—from the East Side slums to the San Juan Heights—Roosevelt deepened his relationship with the American Jewish community.

He was a collector of stories, and his haul from these years had been especially abundant when it came to Jewry. There was the episode of Hermann Ahlwardt, the German hate-monger whom Roosevelt cleverly guarded with Jewish policemen. There was the tale of Otto Raphael, the Jewish immigrant who braved a burning building and earned not just a police badge but Roosevelt's friendship. There was the legend of Sam Greenwald, the Jewish soldier whose courage facing down Spanish bullets alongside Colonel Roosevelt won him a promotion. These stories mattered—to Roosevelt and to American Jewry alike—because they advanced an aspirational vision of national life where Jew and Gentile would stand as equals.

But the question of Jewish belonging at home would soon become eclipsed by the question of Jewish survival abroad. Roosevelt did not yet know, as he inherited the mantle of presidential power, that the momentous years now facing him would coincide with the greatest crisis for global Jewry of his lifetime. The Jewish people prayed that this youthful new president—this teller of Jewish tales—might prevent the next chapter in the Jewish story from being written in blood.

2
ROMANIAN NOTE

At the time that Theodore Roosevelt assumed the American presidency, some five thousand miles away Romanian Jews were suffering under the heel of an oppressive state and society. The Treaty of Berlin had recognized Romania's independence in 1878, and in the ensuing decades, the newly sovereign nation subjected its Jewish community to a relentless succession of indignities. Although Jews had lived there for centuries, they weren't considered citizens. Jews were prohibited from residing in many towns. Hospitals had quotas on Jewish patients. The Romanian government wasn't content to merely bar Jewish students from public schools—it also thwarted a bid by the *Alliance Israélite Universelle*, a French-based Jewish aid organization, to subsidize a Jewish school system. Meanwhile, a series of laws banned Jews from ever more forms of employment, from educated professions like lawyer and broker to working-class occupations such as farmer and peddler. Jewish artisans were disallowed from retailing goods made by their own hands. Abject poverty was all but inevitable for the great mass of Romanian Jews. Thousands of them might have starved to death were it not for the charity of the *Alliance*. And beyond a legal regime of discrimination, the government actively promoted pogroms in which organized mobs ransacked Jewish property and assailed Jewish people.[1]

The Romanian treatment of Jews was all the more egregious in light of the conditions under which the preeminent powers of Europe had granted Romania its independence. The Treaty of Berlin expressly forbade Romania from practicing religious discrimination in its political or economic affairs.² With Romania brazenly flouting that treaty, the country's 400,000 Jews found themselves in a deepening disaster.

Western European and American Jewry fretted about the increasingly desperate situation in Romania. In 1902, a Jewish philanthropist in England, F. D. Mocatta, wrote to the American Jewish leader Oscar Straus about an imminent law in Romania that would ban Jews from some of the few remaining jobs they were still legally permitted to hold. Britain was a signatory to the Treaty of Berlin and thus had some standing to pressure Romania, but Mocatta was dubious that his own nation or the other signatory powers would catalyze action to enforce the treaty's terms. He reasoned that the United States, despite not being party to the treaty, was actually more likely to initiate an effort on behalf of Romanian Jewry.³ In that respect, Mocatta was typical of European Jews who had far greater faith in the American government than their own. Mocatta was hopeful that an American plea to Romania might encourage Britain to then lend its own support to the cause.⁴

Mocatta was prudent in enlisting Oscar Straus, for the latter counted among a small handful of Jews who were positioned to exert real influence on Roosevelt. Straus was a consummate uptown Jew. He had been born in Germany and raised largely in America. An alumnus of Columbia Law School, Straus worked as an attorney before serving as an ambassador to the Ottoman Empire in the 1880s and 1890s.⁵ He had known TR since at least 1900 when, as governor of New York, Roosevelt appointed Straus to a committee tasked with studying the status of indigenous people in the state.⁶ A month before Mocatta sent his letter, Roosevelt tapped Straus to fill one of America's four seats on the newly created international tribunal in The Hague.⁷ The president had some hesitation at first in making the appointment—Straus, after all, was a Democrat—but the owner of the *New York Times*, also a Jew, successfully prevailed upon Roosevelt.⁸

Straus's obligations to The Hague did not preclude him from continuing to reside stateside, and over the course of the Roosevelt administration, he would emerge as TR's most trusted Jewish advisor, offering valued advice on issues far beyond the scope of his official remit. The two men were distinct by many measures. Roosevelt had a commanding

FIGURE 2.1. Oscar Straus. *Source: The World's Work.* Vol. 31, November, 1915, to April, 1916. *A History of Our Time.* Garden City: Doubleday, 1918.

presence; Straus was mild-mannered. Roosevelt could enthrall a crowd; Straus was best suited to backroom diplomacy. Roosevelt epitomized charisma; Straus decidedly did not.[9] Yet there was a great deal for these two statesmen to appreciate in one another. Both staked out moderate positions in the era's struggle between capital and labor. Both saw themselves as embodying an ethical code that transcended the crass

FIGURE 2.2. Jacob H. Schiff. *Source*: The Miriam and Ira D. Wallach Division of Art, Prints and Photographs: Print Collection, The New York Public Library.

materialism of an industrializing America. And both thought that the United States was a fundamentally virtuous nation.[10]

The plight of Romanian Jews fell outside Straus's purview—the matter certainly wasn't before The Hague—but he was sufficiently alarmed that he spent what political capital he had to advance their cause. To press his case for Romanian Jewry, Straus turned to someone who enjoyed, for the time being, even more clout with Roosevelt: Jacob Schiff. Although Schiff was a Republican and Straus a Democrat, they were both German-born members of the Jewish elite in America, and they worked well together on Jewish issues. A contemporary described Jacob Schiff as having "an aristocratic quality in his personality." He had amassed a fortune as a banker in New York and devoted much of his riches to philanthropy, particularly Jewish causes. Schiff possessed a flair for the dramatic. He could be combative or compassionate depending on the circumstances. As America's foremost advocate for Jewry, Schiff was a man whom any president of the era would be wise to cultivate as an ally and adviser on Jewish topics. And Roosevelt was savvy enough to recognize as much.[11]

After Straus and Schiff deliberated in early 1902 on a strategy for influencing Roosevelt's policy toward Romania, they agreed that Straus would draft a memo about conditions on the ground there, which Schiff would then personally deliver to the president.[12] Straus understood that it was a violation of diplomatic norms for any given country to involve itself in another's domestic affairs. At that point in world history, altruism on its own would typically offer an insufficient basis for the United States to press Romania on its persecution of Jews (although exceptions did exist). Straus's memo conceded, "If the matter were of concern ... from only a humanitarian standpoint, I would not have the president's noble heart disturbed." Because Roosevelt would need a pretense to intercede, Straus provided a rationale for action that directly implicated American interests: immigration. Straus explained that as a consequence of Romania's offenses against its Jews, "these people are emigrating *en masse*" to the United States. Romania through its "persecutions" effectively forced thousands of impoverished Jews to flee, which constitutes an "unfriendly act" by Romania toward America—one that "gives our government the right, not only to protest, but to remonstrate against such inhuman laws that discredit the age in which we are living."[13] In truth, Roosevelt wasn't actually opposed to accepting Romanian-Jewish refugees. Not even seven thousand had entered America the prior year. The immigration excuse would be pure pretext.[14]

Straus's memo suggested some possible courses of action that Roosevelt could pursue. TR might encourage a congressional resolution "expressive of sympathy and protesting against the inhuman treatment" of Romanian Jews. Another option was the appointment to Romania of a special commissioner with "diplomatic rank" who would convey America's disapproval to the regime there. Whatever the president might choose to do, any movement from the Roosevelt administration—Straus predicted—would prompt further action from the great powers of Europe that had signed the Treaty of Berlin.[15] Those signatories were Britain, Austria-Hungary, France, Germany, Italy, Russia, and the Ottoman Empire.

Jacob Schiff had occasion in April of 1902 to meet with Roosevelt and deliver Straus's memo. Roosevelt summoned his secretary of state, John Hay, to join that meeting. Hay was measured in his reaction, cautioning that the path advocated by Schiff and Straus was not without "difficulty," but Hay still assured Schiff that he wouldn't simply let the matter rest.[16]

Secretary Hay would become a central figure in the Romanian affair moving forward, a trusted aide whom Roosevelt expected to work collaboratively with Jews like Straus and Schiff on a solution. Although Hay didn't quite share Roosevelt's pro-Jewish instincts, neither did Hay espouse the genteel antisemitism that afflicted so much of the Anglo-Saxon elite of his day. Perhaps Hay was less prone to anti-Jewish prejudice because his background was atypical of the patrician class with whom he fraternized. He wasn't born into the East Coast establishment but rather grew up in rural Illinois. Moreover, Hay owed his riches to the modern railroad industry, not an inheritance from a colonial-era fortune; accordingly, he wasn't troubled by the anxieties of the Old Money set who saw enterprising Jews as rapacious capitalists. Recall that Hay laughed off the paranoid antisemitism of his friend Henry Adams. To be sure, Hay wasn't wholly devoid of bias himself. He once expressed a wish that a friend of his would soon be "getting [as] rich as a Dutch Jew."[17]

At TR's request, John Hay met with Oscar Straus and asked him to produce a second memo on Romania's Jews that could inform the

FIGURE 2.3. John Hay. *Source*: Library of Congress, Prints and Photographs Division.

administration's actions. Straus dutifully drafted a new report, which he sent straight to Roosevelt in May. That report uneasily grappled with the reality that any formal objection to Romania would force the United States to adopt a self-contradictory position. In order to justify its interposition in the domestic affairs of a foreign power, America would have to invoke as a pretext its own interests—in this case, the migration of Jews from Romania to America. Yet the United States was supposed to be a sanctuary for those fleeing subjugation. By bemoaning the influx of Romanian Jews to American ports, the Roosevelt administration might appear hypocritically xenophobic.

Straus was not obtuse to this predicament and tried as best he could to paper over it in his report for Roosevelt. On the one hand, Straus reasoned that America was uniquely positioned to criticize Romania because the United States would "in all probability receive the largest number of those oppressed people." On the other hand, he insisted that reliance on immigration as the basis for a diplomatic protest should *not* be interpreted as a plea "against receiving these refugees in this country, which from the day that the Pilgrim Fathers set foot upon our shores, has been the haven of refuge." Try as Straus might, that inconsistency would continue to present challenges for the Roosevelt administration as it developed its Romania policy.[18]

Some passages of Straus's report notably sidestepped that tension by arguing that humanitarianism alone actually *could* justify an American reproach. He cited a few historical examples, including instructions sent in 1872 from the U.S. secretary of state to American ambassadors across Europe; those instructions had called on the ambassadors to convey to their host nations that America was gravely concerned for the "inhumanly persecuted Hebrews" on Romanian territory. Straus closed his report with an "earnest appeal" for Roosevelt to challenge the Romanian state over its prejudice and to enlist the European signatories to the Treaty of Berlin to follow suit. He optimistically predicted that inveighing against Romania's treatment of its Jewish population "cannot fail to have great influence at this present crisis."[19]

The American public grew increasingly aware of Romanian Jewry's dire condition. A newspaper in Michigan reported that thousands of them were en route to the United States on account of "systematic persecution."[20] Another paper, in Vermont, predicted that this cohort of immigrants is "only the beginning of what promises to be an exodus of Romanian Jews" who were escaping "oppressive legislation."[21]

In Philadelphia—among the leading cities for American Jewish life—the *Alliance* organized a mass gathering to decry the treatment of both Romanian and Russian Jews. Speakers emphasized that Jews in the United States, who enjoyed religious liberty and economic opportunity, shouldered a special obligation to aid their embattled coreligionists overseas. As a local rabbi told the crowd, "The voice of Jewish suffering, of Jewish sorrow . . . must find a responsive chord in every heart." Notably, not all orators that day were Jewish. One Gentile speechmaker insisted that Christians ought to be deeply concerned with the barbarous treatment of any human being, regardless of the victim's faith. The meeting concluded with fundraising for the *Alliance*'s work and a vote in favor of resolutions condemning Romania and Russia.[22]

As the Roosevelt administration considered its options, the president came under pressure to do something on the diplomatic front from Lucius Littauer—a college friend, fellow Republican, and Jewish congressman representing a district in upstate New York.[23] Roosevelt assured Littauer, "Hay is already at work on the Romanian business."[24] Indeed, a plan was afoot to have an American diplomat, Charles Wilson, confront the Romanian authorities about antisemitism. The United States had no embassy in Romania, so Romanian-American diplomacy was handled by Wilson, the regional chargé d'affaires based in Greece (a chargé d'affaires is a diplomatic officer who has lesser rank than an ambassador but enjoys comparable powers in conducting foreign policy).

Secretary Hay tasked a seasoned State Department employee with formulating instructions for Wilson, which would become known as the "Romanian Note." In mid-July, Hay forwarded a draft to Roosevelt for the president's blessing. Hay included with the note a cover letter to Roosevelt acknowledging the same difficulty that Straus had well understood: America wanted to make a humanitarian plea but needed to cite immigration as a pretense to avoid breaching protocol. The United States was, by chance, in the midst of pressing Romania for a naturalization treaty, which would specify the conditions under which each country would formally recognize that a given individual had traded one nation's citizenship for the other's. That endeavor could provide the Roosevelt administration with some grounds for exerting pressure on the topic of Jewish rights, since the absence of Jewish rights was prompting Romanian Jews to seek naturalization in America. "You will see in reading it that it has not been easy to handle," Hay confessed to Roosevelt, "but I have availed myself of what seems our only excuse, the pending naturalization treaty with Romania, to read them a pretty drastic letter on their duty to the Jews. Please let me know if it meets your approval."[25]

The note that Hay submitted for Roosevelt's consideration made the case that, in light of a prospective naturalization treaty, the United States was well within its rights to "scrutinize most jealously the character of the immigration from a foreign land"—especially when that land's maltreatment of its own inhabitants spurred the emigration of destitute refugees to America. Any nation so aggrieved may "point out the evil and make remonstrance" against the offending country. Having established this principle, the note considered the litany of abuses against Romanian Jews: civil disabilities, special taxes, employment blacklists. "In the overcrowded cities . . . they are forced to dwell and engage, against fearful odds, in the desperate struggle for existence," the note continued. The Jews—amid this "state of wretched misery" and "enforced degradation"—have little hope for advancement. They thus confront two options: "submissive suffering" or "flight to some land less unfavorable to them."[26]

Much of the note awkwardly grappled with the tension between the United States' self-professed commitment to sheltering refugees and its complaint that Romania was forcing its Jewish population onto American shores. "The United States offers asylum to the oppressed of all lands," the note proclaimed. But this principle did not constitute a willingness to stand idly by while a bad actor created such inhumane conditions that its impecunious residents had no choice but to embark for American ports. The exodus of the Romanian Jew was not "the healthy, intelligent emigration of a free and self-reliant being" but rather "the mere transplantation of an artificially produced diseased growth to a new place." These Jews arrived as "outcasts, made doubly paupers by physical and moral oppression in their native land." Under such terms, their immigration wasn't "acceptable or beneficial." Such a damning assessment of Romanian-Jewish immigrants risked sounding antisemitic in itself, and so the note took pains to speak well of Jewish immigrants at large: American history showed that "the Jews possess in a high degree the mental and moral qualifications of conscientious citizenhood," so long as they come suitably "equipped in mind and body."[27]

Fabricated concerns about immigration may have given the Roosevelt administration its requisite pretext, but the note still acknowledged and even championed the humanitarian agenda actually motivating its authorship—America was moved "in the name of humanity." Even as the note conceded that it could not "authoritatively appeal" to the Treaty of Berlin's text since the United States wasn't a signatory, it would nonetheless "earnestly appeal" to the treaty's guiding ideals "because they are the principles of international law and eternal justice."[28] Initially intended to be a confidential message to an American diplomat—which would inform his messaging to the Romanian regime—the note's impassioned rhetoric indicates that it was drafted with an eye toward eventual release for public consumption.[29]

Roosevelt had no hesitation in giving the draft his imprimatur. "I think that the memorandum to the Romanian government is admirable," he told Hay. The president also asked that the State Department furnish him with an additional copy that he could show his Jewish ally in Congress, Lucius Littauer.[30] Hay acceded to the request and counseled Roosevelt that Jacob Schiff and Oscar Straus would be interested in the note's contents as well.[31] Appearing as a letter under Hay's name, the note was sent off to Charles Wilson, the diplomat who was to convey its gist to Romania.[32]

The Jews in Roosevelt's circle were uniformly pleased. As Jacob Schiff told Congressman Littauer, "I have read this communiqué with much interest, and I agree with you that it forms a masterful presentation." Schiff and Littauer alike urged the Roosevelt administration to share the note with the signatory nations.[33] Hay agreed that the United States should involve the signatories, writing to Roosevelt, "I think we might do it."[34]

Before the note was dispatched to the signatories, Charles Wilson acted upon it. He met with a Romanian official to discuss the possibility of a naturalization treaty, who explained to Wilson that the king in fact objected to any such treaty. The king was concerned that if a treaty required that all U.S. citizens living in Romania be afforded robust rights, then a Romanian Jew could abscond to America, become a U.S. citizen, and return to Romania with far greater freedoms than his coreligionists who had never left. American citizenship would thereby become an end-run around the regime of Jewish persecution to which Romania was so ardently committed. This, the king would not abide.[35]

Wilson wrote Hay with the details of this meeting. Notably, Wilson's letter made no mention of his having communicated to the Romanian official America's general opposition to the conditions of Romanian Jewry—presumably because Wilson did not. Perhaps Wilson discussed the naturalization treaty only and pressed no further because the official's negative reaction to naturalization made it apparent that any remonstrance about Romanian antisemitism would fall on deaf ears. Or maybe Wilson misunderstood Hay's note by failing to appreciate that the treaty discussion was the pretext, not the point.[36] Either way, Romanian obstinance appears to have only reinforced for the Roosevelt administration that it should indeed forward the note to the signatories. Hay initiated that process just days after hearing from Wilson. The note was accompanied with a request that the signatories take whatever steps they deem suitable to dislodge the Romanian government from its present policy.[37]

The *American Hebrew* periodical broke the news in early August. It reported that John Hay wired a "most forceful remonstrance" concerning the peril of Romanian Jewry. "Our government shows that it is still in the forefront whenever it comes to questions of humanity and justice," the paper boasted.[38] Roosevelt was highly satisfied. As Hay informed his subordinate who drafted the note, "The President is greatly pleased with your circular, and the Hebrews—poor dears!—all over the country think we are bully boys."[39] The coverage in the *American Hebrew* was based on an unofficial leak and lacked the Romanian Note's actual text. Other newspapers held off on commentary until mid-September, when the Roosevelt administration confirmed the story and provided the press with copies of the note itself.

At that point, front-page headlines nationwide carried word of the diplomatic protest. Many papers reprinted much, and sometimes all, of the Romanian Note. "United States Appeals to Save Jews," declared the *Evening News* in San Jose.[40] Although the note was produced at Roosevelt's direction and drafted by one of Hay's underlings, it was Hay who signed it; accordingly, many headlines gave Hay the credit. The *Salt Lake Telegram* announced, "Hay Appeals to the Powers for Suffering Jews."[41] Jewish newspapers, of course, lavished the administration with praise. In New York, the *Hebrew Standard* attributed the Romanian Note to "the head and heart of President Roosevelt."[42] These plaudits for the Republican president were all the more notable given that the *Hebrew Standard* leaned Democratic.

Some journalistic outlets highlighted the note's atypical character. The *New York Times*, for instance, emphasized that the administration's conveyance of the Romanian Note to the signatories constituted an "unusual course" and that the content of the note itself was "remarkable in several respects." The *Times* did not offer specifics as to why the American tactic departed from convention. It was too obvious to spell out that the United States was hardly in the habit of pressuring European countries to adhere to the terms of a treaty to which America was not itself a party. The paper did acknowledge the "double purpose" of the note: "protecting the long-suffering Jews" on the one hand and sparing America a "horde of poor people" on the other.[43]

An editorial in the *Washington Post* expressed concern that this latter rationale about immigration undermined America's altruistic plea and thereby weakened the note. "If our only objection to [Romanian antisemitism] resides in the fear that those hapless people will flee to America and so introduce into our civilization a degrading and abhorrent quantity, we cannot reasonably expect our appeal to exert a very potent influence," the editorialist surmised. The author fully appreciated that impoverished newcomers were being invoked "merely as a justification" for the humanitarian appeal. Secretary Hay may have been hamstrung by diplomatic protocol that rendered human rights an insufficient basis for intervention, but "what he wants to say . . . is that the American people view with horror and indignation the pitiless pursuit of a race by the government of Romania."[44] It is striking the ease with which the *Post* contributor was able discern the administration's pretextual maneuvering. Editorials like this one mattered—with sophisticated polling still decades in the offing, politicians of the day often relied on the press as the best thermometer of the public temperature.[45]

The Roosevelt administration had made its move; the question remained how Europe would react to this uncharacteristic bid by the United States. Some European papers praised America for setting an example that the Continent should follow. A Viennese daily observed that it had been left to "America to admonish the European powers concerning their obligations to civilization" after Europe "bowed itself so impotently and pitiably before Romania's barbarities."[46] Berlin's paper of record lauded America's refusal to "keep silence in the presence of international wrong" and warned that it would be "highly shameful" if Europe did not respond in like manner.[47] The paper fully grasped that America seized on immigration as a pretense for pursuing what was really a humanitarian endeavor, suggesting that "the United States does not need the protection of Europe against pauper immigration" and therefore was motivated in actuality by "feelings of humanity."[48]

Despite these voices of support, other corners of the European press were far less favorable toward the United States. One German newspaper derided the Romanian Note as an exercise in hollow sanctimony, insisting, "The prattle about humanity and eternal justice, especially in an American mouth, is an empty phrase."[49] A number of the European critics accused the United States of hypocrisy for intruding in Old World affairs after long resisting comparable interventions by Europe into the Western Hemisphere. President James Monroe had first articulated in 1823 what became known as the Monroe Doctrine, which held that any European attempt to colonize an independent nation in the

Americas would be interpreted as an act hostile to the United States. Given this history, an Austrian daily condemned the "impertinent meddling" from a nation that "maintains the Monroe Doctrine" and thus "has the least right of any country to exercise a similar influence."[50]

In the Russian capital of St. Petersburg, one of that nation's oldest papers, *Zeitung*, found a different basis for accusing America of a double standard. The United States was then engaged in a brutal occupation of the Philippines, and *Zeitung* conveyed that it "doubts the unselfishness of the American step, since the Romanian Jews are probably much better off than the Filipinos."[51] In the same vein, a paper from the German city of Dresden argued that the United States had precious little credibility not merely because of its maltreatment of Filipinos but also because of "lynch law" whereby countless American Blacks were savagely murdered. "Romania should either remain silent or send a protest to the United States against lynch law and the treatment of the Filipinos, lest the negroes and Filipinos all emigrate to Romania," the paper sneered.[52] This kind of commentary previewed a recurring theme throughout Roosevelt's presidency wherein America's own human rights abuses would undermine his claim to an altruistic agenda abroad.

The European newspapers, divided as they were on the propriety of the Romanian Note, also diverged in their predictions of its impact. Some thought it would prompt action from the signatory nations; others expected continued inertia.[53] Britain fell into the former camp. The British government had already been under pressure from a coterie of powerful Jews and Gentiles within its borders to join any remonstrance that might come from Washington.[54] When the note from the State Department went public, Britain sent a note of its own to the fellow signatories. That British note seconded American concern for Romanian Jewry and sounded out the other European powers about what action they might collectively take. The Foreign Office in London released a statement that its note "follows and supplements the action taken by the American government, which is entitled to full credit for seeking to alleviate the condition of those oppressed people."[55] However, an unnamed member of the Foreign Office candidly acknowledged to the press that Britain was unlikely to inspire the Continent to do anything: "Nothing that will be of any permanent good can result from Secretary Hay's note . . . unless somebody is willing to crush Romania, and no power seems anxious to take on that task."[56] His pessimism proved well-founded.

Two days later, the *New York Times* announced that Germany would definitively not intercede on behalf of Romanian Jewry. Germany's official rationale was the diplomatic custom of abstention from another nation's internal affairs, but the *Times* contended that Germany had financial incentives to refrain. Germans held significant shares of Romanian securities, making the German government hesitant to meddle and thereby risk those investments. Austria and Russia were equally unwilling to act.[57] Several state-funded newspapers in the capitals of the various signatories suggested that these countries were more likely to collaborate on a rebuke of America for undue interference in European matters.[58]

Romania, for its part, showed little willingness to mend its ways. The Romanian minister to Britain gave an interview in which he simply dissembled about the condition of Romanian Jews. He peddled the fiction that Jews were leaving Romania owing to an agricultural decline.[59] This was a particularly audacious lie given that Romania forbade Jews from purchasing farmland, working someone else's land, or even living in rural areas.[60] With nonexistent support from its fellow signatories, Britain had to content itself with a symbolic gesture of its displeasure: the Romanian ambassador was deliberately excluded from a banquet hosted by the Lord Mayor of London.[61]

★ ★ ★

The Romanian Note may have failed to stir meaningful action in Europe, but it did prove strikingly successful in winning over the affection of Jews in the United States. At a synagogue on the Upper East Side, a rabbi delivered a sermon that was quoted at length in the *New York Times* in which he extolled the "noble plea" of the American government to "prevent the upstart monarchy" from "crushing into dust its unfortunate Jewish subjects." The rabbi also lauded the Romanian Note as embodying the principles of the Declaration of Independence.[62]

Ever since the note became public, John Hay had been inundated with messages of thanks from Jews across the country.[63] Jews in Milwaukee who had established a Romanian Relief Committee sent a telegram to Hay that expressed "profound gratitude for the timely protest.... An all-wise Providence will bless our Nation for acts like this."[64] A rabbi in Indiana sent a letter of thanks to John Hay written exclusively in Hebrew. Hay drafted a response in English and then tasked a translator at the State Department with producing a Hebrew version for the rabbi. This marks perhaps the only instance in American history when a secretary of state sent a message on official department letterhead in Hebrew.[65]

The administration was repaid for the Romanian Note with public praise from a key figure in Jewish advocacy and Republican circles: Simon Wolf. Like Jacob Schiff and Oscar Straus, Wolf was a self-made German-Jewish immigrant who emerged as a key spokesperson on Jewish causes. And like Roosevelt, he was a veritable Swiss Army knife of versatility: prominent lawyer, prolific author, former diplomat, outspoken advocate, and energetic philanthropist. Wolf was known as "the Nestor of American Jewry"—an allusion to a sage king from Greek mythology. He enjoyed the ear of many presidents throughout his long career, and Roosevelt was no exception.[66]

Not long after the Romanian Note's publication, Wolf delivered a Yom Kippur address in Washington that was covered in the press. He celebrated the "high resolve and exalted humanity" of the U.S. government. Even as Wolf conceded that the note had been shrugged off by Romania and the signatories—"the absolute effect of this immortal circular may not be apparent"—he nonetheless argued that the note formed a virtuous precedent whose "moral effect will be lasting for all time." John Hay had received much of the public acclaim, but Wolf knew that Roosevelt also deserved credit. In his Yom Kippur remarks, he made sure to show appreciation "for the noble President who inspired it, and the no less noble Secretary who gave it expression."[67] Wolf was equally enthused about the administration in correspondence. He privately told the publisher of a Jewish newspaper that he was "thoroughly satisfied" with the "splendid letter," which was "record making and bound to be of great service to our people at home and abroad."[68]

Jacob Schiff penned an effusive letter of indebtedness to Roosevelt for sending a note of "such momentous importance."[69] In reply, Roosevelt credited Schiff and Congressman Littauer for their involvement in the matter: "It was you, and second to you, Lucius Littauer, who did the most to fix my attention on the matter of the persecution of the Romanian Jews. You have every right to feel pleased with the result."[70] Schiff was gratified by the administration and confident it would undertake additional efforts for Romanian Jewry. As he wrote the head of the *Alliance*, which had been so central in giving humanitarian aid to embattled Jewish communities, "I believe we can count upon the president's willingness to follow up what has already been done by further action, which it might be necessary and practicable to take."[71]

Jacob Schiff's letter didn't specify what "further action" might entail, but Simon Wolf had a concrete idea that he floated to Roosevelt. Recall that the United States did not have a diplomat specifically for Romania; Wolf reasoned that the appointment of one might placate the king and ease his hostility toward Jews. He told Roosevelt, "Such representation would be of great service to both countries and the unfortunates for whom you have interested yourself so splendidly."[72] Regardless of the merit or naiveté of Wolf's proposal, Roosevelt did not pursue it.

The 1902 midterm elections were then looming, and Republicans well understood that they could court Jewish voters on the back of the Romanian Note. A Gentile politico, Charles Treat, advised Roosevelt to dispatch John Hay to Jewish neighborhoods in New York City in advance of election day. "The mere fact of his presence, and words of cheer and advice, would arouse more enthusiasm than all the meetings we have had," Treat insisted. "The appreciation of the Hebrews for Mr. Hay's splendid defense [on] their behalf in the Romanian matter has evoked a tremendous outburst of gratitude."[73] Hay would make no such entrée into the political sphere, but Democrats were nonetheless concerned that Republicans were poised to perform well with Jewish constituents. The *New York Times* reported that the Romanian American Citizens' League—apparently a Jewish organization—would endorse the Republican ticket as a gesture of thanks for the Romanian Note.[74] On the Shabbat before the vote, the Romanian Note was read in a number of synagogues to remind Jews where the Roosevelt administration stood.[75] Measuring the influence of the Romanian Note on the midterms is difficult. Political observers would have to wait another two years to see the impact of Roosevelt himself at the top of the ballot.

For all the goodwill from American Jews, consternation arose from an unexpected corner. Recall that in 1898, the prominent rabbi Joseph Krauskopf had convened with Roosevelt in Cuba and favorably reported on that experience for the American press. But after the midterm elections of 1902, the same rabbi gave a sermon at his synagogue in Philadelphia that criticized the Romanian Note. Most Jewish commentators had been content to overlook the inherent tension in the administration's diplomatic gambit: the United States made a humanitarian plea for the woeful Jews of Romania while justifying its remonstrance by objecting to the influx of those very same Jews to America. The result was a note that could appear sympathetic *and* disdainful—and Krauskopf would not let this inconsistency pass unmentioned. He acknowledged the "humanitarian" element of America's appeal to Romania but lamented that "by far the larger part" of the note was "self-protective." This dissonance, he insisted, accounted for the lack of progress in mitigating the hardships endured by Romanian Jewry. Although in reality the note's stated misgivings about indigent newcomers was a fabricated pretext for the humanitarian entreaty, Krauskopf feared that the reverse was true: altruism was a mere cover for nativism. In his words, the Romanian Note's grievance about immigration "throws the humanitarian phase into questionable form that makes it appear as but a diplomatic sugar coating of a very bitter pill."[76] Possibly as a concession to Roosevelt, the rabbi waited until after the midterms to render his opinion. Or perhaps Krauskopf's timing was simply designed to avoid the impression that his remarks were politically tinged.

Krauskopf may have misinterpreted the administration's motives, but he wasn't wrong about the note's futility. There seemed to be little cause for optimism that Romanian Jews would enjoy better circumstances on the ground. Two weeks after the note became public, Hay had forthrightly acknowledged to Oscar Straus that concrete action from either the signatories or Romania was unlikely. "For the moment Romania seems obdurate, and some of the great powers indifferent, to the moral question involved," Hay conceded, while still offering with vague optimism that perhaps "some good may result from what we have done."[77] Three months later, Jacob Schiff confessed to a prominent German Jew, "I fear nevertheless that there has been no radical change in Romania in favor of the Jews.... But let us not lose hope."[78] There was some small reason for hope—conditions may not have improved for Romanian Jewry, but neither did they worsen. In the wake of the note, the Romanian government abstained from new restrictions on Jews. Still, that would have been little recompense for a Jewish community that was among the most oppressed in the world.[79]

Although the note proved ineffectual for Romanian Jews, its repercussions in other realms were significant. The affair began to solidify what might be called Roosevelt's Jewish kitchen cabinet: Jacob Schiff, the tycoon; Oscar Straus, the diplomat; Lucius Littauer, the lawmaker; and Simon Wolf, the renaissance man. Having consulted these Jewish leaders about the Romanian issue, Roosevelt would turn to them on other matters of Jewish concern throughout his presidency. This approach to statecraft more closely resembled a past era when Court Jews aided European royals than it did our modern age's reliance on professional technocrats.

The Romanian Note also demonstrated the potential for foreign policy initiatives to influence domestic electoral politics. Votes could be had in Jewish neighborhoods in America if Roosevelt was willing to make gestures—even largely symbolic ones—in defense of Jewry abroad. No historical evidence suggests that Roosevelt was motivated by an electoral agenda in this particular instance, but after now glimpsing the value at the ballot box of supporting Jewish causes, the president would be mindful of such considerations in the future.

That the United States confronted Romania at all is notable when measured against the non-reaction of the European signatories, Britain excepted. European Jews realized that their efforts were wasted in requesting the aid of their own governments. Far better for them to rally their American coreligionists to put pressure on Roosevelt.

Moreover, the Romanian Note set an important precedent that the Roosevelt administration would potentially intercede in the internal affairs of another country on a humanitarian basis, even as that humanitarianism was awkwardly couched in (contrived) objections about immigrants. To be sure, there have been moments in American foreign policy when the country clothed its self-interest in the garb of human rights; the Romanian Note stands as a vivid illustration of the reverse.

Months after Romanian Jews ceased to make front-page headlines, Roosevelt maintained his interest in their plight. He asked Hay in March 1903, "Would it be possible to have our Minister, when he goes to Romania, find out what has been accomplished under your note concerning the Romanian Jews?"[80] The minister in question was John Jackson, the newly installed ambassador in Greece whose regional remit covered Romania. Secretary Hay tapped Jackson to uncover whether the note—circulated to the signatories fully seven months earlier—had moved them to bring any pressure to bear on Romania. "The matter is one in which the president has deep interest," Hay emphasized.[81]

The following month, Jackson informed Hay that the European powers had taken no action whatsoever. He also trivialized Jewish affliction in Romania, claiming that the country didn't perpetuate antisemitism. After painting a fictitiously rosy picture of Romanian-Jewish life, Jackson's letter concluded, "Their sufferings have been exaggerated."[82] Jackson's glib disregard for Jewish anguish is striking given the relatively bold intervention that the administration had made the prior summer on behalf of Romanian Jewry. While Jackson took their plight far less seriously than did Roosevelt, imminent events showed just how terrifying life could become for Eastern Europe's Jews. The very next day in Kishinev—a city situated just over the Romanian border, in southwestern Russia—a sudden explosion of anti-Jewish violence would shock the American conscience.

3

KISHINEV PETITION

At the dawn of the twentieth century, Kishinev was a handsome and even elegant city. It served as the capital of the province of Bessarabia and featured a number of stately government buildings. The principal avenue was a wide thoroughfare lined with acacia trees. Amid the upscale streets of the city center, townsfolk patronized stores, banks, and jewelers. Fashionable crowds would congregate in the evenings at the People's Park to enjoy performances by military bands. The pleasing architecture, rich foliage, and Royal Gardens all gave Kishinev the feel of an affluent and modern community. But underneath this civilized exterior, an antisemitic rage burned.[1]

Bessarabia had been annexed into the Russian Empire during the early nineteenth century. Part of the Pale of Settlement, Bessarabia in general and Kishinev in particular were home to a sizable Jewish population.[2] The city's 130,000 residents included 50,000 Jews, another 50,000 Moldavans, and 8,000 Russians. Most of the remainder originated from various Balkan territories. Some of these Jews enjoyed prosperity, but a majority were impoverished laborers and craftsmen. As with other places in the Pale, Kishinev's Jews subsisted under special strictures. They were forbidden from purchasing land or serving in high government posts. And although Jews comprised nearly 40 percent of the population, state schools implemented quotas that kept Jewish enrollment at no more than 5 percent.[3]

The prejudice against Kishinev's Jews began to metastasize into something even more sinister in the late 1890s. Under the direction of a virulently bigoted editor, the city's sole newspaper—the *Bessarabetz*—inundated readers with an endless torrent of antisemitic vitriol. One conspiratorial story after the next painted Jews as traitors to Russia and as threats to Christianity. The *Bessarabetz* circulated widely among municipal bureaucrats, police officers, and the lower classes. Kishinev was fast becoming a tinderbox of Jew hatred. Then came the spark that would ignite a conflagration.[4]

★ ★ ★

In February of 1903, the corpse of a missing Christian boy was uncovered in a village outside Kishinev. The murderer would ultimately turn out be the victim's own cousin, but a rumor abounded that Jews had slain the child. It was alleged that homicidal Jews needed the boy's blood as an ingredient in their unleavened bread for the Passover holiday.[5] This kind of blood libel against Jews was a hoary trope with medieval roots.[6] The *Bessarabetz* recklessly perpetrated the rumor and demanded vengeance against the Jewish community. Fearful that a violent outbreak was imminent, Kishinev's Jews appealed to authority figures for help. The provincial governor offered them words of reassurance but took no action to preempt a pogrom. When the city's chief rabbi asked the Greek bishop to disavow the baseless accusations, the bishop refused, confessing that he wasn't sure the Jews were actually innocent. The police chief, for his part, reportedly said it would "serve the Jews right if they were driven from the city."[7]

On Easter Sunday came the attack. What began with some rowdy youngsters picking on Jews soon escalated into adults ransacking Jewish businesses.[8] A mob plundered a saloon on Armenia Street owned by the Feldstein family. One rioter uncovered a slab of meat in the saloon, climbed atop the roof, and announced to the horde below, "Here are the remains of a Christian child found in the house of the wealthy Jew." When the gang broke into Feldstein's cellar and uncovered champagne, rioters toasted the editor of the *Bessarabetz* newspaper.[9]

Thus began a two-day pogrom whose brutality would evoke worldwide horror when the details later became known. Mobs roamed the streets, pillaging and massacring with abandon. At No. 13 Asia Street—an apartment building whose eight families were all Jewish—pogromists found a tradesman named Mordecai Greenschopin taking refuge in a shed. They forced him out and beat him lifeless with poles. Other residents of No. 13 were then hunted down and savagely killed, with rioters using crowbars as instruments of death. The victims' corpses were left to rot on the street for hours.[10]

In one of Kishinev's most indigent Jewish neighborhoods, a gang stormed Meyer Weissman's small grocery store. He had sixty rubles and offered his assailants the money in exchange for his life. But the gang leader wasn't satisfied with the rubles alone, announcing, "Now, we want your eye; you will never again look upon a Christian child." Weissman had already lost one eye in his youth, and he now pleaded with the mob to murder him—he would rather die than be fully blind. They used a pointed stick to puncture his one good eye, leaving Weissman to live in darkness.[11]

Throughout Kishinev, Jewish women endured appalling gang rapes. Many of these women knew their rapists by name and fruitlessly begged them to stop. One such victim was twenty-four-year-old Rivka Schiff. After she was found hiding with other Jews in an attic, she was raped more than half a dozen times. Rivka personally knew one of her assailants, pleading with him, "You have known me for many years." Her cries fell on deaf ears, as her husband and other Jews watched her assault in horror.[12]

Christian homeowners warded off the gangs by drawing crosses on their windows. When Jews tried to fool the mobs with the same tactic, it proved ineffective, which suggests that the pogromists were given advance knowledge about which homes were Jewish.[13] Most policemen were indifferent and made little effort to protect Jewish lives, but there were some officers who arrested rioters and safeguarded individual Jews. Moreover, a number of Christians hid their Jewish neighbors. Still other Jews took their fate in their own hands. Around 250 of them—bearing guns and clubs—congregated in a courtyard and managed to stave off pogromists. But whatever success that group had was anomalous; elsewhere in Kishinev, Jewish efforts at resistance were too isolated to overcome the mob's numerical advantage.[14]

Late in the afternoon on the second day, Bessarabia's governor authorized the use of military force to break up the pogrom. The soldiers also picked up the corpses littering the streets; many of these bodies had been showered in feathers as a final act of degradation.[15] In the end, forty-nine Jews were killed and many others hospitalized with severe physical trauma. More than a hundred children became orphans. Property damage amounted to over two million rubles (about $40 million in American dollars today). Entire streets had been effectively demolished. Kishinev Jewry lay in ruins.[16]

The first reports of the slaughter appeared in the American press on April 23, two days after it concluded.[17] Soon the papers were casting doubt on Russia's official narrative of the pogrom, which had sought to downplay the extent of the violence.[18] By April 29, the Jewish leader Simon Wolf decided to write Secretary of State John Hay about the "terrible outrages and massacres practiced upon the Jews of Kishinev." He noted that a number of U.S. citizens wished to send aid to relatives in Kishinev who might have been afflicted. Wolf also asked whether the State Department would tap its ambassador in Russia, Robert McCormick, to furnish "prompt and reliable information" about the condition of the victims and to inquire whether the Russian government would permit charitable donations from Americans.[19] The State Department acted on Wolf's request, and Ambassador McCormick cabled back to Washington: "It is authoritatively denied that there is any want or suffering among Jews in southwestern Russia."[20] McCormick here was merely relaying the Russian position, not vouching for its accuracy.

Just as Russia was brazenly denying reality, eyewitness accounts of the pogrom began to surface in American papers.[21] Meetings were organized by various synagogues and Jewish societies in New York, Philadelphia, Cleveland, and Milwaukee.[22] Yiddish newspapers in America initiated fundraising drives.[23] From affluent bankers to impoverished immigrants, Jews nationwide donated what they could. "The heart of Israel is touched," said a member of a relief committee. "It is sore with the sorrow for its martyred brethren."[24] Although the Jewish community in the United States had any number of internal divisions, Kishinev united American Jewry like nothing else.

The Windsor Theater in lower Manhattan staged a specially produced play, *The Destruction of Kishinev*, and donated half the proceeds of the play's five-night run to a relief fund.[25] Other theaters contributed a portion of their revenue from their regularly scheduled performances.[26] In an early indication that the pogrom would awaken the conscience of non-Jews, a Chinese theater in New York sponsored three benefit shows that sold out all five hundred seats each evening.[27]

Daily newspaper coverage divulged graphic details as they became available about the pogrom's carnage. Western journalists debunked the blood libel that had been invoked to justify the violence. They also blamed Russian authorities—central and local—for allowing such atrocities.[28]

Public pressure mounted in the United States for the Roosevelt administration to take some kind of action. In New York, a group of five hundred Jewish veterans of the Spanish-American War passed a series of resolutions calling on the president to coax Russia into prosecuting the pogromists.[29] Appeals for some kind of official response inundated the State Department.[30] And mass meetings were held in Baltimore, Boston, Dallas, Hartford, Philadelphia, and even Texarkana.[31] Some of these gatherings attracted thousands of people.[32] Leading citizens and elected officials—Jew and Gentile alike—joined the fray on behalf of Kishinev's victims. In Chicago, a large assemblage at the Star Theatre heard two public icons inveigh against Russia: the settlement house pioneer Jane Addams and renowned trial lawyer Clarence Darrow.[33]

Meanwhile the Russian ambassador to the United States, Count Arthur Cassini, issued an extraordinary statement to the Associated Press. He blamed Kishinev's Jews for the crimes that had been visited upon them. Count Cassini insisted that the "unfriendly attitude" toward Jews in Russia was justified because Jews opted to work as moneylenders instead of agrarians. The typical Jewish financier took "advantage of the Russian peasant, whom he soon has in his power and ultimately destroys." Thus any animosity toward Jews was "only natural."[34] Given this callous diatribe from Russia's ambassador, Americans could hardly have been surprised when their press began reporting that the criminal probe in Kishinev was led by a prominent antisemite who was all too eager to exonerate the pogrom's culprits.[35]

★ ★ ★

Jacob Schiff, the influential Jewish philanthropist, beseeched John Hay to speak out against Russia. But Hay was resistant. "I might feel precisely as you do in regard to it," Hay wrote Schiff, "but you are free to express your feelings and I am not." Hay believed, as a matter of diplomatic protocol, that the United States had no business interfering with internal Russian affairs. He pointedly challenged Schiff, "What possible advantage would it be to the United States, and what possible advantage to the Jews of Russia, if we should make a protest against these fiendish cruelties and be told that it was none of our business?"[36] It is unsurprising that Hay proved more reluctant here than he had been with the Romanian Note the year prior. Russia was a more powerful country than Romania; Hay well understood that alienating the former was a higher-risk proposition that could meaningfully threaten international trade for American businesses.

As public demonstrations from San Francisco to Yonkers continued apace, Theodore Roosevelt considered his options. The president asked Hay "if it would be advisable for me to contribute one hundred dollars [about $3,500 today] to some fund for the relief of the Russian Jews." He directed Hay to solicit the opinion of other cabinet members as well; the secretary of war quashed the idea.[37] Thus began a pattern that would recur throughout the Kishinev affair wherein Roosevelt exhibited sympathetic instincts toward Jews that his Gentile advisors then tried to rein in.

The president was, of course, receiving a very different message from the Jewish community. Stephen Wise, a young rabbi known for his captivating oratory and inspired activism, personally met with Roosevelt and encouraged him to issue a statement condemning the bloodbath. Rabbi Wise followed up with a letter to TR highlighting instances

FIGURE 3.1. The U.S. government symbolized by Uncle Sam whose proverbial skeleton in the closet is race-based lynching. *Source*: "A Skeleton of His Own," *Puck*, July 29, 1903.

over the past thirty years when the United States had spoken out against antisemitism on humanitarian grounds. Wise also conveyed his anxiety that the Kishinev pogrom was merely a "prelude to further scenes of violence" and stressed that a public word from the president would likely "have the effect of staying the hand of the oppressor."[38]

Roosevelt's instinct was to do *something*, but he would not pursue any particular plan without Hay's assent. A few days after hearing from Rabbi Wise, the president wrote Hay wondering, "Would it do any good for me to say a word [on] behalf of the Jews such as asked for, or would it do harm?" Roosevelt's letter grappled with the uncomfortable reality that Russia had arguably just as much as right to censure America's own problem with extralegal killing. "I suppose it would be very much like the czar expressing his horror of our lynching negroes," he reasoned.[39] Pogroms and lynchings did involve the same grisly factors: targeted violence at a marginalized group, the effective consent of local authorities, and a spurious insistence that the bloodshed was legitimate retribution for some alleged wrongdoing.[40] There is no extant reply from Hay to Roosevelt's letter—perhaps he responded by phone or in person—but we can glean from Hay's later behavior that he surely did not advise the president to speak out about Kishinev.

Public pressure for action against Russia proved unrelenting. The *Philadelphia Inquirer* detailed in late May that there was "little or no abatement during the week in the interest aroused by the reports from Kishinev," adding, "Everywhere in the civilized world . . . the sentiments aroused by this dreadful affair are those of horror."[41] A play entitled *The Story of Kishinev: A Tragedy in Five Acts* was selling out nightly in New York.[42] Gatherings in support of the victims proliferated in large cities and small towns alike; often these meetings adopted resolutions requesting a diplomatic response from the Roosevelt administration.[43] Although there would be some compassionate reaction in Europe to the Kishinev pogrom—a couple protests and fundraising for the victims—it was nowhere near the scale of the outcry in America.[44] This discrepancy is unsurprising. For one, more Jews were living in the United States than in any European country, aside from Russia itself.[45] And Europe's tortured history of antisemitism had taught Old World Jews the hazards of speaking up too emphatically.[46]

The most prominent demonstration in America took place in late May in New York's Carnegie Hall. Before a throng of 3,500 people, Mayor Seth Low celebrated the city as a haven for Jewish life dating back to the days of Dutch colonial rule. He also proudly noted that fundraising for Kishinev's Jews had begun on the Lower East Side even before the pogrom became a newspaper sensation. A number of other Gentile luminaries gave speeches, including the president of Cornell University and a prominent Baptist minister.[47]

The main attraction at Carnegie Hall that evening was an ex-president, Grover Cleveland. His presence elicited an effusive display of affection from the audience. As the *New York Times* observed, "The two upper galleries, thronged to their utmost capacity, were white with waving handkerchiefs and echoed with applause."[48] Cleveland asked the crowd to condemn the atrocities of Kishinev and provide financial relief for the survivors with "all the moral force which our American citizenship gives to us." But then he struck a cautionary note, maintaining that the "dictates of American conservatism and moderation" required the public to "forgo perplexing and extreme demands upon our government" for diplomatic interference with the Russian Empire.[49] A local paper was displeased with the former president's call for restraint, expressing "regret that Mr. Cleveland followed up his warm and manly denunciation of the murders and outrages with a timid plea for the withholding of pressure."[50]

Kishinev continued to command daily attention from the American press, and with good reason. Because it took time for a full accounting of the facts, some novel piece of information from Kishinev was always surfacing. Western journalists had to make the journey to Kishinev, where upon arrival they unearthed new stories based on testimony from victims and witnesses on the ground. They also covered the pogrom's aftermath in Kishinev—the fate of survivors, the response of Russian officials, the consequences (or lack thereof) for the accused. And once these newspaper correspondents left Russian soil and thus no longer had to contend with the Russian censors, they could furnish additional details they had earlier withheld.[51] What's more, the ceaseless sequence of public gatherings within the United States ensured that there were perennially fresh stories on the domestic front. From the American Baptist Missionary Union to the city council of Detroit, rising numbers of Gentiles were organizing in protest of Kishinev's violence. It was a mainstream story, not just a Jewish one.[52] Increasingly, questions about the proper diplomatic play from the Roosevelt administration came to preoccupy journalists.

★ ★ ★

Letters urging action from John Hay deluged the State Department in numbers too numerous to enable replies, but one particular missive did merit a response. Simon Wolf had written Hay asking him to meet with the leaders of B'nai B'rith, the oldest Jewish humanitarian organization in the country (B'nai B'rith means "Children of the Covenant"). Wolf himself was a member of B'nai B'rith's executive committee. The barrage of public pressure apparently was having some effect—it was announced in early June that Secretary Hay would indeed meet with a delegation from B'nai B'rith in two weeks' time.[53]

As the B'nai B'rith meeting in Washington drew near, Russia released a statement seeking to stymie both donations for victims and criticism of its government: "The Emperor has the means at hand to relieve suffering wherever it appears in his empire," and so aid from abroad "must be declined."[54] This line was just spurious posturing—Americans had already sent nearly 200,000 rubles to Kishinev (over $3 million U.S. dollars today).[55] The Russian statement further cited the principle of noninterference between nations and announced, accordingly, that St. Petersburg would refuse "to receive any representations regarding the Kishinev incident from a foreign power."[56]

Caught between Russian obstinance and American outcry, Roosevelt met with Russia's ambassador, Count Cassini, for nearly an hour in Washington on June 12. Neither party offered any public word about that meeting in its immediate aftermath. But behind closed doors, Cassini assured Roosevelt that several hundred suspects were in custody and would be held to account in court. He also informed TR that Russia had replaced the governor of Bessarabia.[57] Undoubtedly, Cassini's principal aim here was to preempt an embarrassing censure of his country from the United States on the global stage.

Foreign policy wasn't the only source of friction between Count Cassini and President Roosevelt. Both statesmen were alarmed by the combustible companionship between their irreverent daughters: nineteen-year-old Alice Roosevelt and twenty-one-year-old Marguerite Cassini. Together, Alice and Marguerite formed a rambunctious duo that romped their way through the socialite scene. "Our friendship had the violence of a bomb," Marguerite later recalled. They were thrill-seekers who scorned social convention; their penchant for fast cars, day drinking, and betting at the race track all scandalized polite society. Newspapers gleefully reported on what Marguerite called their "veritable reign of terror." The American president and Russian ambassador were each convinced that the other's daughter was a nefarious influence on his own.[58]

Meanwhile Simon Wolf and the other members of the B'nai B'rith Executive Committee converged on the Arlington Hotel in Washington on June 14.[59] The pinnacle of luxury, the Arlington served as the accommodation of choice for princes, dukes, and emperors visiting the American capital. Numerous senators took up residence in the hotel's elegant quarters. The Arlington's manager enjoyed wide renown for his diligence in meeting guests' every need. But the B'nai B'rith leaders didn't likely have time to avail themselves of the hotel's ornate parlors or billiard room.[60] They were consumed with preparations for not one but two meetings: after convening with John Hay, they would be granted an audience with Theodore Roosevelt himself. Count Cassini sent word that he wanted to personally speak that day with Simon Wolf and the B'nai B'rith president, Leo Levi. They refused the offer, feeling it inappropriate to take a meeting with the Russian ambassador when they already had one pending with their own country's secretary of state and president.[61]

B'nai B'rith's leaders decided that they would present the Roosevelt administration with two possible courses of action. The first would entail a petition of protest—arranged by B'nai B'rith and signed by leading American citizens of all religions—that the administration would "unofficially or semi-officially" transmit to the czar. The second option

FIGURE 3.2. Alice Roosevelt. *Credit*: Frances Benjamin Johnston. *Source*: Library of Congress, Prints and Photographs Division.

would be for the United States government to organize an international conference addressing "persecutions and oppressions" rooted in "racial and religious prejudices."[62] It is unclear whether B'nai B'rith intended the prospective conference to deal only with Russian pogroms or to confront hatred worldwide.

At 10:30 the following morning, Wolf, Levi, and several other members of B'nai B'rith's executive committee arrived at the State Department to see John Hay. Levi, as president, spoke for the group and offered its recommendation for a petition or conference.[63] He also gave Hay a memo outlining why the Roosevelt administration would be justified in taking either or both measures, despite the fact that no Americans were victims in Kishinev: Russian persecution drove Jewish émigrés to the United States, and their anti-Russian sentiment helped foment hostility to Russia among the American public generally, thereby weakening Russian-American relations. Pogroms were thus implicated in international relations and a proper subject of diplomacy. This was similar, if not quite identical, to the rationale that the administration had used to legitimize the Romanian Note the year prior.[64]

John Hay fully appreciated that this meeting wasn't merely an opportunity for him to hear from representatives of the Jewish community. It was also an exercise in public relations. The press had already widely reported that the administration would receive a delegation from B'nai B'rith. And so Hay responded in the meeting with prepared remarks that were transcribed for public release. Nearly two months since the pogrom, Kishinev still made daily news—Hay could be sure that whatever statement he offered, the first official one from the administration, would become front-page fodder. He began by recognizing the "deep emotion" that the "cruel outrages" in Kishinev had inspired around the world. Hay also noted the estimable role of Jews in American life. "Nobody can ever make the Americans think ill of the Jews," he insisted. "We know them too well." Hay's categorical assertion here was more aspirational than factual given that antisemitism still had some purchase in the United States.[65]

Hay then made clear that he was firmly committed to noninterference, a position he tried to finesse by lauding American Jewry for its "power of self-restraint" and suggesting that the Roosevelt administration "must exhibit the same." He asked his Jewish visitors to pay heed that "no civilized government in the world has yet taken official action—this consideration alone would bid us to proceed with care." Hay also celebrated the czar as a "man whose personal character is even more elevated than his exalted station" and praised Russia as a "great and friendly nation." America was thus obliged to assume that such an "enlightened sovereign" was surely "doing all that lies in his power to put a stop to these atrocities."[66] These obsequious comments, which were sure to make the papers and come to St. Petersburg's attention, reflected Hay's desire to preserve Russian-American relations rather than any heartfelt admiration for the czar. Hay was plainly disinclined to endorse action from the administration.[67]

After meeting for forty minutes, John Hay accompanied the B'nai B'rith delegation to the White House, where the president welcomed the Jewish leaders. They had already drafted the text of a petition that the administration could submit to the czar, and Levi handed it to Roosevelt. It began with a damning recitation of the facts surrounding the Kishinev pogrom, wherein "derelict" local officials allowed mobs animated by "religious prejudice" to butcher "hapless Jews." The petition maintained that the circumstances precipitating the pogrom—a toxic mix of bigotry and lawlessness—weren't unique to Kishinev but pervasive throughout the Pale of Settlement. Haunted by the prospect of additional massacres, Russian Jews faced a difficult choice: (1) abandon their homes and struggle as foreigners abroad or (2) stay in Russia and brace for the next wave of bloodshed. The Jewish exodus from Russia now had the dubious honor of surpassing Spain's Inquisition and rivaling Pharaoh's Egypt, the petition alleged.[68]

While exhibiting little restraint in its rhetoric about pogroms, the petition did strategically soften its tone when discussing the czar. It credited him with helping establish the international court at The Hague. The petition urged the czar to announce that "the humblest subject or citizen may worship according to the dictates of his own conscience." If the czar defended that basic right, he would "add new luster to his reign and fame."[69]

Roosevelt closely read the petition before launching into a lengthy discourse. A stenographer was on hand to record his words for circulation to the press. The president first noted that while the Kishinev pogrom had elicited worldwide sympathy, it was only natural that expressions of compassion were most fervent in the United States. After all, America had always enjoyed a special relationship with the Jewish people, Roosevelt said. He further observed that "anyone who goes through any of the old cemeteries of the cities" on the Eastern seaboard "will see the names of many an American of Jewish race, who, in war or in peace, did his full share in the founding of this nation." In an age when many native-born Americans feared that the recent influx of Jewish immigrants undermined the Anglo-Saxon heritage of the country, Roosevelt here tacitly rejected that nativist logic by emphasizing Jewish contributions to the republic's birth.[70]

Unlike Hay, Roosevelt had longstanding ties to the Jewish community, which enabled him to speak at length about his personal relationships with Jews in a way that Hay could not. Roosevelt warmly recounted the Jewish policemen on his force in New York and the Jewish Rough Riders whom he fought alongside in Cuba. Precisely because of those deep and enduring connections to Jewry, "I have felt a degree of personal sympathy and personal horror of this dreadful tragedy," the president explained.[71]

Roosevelt also referenced his positive meeting with Count Cassini three days prior and relayed that "the government of Russia shares the feelings of horror and indignation." In that moment, it must have appeared to the B'nai B'rith delegation that Roosevelt would echo Hay and invoke Russia's supposed concern for Kishinev's victims as a pretext for American inaction. But in fact TR was willing to go beyond Hay. Roosevelt promised he would "consider most carefully the suggestions that you have submitted to me." The president needed time to contemplate whether "existing conditions are such that any further official expression would be of advantage to the unfortunate survivors." In closing, Roosevelt avowed, "Nothing will have my more constant thought than this subject."[72] Perhaps Cassini's last-ditch effort to avert diplomatic censure from the United States would prove fruitless.

At the end of the hour-long meeting, the parties agreed that the White House could publicize all documentation from that morning—the B'nai B'rith memo, the petition, and the transcribed comments of Hay and Roosevelt. Both the secretary of state and president also acceded to B'nai B'rith's request for signed photographs for display at the organization's headquarters. Roosevelt then had to make haste to attend a festival in Baltimore, and he inquired whether Simon Wolf would care to attend as the president's guest. Wolf, of course, obliged.[73]

★ ★ ★

The meetings at the State Department and White House garnered considerable attention. Many newspapers printed substantial portions—sometimes even the entirety—of the remarks by Roosevelt and Hay.[74] The Jewish press, in particular, trumpeted Roosevelt's sympathetic words to the Jewish delegation. "His answer is in itself a protest and a mighty one," pronounced the *Jewish American*.[75]

As Roosevelt weighed his diplomatic options in the days that followed, some on the home front were satisfied that, given his widely covered caucus with B'nai B'rith, the president had done as much as was prudent. He ought to push Russia no further. The *New York Press*, for instance, maintained that Roosevelt's comments, while fully warranted, also marked "the very limit" of propriety since no American citizens were victims of the pogrom. It would be ill-advised to proceed along the lines B'nai B'rith recommended in light of the "voluntary assurances of Russia that the murderers would be punished and the governor of the province removed." On other hand, the *New York News* was frustrated that Roosevelt hadn't been bolder. "In spite of the thousands of protests and petitions presented to him, President Roosevelt has refused to make remonstrance to Russia," the *News* grumbled.[76]

As the president deliberated whether to forward the B'nai B'rith petition to Russia, Count Cassini spoke to the Associated Press on June 19 in what was surely a calculated bid to influence Roosevelt's decision. Cassini publicly emphasized to the AP what he had already told Roosevelt in private: the Bessarabian governor had been replaced and the guilty would pay for their crimes. The Russian ambassador also stressed his country's commitment to protecting its Jewish residents, a message that offered a stark contrast from the prior month when he had insisted that the Jews provoked the pogrom with their greedy moneylending. In conciliatory fashion, Cassini asserted that the attitude of both the Russian government and the Russian people toward the United States was amicable. "To disturb these relations owing to false impressions conceived in hostile quarters would be most deplorable," he warned.[77]

Count Cassini's claim that Russia was committed to the security of its Jews was, of course, rooted less in reality than in his desire to soothe tensions with the Roosevelt administration. Simon Wolf was infuriated by the Russian ambassador's dissembling. And so Wolf took it upon himself not only to issue a piqued letter to Cassini but also to disseminate it to the press. The letter called attention to the systemic degradations imposed on Russian Jews, declaring that the American people and their government would not be misled by Cassini's attempt to "deceive and obscure." Wolf pointedly suggested that if Russia was truly as "friendly" toward the United States as Cassini contended, then it could "evidence the friendship by deeds and not by empty phrases."[78] John Hay—who had so effusively celebrated Russian-American amity in his remarks to B'nai B'rith—must not have been pleased with the contents of Wolf's publicly released letter.

Nor could Hay have been delighted to learn that Roosevelt resolved to forward B'nai B'rith's petition to the Russian government. In late June, Hay informed Wolf of the president's decision in a letter that soon appeared verbatim in the papers. Hay's letter explained that TR's determination had hinged on the question of whether such a petition would benefit or harm Russian Jews. Roosevelt, in the end, "decided to accept your opinion, and that of numerous and intelligent groups of American citizens of the Jewish faith whom you represent." Hay also underscored that the administration couldn't be sure how Russia might react.[79] Leo Levi, as president of B'nai B'rith, told the press that his organization would work expeditiously to collect signatures for the petition.[80]

Although the historical record doesn't offer insight into why Roosevelt chose B'nai B'rith's approach over noninterference, there can be little question that Roosevelt did so against Hay's counsel. The *New York Times* reported that Roosevelt had initially opted against the petition idea before reversing course: "After consultation with his advisers, he determined not to forward the petition, because Russia might resent it and ... break off diplomatic relations." But then Roosevelt "reconsidered." The president, despite the undoubted misgivings of his secretary of state, was prepared to take a diplomatic risk for Jewry.[81]

Word of Roosevelt's decision was, of course, poorly received in St. Petersburg. According to a "semiofficial news agency" in Russia, the czar's government would deem the petition to be foreign meddling in domestic matters.[82] The *Los Angeles Times* anticipated a "diplomatic rupture" between the two countries. The paper also predicted that Count Cassini, who was scheduled to take an imminent summer vacation, would soon find himself on permanent holiday owing to St. Petersburg's displeasure with the turn of events.[83] Meanwhile, foreign envoys in Washington disapproved of Roosevelt's pending interference into Russia's internal affairs. The French ambassador wrote back to Paris that the American president was currying favor with "the influential Jewish coterie" and thereby setting a "most vexatious precedent ... a very dangerous policy."[84]

With tensions escalating, the Associated Press tipped off the State Department in early July about a story that would break in a few hours: the Russians were now confirming their earlier semiofficial refusal to accept the petition and they were denying that Count Cassini had ever engaged in official discussion about Kishinev with the Roosevelt administration. Because John Hay was vacationing with his daughter in Newport, Assistant Secretary of State Francis Loomis received the news from the AP. Loomis immediately wired the president, who was at his summer home in the town of Oyster Bay on Long Island. Loomis's telegram to Roosevelt disclosed that the AP was about to release the following announcement to the papers: "The Associated Press is authorized to state that the Russian government most positively and absolutely denies the reports that it has offered any official explanation to the American government" through Cassini. The AP statement further relayed that Russia would "categorically refuse" to accept any petition from a foreign power about its domestic life.[85]

Of course, Count Cassini *had* supplied an explanation when he met with Roosevelt on June 12. Maybe Russia was treating that conversation as unofficial and thus felt justified in refuting the notion that it had furnished an "official explanation." Or perhaps the June 12 meeting had indeed been official and the Russians were now lying about it. After all, Russia's instinct for falsehood had been brazen throughout the Kishinev affair: first Russia gainsaid the pogrom's very existence, then it blamed the Jews for their own macabre fate, and finally it insisted that the victims required no charitable aid. An exasperated Roosevelt would later vent to a friend, "What I cannot understand about the Russian is the way he will lie when he knows perfectly well that you know he is lying."[86]

The president was riled that Russia had gone straight to the American press with the message that the petition would be a futile gesture instead of communicating that position through diplomatic channels. He well understood that the Russian government was attempting to indirectly pressure him by dampening public support in the United States for the petition. Roosevelt fired off a furious letter to John Hay, still in Newport. "I am angered over what I regard as the impertinent action of the Russians in this matter," TR fumed. "They are endeavoring to appeal to the people over our heads." He vowed that if Russia persisted in its present manipulation campaign instead of engaging directly with the State Department, then he would remain steadfast in his resolve to transmit the petition.[87] Russia's strategy was backfiring.

Roosevelt crafted a press release for Loomis to distribute to the papers. TR wrote it such that the remarks were attributed to an unnamed "high official" at the State Department rather than to the president himself. The statement made clear that the Roosevelt administration would disregard Russian declarations made outside the formal methods of diplomacy. It also reaffirmed the U.S. government's willingness to follow through on its commitment to B'nai B'rith, promising to "give expression to deep sympathy felt not only by the administration but by all the American people for the unfortunate Jews." Roosevelt's press release clarified that the administration's failure to have thus far transmitted the petition to Russia was "due solely to the delay in furnishing the address to the State Department by the petitioners," lest anyone misinterpret the ongoing lag to mean that the president had opted, as a concession to Russia, not to forward the petition after all.[88]

The newspapers, with their insatiable interest in all things Kishinev, diligently covered this exercise in diplomatic brinkmanship.[89] Count Cassini declined to issue a rebuttal. St. Petersburg was frustrated that the situation had deteriorated under Cassini's watch. He was put under strict orders to pass along to the Roosevelt administration verbatim messages from St. Petersburg and not to improvise his own comments.[90]

Journalists were attuned to the fact that the pro-Jewish statement Loomis released—although nominally ascribed to a "high official" at the State Department—had the all the signs of Roosevelt's doing and none of Hay's. As the *New York Times* reported, "It is the understanding that the utterance given out by Assistant Secretary Loomis was authorized from Oyster Bay, [and] there is reason for the belief that it was without the knowledge of Secretary Hay."[91] Rumors soon began swirling that the divergence between Hay and Roosevelt over the petition might well prompt Hay to resign or Roosevelt to fire him.[92]

Russian antagonism had made the president want to proceed more quickly with the petition. He directed the State Department to impress upon Simon Wolf the importance of providing the petition to Washington immediately. Wolf wrote a pained letter to Roosevelt in early July explaining that it was a "physical impossibility" for B'nai B'rith to summarily complete its collection of signatures. He reminded Roosevelt of a point that the B'nai B'rith leadership had made in person at the White House: the petition must bear the names of prominent citizens of all faiths and from numerous cities nationwide. Gathering signatures from such a religiously and geographically diverse cohort would convey a resounding message about "the universal feeling" throughout the United States toward Kishinev's victims. But an endeavor that vast also required time, Wolf noted, especially with so many of the prospective signers on their summer vacations. In his memoirs, Wolf would later recall feeling the "utmost embarrassment" that he could not instantly comply with Roosevelt's request.[93]

Wolf wrote a follow-up letter to Roosevelt the next day offering the president a chance to change his mind about the petition. "Will it be helping you, the administration, or the American people by not sending the petition?" Wolf inquired. "If so, do not hesitate to say so to me." Although reversing course now would entail a sacrifice for American Jews, Wolf affirmed that his Jewish compatriots would bear that burden in the name of good citizenship. "The Jew has ever aided and suffered or both," he observed. "We are prepared to do so now, if by our suffering the Republic of free conscience is benefitted." But the majority of Wolf's letter set forth why the president should in fact stand up to Russia. The Russian Empire was merely "masquerading" as a "friend" of the United States as it connived to "create public opinion inimical to your action, and to prevent signing of the petition." Moreover, Wolf alleged that Russia bribed certain American editorialists to condemn Roosevelt's handling of the Kishinev affair.[94] Wolf was stretching on this bribery claim. Some of the president's domestic critics were apt to find fault with any policy that his administration pursued; they required no greasing from Russia to see lapses in TR's judgment.[95]

Roosevelt, in turn, asked a Jewish contingency—consisting of Simon Wolf, Oscar Straus, and Leo Levi (the B'nai B'rith president)—to plan for a meeting with him in Oyster Bay, to take place in mid-July, for discussion of the petition.[96] In the intervening days, Roosevelt's personal aide telegrammed Wolf that it would "very inadvisable" for him, Straus, or Levi to speak publicly prior to their meeting with the president.[97] The three Jewish leaders heeded that advice. They convened quietly among themselves several times prior to the Oyster Bay meeting to ensure their own views were in harmony so that they could present a unified opinion to the president.[98] B'nai B'rith, meanwhile, was hastily gathering more signatures.[99]

★ ★ ★

That Theodore Roosevelt and Czar Nicholas II both seemed willing to hazard Russian-American relations over a petition is a striking testament to the power of words in international affairs. The standoff was all the more remarkable considering its potential repercussions for East Asian geopolitics. Both Russia and Japan were pursuing imperial ambitions in the region, with Russia then occupying Manchuria while the Japanese controlled Korea, directly to Manchuria's south. Russia and Japan each saw the other as a threat to its own territorial acquisitions. And the United States, for its part, was frustrated that Russia didn't allow American merchants an "open door" to Manchurian ports. With the Russians facing the prospect of a preemptive Japanese invasion of Manchuria, it hardly behooved Russia to antagonize America into siding with Japan.[100] And yet the czar appeared ready to risk Russia's precarious position in Manchuria to forestall a petition about Jews, just as Roosevelt was prepared to jeopardize his own country's prospects for trade in Manchuria to send that very petition.

Some editorialists questioned whether the petition was worth the peril it portended for an already fraught situation in Asia. "It is while this ticklish condition of things exists in the Far East," wrote one New York paper, "that President Roosevelt goes out of his way to fling an insult at Russia which will surely be resented by that country."[101] But the *Salt Lake Telegram* argued that Roosevelt's approach was admirable precisely because he was daring to privilege principle above profit. The paper acknowledged that Russian-American relations were increasingly estranged and anticipated that if the president proceeded with the petition, "the open door in Manchuria, for which Secretary Hay had been laboring, will be closed by Russia." With so much on the line, Roosevelt's resolute stance was "suggestive of good red blood in the veins." The *Salt Lake Telegram* advised Roosevelt to show no reluctance in conveying America's disdain for "the butchers of Kishinev."[102] Irrespective of their take on the wisdom of the petition, newspapers of all stripes agreed on this much: the stakes were real, and the consequences global.

Amid speculation that Hay would possibly leave the administration over the Kishinev Petition, he denied as much to both the president and the press.[103] But privately Hay confided in his wife that he might well resign. "I am not 'doing fixed time' as in a penitentiary," he told her.[104] Hay's frustration is unsurprising—the Manchurian "open door" had

ONE LITTLE MATCH MAY FIRE THE WHOLE BUNCH.

FIGURE 3.3. Roosevelt could upend great power politics in the Far East by sending the Kishinev Petition. *Source:* "One Little Match May Fire the Whole Bunch," *Camden Post-Telegram*, July 10, 1903.

long been among his signature ambitions, and now Roosevelt was risking that endeavor in service of a Jewish cause that elicited limited sympathy from Hay.

TR summoned Hay to his summer home in Oyster Bay to discuss, among other matters, the Kishinev affair.[105] Hay was annoyed. Not only was the Kishinev Petition possibly closing Manchurian doors, but now

Hay was being dislodged from his holiday excursion with his daughter—all to attend to a president who wasn't always mindful of other people's time. As Hay was preparing to leave for Oyster Bay, he complained to his wife, "I always find TR engaged with a dozen other people, and it is an hour's wait and a minute's talk—and a certainty that there was no necessity of my coming at all." It would, in fact, be more than an hour's wait on this particular occasion. When Hay reached Oyster Bay, Roosevelt was characteristically playing host to a mélange of guests, which included several senators, a poet, and a shipping tycoon. The president asked Hay, "Will you excuse me till I play a game of tennis?" adding, "I have had no exercise all day." At that moment, a Rough Rider veteran suddenly surfaced to see whether he could hold serve against his former colonel.[106]

Hay bided his time ambling about the eighty-acre estate, which Roosevelt had named Sagamore Hill as an homage to an Indian chieftain who had ruled there centuries earlier.[107] The assortment of gardens, meadows, and orchards must have been some recompense for the slighted secretary of state.[108] Sagamore Hill's greatest charm was its vista; the unspoiled views gave the pleasingly false impression that Roosevelt and his guests had all of Oyster Bay to themselves.[109] The property's Queen Anne style house was sizable—three stories, twenty-eight rooms—but more folksy than luxurious. It certainly lacked the splendor of the Newport mansions where high-society types passed the warmer months. Mounted on the walls of the home were taxidermied animal heads that kept a constant vigil over the Roosevelts and their guests.[110]

Not until the evening did TR finally give Hay a private audience. Whatever precisely was said between them remains unknown, but Hay's pique melted away amid Roosevelt's warmth.[111] The next day Hay confessed to his wife, "The president was so cordial and hospitable that I felt ashamed of my surly crossness at having to go there."[112] In the immediate wake of his trip to Sagamore Hill, Hay was irked by journalists who continued to conjecture that his resignation was imminent. "I despair of the newspapers," Hay wrote Roosevelt, fretting that "the stupid rumor will not cease."[113] But Roosevelt reassured him, "Do not ever give a thought to the newspaper and other swine who delight to invent tales about our relations." The president further gushed over "what a really great secretary of state you are."[114] With appreciation for the heartening words, Hay thanked Roosevelt "a thousand times for your kind and generous letter" and described his pleasure in serving a president who "happened to be born a gentleman."[115]

Their rapprochement aside, Hay continued to push Roosevelt to relent on the Kishinev Petition. Seizing on a recent consular report (albeit of questionable accuracy) that Russia was holding the pogromists responsible, Hay counseled that the Roosevelt administration should back off. "The less we do and say now . . . the better, in my opinion," he cautioned.[116] By all accounts, Hay's sentiment was indicative of the State Department at large.[117] It remained to be seen whom, in the end, Roosevelt would heed: his secretary of state or his Jewish advisors.

The Jewish delegation journeyed to Oyster Bay on July 14 to meet with the president. While en route, Wolf remarked to Levi and Straus that whether Russia accepted their petition was immaterial. He reasoned that if the Roosevelt Administration at least *attempted* to submit the petition, that bold act on the world stage—more so than Russia's reaction to it—would ensure that the petition achieved its purpose.[118]

Upon arrival at Sagamore Hill, the Jews were greeted by Roosevelt with his characteristic "cordiality and informality," Wolf later recalled. Roosevelt had invited a few other guests who happened to be on hand to join him and the Jewish delegation at lunch. The whole group spent the meal deliberating over the predicament with Russia. The president's manner of formulating his foreign policy here is striking—a free-flowing conversation with not one member of his State Department but rather Jewish leaders, a British judge, a magazine editor, and his teenage daughter, Alice Roosevelt.[119] Perhaps Alice's notorious friendship with the Russian ambassador's daughter gave her unique insight into Russia's ruling class. Perhaps it compromised her objectivity. Perhaps both.

Straus, Levi, and Wolf were concerned that B'nai B'rith had collected only three thousand signatures so far, and these were disproportionately from citizens in the Northeast. In other words, the petition was too thin in volume and too unrepresentative in geography. But the Jewish delegation also understood that Roosevelt wanted to act immediately—indeed, the president had been eager to move forward with the petition fully two weeks earlier. And so during the meal, Straus, Levi, and Wolf suggested a compromise measure: instead of sending a petition with too few signatures, the administration should instruct its embassy in St. Petersburg to convey the petition without any signatures to the Russian government and inquire whether the czar himself would accept the petition. If the czar was amenable, then B'nai B'rith would take the time to gather more signatures, secure in the knowledge that the completed petition would meet with a favorable reception. But if the czar refused as expected, then B'nai B'rith would still invest the time required to amass signatures, with the resulting document to be deposited in the State Department's archives. There, the petition would endure in perpetuity as a historic symbol of religious freedom. This plan was designed to satisfy Roosevelt's sense of urgency and B'nai B'rith's desire for a comprehensive list of signatories.[120]

The time for Roosevelt to make his final decision was now at hand. In the nearly 3 months that passed since the atrocities in Kishinev, 77 public meetings had convened across America in support of the victims, and 363 speeches were delivered—by rabbis and reverends, senators and judges, editors and lawyers. Substantial sums were raised for survivors.[121] Newspapers had relentlessly covered both the pogrom and its ripple effects around the world. If Roosevelt proffered the petition to Russia, he could do so with confidence that he spoke for a broad-based movement spanning the United States.

But then again, there were compelling reasons for Roosevelt to reverse course in the eleventh hour. By submitting the petition, he might not only imperil American trade in Manchuria but provoke Russia to dissolve all diplomatic ties with the United States. No one could be sure of the unintended consequences that such a rupture could foment. The president's own secretary of state had repeatedly advised against estranging St. Petersburg. Some voices in the American press were arguing that Roosevelt had already fulfilled his humanitarian duty with his compassionate statements about Kishinev's Jews and that it would be reckless for him to alienate Russia any further. He could seize on newspaper reports that Russia was bringing the guilty to justice as a convenient pretext for noninterference. Even Simon Wolf had offered to withdraw the petition if it suited the president, affording Roosevelt cover with domestic Jews in the event that he changed his mind. And perhaps most significantly, no other head of state in the world had dared to challenge Russia over the pogrom. If Roosevelt sent the petition, he would stand alone in the global arena.[122]

And so he did. The president announced to his lunch companions at Sagamore Hill that he would proceed precisely as the Jewish delegation recommended and transmit the petition now, sans signatures. The group retired to Roosevelt's study where he declared, "Now let's finish this thing up." Roosevelt crafted language for a cable to the American embassy in Russia, incorporating feedback from his guests. When the cable was finished, Oscar Straus was entrusted with hand-delivering it to the State Department.[123] He, along with Wolf and Levi, caught the 4:18 p.m. train out of Oyster Bay.[124]

The president notified Hay via telegram that Straus was en route with a cable, which Hay was to forward without delay to St. Petersburg. The remainder of the telegram reflected TR's perceived need to defend his decision to Hay—Roosevelt insisted that this course of action would appease B'nai B'rith, demonstrate cordiality to Russia, and conclude the affair at long last.[125]

That same day, the president also felt compelled to justify his position to Edward Everett Hale, the esteemed writer and minister. Hale had recently urged Roosevelt in a letter to "take an old man's counsel" and "think three times before you offer advice to the czar."[126] Roosevelt replied that he wasn't "offering advice at all" but merely inquiring whether the czar would "receive a petition couched in respectful language." He assured Hale that the administration's decision-making process was duly deliberative: "We decided to send the petition only after careful and rather prayerful consideration."[127]

B'nai B'rith president Leo Levi issued a statement to the press the next day concerning the Oyster Bay meeting but divulged no specifics owing to Roosevelt's request for continued discretion. Still, Levi provided strong hints: "Our views and those of the president are in perfect accord." With B'nai B'rith collecting more signatures by the day, Levi's press release celebrated the petition as a broadly American—rather than narrowly Jewish—endeavor. He also maintained (implausibly) that the petition shouldn't be interpreted as a bid to intervene in Russia's internal affairs.[128]

That very morning, Straus personally handed the cable to John Hay.[129] Hay wired it at once and, at Roosevelt's request, shipped the original cable to B'nai B'rith as a keepsake.[130] With the American ambassador to Russia having taken leave to attend a wedding in Chicago, the cable was instead addressed to John Riddle, the chargé d'affaires who was administering the embassy in the ambassador's absence. The cable instructed Riddle to meet with Russia's foreign minister, share the text of the petition, and ask whether the minister would forward it to the czar.[131] With this fateful message dispatched to the U.S. embassy in St. Petersburg, the State Department stood by for word of Russia's response.

What Hay and Roosevelt did not know was that before the cable reached Riddle, the Russian foreign minister had already summoned Riddle to discuss the petition. The Russian authorities, as it turned out, had been carefully reading newspaper reports about the imminent prospect of a petition to be forwarded under the auspices of the U.S. government. Anticipating this eventuality, the foreign minister in St. Petersburg raised the issue with the czar, who was adamant that the petition be refused. Czar Nicholas regarded his authority over Russian territory as absolute and could not brook any petition that concerned Russia's domestic life. The foreign minister, in turn, met with Riddle to explain the czar's position and reasoning.[132]

In their conversation, the foreign minister told Riddle that if he were to personally hand over the petition, it would be handed back unread; if the petition were delivered by courier in an envelope, it would be returned unopened. But the foreign minister also conveyed that the czar entertained a "kindly feeling toward America." Czar Nicholas plainly didn't want Russia's refusal of the petition to undermine relations between the two nations. In that spirit, the foreign minister made clear to

Riddle that he was offering this information "informally" in the hopes of precluding the "discourtesy" of having to rebuff any attempt by Riddle to physically transmit the petition.[133]

Shortly thereafter, the cable from Hay arrived at the U.S. embassy in St. Petersburg. Since Riddle had already discussed the petition with the foreign minister, Riddle felt that he had in effect followed the cable's directive; he didn't think it necessary to meet a second time and have the same conversation again. Riddle relayed to Hay all that the foreign minister had said and also shared his own determination that he had, for all intents and purposes, done his duty. "I shall consider your instructions as already carried out by the present report unless I am ordered to take further steps," he concluded.[134]

Hay forwarded Riddle's message to Roosevelt at once.[135] TR saw no need for Riddle to undertake the formality of literally handing over the petition only to have it handed back. It was sufficient that Hay had wired the cable to Riddle and that Russia had given its answer, even if the sequence of those two events was the reverse of what had been expected. From the president's perspective, his pledge to B'nai B'rith was fulfilled. And, critically, the controversy had been resolved without Russia cutting off diplomatic ties to the United States. Roosevelt authorized Hay to release to the press both TR's cable to Riddle and a brief summary of Riddle's reply back to Washington. The president also directed Hay to tell the Jewish leaders from the Sagamore Hill meeting that they could now speak freely on the matter.[136]

★ ★ ★

Breaking news of the petition received comprehensive coverage from the papers. The *Philadelphia Inquirer* described Riddle's discussion with the Russian foreign minister as tantamount to submission of the petition. Riddle had put "Russia in possession of the petition fully as much as if it had been delivered with all the formality of many sheets of paper and thousands of signatures."[137] An editorial in the *New York Times* minimized Russia's rejection of the petition as a trivial afterthought; the publicity surrounding the petition had ensured that its message was heard. Russia was now "on notice that the civilized world views with amazement and pain its failure to prevent within the dominions of the czar the murder of men and women for reasons of faith."[138] Back in St. Petersburg, the Russian Foreign Office spoke to the Associated Press, reiterating Russia's resistance to external interference but also its commitment to amicable relations with America.[139]

Leo Levi, on behalf of B'nai B'rith, trumpeted the outcome as a victory in his own remarks to the press. He celebrated the people of the United States for memorializing in a petition their outrage over Kishinev, and he lauded the Roosevelt administration for forwarding it to Russia. The initial plan as conceived in June had been to furnish Russia a petition *with* signatures, and Levi felt it important to clarify that the subsequent proposal to submit a signatureless petition came from the B'nai B'rith leadership, not from Roosevelt. Levi appeared to be concerned that the public might misinterpret the unsigned petition as some kind of half-measure that the administration had pressured the B'nai B'rith leadership into accepting. In his words, "We, upon our own initiative, and without any suggestion whatsoever, besought President Roosevelt to alter his decision to send the signed petition, and to transmit its text instead." Levi also noted proudly that the petition would ultimately endure in the State Department archives where it would "forever testify to the lofty humanity" of the American people, their president, and his administration.[140]

In a letter to Roosevelt, John Hay praised him for besting Russia in diplomatic brinksmanship. "They would have scored by receiving the petition and pigeonholing it. I think *you* have scored, as it is!" Hay exclaimed. "You have done the right thing in the right way, and Jewry seems really grateful." Given Hay's earlier resistance to the petition, perhaps this letter was a somewhat contrived bid to shore up his own relationship with the president after their widely publicized disagreement over Kishinev. Or maybe—with the deed done and Russian-American relations still intact—Hay was freed from his anxiety about a diplomatic rupture and could now more easily see wisdom in Roosevelt's judgment. Hay's letter was also uncharacteristic in its blunt disparagement of the Russians, which was absent from his earlier correspondence with

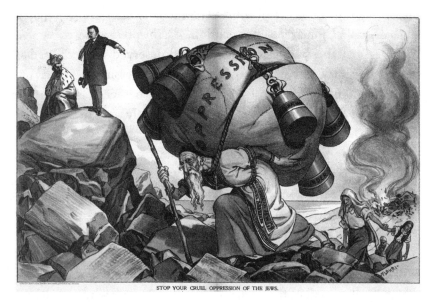

FIGURE. 3.4. Roosevelt admonishing Czar Nicholas II as Russian Jews flee a pogrom. *Source*: "Stop Your Cruel Oppression of the Jews," *Judge*, circa September 1905.

the president about the Kishinev affair. "What inept asses they are," Hay scoffed. He denigrated the Russians' habitual dishonesty, predicting that they would still "lie to us as volubly as ever."[141] Roosevelt, for his part, was pleased with the outcome, writing Hay, "I think the Russian business is in pretty fair shape."[142]

The president's Jewish constituents were apt to agree. On behalf of the B'nai B'rith executive committee, Simon Wolf thanked Roosevelt for honoring his commitment. "The people of the United States, especially your Jewish fellow citizens at home and abroad, bless you," Wolf wrote. "You have lifted the veil, and the light of reason and humanity is streaming in."[143] Roosevelt replied in kind, conveying his appreciation to Wolf for his "admirable good sense" throughout the affair.[144] Other expressions of gratitude from the Jewish community to Roosevelt were more public. Oscar Straus, for instance, authored a note to the president that appeared verbatim in several newspapers. With purple prose, Straus gushed that Roosevelt had ushered in "an era in that highest realm of diplomacy, the diplomacy of humanity, which marshals the enlightened spirit of civilization against persecution."[145] The president was pleased with the favorable publicity and felt it well-deserved. He indicated as much to Lucius Littauer, the upstate Jewish congressman who had befriended TR in college. Roosevelt asked "Litt" whether he had seen the Straus letter in the press and crowed, "We certainly went to the limit in taking the lead on behalf of humanity."[146]

Curiously, one ally of Roosevelt's in the Jewish community opposed the president's approach to the Kishinev affair: Jacob Schiff. Three weeks after the petition was cabled to St. Petersburg, Schiff wrote the president, "Petitions to the czar's government profit no one." His appraisal of Roosevelt on this count was a marked deviation from Jewish-American opinion at large. Instead of a petition, Schiff preferred protests like "the Carnegie Hall meeting in N.Y., and in other cities," which "will not fail of their purpose."[147] It is unclear why he believed public protests were more effective than petitions in preempting pogroms. Roosevelt's reply, while respectful in tone, ceded no ground. "The action of the government concerning the petition was in effect (only to an infinitely greater degree) doing just what the Carnegie Hall meeting attempted to do," the president insisted.[148]

Schiff wasn't the only critic of Roosevelt in the Jewish community. The Democratic-leaning *Hebrew Standard* suggested that the president was motivated only by "Jewish votes" and that "no one suspects Mr. Roosevelt or Mr. Hay of any very burning feeling of indignation" over Kishinev.[149] But the *Jewish American* defended TR on that score: "It requires a mighty mean little soul to believe that President Roosevelt took the stand he did in the Kishinev matter for sake of catching a few Jewish votes."[150] The fairest assessment is that both newspapers had some purchase on the truth—Roosevelt was certainly alive to the electoral benefits of the Kishinev Petition, but he also felt genuine compassion for the pogrom's victims.

In the months that followed, B'nai B'rith collected thirteen thousand signatures for the petition. The loose pages from around the country were collated, bound in leather, and put in a custom-made ebony box, together with a volume detailing the petition's origins. Simon Wolf had the honor of hand-delivering the petition to John Hay in late October. Wolf also gave Hay a letter from B'nai B'rith president Leo Levi expressing gratitude to the administration. Levi well understood the novelty of the government's submitting a petition from private citizens to a foreign power about its internal affairs. "If it be without precedent, it is the more precious for becoming one," he wrote. Hay replied that the petition would be "sacredly cherished" in the State Department annals.[151]

★ ★ ★

The consequences of the Kishinev pogrom would be long-lived and far-reaching—for global Jewry, for American politics, for international relations, and for Roosevelt's role in all the above. Outrage beyond the borders of the Russian Empire did little to palliate conditions for Jews within them. The editor of the *Bessarabetz* newspaper, who had used its pages to incite the butchery in Kishinev, was undeterred in his bigotry. Just months after the pogrom, he became the first-ever publisher of *The Protocols of the Elders of Zion*, which outlined an alleged conspiracy for Jewish world domination and would emerge as the most widely circulated antisemitic text of the twentieth century.[152]

Meanwhile, the trials of the pogromists in Kishinev, conducted in secret, were largely a farce. The court made a full airing of the facts impossible, and prosecutors with honest intentions resigned in frustration. In the end, only a few perpetrators among the hundreds of defendants were found guilty. Even those who were convicted typically received light sentences. Jewish victims, moreover, were given no legal recourse to seek compensation for stolen or damaged property.[153] The American explorer and Russia expert George Kennan (a distant cousin of the more famous statesman by the same name) personally translated excerpts from the trial transcripts for Roosevelt. Kennan told the president that Russia was run by "a government of cruelty, duplicity, and medieval barbarity."[154]

Although Americans hoped that the Kishinev Petition would shame Russia into forestalling further slaughter of Jews, in fact Kishinev marked only the beginning of a new phase of Jewish bloodletting.[155]

The massacre in Kishinev and subsequent pogroms made plain that Russian Jews could not subsist under the czarist regime.[156] Some of these Jews allied with revolutionary agitators in Russia who hoped to depose the czar. Others moved to the Holy Land, as Kishinev gave new life to Zionism—the movement to create a Jewish homeland in Palestine. But far more Russian Jews chose a third option: migration to America.[157] As we will see, the accelerating influx of Jewish immigrants to the United States stoked nativist anxieties and presented the Roosevelt administration with discomfiting challenges.

The fallout from Kishinev reverberated beyond Russia, Palestine, and America all the way to Asia. Roosevelt felt newly emboldened to confront Russia about the Far East. He remained frustrated that Russia didn't provide an "open door" for American trade in Manchuria.[158] Merely four days after Roosevelt resolved to send the petition, he informed John Hay, "I have not the slightest objection to the Russians' knowing that I feel thoroughly aroused and irritated at their conduct in Manchuria." The public uproar in the United States over Kishinev had impressed upon Roosevelt the depth of anti-Russian sentiment at home—animosity that might afford him wide latitude if the dispute over Manchuria intensified. "I am year by year growing more confident that this country would back me in going to an extreme in the matter," the president told Hay.[159] About two weeks later, Roosevelt wrote Hay again to express his annoyance with Russia's control of Manchuria. "I am beginning to have scant patience," he confessed. Smirking at Russia's appetite for deceit, the president added, "They never find any treachery *really* difficult."[160]

His increasingly anti-Russia posture stood to benefit not just the Jews but the Japanese as well. Japan was eager to see Manchuria rid of the Russians, and the Japanese press anticipated that America's disaffection from Russia over Kishinev might well redound to Japan's benefit in Far Eastern affairs.[161] Sure enough, within a few months Roosevelt was staking out a markedly pro-Japan position in the region. That October, the United States and Japan signed complementary treaties with China calling for an "open door" in three key Manchurian cities. Although those treaties wouldn't actually be operable so long as Russia colonized

CZAR—"EXCUSE ME, I'M TOO BUSY WEEPING OVER THIS DELAWARE AFFAIR."

FIGURE 3.5. "Excuse Me, I'm Too Busy Weeping over This Delaware Affair." *Source: Brooklyn Daily Eagle*, July 2, 1903.

Manchuria, they did the symbolic work of signaling America's burgeoning affinity for Japan. Indeed, the Russian ambassador in Tokyo now considered the Americans and Japanese allied against his own nation.[162] And so—even before B'nai B'rith had finished preparing the petition for its hand-off to the State Department—the ripple effects of Kishinev had circumnavigated the globe.

Closer to home, contemporary observers in the United States saw disturbing parallels between carnage in Kishinev and lynching in America.[163] The *Springfield Daily Republican* in Massachusetts lamented, "Melancholy is the fact that we have Kishinevs of our own."[164] On the very day that Roosevelt and his Jewish advisors were drafting the historic cable to the St. Petersburg embassy, the *Salt Lake Telegram* published a list of all American lynchings in the first six months of 1903. Forty-six lives—forty Blacks and six whites—had been lost, nearly matching the death toll from Kishinev. "Russia may well advise us to do a little house-cleaning at home before we try to reform Russia," the *Telegram* advised.[165]

Some newspapers tried to minimize the comparison between Russian pogroms and American lynchings. They suggested that Roosevelt's critics, who accused the president of applying a double-standard to Russia, weren't genuinely outraged about lynching but merely seeking to score "a point against the administration."[166] Roosevelt himself privately told John Hay that pogroms and lynchings were not equivalent, that Jewish victims of pogroms "infinitely" outnumbered Black victims of lynchings in the years since the American Civil War.[167] The president was wildly inaccurate here—Black fatalities had exceeded Jewish ones by orders of magnitude.[168] Roosevelt's erroneous claim betrays that he more easily felt sympathy for Jews than for Blacks. Even as he gravely misrepresented the depths of Black suffering, the similarities between lynchings and pogroms were too obvious for the president to entirely ignore. In the letter to Congressman Littauer, after Roosevelt indulged in some self-congratulations for his handling of the petition, he added, "I wish to Heaven our course were clearer in the lynching business!"[169]

Much of the Black press bristled that white America seemed much more willing to denounce lawless violence abroad than at home.[170] Other Blacks sought to make common cause with Kishinev's Jews. A meeting of the self-described "negro members of the Louisville bar" issued a statement in support of the pogrom's victims. These Black lawyers alluded to lynchings by noting that they, too, were "acquainted with sorrow" and "the oppressor's wrongs." In a spirit of solidarity born from shared suffering, they decried "the hapless condition of our Hebrew brethren" and called on the government to welcome Jewish refugees to America.[171]

And there were Jews, in turn, who translated their dismay over pogroms into support for the anti-lynching movement. Anna Strunsky was the most notable example. A Russian-born Jewish immigrant to America,

Strunsky returned to the Pale of Settlement to investigate pogroms as a journalist. It was painfully obvious to her that antisemitic bloodshed in her native land resembled anti-Black violence in her adopted home. She went on to become a founding member of the National Association for the Advancement of Colored People, or NAACP.[172]

As the Kishinev Petition dominated headlines in 1903, Roosevelt was already looking ahead to its implications for 1904. He had inherited his office from his fallen predecessor and would soon seek to capture the presidency in his own right. The Jewish vote mattered in states that would be essential to his success at the polls. Roosevelt had long courted Jewish support in his days as a New York politico; his elevation onto the national stage in no way diminished his interest in cultivating Jewish constituencies. The president cheerfully informed Congressman Littauer that Oscar Straus, the most prominent Jewish Democrat in the country, would back Roosevelt's reelection bid: "Straus, by the way, volunteered the statement that, whoever was against me for president, he should support me."[173] Jewish endorsements would mean something to Jewish voters. So would Jewish diplomacy—between the Romanian Note and Kishinev Petition, Roosevelt had done much to bolster his stock with this key slice of the electorate. But neither episode had directly implicated U.S. citizens of Jewish faith. Come 1904, Jewish voters would focus their attention on Russia's brazen assault against the rights of American Jews themselves.

4

PASSPORT QUESTION

Henry Pinkos was diligent in his work, mild in his manner, and American in his citizenship. This peaceful tradesman led a quiet life in St. Petersburg with his wife and their child in the early 1880s when the local police suddenly ordered the Pinkos family to vacate the Russian capital. The reason for their ouster was uncomplicated: they were Jews. Henry Pinkos sold his modest property and purchased tickets for an outbound ship departing the empire. The boat was scheduled to set sail from Kronstadt, a small town on an island some twenty miles west of St. Petersburg. After having his family's bags loaded onto the ship at Kronstadt, Pinkos presented the police there with both his U.S. passport and the order evicting him. Here his troubles quickly compounded. The police in Kronstadt denied him permission to exit Russia on the grounds that the order from St. Petersburg only expelled him from that city, not from the Russian Empire at large. Then the ship captain refused to refund the Pinkos family for their tickets even though they couldn't embark. And the final blow: the boat sailed off with their luggage still on board. The Pinkoses were left destitute. They were instructed by the Kronstadt police to return to the very city from which they had been banished. Back in St. Petersburg, the family subsisted on private donations until, eventually, they did manage to secure passage out of Russia.[1]

Henry Pinkos's nightmarish experience was of a piece with Russia's arbitrary approach to Jewish rights. Russian law technically banned Jews from St. Petersburg and many other cities. However, exceptions abounded—sometimes explicitly by way of official exemption, other times tacitly by authorities choosing not to enforce restrictive laws too severely. Local officials were given wide latitude to implement or relax civil disabilities on Jews. This ambiguous state of affairs meant that a Jew could, with little notice, face eviction from a given municipality on religious grounds.[2]

That Henry Pinkos held American citizenship did not protect him from this kind of cruel caprice. But it should have. An operative treaty from 1832 then governing Russian-American relations specified that the inhabitants of each nation shall freely enter the other and enjoy the "same security and protection as natives of the country."[3] The U.S. government, acting discreetly through diplomatic channels, conveyed to Russia that Pinkos's expulsion was a violation of the foregoing treaty.[4]

The Russians were unmoved. They argued that because Russia drew legal distinctions between its own Jews and Gentiles, and had been doing so prior to 1832, it ought to be fairly presumed under the 1832 treaty that Russia could also draw distinctions between Jews and Gentiles from America. Russia, moreover, insisted that it already had significant trouble with its own Jews, who were allegedly a troublesome people in league with revolutionaries. Taking on more Jews from abroad was unacceptable.[5] Russian paranoia about Jews was unhinged. Although an underground revolutionary movement in Russia did claim some Jewish members, in reality most Russian Jews were too focused on the daily survival of their hardscrabble lives to engage in subversion.[6]

Tensions only worsened after the Pinkos incident. No later than 1886, the Russian government began directing its consulates abroad to refuse visas to foreign Jews who wished to visit Russia. When Americans did apply for visas at Russian consulates within the United States, they faced interrogation about their religious identity; applicants professing Judaism were denied entry papers.[7] By 1895, the issue became sufficiently prominent to merit comment in the State of the Union message. President Grover Cleveland derided the Russian consulates for having the audacity to pressure American citizens—on U.S. soil, no less—to reveal their faiths. He condemned these antisemitic inquisitions as an "obnoxious invasion of our territorial jurisdiction."[8]

At particular risk were American Jews of Russian birth. Some of these naturalized citizens desired to visit Russia for familial or commercial reasons. If they tried to reenter Russia, they were liable to be turned away. And even if they managed to circumvent the bar on Jews, once in Russia they could face severe punishment for having adopted U.S. citizenship without Russian permission. In August of 1901—five months into the McKinley administration—the State Department issued a circular warning Jewish Americans of Russian origin about the hazards of Russia's visa policy.[9] William McKinley drew his dying breath six weeks later, and Theodore Roosevelt inherited the "Passport Question" that had bedeviled so many administrations before his.

The following year, a Democratic congressman of Jewish faith named Henry Goldfogle decided to press the Roosevelt administration on the issue. Goldfogle was then in his first of seven terms in Congress and represented the epicenter of immigrant Jewish life in America: the Lower East Side. At his initiation, the House of Representatives passed a resolution calling on Secretary of State John Hay to furnish information about Russia's visa policy and what steps, if any, the State Department had taken to rectify the situation.[10] Hay's written response to Congress, which was released to the press, noted that Russia's restrictions against Jews from the United States applied with equal force to Jews from other nations. Hay also detailed that the State Department for many years had been engaged in "efforts to secure uniform treatment of American citizens in Russia." Those efforts "have not been attended with encouraging success," but diplomatic protest would continue unabated, Hay assured the House.[11]

Four weeks later, a spirited public meeting was held at the Educational Alliance, a Jewish settlement house on the East Side, to rally against Russia's ban on American Jews. A series of Jewish luminaries addressed the packed crowd. One speaker elicited ardent applause after connecting the Passport Question to pride in Jewish facial features. He argued that Jews shouldn't content themselves with merely looking

Jewish; they needed to advance Jewish values as well. In his words, a "hooked nose and kinky hair" alone do not "make an Israelite." Being an Israelite also required "loyalty to ideals," which in this case meant opposition to Russian "despotism and tyranny." The speaker elaborated, "That Hebrew who relies on a great big nose ... well, he's not Israel at all." Some high-profile Gentiles gave speeches, including a former congressman and a prominent Catholic priest. Their presence and words affirmed that the rights of Jews with U.S. passports should concern Americans of all backgrounds. To reinforce that point, Congressman Goldfogle insisted in the final remarks of the day, "The question before us is not a Jewish question. There is nothing of racial character in it. It is a matter of pure Americanism."[12]

Soon the macabre sensationalism of the Kishinev pogrom relegated the Passport Question to the margins for both American Jews and the Roosevelt administration. But when Kishinev receded as a front-page issue, passports reemerged as the focal point of Jewish concern. Just three weeks after B'nai B'rith delivered the Kishinev Petition to the State Department, Congressman Goldfogle indicated to the press that he planned to make noise about Russia's visa policy.[13] An election year was looming, and Republicans were poised to overperform with the Jewish vote thanks to the Romanian Note and Kishinev Petition. The unresolved Passport Question thus presented an opportunity for Goldfogle to reclaim ground for the Democratic Party.

In January 1904, he introduced a second passport resolution in the House that differed from his 1902 resolution. Whereas the first resolution had merely made a factual inquiry and was addressed to John Hay, this second resolution called for action and was directed at Roosevelt. It asked the president to initiate negotiations of a new treaty with Russia that would guarantee the unfettered admission of American citizens regardless of their faith.[14] After a hearing on the topic by the House Committee on Foreign Affairs in February, the House adopted the resolution in April in a bipartisan vote.[15] Both parties saw the defense of Jewish Americans as a winning issue.

The *New York Times* treated the Goldfogle resolution as a well-intended but ultimately futile exercise. The paper reported that any diplomatic push by the United States had "little prospect of success." According to the *Times*, Russia feared that a Jew bearing a U.S. passport would, under the pretext of peacefully conducting international business, "gain access to Russian territory and prosecute his real mission of political disturbance and possibly nihilistic violence."[16] In Russian eyes, Jews at home and abroad were radicals who threatened the czar's empire.

★ ★ ★

The Goldfogle resolution may have been unlikely to alter Russia's policy, but it did stand to improve Democratic performance with the Jewish vote in the upcoming election. And so Roosevelt began to make countermoves. The Republican National Convention was fast approaching and would provide a critical opportunity for the party to signal its commitment to Jewish causes, including the Passport Question. Presidential candidates of the era did not themselves attend the conventions, so Roosevelt was relegated to behind-the-scenes strategizing. In early June, TR wrote a letter to Elihu Root—who had recently stepped down as war secretary—with advice for the keynote speech that Root was to deliver at the convention a few weeks hence. "I hope that you can make some allusion to the action taken as regards Kishinev and the Jew passports," Roosevelt urged. "It will be a good thing to recite what has been done in the Kishinev matter, and the steady and unwearied efforts of the State Department to secure passports from Russia for all well-behaved Americans, whether Jew or Gentile." Although Roosevelt wanted Root to take up these Jewish causes in a speech, the president nonetheless cautioned, "We can hardly put this in our platform."[17]

Roosevelt didn't delineate why the platform ought not remark on the Kishinev Petition. As for the Passport Question, he told Oscar Straus that it wasn't a proper subject for the platform because such a plank would smack of naked political opportunism. "Unless we mean to do something further than simply protest," TR explained, "it would look like an effort to catch votes, for such statements in the platform could not be regarded for any other purpose."[18] Roosevelt's reasoning here is arguably tenuous. After all, he felt that the Passport Question ought to be included in a convention speech, which surely would be a transparent bid to "catch votes."

Perhaps that inconsistency reflected a president caught between two competing imperatives: courting Jewish voters and preserving Russian relations. The American and Russian governments were then engaged in secret discussions (which became public only years later) concerning a wholly distinct issue—namely, a potential agreement ensuring that any given corporation based in one country would enjoy legal standing in the other.[19] Roosevelt may have been worried that pressing Russia too hard on the Passport Question in public might compromise ongoing negotiations in private. TR *was* amenable to a platform that included abstract language about the rights of U.S. citizens overseas, but only so long as the plank was framed in generalities without express reference to either Jews or Russia.

To that end, the president tapped a Jewish ally of his from New York, Judge William Cohen, for input on the platform.[20] This was the selfsame Cohen who had praised Roosevelt's dignified composure at McKinley's deathbed in a gracious letter that TR made a point of keeping. Once, Roosevelt flattered Judge Cohen by calling him a "bold man," and Cohen in turn gushed with delight, "If *you* call a fellow a 'bold man' he must be a two-footed lion."[21] When TR solicited Cohen's help with the 1904 platform, Cohen proposed some language on a slip of paper that he sent to Roosevelt. The slip doesn't survive today, but apparently Cohen's phrasing satisfied the president's dueling desires to appeal to Jewish voters on the one hand without doing so too overtly on the other.[22] As Roosevelt shared with a Republican senator the following day, "I enclose you this letter from Cohen. I think that the slip which he inserts is good, and saves us from making any direct allusion to either the Kishinev massacre or the passport business."[23]

The delegates convened for the Republican National Convention in late June at the Chicago Coliseum. Opened four years earlier, the Coliseum was an architectural marvel. Massive arches held up the roof, which obviated the need for pillars and thereby endowed the arena with a grand sense of capaciousness. Floor seating, when combined with a balcony that lined all four walls, allowed for ten thousand attendees.[24]

Although the delegates didn't fill the arena to capacity, they loudly voiced their enthusiasm during the convention proceedings. The first mention of Theodore Roosevelt in a speech occasioned particular exuberance. As one journalist reported, "Cheers rang through the hall, and many men sprang upon their chairs and waved hats, handkerchiefs, and banners."[25]

Elihu Root took the stage for his keynote to great applause. Pacing with his feet and gesticulating as he spoke, Root offered the kind of specificity on Jewish issues that the platform would studiously avoid.[26] He explicitly referenced not only the Kishinev Petition but also the Romanian Note. "When the Romanian outrages and when the appalling massacre at Kishinev shocked civilization and filled thousands of our own people with mourning," Root recounted, "the protest of America was heard through the voice of its government, with full observance of diplomatic rules, but with moral power and effect."[27] Curiously, Root's speech made no mention of the Passport Question despite Roosevelt's request that he do so. Root's omission may have been strategic; after all, the president had scored important symbolic victories with the Romanian Note and Kishinev Petition but lacked a public win on the Passport Question.

The day after Root's keynote, the convention unanimously adopted a platform that included a plank along the lines Judge Cohen had suggested—probably his exact wording—as it nodded to Roosevelt's response on Kishinev without direct comment on Jews or Russia. "Whenever crimes against humanity have been perpetrated which have shocked our people, his protest has been made, and our good offices have been tendered, but always with due regard to international obligations," the plank read. The Republican platform was similarly vague about the Passport Question, avoiding mention of Jews, of Russia, or even of passports: "We commend the vigorous efforts made by the administration to protect American citizens in foreign lands, and pledge ourselves to insist upon the just and equal protection of all of our citizens abroad."[28] With this, the party achieved Roosevelt's goal of a platform that implicitly gestured toward Jewry. The platform may have lacked specificity, but it was still unprecedented; prior platforms from

FIGURE. 4.1. Theodore Roosevelt here gavels in his own nomination. In reality, he followed custom by absenting himself from the convention. *Source*: "All in Favor of the Nomination Will Say Aye!," *Puck*, June 15, 1904.

both parties had neglected to make even discreet allusions to the Passport Question.

★ ★ ★

In the immediate wake of the Republican National Convention, the Roosevelt administration grasped for tangible progress on passports. John Hay cabled the U.S. ambassador in St. Petersburg, Robert McCormick, sharing with him the text of the congressional resolution on the Passport Question. Hay instructed McCormick to convey to the Russian foreign minister the disapproval—by Congress and Roosevelt alike—of Russia's ongoing visa restrictions. In Hay's words, the discrimination against American Jews amounted to "needlessly repressive treatment." Hay further relayed Roosevelt's bemusement that Russia perceived itself as somehow benefitting from its prohibition against U.S. nationals of Jewish faith, whom TR considered exemplary members of American society. "In the view of the president," Hay related, "it is not easy to discern the compensating advantage to the Russian government in the exclusion of a class of tourists and men of business" who were endowed with "intelligence and sterling moral qualities." This communication was confidential—at least for the time being. Whether and when to publicly release the foregoing cable would ultimately become a source of debate within Roosevelt's circles, but for now, the State Department quietly awaited a response.²⁹

★ ★ ★

Democrats convened the following week for their party convention at the St. Louis Exposition and Music Hall. The venue was festooned with colorful fabrics for the occasion, and the seals of each state in the Union hung from the ceiling. The ventilation, however, did not live up to the decoration. As the crowd grew, temperatures rose and overheated attendees resorted to vigorous fanning. One journalist recorded that the hall looked like a "yellow flutter as the palm leaf fans bobbed back and forth."³⁰ The Democrats nominated Alton Parker, an obscure figure with a judicial background, to challenge Roosevelt for the presidency.

Before the Democratic convention, Judge Cohen had warned Roosevelt that "our adversaries intend [on] making some reference" in St. Louis to the "recognition of our passports in Russia."[31] Indeed, the Democratic platform now offered a plank on the Passport Question that was more extensive in length and specific in detail than the Republican version. While avoiding the words "Russia" and "Jewish," the plank nevertheless made explicit mention of passports and religious discrimination in a way that the Republicans had not. It also echoed the Goldfogle resolution by calling for treaty negotiations, which the Republican platform had avoided.[32] Jacob Schiff would soon thereafter candidly acknowledge to Roosevelt that although "the platform of both parties makes special reference to this vexatious question, the Democratic platform [does so] even somewhat stronger than our own."[33]

In a convention speech, a Democratic congressman from Mississippi named John Sharp Williams took aim at the Republican plank about U.S. citizens traveling abroad. Williams—whom Roosevelt once derided as a "drunken skunk"—accused Republicans of hypocrisy: in one breath, the Republican administration resigned itself to Russian discrimination by issuing a State Department travel warning that American Jews wouldn't be protected in Russia; in the next breath, the Republican platform pledged fealty to equal justice for U.S. passport holders of all faiths. Congressman Williams suggested that "our fellow-citizens of Russian birth and Jewish extraction" would read the GOP platform with "singular astonishment" at its insincerity.[34] His criticism here was arguably unfair given that a party platform was widely understood to be an aspirational policy agenda whereas the travel warning was simply a sober description of facts on the ground. Republicans could take some solace that, according to press reports, convention delegates in St. Louis had "kept up a constant hum of conversation that smothered Mr. Williams's voice."[35]

As the Democrats made a strong play for the Jewish vote, Roosevelt wondered whether he would win the grand prize of Jewish endorsements: Oscar Straus. True, Straus was a Roosevelt appointee and a trusted advisor who had already signaled to TR a year prior that his endorsement was forthcoming. But Straus was also a Democrat—perhaps he wouldn't abandon his party after all. The president asked his campaign manager, "Do you know if Oscar Straus intends to support me or not?"[36] Roosevelt did not have to wait long for the answer. Four days later, Straus personally informed the president he would "dedicate my best services to your election" despite having "always been a liberal Democrat."[37] Roosevelt was relieved, replying to Straus, "I need hardly say how deeply gratified I am."[38] Straus soon publicly endorsed the president and announced he would likely stump for Roosevelt.[39] In an article about the endorsement, the *Jewish Voice* newspaper described Straus as "probably the most distinguished Jew of the country," a stature that on its own would render his advocacy of Roosevelt significant. But Straus's blessing was all the more noteworthy—the *Jewish Voice* observed—because he was crossing party lines to back the president.[40]

Another Roosevelt devotee in the Jewish community, Simon Wolf, knew that Straus would be a key ally in rebutting Democratic attacks. As Wolf told a Roosevelt aide, "You will remember that months ago I told you that Oscar Straus would be with us, there will be plenty of others, to offset John S. Williams's slur as to the Jewish question." Wolf also expressed a desire to counter "the slurs of Goldfogle, who claimed that the resolution passed by Congress had been pigeonholed." Wolf's annoyance with these congressional Democrats did not undermine his optimism about the results to come in November. "Every day convinces me more of our success," he shared. "As usual they shout and brag, but we will have the votes."[41] Wolf must have felt especially endeared to Roosevelt at this moment, as just two months earlier the president had appointed Wolf's thirty-six-year-old son to a judgeship.[42]

★ ★ ★

Meanwhile, preparations were underway for Roosevelt's nomination ceremony at his Sagamore Hill estate. Roosevelt told his campaign manager that he wanted Jewish representation in the audience. "It seems to me that if we could have one or two of our good Jewish friends out here . . . it would be all right," the president wrote from Oyster Bay. Naturally, Oscar Straus and Jacob Schiff would top the list, but Roosevelt wondered, "Would three be too many?" He wanted to include James Speyer, whose profile was similar to Schiff's: German by birth, New Yorker by choice, successful in banking, and generous in philanthropy. "They all three have been genuine friends," Roosevelt explained to his campaign manager.[43] Ultimately, three Jews among 125 guests did not prove too many; the full Jewish trio received invitations and, of course, each man accepted the honor.[44] In late July, a special train from New York delivered guests to Oyster Bay for the ceremony. The day's perfect weather augured well for the event. Roosevelt delivered a speech midday from a large porch adorned with American flags before the gathering of supporters.[45] The president's own family members served the visitors at the ensuing banquet.[46]

With this bit of campaign pageantry behind him, Roosevelt turned his energies toward the final element of the nominating process: his formal letter of acceptance. Such letters were published in newspapers and thus offered presidential contenders important outlets to court voters. For an incumbent like Roosevelt, the acceptance letter offered the *only* outlet to make his own case for his candidacy. Alton Parker as the challenger could give stump speeches, but protocol dictated that Roosevelt as the sitting president had to refrain from active campaigning and rely instead on surrogates.[47] The passive demands of incumbency ill-suited the tenacious Roosevelt. A congressional ally wrote him, "I think it depresses you a little to be the only man in the country who cannot take part in the campaign for the presidency." The word "little" understated the president's discontent. As Roosevelt told his son Kermit, "I could cut [the Democratic nominee] into ribbons if I could get at him in the open. But of course a president can't go on the stump . . . and so I have to sit still and abide by the result."[48] Given these strictures, Roosevelt's acceptance letter was of paramount significance to his reelection bid.

Jacob Schiff encouraged the president to use that letter as an opportunity to signal his commitment to securing Jewish-American rights in Russia. "Assuming that you are about to enter upon the preparation of your letter of acceptance, I should like to suggest that the Passport Question receive some forcible treatment," Schiff urged. He conjectured that the Jewish vote might determine New York state's Electoral

College votes and thereby swing the presidential race. "It is not at all unlikely, that the East Side of New York City, which casts upwards of a hundred thousand votes, is going to decide the coming state election and through this possibly the national election," Schiff speculated, "and it will therefore be well that these voters thoroughly understand where we stand on a question so vital to them." Lest Roosevelt entertain thoughts that Schiff was simply pushing a self-interested Jewish agenda, Schiff insisted that the impetus for his writing the president was a desire to recommend a "successful issue" for the campaign more so than "any other motive."[49]

Schiff's true aims extended beyond the ballot box. He believed that a change in Russian policy toward American Jews would have a cascading effect, leading ultimately to legal equality for Russia's Jewish population. As Schiff predicted in a letter to a German-Jewish leader, if the Jews of other nations could enter Russia and enjoy the liberties rightly afforded them as foreign nationals, "then the Russian government will not long be able to insist on maintaining the scandalous restrictive laws against her own Jews."[50] Two classes of Jewry—one of foreign citizenship enjoying basic freedoms, the other of domestic subjecthood denied those same freedoms—would prove untenable.

The Russians, it appears, were proceeding from the same logic as Schiff. A Russian official personally told Schiff that discrimination against American Jews was a precondition for continued discrimination against Russian Jews.[51] This was the very same reasoning that the Romanian king had provided in refusing America's request for a naturalization treaty. Both Russia and Romania appreciated the dangers of having two categories of Jews with differing sets of liberties. The state-sanctioned prejudice against domestic Jews could buckle under the weight of this inconsistency.[52] In turn, the demise of legally enforced antisemitism could well harken the demise of autocracy in those nations. One lesson from Western European countries was that pro-Jewish reforms often worked in tandem with more sweeping liberalization—e.g., the adoption of civic equality, individual freedom, and the rule of law. The despots of Russia and Romania were hardly keen to see liberalism take root on their soil.

Roosevelt proved amenable to Schiff's counsel that he take up the Passport Question directly. "I agree entirely with you and shall dwell upon that matter in my letter of acceptance," TR replied.[53] Three days later, the president followed up with a draft for Schiff's perusal and encouraged him to "make any emendations you desire and send it back to me with your suggestions."[54] Roosevelt also requested advice on the letter from Oscar Straus and Nathan Bijur, a major figure among Jewish Republicans in New York.[55] All three provided him with feedback.[56]

Straus, for his part, advocated that the president adopt language making clear that his administration's attempt to secure entry to Russia for American Jews was a matter of neutrally applied principle rather than a concession to Jews as a special interest. As Straus put it, Roosevelt should convey it had been "high motives that prompted action, [i.e.] that it was not to favor any particular class but to maintain equality of all in their right to protection, be they native born or naturalized, Christian or Jew."[57] This was precisely the kind of messaging that would have appealed to Roosevelt, who was fond of denying that he engaged in identity politics.

As Roosevelt continued to fine-tune his letter, the diplomatic front in St. Petersburg saw some movement in late August. John Hay's cable to Ambassador McCormick—which had communicated American opposition to Russia's visa restrictions back in early July—was left unattended for several weeks owing to the ambassador's absence from Russia. After McCormick finally returned to the embassy and read the cable, he sent a letter to the Russian foreign minister informing him that Congress and the president alike were concerned about discrimination against American Jews at Russian hands. McCormick explained that religious freedom was a "principle which lies at the foundation of our government." Therefore the passport issue presented a "live question . . . liable to become acute" and had the potential to "seriously disturb the friendly relations" between the United States and Russia. Given the potential diplomatic cost to Russia of preserving this "needlessly oppressive" policy, Russia ought to reconsider its Jewish ban, if not on principle then at least as a matter of "expedience and reciprocal convenience" in its relationship with America.⁵⁸

The text of McCormick's letter wasn't disclosed to the press, but the Roosevelt administration did quickly inform newspapers that McCormick had made overtures to the Russian foreign minister about passports.⁵⁹ Journalists had slim hope that McCormick's efforts would prompt Russia to reconsider its treatment of American Jews. "While Russia has not yet rejected the proposal of the United States . . . it is particularly certain that she will decline," the *New York Times* asserted. Just like Jacob Schiff, the *Times* appreciated that the Passport Question was so weighty because of its implications for domestic policy within Russia: "Compliance with the wishes of the United States would entail a complete change in the laws of the empire, in so far as they affect the Jews."⁶⁰ And that kind of change was of little interest to the Russian regime. But Russia didn't summarily issue a response to McCormick, and so the American ambassador was left waiting to see whether Russia actually would prove obstinate.

Roosevelt finally released his acceptance letter for the Republican nomination in mid-September. Some newspapers published the 14,000-word letter in its entirety, while others reprinted select passages owing to its "extreme length."⁶¹ The president's letter touted his diplomacy on Jewish issues, asking, "Do our opponents object to what was done in reference to the petition of American citizens against the Kishinev massacre, or to the protest against the treatment of the Jews in Romania?" Roosevelt further acknowledged that Russia "refuses to admit and protect Jews" from the United States, and he defended his administration for having "consistently demanded equal protection abroad for all American citizens." The Democrats' insistence that he initiate negotiations with Russia over the Passport Question "shows either ignorance of the facts or insincerity"—after all, his administration was already applying "steady pressure." Roosevelt stood by his foreign policy for its commitment to humanitarianism. "Discrimination and oppression because of religion, wherever practiced, are acts of injustice before God and man," he declared, "and in making evident to the world the depth of American conviction in this regard we have gone to the very limit of diplomatic usage."[62]

Oscar Straus extended to Roosevelt his "heartiest congratulations" on the letter, which he found "honest, just, and noble in spirit, a great state paper reflecting the author in every line."[63] The president responded with a request. With the election less than two months away, he was eager to more fully reap credit for the pressure that his administration was then bringing to bear on Russia. Neither the text of Hay's cable from July nor of McCormick's letter from August had been disseminated to the public. Roosevelt told Straus that it might become "necessary to publish the State Department dispatches showing what we have done in connection with the Passport Question. I should like your judgment as to just how far we should go." The president added that other participants in the decision-making would include George Cortelyou, who headed the Republican National Committee. That Roosevelt involved the RNC chair in a decision about declassifying diplomatic correspondence offers striking testimony to the intimate relationship between domestic politics and foreign policy.[64]

Some prominent Jews who were Roosevelt sympathizers had already quietly suggested to Cortelyou that releasing the correspondence would backfire. After all, it had been a Democrat, Henry Goldfogle, who sponsored the congressional resolution that spurred the administration into action, and so the Democrats were possibly poised to benefit from any publicity.[65] Oscar Straus took a different view. After reading the diplomatic dispatches, an elated Straus told Nathan Bijur, who had also seen them, "I had no idea that the matter had been so fully and forcefully presented to the Russian government, and I am especially pleased with Secretary Hay's instructions, wherein he places the subject upon so high and broad a plane." Although Straus was sure that declassification would enhance Roosevelt politically, Straus nevertheless told Bijur that TR ought to hold his fire: "Regarding the publication of these dispatches, my judgment is not to do so for the present, but to wait." If the

Democrats renewed their line of attack that Roosevelt had been weak on the Passport Question, Straus reasoned, then the president could play his hand.[66]

Bijur agreed. Later that day, Bijur relayed to John Hay that he and Oscar Straus alike thought "it would be better not to publish these dispatches at the moment, but to await a favorable opportunity."[67] Bijur soon thereafter penned a letter to Chairman Cortelyou that expressed the same message in more vivid language: "It is very important that nothing be done about this Russian correspondence until the psychological moment"—that is, until declassification would have maximal psychological impact on the electorate.[68] Ultimately it was Hay who conveyed the Straus-Bijur position to the president, and in so doing the secretary of state lent his own imprimatur to their measured approach, writing to Roosevelt in late September, "I think [Bijur] and Mr. Straus are probably right in thinking it better not to publish the Russian matter just now."[69] A resigned Roosevelt conceded, "All right, I shall have nothing done about that Russian Jew matter at present."[70]

But then Simon Wolf pitched an idea to Roosevelt that resonated with the president: Wolf could be the one to publicly trumpet the administration's diplomatic play, if only he were given access to Hay's cable. Roosevelt anticipated that Wolf—having taken over the leadership of B'nai B'rith—could functionally serve as a surrogate under the useful banner of a nonpartisan organization. "Simon Wolf has been in, anxious to get the Hay correspondence about the Jews," Roosevelt shared with Chairman Cortelyou. The president was well aware that his inner circle presently opposed declassification, and so he floated to Cortelyou a halfway measure: the administration could provide Simon Wolf with a summary of the cable rather than a verbatim copy, which Wolf could then use in public remarks. "Why wouldn't it do to hand him a statement . . . which would give the facts of the case?" asked Roosevelt.[71] But Cortelyou was unenthused. For one, he didn't trust Wolf. "Wolf thinks he can do a great deal more than I believe he can," Cortelyou wrote the president, adding, "his influence stirs up a lot of antagonism." Cortelyou had more faith in the tempered judgment of Nathan Bijur. As Cortelyou told Roosevelt, "I have been over the matter of the Hay correspondence about the Jews with Nathan Bijur ... and we are holding it, to be given out at just the right time."[72]

TR did not have the cable released to Wolf, but he still struggled to heed the call for patience on declassification more generally. The following week a restless Roosevelt appealed directly to Bijur, asking him to see "Chairman Cortelyou to discuss with him as to whether we should not send out that State Department statement on the Passport Question?" Roosevelt was anxious about the Democratic push for the Jewish vote. He warned Bijur, "I hear Goldfogle's speech on the Passport Question is to be issued in immense numbers by the Democratic Committee"—this was most likely a reference to a noteworthy speech that Goldfogle had delivered in Congress just before the House approved his resolution.[73] But before Bijur could meet with Cortelyou, the next day brought momentous news: word from St. Petersburg had finally arrived.

Ambassador McCormick forwarded to Secretary Hay a letter from the Russian foreign minister that was shockingly conciliatory. Russia had authorized a "special commission" with the aim of "generally revising the passport regulations." The foreign minister also promised to communicate the American position on the subject to this special commission as it proceeded with its work.[74] In reality, Russia would make no effort to redress the grievances of American Jews. But Russia saw value in posturing as though it would, thanks to events transpiring thousands of miles from the halls of power in Washington and St. Petersburg.

Russian-Japanese tensions in the Far East had, by that point, degenerated precipitously. Recall that Russia controlled Manchuria in China, and the Japanese feared that Russia's ambitions in the Far East might extend to nearby Korea, which Japan itself had colonized. To avert armed hostilities, Japan proposed an agreement with Russia whereby each power would respect the other's sphere of influence. But the Russians did not deign to respond to Japan's proposal, much less accept it.[75] Convinced that military action was its only recourse, the Japanese launched an attack on Port Arthur—Russia's key seaport in Manchuria—in February of

1904.[76] Thus began a full-blown war that would have reverberating effects on Jewish causes.

Japan's special finance minister journeyed to Western capitals in the spring of 1904 for the purpose of securing war loans. He made little headway until a chance encounter at a dinner in London found him seated next to Jacob Schiff, who happened to be passing through town. The Japanese minister would later recount how Schiff was "justly indignant at the unfair treatment" and "notorious persecutions" that Russia inflicted on Jews.[77] Even before the dinner, Schiff had actively lobbied Jewish bankers in Europe to deny Russia loans for its war effort; now Schiff was presented with a unique opportunity to subsidize the other side of the conflict. Within a matter of days, his banking firm in New York was underwriting a multimillion-dollar bond for Japan.[78]

The Russian interior minister, Plehve, then invited Schiff to come to Russia for a discussion of Jewish rights—this was a self-interested bid to placate Schiff in the hopes that Russia could secure war financing in the loan markets if Jewish bankers relented in their opposition.[79] In a letter to Theodore Roosevelt, Schiff relayed that he had issued to Plehve an ultimatum: "I replied that I would never come to Russia by toleration, and that if I was wanted there, the government would first have to remove the restriction against foreign Israelites in general."[80] This much was untenable to the likes of Plehve.

However, two developments over the summer moved Russia to soon adopt a more accommodating stance on passports. When Plehve was traveling by carriage in St. Petersburg, a revolutionary agitator tossed a bomb at its wheels and assassinated the minister. The man who replaced Plehve was comparatively moderate in his politics.[81] What's more, Japanese forces were pressing ahead with a long and bloody siege of Port Arthur at the very moment when Ambassador McCormick cabled the Russian foreign minister about the Passport Question.[82] With Russian antisemitism proving a tangible obstacle to war funding, it is unsurprising that Russia—on its backfoot militarily and financially—tried to assuage the United States on passports. If Russia softened its hard line, then perhaps Jewish bankers like Schiff would soften their own.[83]

Russian assurances about passport reform would ultimately prove hollow, but that much would not become clear until after the election. For now, the State Department quickly issued an announcement about those assurances, thereby offering Roosevelt the appearance of a win at the height of campaign season. The *Duluth News-Tribune* announced, "Jews May Get a Better Deal."[84] Even more optimistic was the *Morning Oregonian* front-page: "Plea Not in Vain—America Wins Victory at Russian Court."[85] Coverage in the *Washington Post* emphasized the unexpected nature of the result in light of Russia's previous recalcitrance. "This is the first time the Russian authorities have not brusquely declined to entertain American representations upon this question," the *Post* observed.[86] Roosevelt could rest on this favorable news for now and hold off on declassifying the State Department correspondence until an even more opportune moment. As for Jacob Schiff, he remained resolute in his support for the Japanese and helped arrange additional loans to finance their forces.[87]

Two days after Ambassador McCormick shared with John Hay the mollifying language from the Russian authorities, McCormick wrote Hay unofficially in order to communicate with total candor. "I have something to add to my dispatch," McCormick informed him, continuing ominously, "I thought it best not to include what I have to say in my official note." The ambassador related how he had personally conversed with the Russian foreign minister, Count Lamsdorff, who had been unrestrained in his criticism of Jewry. As McCormick now paraphrased it for Hay, Lamsdorff considered Jews a "veritable plague" who "exploited the Russian peasant" through usury. This Jewish profiteering explained why "the feeling against the Israelite in the lower social stratum was most bitter," said Lamsdorff. He insisted that "this feeling had to be reckoned with"—in other words, the Russian government was obliged to "protect the peasants" from rapacious Jews. This was the same antisemitic canard that the Russian ambassador to the United States, Count Arthur Cassini, had peddled to the American press after the Kishinev pogrom: Jews invited persecution through their own predatory behavior.[88]

Ambassador McCormick's missive to Hay is striking because he made plain that he found Lamsdorff's indictment of Russian Jews to be credible. McCormick relayed to Hay that Cecil Spring Rice—the chargé d'affaires at the British Embassy in St. Petersburg—had "an example of this leech-like exploitation." Spring Rice described a habit among "the shrewder Jews" who would approach Russian peasants en route to market where the peasants planned to sell produce from their farms. The Jews, purportedly, offered the peasants prices below what the produce would fetch at market, which the "stupid thriftless" peasants tended to accept. "This example goes to explain the feeling existing throughout Russia towards the more thrifty Israelite," McCormick told Hay.[89]

As it happens, Spring Rice—whose first diplomatic assignment twenty years earlier had been in Washington—enjoyed warm relationships with prominent Americans. McCormick's letter to Hay described Spring Rice as "a gentleman who is a friend of yours as well as of mine ... who was long enough in Washington to have made many friends there, and among them, President Roosevelt."[90] In fact, Roosevelt and Spring Rice had known one another even before either of them landed in Washington. They were in their twenties when they first met as fellow passengers on a transatlantic ship. By the time the ocean liner docked in England, Spring Rice had accepted Roosevelt's offer to serve as the best man at his wedding.[91] It is unsurprising that Roosevelt's social circle included friends who lacked his own relative liberality toward Jews, given the prevalence of antisemitism among the elite classes.

Ambassador McCormick, for his part, not only took Spring Rice at his word about Jewish trickery but also trusted Russian officials in their besmirchment of Jews as radicals. The ambassador conveyed to John Hay in his foregoing letter, "I learned from Minister Plehve some months before his tragic taking off ... that 70% of the Socialists in Russia are Jews." McCormick credulously regurgitated Plehve's antisemitic talking points for Hay: "The stringent passport regulations are directed mainly against the German and Polish Jew, who are the most violent propagandists of the doctrine of socialism in its most extreme form."

Here was an American ambassador willing to uncritically believe the worst about a persecuted minority within Russian borders.⁹²

Even so, McCormick was skeptical that Russia could subjugate Jews in perpetuity, and in his letter he ultimately walked himself back to a position more in accord with official State Department policy, telling Hay, "The anti-Jewish laws, the passport system itself, and the censorship of the press, are but a part of the rotten underpinning of a system which, in my judgment, must soon give way under the influence" of international censure. McCormick's letter, then, amounted to a mixed conclusion: the persecution of Russian Jews had some justification behind it, and yet Russia's antisemitic agenda was bound to yield in the face of foreign pressure.⁹³

As the election neared, Jewish newspapers increasingly spilled ink about Roosevelt. The Republican-leaning *Reform Advocate* in Chicago reprinted an editorial that maintained, "Jews would be churlish ingrates if they did not recognize the efforts that the United States continues to put forward on behalf of their race." Recalling TR's role in the Romanian Note, the Kishinev Petition, and now the Passport Question, the writer declared, "We hail President Roosevelt as the nearest approach to the political knight-errant that exists in the latter-day world." The editorial also approvingly noted that another paper dubbed Roosevelt "The New Moses."⁹⁴

TR received comparably favorable coverage in *Menorah*, which billed itself "a monthly magazine for the Jewish home." A Jewish undergraduate at Harvard named Joseph Lebowich authored a piece for *Menorah* entitled "Theodore Roosevelt and the Jews." Lebowich reminded readers of the iconic stories connecting Roosevelt to Jewry, like TR's provision of a Jewish police detail for an antisemitic speaker. Even as Lebowich targeted Jewish voters in a Jewish periodical, he praised the president for rejecting identity politics: "In his dealing with the citizens of Jewish faith or race, President Roosevelt has always treated them not as Jews but as citizens of the United States." Lebowich contrasted TR with the "unscrupulous politicians of our country" who "split the voters into sects and classes."[95]

Few would guess that a sitting president in the midst of a reelection campaign would have time to read a piece in an obscure ethnic periodical authored by a college student. And yet Roosevelt enthusiastically wrote Oscar Straus, "I like that article by Mr. Lebowich. Do you know him? If so, I wish you would tell him how much I appreciate it—and add that I wish he had been among the Harvard men in my regiment," referring to the Rough Riders.[96]

The president especially appreciated Lebowich's argument that Rooseveltian politics were based on a common civic identity as Americans rather than a plurality of religious identities as Jews, Protestants, and Catholics. "I am particularly pleased with the way he has grasped exactly what my attitude is," Roosevelt remarked. Whereas "various Democratic papers" have "endeavored to show that I have appealed to the Jew vote, the Catholic vote, etc.," in reality—or, at least, in the president's self-perception—he had sought to "make it evident that each is to have a square deal, no more and no less," irrespective of religious background. Roosevelt predicted that in the fullness of time "there will be presidents of Jewish faith, presidents of Catholic faith," and his stated aspiration was to behave himself just as he hoped future Jewish or Catholic presidents would behave toward their fellow citizens—namely, "without regard to the several creeds they profess or the several lands from which their ancestors have sprung."[97] Lebowich and Roosevelt alike may have been enamored of the idea that America could boast an identity-neutral civic sphere, but that was more of a comforting conceit than a lived reality. Jewish voters cared about Jewish issues, and politicians like Roosevelt courted them accordingly.

Straus was thrilled to receive the president's note. "I thank you for your splendid letter, which I know expresses the innermost feelings of your heart," he gushed. Straus shared that he had relayed Roosevelt's approval directly to Lebowich, which would surely "be a source of great pride and gratification to him."[98]

Not all commentary in the Jewish press was as positive as Lebowich's. The Democratic-leaning *Hebrew Standard* in New York published a guest column from a *New York Times* staffer named Louis Wiley, who derided Roosevelt's recent diplomatic play with Russia as an election-year stunt. "Not until June 1904, on the eve of the presidential campaign, did President Roosevelt begin any action in the matter," Wiley sneered. Prior to election season, the Roosevelt administration had assumed a posture of "utter indifference" as "clearly demonstrated by the fact that it remained silent until after the passage of the second Goldfogle resolution in April 1904." Wiley added, "President Roosevelt should have taken the initiative—that was his privilege and his duty. At least, he might have made some effort when Representative Goldfogle first agitated the matter in Congress in 1902. Yet not a line of diplomatic correspondence between Washington and St. Petersburg, not an effort of any kind was made by the administration tending to correct the abuse." Accusing Roosevelt and the Republican Party of "insincerity," Wiley belittled the president's foreign policy with Russia as "comic-tragic performance."[99]

The very day this editorial appeared, in late October, the Democratic nominee Alton Parker made a surprise appearance on the Lower East Side. He surfaced at a Yiddish theater to see a Judaized rendition of *King Lear*, in tow with local Tammany leaders and Congressman Goldfogle. After the show, Parker enjoyed a meal at Lorber's, a nearby haunt on Grand Street. His dining party included the play's lead actor, some East Side politicos, and a local rabbi who ran a settlement house.[100]

Notwithstanding Parker's late-stage bid for the East Side vote, the conciliatory word from St. Petersburg about passports had been a significant win for the president, and now his administration optimized its impact for his campaign. The Department of State declassified Secretary Hay's July cable to Ambassador McCormick just six days before Americans headed to the polls. The "psychological moment" had finally arrived. Excerpts from the cable appeared in newspapers nationwide.[101] The press projected an air of certainty about an imminent change in Russian policy—articles featured headlines like "Russia Will Favor Jews" and "American Jews to Be Protected."[102]

★ ★ ★

Roosevelt delivered a crushing blow to his opponent on election day. His victory of nearly twenty percentage points was the largest in almost a century and translated to a 336-to-140 margin in the Electoral College. Although he lost the South, the president triumphed in the North and West in an unbroken wave stretching from Maine to California.

His success with Jewish voters was, frankly, astounding. On the Lower East Side—solidly Democratic terrain—Roosevelt didn't merely outperform conventional Republican results. He actually *won* the East Side. His victory in that neighborhood, slim as it was, blew away McKinley's showing four years earlier. The Lower East Side's sixteenth assembly district is instructive. That district was overwhelmingly Jewish and reliably Democratic. Among its residents who cast ballots for either major party in 1900, McKinley lost by sixteen points. But in 1904, Roosevelt narrowly edged out his opponent on that same turf by a quarter percent. Another measure of TR's popularity throughout the Lower East Side was his vote count relative to down-ballot Republicans. There were twelve such GOP candidates, running for everything from governor to assemblyman; in East Side districts, Roosevelt outran them all.[103]

Even as TR surpassed these other Republican office-seekers, they benefitted immensely from his coattails. Races that would normally result in Democratic landslides were suddenly competitive. Democrat Henry Goldfogle, for instance, represented the Lower East Side in Congress for many terms. Between 1900 and 1910, Goldfogle consistently dominated his Republican opponent by an impressive average of nearly thirty points—except in 1904. With Roosevelt at the top of the ballot that year, Goldfogle nearly lost his seat as his usual margin of victory plummeted to a measly 2 percent.[104] Meanwhile, the aforementioned sixteenth assembly district—which had unfailingly sent a Democrat to the New York legislature in annual elections for three decades—saw the Republican candidate for the statehouse pull off a stunning upset.[105] Roosevelt had remade the political map with Jewish voters, and the Republican Party at large was reaping the rewards.

Members of his Jewish kitchen cabinet sent words of congratulations. After receiving a telegram from Jacob Schiff, Roosevelt replied, "I understand to the full all that you have done in this election and am very grateful for it."[106] Of course Oscar Straus was elated, confessing to the president, "It has required some time for me to get over the ecstasy of my delight upon the result." He credited Roosevelt's reelection to ordinary Americans rather than to the elite. "It was not the frock-tail gentry, but the plain people who, uninfluenced by Democratic bogies, best understood you," Straus crowed.[107]

Even elements of the Jewish press that had chided Roosevelt now conceded that his historic triumph was attributable to his positive qualities. The *Hebrew Standard* acknowledged that the "enviable and widespread personal popularity of the president" accounted for "the great disintegration of the Democratic Party." Roosevelt may not have been the paper's preferred candidate, but the *Hebrew Standard* nevertheless granted, "The future of a great country lies in the hands of a great man."[108] Similarly, the *B'nai B'rith Messenger* in Los Angeles—which had given a platform to anti-Roosevelt voices during the campaign—now offered, "We are quite satisfied as to the people's choice."[109]

In the wake of Roosevelt's victory, his detractors surely anticipated that the president would take the path of least resistance on the world stage and ease off St. Petersburg. There was, after all, truth in the critique that he turned up the pressure on Russia only in the heat of campaign season. And Roosevelt wasn't worried about facing voters again—he had announced on election night that his second term would be his last (which wasn't a constitutional requirement, as presidential term limits were still a half-century in the offing). What's more, the Russian foreign minister had assured Ambassador McCormick that passport reform was under consideration, a revelation that could provide Roosevelt a solid pretext to relent on the issue. And yet as the president toiled on drafts of his State of the Union message, he was determined to fulminate against Russia for its treatment of both American and Russian Jews, even at the risk of alienating the Russian government.

State of the Union messages in that era were sent in writing to Congress rather than spoken aloud at the Capitol. Roosevelt summoned

Oscar Straus and select others to a dinner at the White House to discuss the contents of his forthcoming message. After the meal, the party adjourned to the president's private study where he reached into a desk drawer and pulled out a draft of various sections of his State of the Union. He turned to Straus for advice on the Jewish-related portions. Roosevelt also shared with the group his frustration that Russia so readily analogized pogroms to racial lynchings in the American South. TR continued to erroneously insist that there were far more pogrom victims. As Straus later recalled, "He argued that the lynchings were comparatively few, and, though bad enough, were nothing compared to the wholesale murder in cold blood under official sanction and perhaps instigation." Roosevelt further remarked that he, unlike the czar, was actually willing to engage foreigners about the shameful propagation of violence in his own country and furnished an example: when a collection of British citizens sent Roosevelt a petition about lynching, he accepted it and issued a reply denouncing the practice.[110]

The State of the Union, in its final form, was unequivocally disparaging of Russia. The president championed "the right for our Jewish fellow-citizens to receive passports and travel through Russian territory." Deriding Russia's policy as "unjust and irritating," Roosevelt insisted there weren't countervailing benefits that could plausibly outweigh the diplomatic animosity Russia was fomenting: "No conceivable good is accomplished by it." So long as American Jews were denied free passage into Russia "merely on racial and religious grounds," the administration was "entitled to protest."[111]

TR didn't limit his censure of the Russians to their visa policy. He also defended his decision to forward the Kishinev Petition to St. Petersburg. "There are ... cases in which, while our own interests are not greatly involved, strong appeal is made to our sympathies," he affirmed. Casting aside the diplomatic orthodoxy that prohibited intrusion into another nation's internal affairs, Roosevelt argued that "there are occasional crimes committed on so vast a scale and of such peculiar horror" that it becomes "our manifest duty ... to show our disapproval." He cited the "massacre of the Jews in Kishinev" as just such an atrocity. The president effectively acknowledged the Russian retort that a hypocritical

America was bedeviled by lynchings—he conceded that the United States suffered from "brutal lawlessness and violent race prejudices here at home."[112] But Roosevelt would not let the scourge of racialized terror within America's borders muzzle his protest against evil perpetrated beyond them.

His allies in the Jewish community naturally celebrated the president's tough-minded treatment of Russia in his State of the Union. The *Reform Advocate*, edited by a Jewish Republican, contrasted Jewry's history of transient wandering with the permanent homeland that Roosevelt's America provided. "Mr. Roosevelt's last message bears testimony to the fact that we are not homeless waifs," the paper pronounced, "but that the Jew in America is a Jewish American and as such has a flag and a country that will speak for him."[113] Meanwhile, B'nai B'rith president Simon Wolf published an editorial celebrating the State of the Union, which "most gloriously vindicated" the government's defense of American Jewry against Russian discrimination. Wolf juxtaposed TR's principled stance with the allegedly self-serving machinations of the president's critics, lamenting how the "Passport Question unfortunately has been made the shuttle-cock by scheming politicians for their own selfish ends"—a veiled reference, no doubt, to Goldfogle and his supporters in Congress.[114]

Roosevelt wasn't the first American president to deem the Passport Question worthy of space in the State of the Union. Chester Arthur in 1883 and Grover Cleveland in 1895 had both raised the issue in their annual messages. Even so, the *New York Times* reported that foreign envoys in Washington were abuzz about Roosevelt's blunt reproach of Russia, which was "amazing" in its departure from the international norms that prevailed in European capitals. But this was Washington, not Vienna or Berlin; Old World customs did not rule American politics. One unnamed diplomat told the *New York Times* that the European powers had "come to regard the United States as entitled to exceptional toleration in matters of this kind." According to the *Times*, foreign emissaries in Washington were speculating that St. Petersburg would likely refuse to amend its passport policy after Roosevelt admonished Russia so publicly.[115] The *Dallas Morning News* similarly predicted, "Roosevelt's tart reference to Russia ... will be received with much distaste at the court of the czar."[116]

One measure of dissatisfaction by the Russian government was the defensive reaction of *Novoe Vreyma* (New Time), a semiofficial newspaper in St. Petersburg that predictably lampooned the United States for its own raft of extralegal killings. The paper tallied the lynching of thirty-two Blacks in America over the prior seven months. *Novoe Vreyma* suggested that Russia's objection to the admission of American Jews was rendered in the same spirit that "the people and government of Louisiana" would surely refuse "to be overrun by the dark races of Russia."[117]

Given that Russia had recently provided assurances to Ambassador McCormick about passport reform, it is striking that Roosevelt would take such a provocative stand. The president surely felt emboldened by the steady stream of headlines about Japan's tenacious siege of Port Arthur in its war against Russia. With Russia in a weakened condition and still in need of financing, Roosevelt had seized an opportunity to apply pressure on Jewish issues. The *Cleveland Plain Dealer* reported that "military and naval disasters" would likely force Russia's hand on passport reform. St. Petersburg was facing a reality that "the great Jewish bankers in the countries where Russia must borrow money" would persevere in their favoritism toward Japan so long as Russia persisted in its hostility against Jews. If the Passport Question was resolved to the satisfaction of Jewry, "at least one good will have resulted from the war," the *Plain Dealer* reasoned. But then the paper sounded a note of caution, recalling that Russia had a penchant for "devious political and diplomatic ways."[118]

Indeed, the unreliability of Russian diplomacy combined with Russia's increasingly perilous war footing meant that the situation was unpredictable. No one could be certain what unintended effects the bombardment of a port in the Far East would have for Jews thousands of miles away. Maybe a newly vulnerable Russia would succumb to the exigencies of the moment and offer Jews—foreign and native alike—the dignity of equal standing with Gentiles. Or perhaps a nation long steeped in antisemitism would, in a time of crisis, plunge itself deeper into the abyss of Jew-hatred.

5

PEACE AT PORTSMOUTH

By the thousands, eager spectators descended on Washington to witness the inauguration of Theodore Roosevelt. They spent the morning of March 4, 1905, under a canopy of clouds that threatened rain, but as the noon hour approached so did the sunlight. Roosevelt had sufficient opportunity to savor his two-mile journey from the White House to the Capitol—after all, his horse-drawn carriage was escorted by slow-moving Civil War veterans "who were fast approaching the Scripture limit of life," one reporter remarked. A steady wind ensured that the countless American flags lining the route down Pennsylvania Avenue were blowing with dutiful enthusiasm.[1]

Outside the east wing of the Capitol, an immense horde awaited the president. Those sufficiently agile to climb trees enjoyed superior vantage points to the throngs below. When Roosevelt finally emerged on the dais, the mass of onlookers erupted with excitement. A journalist recorded, "The shouting began, swelling into a roar like Niagara, rising to cyclonic effects." Roosevelt was accompanied by esteemed personages from across the federal government—members of Congress, justices of the Supreme Court, leaders of the navy and army—as well as foreign dignitaries. Per tradition, the chief justice administered the presidential oath of office upon a Bible. Once Roosevelt finished reciting the words prescribed by the Constitution, he touched his lips to the holy book and commenced his inaugural address.[2]

Nearly four years earlier, Roosevelt had been hastily sworn into office in a parlor in Buffalo, amid the fright and grief of McKinley's assassination.³ Now TR stood on the steps of the Capitol before an adoring multitude, not as a deputy who had become head of state by default but as the winner of the presidency in his own right. Top of mind for the newly emboldened Roosevelt was America's emerging place in the global arena. "We have become a great nation," he declared to the crowd, "forced by the fact of its greatness into relations with the other nations of the earth, and we must behave as beseems a people with such responsibilities."⁴ Roosevelt and the country alike had reached remarkable heights of power despite their relative youth. Jews on both sides of the Atlantic wondered how he would deploy that power on the world stage.

TR wasted little time advancing his agenda overseas. Within a week of the inaugural festivities, he redoubled his efforts to serve as peacemaker between the warring Russians and Japanese. Roosevelt's motivations for seeking a negotiated peace were complex. When the conflict had begun in February 1904, the president and the American public at large favored Japan. He had little regard for a czarist regime that oppressed its people at home and was deceitful in its diplomacy abroad.⁵ Unsurprisingly, Roosevelt's closest Jewish advisor, Oscar Straus, had been of similar mind. "Japan is certainly battling on the side of civilization," Straus wrote Roosevelt as the war commenced. "May wisdom and victory be on her side."⁶

Japan's superiority in troop training, weapons technology, and intelligence gathering all redounded to Russia's detriment.⁷ Roosevelt thrilled to Japan's surprising string of successes early in the war. But by late 1904, the president's delight morphed into dismay. The Japanese seemed poised to unconditionally crush Russia and dominate the Far East—and not, Roosevelt feared, in a manner conducive to American interests. He expressed to the British ambassador in St. Petersburg his worry that Japan privately drew no distinctions between Russians and Americans, all of whom the Japanese supposedly considered "white devils inferior to themselves."⁸ If Roosevelt could mediate an end to the war before Russia's total defeat, he might well secure peace terms ensuring a balance of power in the Far East, one that would benefit America's own ambitions in the region.[9] And beyond the level of pragmatic geopolitics, the president genuinely believed that war was an evil to be truncated, whenever possible. As he later reflected about the Russo-Japanese War in his autobiography, "The losses of life and of treasure were frightful."[10] True, this was the same Roosevelt who had lusted for blood in Cuba. But TR had a talent for effortlessly inhabiting a contradiction.

On March 10, Roosevelt instructed his secretary of state, John Hay, to make discreet overtures to the belligerent parties indicating that the American president was willing to broker a peace. Both Russia and Japan, exhausted by war but hamstrung by pride, suffered from an inertia that threatened to prolong the bloodshed.[11] The Japanese enjoyed the upper hand and wanted to cease hostilities in theory, but only on one-sided terms that Russia was destined to reject. Meanwhile, Russia seemed determined to carry on a losing struggle; such was the arrogance of an autocracy that believed itself immune from facts on the ground. "Did you ever know anything more pitiable than the condition of the Russian despotism?" Roosevelt asked Hay. "The czar is a preposterous little creature." TR further conveyed his frustration that Czar Nicholas was unwilling to free himself from a quagmire of his own making. "He has been unable to make war, and he is now unable to make peace," the president lamented.[12]

The Japanese eventually signaled their amenability to Roosevelt's involvement in late April. They wanted to conduct any peace negotiations with Russia directly, but they were open to TR's help in clearing what would surely be a difficult path to even reach the bargaining table in the first place.[13] With Japan on board, Roosevelt concentrated his efforts on coaxing Russia toward the same end. The czarist regime proved obstinate, however. The Russians were letting their vainglory override their material interests, for they could hardly afford to fight much longer.

Russia was then enduring not only an embarrassing succession of military defeats but significant upheaval at home. Earlier that year in

St. Petersburg, a peaceful demonstration calling for labor reforms ended with Russian troops firing into the crowd, killing 130 people. That massacre—known as "Bloody Sunday"—damaged the czar's standing with the Russian populace and touched off months of domestic unrest.[14] Russia's internal strife swept diverse segments of society, from peasants to professionals and from cityside to countryside. Waves of worker strikes resulted in deadly clashes between protestors and soldiers. Radicals orchestrated political assassinations, including the murder of a high-ranking official in the czar's own family. Some faction of the Russian navy even began whispering about inciting a mutiny. The unrest wasn't centrally organized; the fragmented nature of the resistance allowed the czar to maintain power for the time being. But he was badly weakened, and it was unclear how much longer his grip on Russia would hold. (Lenin would later refer to the 1905 tumult as the "dress rehearsal" that presaged the Bolshevik Revolution of 1917.[15])

Russia's lackluster military performance against Japan exacerbated the rebellion within Russian borders. In symbolic terms, the Russian losses in the Far East epitomized the ineptitude and corruption of the czar's autocracy; in practical terms, the war exacted a severe toll on the Russian economy.[16] Still, the czar blindly pushed forward in his conflict with Japan—until a devastating naval loss in late May, combined with considerable cajoling from the Roosevelt administration, finally brought Russia to the table.[17]

Oscar Straus, with his characteristically effusive prose, congratulated TR for this "recent triumph in that humanitarian diplomacy," which had sealed Roosevelt's stature as "the world's greatest peacemaker."[18] The president knew, though, that the difficult work had only just begun. Simply getting the two parties to agree on a city for negotiations was proving onerous. "I have been having a curious time," Roosevelt told Straus. "I have been endeavoring to get Russia and Japan to go to The Hague. Curiously enough, Russia is most reluctant and Japan positively refuses."[19] Both sides were, however, willing to accept Washington, DC. Roosevelt personally harbored doubts about Washington on account of the heat that engulfed the American capital every summer. He began considering New England coastal communities, which could offer the twin benefits of balmy weather and relative seclusion. Posh locales like Bar Harbor and Newport held strong appeal, but it was the picturesque town of Portsmouth on the New Hampshire shoreline that won the honors of playing host.[20] Neither Russia nor Roosevelt yet knew that the Portsmouth conference, for all its focus on the Far East, would present an unexpected opportunity for American Jews to confront Russian officials face-to-face about the pernicious antisemitism that found free rein under czarist rule.

In the midst of these preparations, Secretary Hay's health rapidly deteriorated. His ultimate fate was approaching faster than anyone realized or wanted to believe. On July 1, with the peace conference mere weeks away, John Hay took his final breath.[21]

American Jews in particular felt the loss of a statesman whose efforts on the Romanian Note and Kishinev Petition they wouldn't soon forget. That Hay had only begrudgingly participated in the latter initiative was readily overlooked in the wake of his death. It is a striking fact that the only memorial service in New York honoring Hay took place at a Jewish house of worship, on the Lower East Side. Although temperatures in the city that day reached 87° Fahrenheit, with the humidity lending the air a "sultry" quality, Jews packed tightly into the Romanian synagogue on Rivington Street. Women and children sat in the balcony, which featured an American flag adorned with black streamers, as befitting a mourning ceremony. The men, gathered below, uniformly wore black ties. Attendees who had never met Secretary Hay openly wept as if a beloved family member had passed.[22]

The service was late to begin owing to the delayed arrival of Henry Goldfogle, the Jewish congressman who represented the district. For an interminable hour, the crush of people in the synagogue waited in the heat. Finally Goldfogle surfaced, and he delivered an address that notably set aside his partisan differences with Republicans. Although he had a history of accusing the Roosevelt administration of feckless disregard for Russian Jewry, Goldfogle now saw fit to praise not just the late secretary but the sitting president as well. "With Theodore Roosevelt, in calling attention to the indignation of Americans at the Russian outrages on the Jews, [John Hay] made himself heard even in darkest Russia," Goldfogle affirmed.[23] That same day a similar service was held to commemorate Hay in a Philadelphia synagogue.[24] And the Union of Orthodox Jewish Congregations, which spanned both the United States and Canada, wired a telegram of condolence to Hay's widow.[25]

The new head of B'nai B'rith, Adolf Kraus, was making his own arrangements in advance of the peace conference. Kraus was politically adept—he had managed a successful mayoral campaign in Chicago—and he saw in Portsmouth a potential forum to champion the cause of Russia's Jews.[26] Perhaps the embattled Russian regime, reeling from military defeat and internal discord, could be persuaded in this moment of crisis to relent in its persecution of Jewry. Russia was dispatching one of its leading officials, Count Sergei Witte, to America for negotiations with the Japanese. Witte was considered a reformer, at least by Russian standards. And his wife, a convert to Christianity, had originally been Jewish.[27] Maybe he would agree to meet with a contingent of American Jews during his stay in New Hampshire about what was often called "the Jewish Question." This phrase referred to debates in various European nations about whether their Jewish residents should remain consigned to second-class citizenship. By Roosevelt's day, many European countries (but certainly not Russia) had favorably answered the Jewish Question with "emancipation," or the removal of civil disabilities imposed on their Jewish subjects. If American Jews could convince Witte of emancipation's merits, then perhaps Witte in turn could convince the czar.

Kraus contacted a Russian consul to see whether such a meeting could be scheduled.[28] Count Witte was, in fact, eager to meet with representatives of the Jewish community. This would be a strategic play on Witte's part. He believed that America's Jews had prejudiced their fellow citizens against Russia—with real consequences. The broad antipathy to Russia within the United States meant that Japan had been able to float war bonds on the American market while Russia could not. If negotiations in Portsmouth failed and the conflict dragged on, Witte hoped that a meeting with Jewish leaders would improve Russia's image in the United States and thereby enhance the Russian war effort. He seemed to think that his optics campaign in America wouldn't necessarily result in U.S. banks' financing Russian forces—that was too quixotic—but he might achieve the more attainable goal of leading American investors to cut off their financial support for Japan. It would take real work, Witte recognized, to reverse Russia's diminished standing.[29]

When word came that Witte was amenable, Kraus began assembling a delegation of Jews to convene with the Russian statesman. Naturally, Kraus solicited Jacob Schiff, the de facto spokesman for American Jewry and an ally of the president's. Schiff, however, had reservations. "I have been urged to meet Mr. Witte and Baron Rosen [the Russian Ambassador to the United States] to discuss with them Jewish affairs, but I have fought shy of them," Schiff privately told the publisher of a Jewish newspaper. "First, because I know it can do no good; and secondly, because I do not wish to have it said that I went to discuss Russian finance with Mr. Witte."[30] Schiff had been the single-most powerful force stonewalling Russia's bid to secure war funds, and he was hardly inclined to lend his ear to the pleas of a country that itself remained deaf to the lamentations of its Jewish inhabitants. But the meeting with Witte was moving ahead either way, and Schiff would ultimately put aside his misgivings to participate.

Three others were tapped for the occasion. Of course, Oscar Straus would be part of the deputation. He was the most politically powerful Jew in America thanks to his close relationship with Roosevelt. And by dint of Straus's ambassadorial experience, he possessed a diplomatic finesse that Schiff hadn't seemed to cultivate in his career as a banker. Joining them was Adolph Lewisohn, whose profile was similar to Schiff's: a German-born New Yorker who had acquired a large fortune and was active in philanthropy.[31] Rounding out the party was the brilliantly named Isaac Newton Seligman. The Seligmans, among the wealthiest and best-connected Jewish families in the country, enjoyed longstanding ties to TR.[32] Although the Roosevelt administration had no official role in the pending encounter between Witte and this Jewish cohort, the president was keen to be discreetly involved from a distance. And so Roosevelt met with Straus and Seligman in advance of the conference, calling on them to keep him apprised of developments in Portsmouth.[33]

★ ★ ★

As Count Witte's ship approached New York, he found that a cadre of reporters and onlookers hadn't been content to wait on shore for his arrival and instead filled a "whole flotilla of small vessels" to greet him in the waters. He could not have been difficult for them to spot—Witte had a massive frame, six feet six inches with broad shoulders. Once docked, Witte rode to the city's finest hotel, the St. Regis, where he was led to a lavish suite that boasted a sizable Russian flag draped from his balcony for the occasion. He also enjoyed the protection of the Secret Service, at Roosevelt's behest. The Russian statesman, who was to have a brief stay in New York before heading north, saw his limited time in the city as an initial opportunity to begin a strategic campaign to win over public opinion. On his second day in New York, Witte traveled to the Lower East Side—or "the Jewish ghetto," as Witte called it—where he conversed in Russian with some of the Jewish immigrants there. Witte later explained in his memoirs that, "in view of the considerable influence of the Jews on the press and on other aspects of American life," he had felt it was imperative that he not "exhibit any hostility toward them."[34]

He then took the train to Oyster Bay to see Roosevelt at his Sagamore Hill estate, which Witte thought "looked like an ordinary summer house of a burgher of small means." Witte was even less impressed by the meal inside. "The luncheon was more than simple and, for a European, almost indigestible," he later complained. According to Witte, Roosevelt was an apt representative of his country in culinary matters: "I noticed that, generally speaking, people ate very poorly in America." Although Witte came from a nation maligned on the world stage for its barbarity, he was offended by the lack of tablecloths and wine at TR's lunch. The president used the visit to press Witte into considering treaty terms that the Japanese would find acceptable, an early indicator that Roosevelt—though not formally part of the negotiations—would exercise clout as they proceeded.[35]

★ ★ ★

When the delegations from Japan and Russia surfaced in Portsmouth several days later, this sleepy seaside village of colonial homes and leafy streets came alive.[36] Onlookers packed the roadsides to catch a glimpse of the diplomats as they rode in open buggies down a processional route that was festooned with banners and flags. New Hampshire state troops, bedecked in blue and yellow, kept the throngs at bay. Spectators cheered the Russian and Japanese envoys alike; Witte repaid the honor by repeatedly lifting his silk hat. The parties disembarked at the courthouse where the governor ceremoniously welcomed them. At the expense of the American taxpayer, the dignitaries stayed at the Wentworth, a luxury hotel that exuded opulence. The Japanese took the elevator to their suites, whereas the Russians opted to labor up the stairs—perhaps a fitting metaphor given that the negotiations ahead would be more difficult for the Russians, whose bargaining position was far weaker.[37]

Portsmouth didn't technically host the bilateral meetings between the delegations. Every day, the parties would travel just across the Piscataqua River to Maine where the U.S. Navy maintained a facility outfitted with communications infrastructure that would enable the diplomats to easily cable Tokyo and St. Petersburg. The American officials playing host undertook extensive efforts to ensure that the daily cuisine was nothing less than sumptuous. But Witte remained underwhelmed, confining himself to a meager diet of vegetables and grains.[38] "It is highly dangerous to eat the ordinary food which is served in America," Witte later reflected. "I have arrived at the conclusion that Americans have no culinary taste and that they can eat almost anything that comes in their way, even if it is not fresh."[39] When a Japanese negotiator fell ill during the peace talks, Witte blamed the food. Nor was Witte

FIGURE. 5.1. Sergei Witte outside the Wentworth. *Source*: Library of Congress, Prints and Photographs Division.

terribly pleased with the Wentworth's accommodations, the hotel's grandeur notwithstanding. For one, the light in his room was disagreeable to his eyes. And when he tried to squeeze his sizable body into the bathtub, Witte twisted his ankle in the process.[40]

★ ★ ★

Reporters had poured into Portsmouth from across the country and around the world: London, Paris, Frankfurt, Rome, and Tokyo.[41] On his fifth day in town, Count Witte finally sat down for an extended interview with a newspaper, giving an exclusive to the *Boston Globe* during a break in the peace talks. Witte's cadence of speech was "animated" yet "deliberate" as he shared strikingly frank views about Jewish people. "The Jews in America possess great influence and have quite naturally used that influence to destroy American sympathy [for Russia], to do all that is possible to enlist sympathy for the Japanese," he griped. Witte must have realized that he sounded conspiratorial and even antisemitic because he then quickly hedged, "I do not say this with any bitterness." Despite Witte's self-directed resolution to present a friendlier face to Jews, it appears he could not help but peddle the hackneyed conceit of the Jew as duplicitous puppet-master.[42]

Witte utilized his interview with the *Globe* to reiterate the Russian sentiment expressed during the Kishinev affair: external interference into internal matters was beyond the pale—in both senses. He conveyed that the "Jewish Question" was strictly a "domestic matter that must be dealt with by Russia herself" and lay outside "the domain of international discussion." To buttress his point, Witte relied upon the popular Russian tactic of referencing race-based lynching in the United States. He contended, "Every country has its own great questions to settle that can only be settled by itself. I need only refer by way of illustration to the negro in America." He then curtailed his commentary by suggesting that it was wise for him not to say too much in advance of his meeting with the Jewish leaders. But Witte had said plenty already.[43]

★ ★ ★

That same day, members of the Jewish contingent turned up in Portsmouth.[44] Oscar Straus spoke to the press upon arrival and called for the repeal of hundreds of discriminatory Russian laws targeting Jews. He evoked the Declaration of Independence in his remarks: "We will ask M. Witte that the Jews in Russia be accorded the same right to pursue life, liberty, and the pursuit of happiness that others in that country have." (The "M." before Witte meant "Monsieur," a nod to French as the language of diplomacy.) Straus then added, "This is what we ask. No more, no less, to use President Roosevelt's effective phrase." He was referencing Roosevelt's famous line that everyone merits "a square deal, because he is entitled to no more and should receive no less."[45] Straus also sought to preempt speculation in the press that he was there to purchase civil rights for Russian Jews in exchange for war loans. "This is [in] no way involved with any financial question," he clarified. "It is purely and simply a question of humanity."[46]

Loans were indeed not on the agenda, but the *New York Times* discerned that the topic couldn't have been far from Witte's mind. "When this war began and [Russia] turned to the financial centers for money," the *Times* recounted, "she found every Jewish banking house in the world closed to her." Consequently, a Russian regime that just two years prior had refused to accept a petition sent by an American president would now subject itself to a remonstrance by American citizens. It was an "extraordinary spectacle," proclaimed the *Times*.[47] To be sure, no explicit quid pro quo was on the table, but many observers thought that if the Russians made moves toward Jewish emancipation, their financial troubles might well ease.

★ ★ ★

Witte received his Jewish visitors in his room at the Wentworth Hotel at 8:45 in the evening, joined by the Russian ambassador and Witte's interpreter. The Jewish delegation revived a line of reasoning that had appeared first in the Romanian Note and then in the Kishinev Petition: the prejudicial treatment of Russian Jews prompted "an influx en masse" of refugees to the United States, rendering the issue international in character. Therefore, the czar's regime couldn't rightly claim that the Jewish-American representatives before him were "meddling with affairs" internal to Russia. While immigration gave them just cause to state their grievances, they insisted that immigration itself wasn't a viable solution to the Jewish Question. There were too many millions of Russian Jews to simply displace them to other nations. "The Russo-Jewish question must be settled in Russia," they averred.[48]

The Jewish leaders also assured Witte that Russia had nothing to fear from granting civil equality to its Jewish population. After all, Jewish emancipation in France, Germany, and England all demonstrated that once the Jew is granted the full prerogatives of citizenship, he becomes "a lover of his country and supporter of the government." And, of course, in "the United States the Jew has become an ardent American"—so ardent that American Jews of Russian origin were helping rally the U.S. government against their former homeland. The Jewish delegation asserted that "Jewish influence in the United States" was substantial and increasing daily thanks to the arrival of Russian-Jewish refugees. Emphasizing Russia's self-interest, the Jewish representatives urged Witte to consider the detriment to Russia of an icy relationship between the eagle and the bear: "Can it be expected that the influence, which the American Jew is thus gaining upon public opinion, will be exerted to the advantage of the country which systematically degrades his brethren in race and makes their fate almost unendurable?"[49] If Witte worried about Jewish persuasive power in America, then the Jewish delegation was more than happy to leverage his concerns toward their own ends.

Witte, for his part, sought to stake out some middle ground between the typical Russian denial of Jewish persecution and a candid acknowledgement of that reality. He conceded, "Jews in Russia [are] in a very difficult position," yet he still alleged that "the horrors of the Jewish situation in Russia had been presented to the world in a somewhat exaggerated light."[50] Witte also expressed optimism for Russia's Jews thanks to a new development: Czar Nicholas, under pressure from domestic unrest, had recently agreed to institute an assembly—the Duma—that would represent the people's interests. Once the Duma convened, it would likely repeal antisemitic laws, Witte told the Jewish delegation.[51] His prognosis here lacked credibility because the Duma was to exercise merely consultative rather than binding powers, providing a nominal gesture toward liberalism while allowing the czar to preserve absolutism in practice.[52]

The meeting wasn't without its tenser moments. In one instance, Jacob Schiff motioned toward Witte's translator—a Russian national of Jewish faith—and pointedly pressed Witte, "Will you please tell me why you, as a Russian, have full rights in your country while he, also a Russian, has none?"[53] Witte responded with an expression of support for the emancipation of Russian Jews but argued that any progress should be incremental. He conjectured that the "immediate and complete removal of their legal disabilities would, in my opinion, do them more harm than good" because it would provoke hostility from the Russian people.[54]

Unsurprisingly, that answer didn't satisfy Schiff and the others. They countered that if the Russian populace was going to take umbrage at each piecemeal step toward Jewish liberation, all the better for the regime to implement equality "by one single action." The swift and total emancipation of Jewry would limit Russian hostility to one discrete point in time. Alternatively, Witte's proposal to have emancipation "dragged on through partial measures" would only serve to stoke "anew the irritation" among Russians toward their Jewish neighbors in an endless succession of aggravating reforms.[55]

Jacob Schiff was particularly irked when Witte recommended that American Jews use their supposed clout with their Russian coreligionists to sway them away from revolutionary movements and toward loyalty to the czar. Witte was proceeding from the common view in Russia that its Jewish population comprised dangerous traitors. The reality was that only a small minority of Russian Jews were seditious agitators. Most the czar's Jewish subjects were far too preoccupied with the relentless struggle of daily life; insurrection simply wasn't on their agenda. But Schiff did not reject the allegation that many Russian Jews were subversive of state authority. Instead, he argued that they were justified in their radical bid to create a Russian republic. With an edge in his voice, Schiff asked rhetorically, "Is it not probable that the young men became revolutionists in the hope that a republic will grant them just laws which are denied under the rule of the Emperor?" Witte, in turn, dismissed revolutionary aspirations as quixotic, declaring that the end of the czarist dynasty—the Romanovs—would not materialize in their lifetime. "The Romanovs will rule Russia for at least another hundred years," he insisted.[56] He was off by about ninety.

Despite some friction—at one point, Schiff pounded his fist on the table—both sides were reasonably cordial.[57] Witte would later recall that Schiff's stridency was "toned down by the more balanced judgments of the other members," and he singled out Oscar Straus for making an especially "excellent impression."[58] In the same spirit, Seligman would describe Count Witte as "a gentleman inspired with broadminded views and having a thorough grasp of the situation." Even if Witte was disinclined to recognize the full depths of Jewish deprivation, the willingness of a high-ranking Russian official to admit any of it was a breakthrough of sorts. Witte offered to resume his discussion with the Jewish leaders in New York City, after he concluded the peace talks.[59]

Reporters had been patiently awaiting the reappearance of the Jewish delegation from Witte's suite, as a meeting that was supposed to take one hour stretched to three. Finally, the Jewish leaders emerged just before midnight. Jacob Schiff gave a mixed statement to the press—he surmised that their conference with Witte "could not well lead to any practical result" for Russian Jewry but nevertheless vaguely anticipated that the "frank exchange of views" on the subject would "bear beneficial consequences" in the fullness of time. Oscar Straus added, "There is nothing more for us to do; our mission is done."[60]

As with the peace negotiations themselves, Roosevelt was officially uninvolved with the Jewish contingent's endeavor but still proved an important behind-the-scenes player from Oyster Bay. TR had requested that the Jewish participants keep him updated on their gathering with Witte; three of the five dutifully dashed off letters to the president. Jacob Schiff reconstructed at length the contents of the discussion and requested Roosevelt's input. "We have become so accustomed to look to you, dear Mr. President, for advice and guidance in dealing with the momentous questions which at this time touch the weal of our race," Schiff wrote.[61] Isaac Newton Seligman relayed to Roosevelt that Witte expected—or at least claimed to expect—that the pending Duma in St. Petersburg would institute pro-Jewish reforms. Seligman had his doubts. "The past promises and subsequent non-performances on the part of Russia naturally lead us to feel distrustful, and we have some misgivings as to his utterances," Seligman confessed, even as he acknowledged having a "favorable" opinion of Witte.[62] Meanwhile, the president's most trusted Jewish confidant, Oscar Straus, told Roosevelt that Witte had expressed a preference for "gradual emancipation" and that they in response had demanded "equal rights—no more no less—and without delay."[63]

Roosevelt wanted to personally lend himself to their ongoing cause. But his first priority was coaxing the Japanese and Russians into a peace accord. "I am greatly interested in what you tell me about the Russian Jew question," the president assured Straus, "and will of course do anything I can, subsequent to the peace negotiations being out of the way, as I do not want to complicate the latter."[64] Indeed, Roosevelt would soon find himself frenetically working back channels to ensure that the precarious discussions between the warring parties did not end in failure.[65]

The Jewish summit with Witte garnered front-page headlines nationwide. From the *Colorado Springs Gazette* to the *Augusta Chronicle*, Americans read about the Jewish leaders who confronted the Russian official over the plight of their embattled coreligionists.[66] The *Cleveland Plain Dealer* declared that the Jewish meeting was "far overshadowing" the peace negotiations.[67] One newspaper correspondent vividly captured the significance of the moment. "Great and dramatic is the spectacle presented tonight," he marveled. "Picture, if you will, the mighty bear, rampant and aggressive, with its teeth so often displayed in harsh snarls . . . humbled before the much despised Jew."[68] After years of practiced obstinance, Russia was now hearing a humanitarian message, from Jewish lips no less.

Opinions in the mainstream press differed over the meeting's potential to appreciably impact the lives of Russian Jews. The *Idaho Daily Statesman* suggested that Witte would surely "carry home with him some new view of the entire subject" after he had not only conversed with the Jewish delegation but also seen firsthand the flourishing Jewish-American community, a model for what Russian Jewry could become if granted equality.[69] But the *Cleveland Plain Dealer* was less sanguine. That paper derided Witte as irrelevant next to the czar, in whose imperial hands the fate of Russia's Jews ultimately rested. Witte was "not supreme" and consistently "overruled" back home by "his weathercock of a master."[70]

When the Jewish representatives returned from Portsmouth to their respective cities, they tried to strike an optimistic note about the near future in their remarks to journalists. B'nai B'rith president Adolf Kraus, who had initiated the meeting with Witte, announced in Chicago, "Better times are coming for our people," and he predicted that the new Duma would dismantle the country's antisemitic legal code.[71] Meanwhile, Seligman—despite confiding in Roosevelt his wariness of Witte—told the New York press that Witte would relay "our message to the emperor in a convincing way that we are confident will bear fruit."[72] Kraus and Seligman were of course incentivized to publicly depict their encounter with Witte as a promising step forward, lest they preemptively undermine their goals.

Other voices in the Jewish community were less hopeful. The Democrat-leaning *Hebrew Standard* reported skepticism in New York among Russian-Jewish immigrants, who were cautioning that "Witte will promise a great deal" but "he will in reality be able to accomplish little."[73] Jews actually living in Russia were also leery. As the Associated Press wired from St. Petersburg, "Prominent Jews here ... are pessimistic regarding the outcome of the promised reforms and have little hope of favorable Jewish legislation from the Duma."[74] Witte's reputation for relative liberality appeared insufficient to outweigh Russia's inveterate Jew-hatred.[75]

FIGURE. 5.2. After rejecting the Kishinev Petition, which lays scattered on the ground, a defeated czar is depicted as having to accept "Jewish loans" to compensate for the war's cost. In reality, Jewish financiers had no desire to offer loans to Russia. *Source*: "Kishineff Must Be Paid For—with Interest," *Puck*, September 6, 1905.

The members of the Jewish delegation were frustrated that the press frequently depicted their meeting with Witte as exactly what it was not: a trade of loans for Jewish rights.[76] In South Dakota, for instance, the *Aberdeen Daily News* erroneously reported, "The well-known ability of the Jews to drive a good bargain is demonstrated again in the proposition of American bankers of that race to loan the czar all the money he needs, provided he will grant reforms in Russia which will deliver the Jewish race from persecution." The paper earnestly "hoped that the bankers will succeed in driving their bargain."[77] Although intended as a compliment, this commentary reinforced tropes about Jews as cunning moneylenders.

Oscar Straus made sure to disabuse Roosevelt of any misinformation he might have picked up from the newspapers. "Contrary to press reports, the conference had nothing to do with finances," he stressed. "The subject was not referred to."⁷⁸ Isaac Newton Seligman, too, took pains to assure the president that they never contemplated funding Russia's war efforts in exchange for Jewish emancipation. "The papers manufactured that matter out of whole cloth, and there is not a particle of truth in such published reports," he vented.⁷⁹ The Jewish leaders had already given statements to the press back in New Hampshire categorically refuting rumors of a quid pro quo.⁸⁰ Witte himself corroborated their claims, but the *Cleveland Plain Dealer* remained unconvinced that war loans had been off the table: "The numerous denials were cleverly calculated, both by M. Witte and these representatives of great banking houses, to befog the casual observance as to the real object of their visit."⁸¹ Jews and Russians alike could not so easily escape stereotyping about duplicity.

With Russia bedeviled by ongoing turmoil at home and abroad, no one could be sure of Russian Jewry's imminent fate. A Jewish scholar in New York, Isidor Singer, published an open letter to Count Witte that reflected the moment's uncertainty. Singer posited that the Russian treatment of Jews would be a bellwether for the very survival of the czarist regime. If Russia applied "the principle of American life and American government" to itself, then perhaps the regime could endure in a reformed condition. But Singer held out the possibility that Russian backwardness was incorrigible under czarist rule, leaving revolution as the only alternative. In Singer's words, perhaps "the malady is rooted so deep, that the amputation of the empire is the only means of salvation." His letter also approvingly alluded to Roosevelt, suggesting that even if the peace talks with Japan failed, at least Witte "had the great advantage of making the personal acquaintance of the American people and [their] sturdy president."⁸²

★ ★ ★

It looked as though the Russo-Japanese talks were, in fact, careening toward collapse but for the efforts of the sturdy president himself. The warring parties found themselves mired in an intractable standoff over land claims and indemnities, spurring Roosevelt to fire off a rapid succession of cables from Oyster Bay to Portsmouth, St. Petersburg, and Tokyo. A principal obstacle to peace was convincing the pride-wounded Russians to make concessions that offended their sense of honor, even though the proposed terms were reasonable given Russia's poor military showing. At first, Roosevelt appeared unable to finesse a compromise that both sides could stomach. But in the waning days of August, just as it seemed the diplomats would return home empty-handed, they agreed to terms.[83] "It's a mighty good thing for Russia and a mighty good thing for Japan," Roosevelt told a congressman, adding that it was "a mighty good thing for *me*, too!"[84]

Indeed. Heads of state and newspaper editorialists the world over lauded Roosevelt for his pivotal part in a conference he never actually attended.[85] After facing criticism earlier in his presidency that he pursued a reckless brand of "cowboy diplomacy," Roosevelt could justifiably claim the mantle of peacemaker in the wake of Portsmouth.[86] Oscar Straus gushed in a letter to the president that many people who "only a few months ago looked upon you as the scourge of war now praise you as the angel of peace."[87] For Roosevelt's role in the Russo-Japanese negotiations, he won the Nobel Peace Prize—the first American to receive a Nobel in any category. He resolved that the prize money be spent in pursuit of improved relations between capital and labor, tapping Straus as a steward of that endeavor.[88]

The signing ceremony of the peace treaty took place in early September in a brick building in the navy yard where the diplomats had spent weeks wrangling over terms. After three previous days of gloomy weather, the sun now appeared as if on cue. All of Portsmouth waited eagerly for the signal—a nineteen-gun salute from the navy yard battery—that would indicate the diplomats had affixed their names to the historic document. The salute was expected at three o'clock that afternoon, but at the appointed hour one agonizing minute after the next elapsed without any discharge from the battery's gunner. Finally, upon the last pen stroke in the conference room, a clerk ran outside to announce, "All signed at 3:47," prompting a navy seaman to wave a red flag at the gunner some fifty yards away.[89] "The opening shot of the salute rang out on the clear air of the soft September afternoon," recorded one journalist, "proclaiming peace between Russia and Japan."[90]

A cacophony ensued. Portsmouth's churches tolled their bells, ships in the harbor blew their whistles, and a marine band in the navy yard "burst out into a fanfare." Amid the noise, a State Department official phoned Oyster Bay to inform Roosevelt of the news. Champagne was opened for the diplomats back inside the conference room, where the American president was toasted even before the Russian czar or Japanese emperor—a testament to Roosevelt's centrality to the negotiations.[91]

At five o'clock, the Russian delegation journeyed across the Kittery Bridge into Portsmouth, which was densely packed with festive crowds. Witte was due to attend a special service at a local church but struggled to make his way through the crush of onlookers. They kept extending their hands to him—and understandably so, given that handshakes were "the usual expression of attention with Americans," he recalled. Finally, Witte entered the church, which was delightfully adorned with floral arrangements. A Russian Orthodox priest walked with rabbis in a procession behind a choir that was intoning a song of peace, a sign that the war's resolution might well hasten a fresh start for Jewish-Christian relations in Russia.[92]

Four days after the peace conference concluded, Witte was back at Oyster Bay as Roosevelt's dinner guest. The president had hosted the Japanese diplomats earlier that afternoon for lunch, and now he provided a final—perhaps inedible—meal to Count Witte. Following that supper, Roosevelt sent a letter to a retired British statesman, George Otto Trevelyan, that reflected his mixed feelings about Witte. "I suppose Witte is the best man that Russia could have at the head of her affairs at present," Roosevelt offered in Witte's favor before disclosing, "I cannot say that I liked him, for I thought his bragging and bluster not only foolish but shockingly vulgar."[93] Witte's diplomatic credentials aside, he wasn't known for his subtlety or tact.[94]

The president may have felt self-professed "contempt" for Witte, but Roosevelt was also encouraged by their discussion at Oyster Bay, which covered the oppression of Russian Jewry. Weeks earlier, TR had promised Straus that he would personally take up the cause with Witte after the peace negotiations, and Roosevelt appears to have stayed true to his word. Precisely what the president said to Witte remains unknown, but he did share with Trevelyan that he had aimed to "get a little alleviation of the condition of the Jews out of this peace conference, as what you might call a by-product." And Roosevelt saw cause for hope, relaying to Trevelyan, "Witte also expressed his views about religious freedom and freedom of conscience in a way that would command hearty support from you or me."[95]

The president felt sufficiently optimistic to send Witte a follow-up letter about an issue that the Jewish group in Portsmouth hadn't broached: the Passport Question. Despite assurances the prior year that Russia would reassess its visa restrictions on Jews with U.S. citizenship, the prohibition of American Jews remained in effect. "In furtherance of our conversation of last evening, I beg you to consider the question of granting passports [i.e., visas] to reputable American citizens of Jewish faith," Roosevelt pressed. He emphasized that the stakes weren't confined to American Jewry but implicated the whole of Russian-American relations; reform on this front would "remove the last cause of irritation between the two nations" and ensure the perpetuity of their "historic friendship." TR acknowledged Russia's right to ban any given U.S. citizen from its territory, provided such a decision hinged on that citizen's rectitude rather than religion.[96] The president's letter came with a request that Witte forward it to the czar himself.[97] Roosevelt's bid here for passport reform was, and would long remain, hidden from public view—in other words, he wasn't posturing to score points with a domestic audience.[98]

On Witte's final morning in New York City before returning to Russia, he and the Russian ambassador visited their Japanese counterparts at the Waldorf-Astoria for a farewell. Then, at the St. Regis, Witte reconvened with the Jewish representatives he had met in Portsmouth—or at least most of them. Three of the five were present for this second gathering: the banker, Isaac Newton Seligman; the diplomat, Oscar Straus; and the B'nai B'rith president, Adolf Kraus.[99] The latter had traveled all the way from Chicago for what was a merely ceremonial sendoff. Having already aired their views fully in New Hampshire, all parties were content to treat this latter occasion primarily as an exercise in politesse.[100]

Afterward, Seligman told the press that Witte had just now pledged "as far as he can personally assist, all will be done to give the Jews their full constitutional rights," though Seligman noted that Witte had been speaking as an "individual" rather than in an "official" capacity.[101] To what was surely Seligman's annoyance, he continued to fend off queries from reporters about whether Jewish-run banks would provide loans for Russia. "The matter of a loan was not even suggested," he insisted. Meanwhile, Witte lunched at the ritzy Union Club on Fifth Avenue before beginning his long voyage home. From on board his steamer prior to sailing, Witte gave an ambivalent statement to the papers. He did express hope for a "new era" of religious equality but cautioned that "it takes time to change sentiment and work political reforms." Witte then added with vague foreboding, "Regrettable things cannot always be foreseen or prevented."[102] As he well understood, cessation of war beyond Russia's borders would not necessarily forge peace within them. It remained to be seen whether ongoing domestic strife would ultimately improve or imperil life for the czar's Jewish subjects.

★ ★ ★

Witte returned home to a Russia roiled by turmoil that was alarming even by the standards of 1905. A cascading series of strikes across different industries turned into a general strike by October that brought the nation's cities to the brink of paralysis. Witte pleaded with the czar that only a transition to a constitutional monarchy would placate the revolutionary fervor sweeping the country. The reform-minded Witte drew up a memorandum for Czar Nicholas's consideration that called for civil liberties, voting rights, and a Duma with real legislative powers; under this scheme, the czar would retain his status as emperor, and prospective laws would be subject to his veto. Nicholas did not thrill to the idea of significantly diminishing his autocratic control, but the dysfunction of Russian society was too plain for even an intransigent despot to ignore. At the month's end, the czar begrudgingly issued the October Manifesto, based on Witte's memorandum, in which "freedom of conscience" was affirmed as a core element of "genuine personal inviolability."[103] This was a remarkable concession for millions of Jews who had endured relentless subjugation.

Witte's promise to the American Jewish leaders that he would do all he could for their coreligionists in Russia was now improbably realized in an official decree bearing the czar's signature. Yet even as its ink was freshly drying, the manifesto became a dead letter. The day after its promulgation, thousands of Russians would greet the news of civic freedom for their Jewish neighbors with an explosion of antisemitic violence never before seen in the dark history of their empire.

6

POGROMS

As word of the October Manifesto spread throughout Russia, some Jews and liberal Gentiles took to the streets in celebration. Their outburst of excitement was decidedly *not* an expression of gratitude to the czar for bestowing new rights. To the contrary, these reformers viewed the manifesto for what it was: an act of desperation from a flailing leader. The anti-czarist crowds sensed the regime's weakness and pressed their advantage in cities across Russia. They marched with banners to jails, police stations, and governors' homes where they called for political prisoners to be set free.[1] "Hurrah, freedom to all!" they chanted. "Down with the autocracy, down with the czar!"[2]

But these Jews and their like-minded compatriots were not the only ones in the streets that day. A loose collection of reactionary organizations—dubbed the "Black Hundreds" by their critics—began massacring Jews with abandon.[3] The assailants savagely beat Jews to death while berating them, "Here is your freedom, here is your constitution, here is your revolution."[4] In one community after the next, mobs torched local synagogues before moving on to Jewish homes and Jewish businesses.[5] That most of the Jewish victims were not actually liberal agitators was of little moment to the pogromists.[6]

On hand that day in Kyiv was the acclaimed Yiddish writer Sholem Aleichem (whose short stories about Tevye, the fictional milkman, formed the basis for *Fiddler on the Roof*). Aleichem gave a firsthand account for the press of a devastating pogrom there. He related how the city's Jews pleaded with Christian acquaintances to offer them refuge but were refused and left for slaughter. Pogromists had no inclination to spare even the most vulnerable. "Jewish girls were dishonored," wrote Alecheim, "children were rent in twain."[7] The very worst of the genocide took place in Odessa, where the streets were littered with Jewish corpses. One journalist described the "revolting barbarity" inflicted on Odessa's Jews. "Heads were battered with hammers, nails were driven into the bodies, eyes were gouged out, and ears severed," the report read. Some of the city's Jews were strangled to death, others burned alive.[8]

These blood-soaked scenes unfolded on a staggering scale throughout the Pale of Settlement and in some cases beyond it. Over the course of twelve days, pogroms erupted in well over six hundred cities, towns, and villages. The forty-nine Jewish deaths in Kishinev were now eclipsed by ghastly orders of magnitude. By some counts, more than three thousand Jewish souls lost their lives in the 1905 pogrom wave, with thousands more injured. Two hundred thousand Jews sustained property damage, entailing losses of 63 million rubles (over $1.1 billion U.S. dollars today). Russian Jewry was in abject ruin.[9]

The pogromists—waving Russian flags and singing nationalistic tunes—were self-professed patriots who viewed their butchery of Jews as an expression of loyalty to the czar. In one sense, their rationale was incoherent: they were violently raging against a manifesto that the czar himself had decreed.[10] But in another sense, the Black Hundreds and their ilk were supremely faithful czarists; after all, the October Manifesto was a begrudging concession that scarcely veiled Czar Nicholas's opposition to liberalization in general and to Jewry in particular.

The czar showed no compassion for the pogrom's victims and felt that they deserved their grisly fate. As he told his mother, "The people became enraged by the insolence and audacity of the revolutionaries and socialists; and because nine-tenths of them are Yids, the people's whole wrath has turned against them."[11] Nicholas here insinuated that the pogroms were spontaneous, which is not entirely accurate. Although some of the antisemitic attacks were indeed unplanned, in other places the Black Hundreds had been plotting and waiting for an opportune moment to savage the Jewish population.[12]

FIGURE. 6.1. The Russian people react to the October Manifesto and its promises of freedom by slaughtering Jews. *Source*: "The Russian Idea of Freedom," *Brooklyn Daily Eagle*, November 3, 1905.

The degree of government complicity varied by place. Some authorities on the ground tried to mollify the mobs, but many other officials passively consented to the brutalities or even partook in them.[13] When Odessa's governor was beseeched to intervene on behalf of Jews, he coldly responded, "You wanted freedom—here is the Yid's freedom."[14] The inconsistency among local authorities paralleled a divide at the highest echelons of the Russian state. On one side was Sergei Witte, whom Czar Nicholas had named the Russian premier—effectively, the prime minister—on the very day that Nicholas signed the October Manifesto.[15] On the other was Dmitri Trepov, the governor-general of St. Petersburg, who favored pogroms.[16] Each man appeased a different constituency: Witte, the reformers; Trepov, the reactionaries. As Lenin keenly observed, "Both Witte and Trepov are necessary: Witte to beguile some, Trepov to suppress others; Witte—for promises, Trepov—for deeds."[17] Trepov cultivated close ties to Nicholas and reinforced the czar's own inclination toward antisemitism. "The Emperor was surrounded by avowed Jew-haters such as Trepov," Witte would later recall in his memoirs.[18]

The atrocities visited upon Russia's Jews were part of a broader turbulence upending Russian society. Witte had hoped that the October Manifesto would soothe tensions, but the perilous situation on the ground seemed only to worsen. In the cities, laborers refused to work. In the countryside, peasants resorted to arson and theft. In the military, mutinies abounded. Railroads came to a standstill. Universities were hotbeds of dissent. Educated elites abstained from their professional obligations.[19]

The American ambassador's aide, H. Custis Vezey, sent a letter back to Washington that offered a revealing glimpse of the fear and furor gripping Russia. "Today a great many people in St. Petersburg were in dread of being murdered in their beds, and they are hardly to be blamed," Vezey shared. "There was a rush on the gun shops and nearly all their stock was sold out yesterday as everyone is arming for the expected riots, no one placing any confidence whatsoever in the police or the troops doing their duty." He further relayed reports that the czarist regime was actively spurring the Black Hundreds—made up of "hooligans, toughs, and the ignorant multitude"—to terrorize Jews and other reformist elements.[20] While the instinct to kill Jews amid a crisis was familiar to many Russians, at this moment of particularly acute social rupture, Jewish blood flowed at an unprecedented pace.

★ ★ ★

After the horrors of Kishinev in 1903 and before the mass carnage of 1905, pogroms had periodically broken out in Russia. But the violence was comparatively limited in that timeframe. Kishinev had taught Russian Jews that they would need to mobilize in their own self-defense, and in a number of attacks predating the October Manifesto, Jews were able to partially defend themselves and mitigate casualties.[21] Pogroms, accordingly, became a secondary concern for most American Jews. To be sure, the American press did report on the sporadic assaults against Russian Jewry, and Jacob Schiff at times nudged Theodore Roosevelt on the issue.[22] Yet it was the Passport Question, rather than pogroms, that assumed prominence amid the 1904 presidential race. And the following year, when the Jewish delegation met with Sergei Witte in Portsmouth, they chose to focus their remonstrance on legal forms of discrimination against Russian Jews, not on extralegal violence.

But the bloodbath of fall 1905—whose sheer scale had overwhelmed Jewish bids at self-defense—once again made pogroms the galvanizing cause for American Jews and many of their Gentile compatriots. Major papers in the Jewish population centers, like the *New York Times* and *Philadelphia Inquirer*, dedicated their front pages to the pogroms.[23] And the news coverage reached communities with far fewer Jews too. From the Deep South and New England to the Great Plains and Pacific Northwest, local papers carried word of the macabre developments in Russia.[24] The *St. Albans Daily Messenger*, on the northern edge of Vermont, printed reports of the "wholesale plunder of Jews."[25] In Alabama, the *Montgomery Advertiser* described how Jews were "being hunted down in the streets."[26] And the *Evening World-Herald* in Omaha relayed, "The mobs swear they will not leave a single Jew alive."[27] The question for America—its Jews, its Gentiles, and its government—was whether and how to mount a response to a calamity of unconscionable magnitude.

America's most outspoken Jewish leader, Jacob Schiff, concentrated his initial efforts at government authorities not in the United States but in Russia. He cabled Witte directly in early November: "The American people stand aghast at atrocities in Odessa and elsewhere." Schiff's cable blamed the Russian state for allowing the slaughter to persist and warned that Russia could never "expect the moral support of other nations" under such circumstances.[28] Witte's reply came two days later. He insisted, unconvincingly, that the Russian government was "horrified" by the "savage outbreaks." Witte was at least honest about the reigning unrest: "As long as the country is in such [an] excited state, the local authorities are often powerless."[29] So was Witte. He did admonish local authorities to stop the pogromists but to little avail.[30]

Witte's feebleness was a symptom of both a teetering regime and his own beleaguered position within that regime. Even before the October Manifesto, political circles in St. Petersburg erroneously suspected that Witte might be conspiring with Jews to engineer a coup. The October Manifesto itself, with its proclamation of religious liberty, could have only served to stoke fears of a Witte-Jewish alliance.[31] Against this fraught backdrop, Witte was reduced to little more than an impotent figurehead in his new role as premier. He later lamented, "I wielded little power and bore all the responsibility" while the antisemitic Trepov, who enjoyed the czar's fidelity, functioned in effect as "the irresponsible head of the government."[32]

Oscar Straus journeyed to the White House bearing in hand the text of Witte's unpromising cable to Schiff. Straus and Roosevelt discussed what steps, if any, TR might take on behalf of Russian Jewry. Afterward the president consulted with Elihu Root, who had succeeded John Hay as secretary of state and whose affinity for Jews was limited. Roosevelt resolved that he would not press the cause of Jewry with the Russian government. The White House released a statement to the newspapers explaining that Russia was far too anarchic to render diplomatic entreaties of any value. "In the conditions of social disorder which actually exist in Russia," the statement read, "the president does not see that any action can be taken by this government at present which will be of any benefit to the unfortunate sufferers for whom we feel such keen sympathy."[33]

Roosevelt's reasoning here was probably genuine. After all, he had been willing to exert pressure, both publicly and privately, on the Russians at various points throughout his presidency. What made this juncture different was the shambolic state of affairs bedeviling the

Russian Empire. The October Manifesto—the kind of reform that American Jewry had long sought—had resulted not in liberation but rather devastation for Russian Jews. In all likelihood, Roosevelt sincerely believed that speaking out now would be negligible or even counterproductive. Secretary Root's counsel mattered, too. He almost certainly helped persuade Roosevelt that inaction was advisable. But most American Jews did not share that calculus; they wanted a robust response from their government. Whatever the president's rationale, the goodwill he had earned from previously supporting Jewish causes would not insulate him from criticism moving forward.

With Russia devolving, Roosevelt fretted that his chief envoy to St. Petersburg was absent from his post. The president had appointed a new American ambassador to Russia, George Meyer, who had overlapped with Roosevelt at Harvard. But Meyer, at this crucial crossroads in Russian history, was back in his native Massachusetts visiting his wife and children. "I think you should be in St. Petersburg now and that you ought not to delay one day," Roosevelt telegraphed.[34] Meyer proved reluctant to leave quite yet. He was a dedicated family man whose daughter was ailing from appendicitis and had just undergone an operation. Meyer told the president that he hoped to wait "until she is out of danger."[35] In turn, Roosevelt expressed obligatory concern for the daughter's well-being but reiterated the urgency in Russia. "I should have asked you to start for St. Petersburg three weeks ago," Roosevelt reflected regretfully. "During these three weeks, the one place where it was really very important that we should have an ambassador was St. Petersburg.... You should be there at the earliest possible moment."[36] But Meyer lingered as Russia imploded.

American Jewry—divided by class, religiosity, politics, and country of origin—united in the face of Russian butchery. Elements from New York City's diverse Jewish communities convened at Temple Emanu-El to establish a relief committee that would channel funds to victims in Russia. The initial contributions from that evening totaled an impressive $56,800 ($2 million today). Roosevelt's two most important Jewish advisors, Jacob Schiff and Oscar Straus, were featured speakers. Schiff recounted to the crowd his fruitless cable to Witte and relayed that he was coordinating relief efforts with prominent European Jews, including Lord Rothschild in Britain. When Schiff read aloud telegrams from Russian Jews pleading for assistance, the crowd cried out: "We will help!"[37]

Oscar Straus, in his own remarks at the gathering, tried to buffer the administration from possible complaints about its passivity. He recalled his recent trip to the White House where he had convened with Roosevelt. "I found our great president as shocked and horrified as we are, and with his heart full of sympathy for our stricken people," Straus assured the audience. He added, "I did not ask him to take any step" because presidential action might unwittingly prompt "greater catastrophes" and exacerbate the "unbearable burden" upon Russian Jewry. In an early indication that Straus's prestige in the Jewish community would not suffice to shield Roosevelt, a subsequent orator took the floor and called for thousands of "Hebrew defenders" to march on Washington in a bid to jolt the president into motion.[38]

The pressure on Roosevelt was only just beginning. Shortly after the Emanu-El fundraiser, newspapers throughout the country printed a plea sent to the president by Simon Wolf, the former head of B'nai B'rith. Wolf's message tried to appeal to Roosevelt as a decisive leader: "The man that sidetracked precedents by ending the coal strike, the man that conjured [peace] between Russia and Japan, and who has in a hundred ways shown marvelous versatility and courage—can he not take the initiative and bring about [a] concert of action to stem the cruelties in Russia?"[39] Wolf had long been an ardent Roosevelt supporter who worked hand-in-glove with the president on the Kishinev Petition, the administration's signature achievement for Jewry. It is thus striking that an ally like Wolf was now pushing Roosevelt so publicly.[40]

Not all voices in the Jewish community were inclined to resort to flattery in the hopes of cajoling the president. A Democratic-leaning paper, the *Hebrew Standard*, was underwhelmed by Roosevelt's claim that Russian disarray precluded American intervention. "It is said that there is no responsible government in Russia," the paper noted. "All the more reason that the rest of the 'civilized' world should step in." True, the president had voiced compassion for the Jewish victims in Russia, but the *Hebrew Standard* thought that such "honeyed phrases" rang hollow as the corpses piled high. The paper bemoaned, "President Roosevelt is sympathetic. We Jews are sick of sympathy. . . . We demand action." The *Hebrew Standard* also accused America of hypocrisy, recalling that the nation had gone beyond diplomatic protest and actually taken up arms for what was considered a humanitarian cause: Cuban rebellion against Spanish rule in 1898. It was little coincidence that the editorialist here alluded to a war with which Roosevelt himself was so closely associated.[41]

As the press printed graphic first-hand accounts of the carnage, donations from across the United States flooded into the relief committee's coffers.[42] Newspapers would announce in each successive issue the latest philanthropic totals, which tallied more than $500,000 (over $17 million today) after just nine days.[43] Some of the country's most renowned Gentiles, including Andrew Carnegie, gave substantial sums to the relief committee.[44] Jacob Schiff praised his Christian friends for their largesse, writing one of them, "It is encouraging to feel that in misfortune, at least the whole world is akin."[45] Although Schiff's comment about the "whole world" was overbroad—Western Europe, for example, wasn't quite so forthcoming with its commiseration—the vast outpouring of compassion from Americans was undeniable.

Meetings were organized throughout the United States, usually in synagogues, to pay respect to the dead and give succor to the living.[46] Many of these gatherings called on Roosevelt to abandon his passivity. At a packed synagogue in Pittsburgh, attendees passed resolutions that beseeched the president to intervene in Russia.[47] So did a group of Jewish veterans of the Spanish-American War based in Harlem.[48] Although

FIGURE. 6.2. Americans donate fulsomely to the pogrom survivors. *Source*: "Hands across the Sea," *Chicago Tribune*, circa November 1905.

Jews organized most demonstrations, many Gentiles participated and even hosted. The Warren Avenue Baptist Church in Boston, for instance, invited a local rabbi named Charles Fleischer to address the congregation. "We have been told that neither as president nor as man can Theodore Roosevelt say anything to Russia in the present crisis," Fleischer told the churchgoers, adding, "I do not believe it." Rabbi Fleischer acknowledged that an American entreaty to Russia would be "unconventional and undiplomatic" but urged Roosevelt to buck any "custom which makes such cowards of us all."[49]

Christian clergymen joined in the admonitions. At a Baptist church in New York, an interfaith audience of Jews and Christians heard the pleas of a prominent preacher who suggested that Roosevelt—if constrained from speaking out on the nation's behalf—should at least speak out on his own. "Perhaps our fearless president can do nothing as president, but I tell you that he can do almost anything simply as Theodore Roosevelt," the reverend declared, eliciting an enthusiastic reaction from the crowd.[50] A similar scene unfolded at Grand Central Palace in midtown Manhattan, where the famous Christian theologian Lyman Abbott announced to an assemblage of six thousand Jews, "It is time for the United States government to interfere in the cause of humanity."[51] Notably, Abbot enjoyed a warm relationship with TR; that even Abbott would conspicuously pressure the Roosevelt administration testifies to the depth of resistance facing the president.[52]

Public officials began turning up at mass meetings where crowds matched moral outrage with financial contributions. The mayor of St. Louis surfaced at one such interfaith gathering in a synagogue.[53] Baltimore hosted a bipartisan affair at its city hall with the Republican mayor and Democratic governor of Maryland.[54] Meanwhile, at the Atlantic City pier, the Republican governor of New Jersey rallied a crowd of thousands, and a local congressman, also a Republican, expressly appealed to Roosevelt for action.[55] The presence of elected officials at these demonstrations—many of whom belonged to Roosevelt's own party—could have only intensified the pressure on the administration.

Secretary of State Elihu Root was more concerned about subduing American Jewish fervor than in alleviating its cause. In mid-November, Root met in person with Ambassador Meyer, who had journeyed from Boston to Washington and would shortly sail for St. Petersburg. Meyer recorded in his diary that Root asked him to prod Witte for some kind of statement that would "reassure the Jewish element [in America] and quiet public sentiment." Root also derided Jewish protests in the United States as self-interested, telling Meyer that "certain Jews in

America were merely striving for notoriety."⁵⁶ Root's comment here is deeply cynical given the desperate plight of Russian Jewry at that moment. Even an incorrigible antisemite like the British diplomat Cecil Spring Rice, a close friend of the president's, wrote to the first lady that he was aghast at the "inconceivable brutality" of the "savage attacks."⁵⁷

Over the ensuing days—as mass meetings, fundraising drives, and press coverage continued apace—it must have become increasingly clear to Root that he could not idle his way through the crisis. He personally sent a sizable check to the relief committee along with a note, republished in the papers, that was partly an expression of sympathy and partly a defense of the administration's inactivity. Root conveyed his compassion for "the unfortunate Jews who have been subjected to such dreadful cruelties" while nonetheless insisting that "we have little power to help them." He hoped that the "present disorder" would yield in time to a "better day of security and freedom" in the Russian Empire.⁵⁸

Around that same time, Root reached out to the embassy in St. Petersburg for more information. "Many influential Hebrews in this country are greatly distressed over reports of Jewish loss of life and suffering in recent outbreaks," he relayed. Root asked for numbers concerning the pogroms' victims—the deceased, the ailing, and the dispossessed.⁵⁹ With Ambassador Meyer on the long journey back to Russia, it fell to his deputy to notify Washington of whatever details could be confirmed about Jewish "destitution" across the empire.⁶⁰ The situation remained perilous for Russian Jews. Although the initial twelve-day killing spree of Jews had subsided, pogroms were still breaking out with some regularity. Survivors were left tending to their ravaged communities across the Pale. And Russian society more broadly continued to convulse with chaos.⁶¹

★ ★ ★

In late November, Roosevelt showed that he was willing to lobby on behalf of Jews overseas—albeit in the Arab world. The president was then helping organize the Algeciras Conference, set to take place the following year in Spain. There the great powers of Europe, together with the United States and Morocco, would convene to arbitrate tensions between France and Germany over their conflicting ambitions for Morocco's future. Just as the Russo-Japanese peace negotiations had presented America with an opportunity to press for concessions on Jewish rights, the Algeciras Conference held out the same promise that the United States might successfully shoehorn Jewish issues into an unrelated international event. Per usual, it was the ubiquitous Jacob Schiff who had brought up the matter with the Roosevelt administration, sharing with Elihu Root a report about conditions of Moroccan Jewry produced by the French-Jewish organization *Alliance Israélite Universelle*.[62]

That report—which turned out to be riddled with inaccuracies—outlined the putative degradations of Jewish life. Jews were confined to residences in ghettos that were locked in the evenings. Walking canes were forbidden for Jews, even for the elderly or infirm among them. Nor could Jews wear shoes; locals would toss hot coals and glass shards at Jewish feet as something of a hobby. Severe restrictions limited Jewish travel and emigration. Moroccan courts banned Jewish testimony. The government levied special taxes on Jews and tightly regulated Jewish commercial activity, even forcing Jews to work on Shabbat.[63]

The administration would find out two months later that these allegations of Moroccan prejudice were variously erroneous or misleading.[64] But Schiff, Root, and Roosevelt took them at face value for the time being and proceeded accordingly. At the president's behest, Root instructed Henry White—the American ambassador who would represent the United States at Algeciras—to inject the Jewish Question into the conference agenda. Perhaps America could rally the great powers to support religious liberty in Morocco.

Secretary Root conveyed to Ambassador White that Moroccan Jews "appear to suffer from painful and injurious restrictions" that would be "hard now to ignore." He enclosed the report from the *Alliance* and stressed that Roosevelt himself wanted White to prioritize the issue: "It is the president's wish that you give the subject your earnest attention and endeavor in all proper ways to impress its importance upon your colleagues in the conference."[65] Accompanying these formal instructions to White, Root included a private note underscoring the utility of standing up for Jews in Morocco in order to counterbalance the administration's policy of abstention in Russia. "It would be very opportune," Root explained, "because our immense Jewish population is now naturally much excited over the cruelties in Russia, and it is very difficult for many of them to understand why our government cannot interfere."[66] This pending diplomatic play regarding Morocco was not yet made public nor did it promise to yield results until the conference concluded in the spring of 1906. But, if successful, it might eventually reverse some of the present damage to Roosevelt's relationship with American Jews.

The president's amenability to American interference in Morocco, even as he remained motionless on Russia, offers an instructive comparison. Plainly, Roosevelt was still prepared to leverage his nation's influence for the benefit of Jewry abroad, provided he found the particular conditions favorable. His approach to the Algeciras Conference thus lends credibility to the idea that Roosevelt wasn't coldly seizing on Russian upheaval as a convenient pretext to pursue a do-nothing policy; rather, it appears he honestly believed that U.S. intervention on behalf of Russian Jews might only worsen their situation. It is otherwise difficult to comprehend why he resisted the politically popular option of capitulating to America's public uproar over the pogroms.

Given Roosevelt's restraint on Russia, Schiff resolved to make diplomatic moves of his own with St. Petersburg. He communicated directly to Witte his view that the Russian authorities had "instigated" the atrocities. Schiff well knew that the premier stood apart from the reactionary elements within the state apparatus, and he told Witte that he was praying for Witte's success. Recall that in Portsmouth, Witte had warned Schiff and his fellow Jewish leaders that a sweeping enactment of religious freedom in Russia would foment antisemitism. Schiff now acknowledged Witte's grisly prescience on that score but still argued against Russian appeasement of the antisemitic mobs, insisting that it was "doubly proper and important that no step backward be taken, and that the Jewish subjects of the czar be vouchsafed every civic right." Failure to do so, Schiff warned, would ensure that Russia remained a pariah state on the global stage.[67]

★ ★ ★

Against the backdrop of untold Jewish suffering in Russia, synagogues across the United States took a brief respite from their sorrow to celebrate a landmark occasion at home: the 250th anniversary of communal Jewish life in America.[68] The most illustrious commemoration took place in New York's Carnegie Hall in late November. More than five thousand people squeezed into the famed venue, which was grandly decorated for the event. Coats of arms, representing each state in the Union, adorned the boxes on the lower tier. The mezzanine featured a series of golden shields, symbolizing the Holy City of Jerusalem. And American flags festooned the packed galleries above. Jacob Schiff presided, with notable speakers including the mayor and governor as well as former president Grover Cleveland. Among the evening's highlights was a performance by fifty cantors, clad in black and arranged in a semicircle, who sang the Jewish hymn "Adon Olam" in accompaniment with the New York Symphony Orchestra.[69]

Prior to the event, Schiff had asked that Roosevelt furnish a letter to be read aloud at Carnegie Hall. The president may have rebuffed Jewish pleas for the past month regarding Russia, but this much he could do. As TR's words were recited to the crowd by one of the evening's speakers, loud applause broke out every few sentences.[70] Roosevelt's letter explained that he didn't normally accede to such requests for various celebrations—the solicitations were unending and he had to avoid favoritism—but he would "make an exception in this case because [of] the lamentable and terrible suffering to which so many of the Jewish people in other lands have been subjected." The Jewish-American experience, the letter declared, demonstrated that Jews exhibit "fine qualities of citizenship" when they "enjoy the benefits of free institutions and equal treatment before the law." Although Roosevelt didn't mention Russia by name, few in Carnegie Hall could have missed his implication that Russia ought to look to America for the right answer to the Jewish Question.[71]

The remainder of the letter described the Jewish community in terms that seemed designed to implicitly counter antisemitic stereotypes.

Whereas American nativists saw Jewish immigration as a threat to the country's founding character, Roosevelt trumpeted the historical truth that Jews had been central to American democracy from its inception. "During the Revolutionary period," he recounted, "they aided the cause of liberty by serving in the Continental Army and by substantial contributions to the empty treasury of the infant republic." Some in Roosevelt's genteel circles engaged in a kind of moderate antisemitism wherein assimilated Jews of Central European origin passed social muster, while the indigent masses from Eastern Europe were met with contempt. Yet the president hailed both Jewish subgroups, lauding the work ethic and patriotism not just of established Jewish families but also the more recent Jewish "refugees reduced to the dire straits of penury and misery."[72]

Roosevelt further insisted that Jews could be Jews *and* Americans; they needn't shed their particular religious identity to lay claim to a common civic one. "While the Jews of the United States . . . have remained loyal to their faith and their race traditions, they have become indissolubly incorporated in the great army of American citizenship," TR proclaimed. Many Gentiles would make homogenization the price of acceptance for Jews, but the president here advanced a decidedly pluralistic vision for Jewish-American life.[73] (Two years later, when a hotel in New York tried to exclude Jews, a judge ruled against the hotel and quoted Roosevelt's foregoing letter in his legal opinion.[74])

New York City resumed its role as the epicenter of Jewish protest the following week. Amid a mass demonstration whose size was surely unprecedented in American Jewish history, the usual bustle of activity on the Lower East Side came to a standstill. A mournful procession of some one hundred thousand Jews wound its way through the cramped streets of their neighborhood, culminating in Union Square. Along the route, the sounds of weeping mingled with funeral melodies and prayers.[75] Meanwhile, the relief committee announced, less than three weeks since its fundraising campaign began, that it had topped an astounding $1,000,000 in donations (over $35 million today).[76]

Jewish leaders decided to press the Roosevelt administration yet again in early December, undoubtedly hopeful that the unrelenting public agitation would soften the government's stance. When a relief committee member issued a plea to Elihu Root's deputy, the State Department line remained unbending: "I sincerely wish that this department had the power to relieve the unfortunate people with whom we sympathize so deeply." Simon Wolf—the former B'nai B'rith president who unsuccessfully pressured Roosevelt the month prior—now tried his luck with Secretary Root. But Root's view was fixed: so long as Russia was seized by acute instability, diplomatic overtures were ill-advised. Root's reply to Wolf, which was reprinted in the press, assured him that "the problem is one which strongly attracts the sympathetic attention of this government." Should the Russians adopt a "more liberal form of government," along with the resumption of law and order, then the Roosevelt administration might well attempt to "exert efficient and good influence toward the liberal treatment of all Jews in Russia."[77] Yet the set of preconditions that Root spelled out for American intervention looked increasingly elusive as Russia's nihilistic spiral showed few signs of slowing.

Back in St. Petersburg, Ambassador Meyer's aide, Vezey, conveyed a deep sense of distress in a letter to Meyer, who was making his way through Europe en route to Russia. "One has the feeling of living over a volcano," Vezey remarked. He anticipated the prospect of fresh violence on an alarming scale: "Now all are armed, and if it comes to a conflict, it will not be so easy to put down the rabble."[78]

When Meyer himself finally set foot back on Russian soil, his assessment of conditions on the ground was equally bleak. He told Senator Henry Cabot Lodge that the Russian "government is showing the same incompetency as to handling the internal situation as they did in the late war." By Meyer's lights, Witte was mired in a nigh impossible situation, bereft of support from any faction: "The reactionists are plotting against Witte, and the liberals do not believe in his integrity." Nor did Witte have the political instincts to navigate such treacherous terrain. "He is a financier, not a statesman or even a practical politician," Meyer sneered. Ambassador Meyer was also skeptical that the Russian populace could be pacified, relaying to Senator Lodge, "the people are all nearly crazy here and are not contented with any concessions." Amid frighteningly volatile circumstances, no one could be sure what each new morning might bring. "One day we are told there will be a general strike, another that Witte is to resign and a military dictator to succeed him," Meyer reported. "Everything in fact is rumored, from the flight of the czar down."[79]

Even Jacob Schiff now conceded to Roosevelt that, at the present moment, diplomacy would be futile. With "Witte's government tottering" and "not likely to last many days," any protest from the Roosevelt administration would probably come to naught, Schiff acknowledged. For TR, that reality meant his only option was inaction. For Schiff, it meant justification for a far more audacious move: military invasion—or at least the threat of it. Schiff reminded Roosevelt of recent precedent for America's resort to armed intervention on humanitarian grounds, precedent that the Rough Rider knew intimately. "You willingly took your own life into your hands to help to prevent the oppression of the Cuban people," Schiff recalled. Surely the "horrors now occurring in Russia" would similarly warrant martial measures to preempt additional "slaughter," which Russia's own government "declares it is powerless to prevent." More specifically, Schiff advised Roosevelt to solicit congressional authorization for a multilateral effort in tandem with the great powers of Europe. A mere signal of possible military operations would likely serve the intended purpose, Schiff predicted, thus sparing the United States from actually hazarding American lives. The specter of foreign troops on Russian soil would "rally national self-respect in Russia" and facilitate the ascension of a "proper party of law and order." If Roosevelt took that kind of bold step—or, perhaps more accurately, that kind of bold bluff—the American people would stand firmly behind their president, Schiff insisted.[80]

Roosevelt balked. Although his replies to Schiff were typically prompt, in this instance TR uncharacteristically dithered for nearly a week before responding to the letter. "I did not answer it because, my dear Mr. Schiff, I must frankly say that it would be difficult to answer it without hurting your feelings," Roosevelt confessed. The remainder of the president's missive bordered on caustic. He derided Schiff's proposal as "simply nonsense." No pressure on Russia could possibly bear fruit when "there is revolt in every quarter of the empire among every class of people and the bonds of social order everywhere are relaxed." Roosevelt would not turn the czar's Winter Palace into the next San Juan Heights nor bluff as if he might. "We should act in accordance with the [Great] Plains adage when I was in the ranch business, 'Never draw unless you mean to shoot,'" the cowboy-turned-president told Schiff. Hollow threats of military intervention would not only fail to benefit Russian Jewry but confine America to a "humiliating and ridiculous" position. And Roosevelt dismissed Schiff's idea for a transatlantic coalition as "of course wholly chimerical."[81]

Roosevelt's retort to a loyal, and powerful, ally is striking for its barbed tone. The president himself apparently sensed as much, mustering a conciliatory word for the well-intentioned Schiff in a postscript. "I sympathize thoroughly with your feelings, wrought up as they are and ought to be by the dreadful outrages," he offered, adding, "Anything I can do I will do, but I will not threaten aimlessly and thereby do harm."[82] Roosevelt resolved to bide his time unless and until Russian affairs less starkly resembled a descent into anarchy.

At least the president could still count on the only Jew in America who rivaled Schiff in stature: Oscar Straus. Roosevelt divulged to Straus, "By the way, our good friend Jacob H. Schiff became hysterical over what I could do about the dreadful atrocities perpetrated upon the Jews in Russia. I enclose a copy of my letter to him." TR was grateful that Straus wasn't making comparable demands: "Thank Heaven, you kept your head, as you always do, my dear fellow!"[83] Straus replied that he had attempted to leverage his own credibility with American Jewry to "buffer" Roosevelt from critics. But those voices agitating for American action were unmoored from reality, lamented Straus, as "they crown you with a halo of international omnipotence" even though events in Russia lay beyond the president's control. Straus concurred with Roosevelt that bids at external inference in a country lurching toward collapse would prove ineffective at best and inimical at worst. He further posited that Russia's upheaval was on the same inescapable trajectory as the ill-fated French Revolution. "The logic of history, said Bismarck, is as exacting as Prussia's accounting office," Straus quipped, borrowing language from the quotable German statesman.[84]

Having reassured Roosevelt of his personal loyalty, Oscar Straus did gently nudge the president on the question of immigration. Should the Jewish exodus from Russia to America intensify, Straus opined, it might behoove the president to make a statement embracing the newcomers. But then Straus tempered his proposal, anticipating that events would render such a statement unnecessary. He expected that Russian-Jewish immigration would actually diminish "as the hope for enlarged rights and ultimate freedom in Russia near realization." Given that Straus thought Witte's government was doomed to failure, these latter remarks imply his belief that, somehow, a liberal democracy in Russia would emerge from the bedlam.[85]

Witte himself shared in Roosevelt's belief that no progress could be made for Russian Jews under prevailing conditions. In the first lethal weeks following the October Manifesto, the embattled premier had clung to delusions that he might yet operationalize its liberal promises.[86] But by December, he came to concede that the outlook for Jewry was hopeless. Witte remarked to the Western press that no one could escape the manifesto's unwitting lesson: if the Russian state were to "proclaim equality of rights" for Jews, it would "provoke appalling bloodshed." Under that scenario, the only way for the authorities to protect Jews from pogromists would be for "the Russian government to shoot down the Russian people, and that is inconceivable." This was the unforgiving calculus of a society rotting with antisemitism—Russia's Jews could endure *either* the indignities of second-class citizenship and periodic carnage *or* nominal pretenses to first-class citizenship and mass carnage.[87]

A Jewish paper in San Francisco, *Emanu-El*, was exasperated that Roosevelt seemed content to leave Russia to its own barbarity. "Every country may slaughter its Jews to suit itself; that is the courteous rule of non-interference in the internal affairs of other nations," *Emanu-El* wrote with disdain. "President Roosevelt, Russia's great and good friend, finds it impossible to even lodge a protest on behalf of the

American nation."⁸⁸ To be sure, the principle of noninterference had given the administration some hesitation in censuring Russia in prior episodes, but *Emanu-El* was off the mark at this particular juncture. Roosevelt was now citing a different rationale entirely—the havoc enveloping Russian society—to justify presidential passivity.

Meanwhile, the fundraising drive for pogrom survivors continued to elicit the generosity of American donors and even some celebrities. A benefit performance at Broadway's Casino Theatre featured Sarah Bernhardt, a famous French actress of Jewish birth and Catholic upbringing who identified with both religious traditions. A number of other actresses were on hand in the lobby, selling flowers and playbills at prices that were benevolently inflated to boost the philanthropic total. "The prices, however, were no more objectionable than the smiles that went with them," the *New York Times* reported, "and this feminine lobbying proved a popular and profitable device." The one-act play was followed by a special appearance from the legendary Mark Twain, who regaled the packed audience with his masterful storytelling.⁸⁹

Not long after the performance, a Russian revolutionary in exile asked Twain whether he was rightly proud of America's considerable philanthropy for pogrom victims. Twain was not. He claimed, inaccurately, that Jews alone contributed to the relief efforts, and Twain expressed embarrassment that his fellow Christians—whom he referred to as "Americans"—withheld their charity. "That money came not from Americans, it came from Jews," Twain alleged. "Suffering can always move a Jew's heart and tax his pocket to the limit. He will be at your mass meetings. But if you find any Americans there put them in a glass case and exhibit them. It will be worth fifty cents a head to go and look at that show." Twain's distinction between "Jews" and "Americans" implied that one could not belong to both groups; he was distancing Jews from American identity even as he was exalting Jews above Gentiles.⁹⁰ Sometimes Jews themselves in the United States used "Americans" in that same exclusionary sense. The most respected Jew in the country,

Oscar Straus, employed "American" as a synonym for Anglo-Saxon in a press interview where he was inveighing against antisemitic stereotypes.[91] Twain and Straus, then, both demonstrate a counterintuitive reality: the contemporary defense of Jews at times relied upon tropes that are recognizably prejudicial by modern lights.

Two Democratic congressmen from New York City stepped into the yawning gap that separated America's public uproar from Roosevelt's strategic inertia. The first, Henry Goldfogle, submitted a resolution to the House decrying the butchery of Russian Jews. Goldfogle's resolution employed measured language with respect to the Roosevelt administration, asking "respectfully" that the president make diplomatic overtures to Russia "if he finds it not incompatible with the public interest."[92] His colleague, William "Plain Bill" Sulzer, was less temperate in a stemwinder from the House floor that drew applause from fellow representatives. He remarked with incredulity, "I know it is said by those who speak for the administration that our government can do nothing, that the president and secretary of state cannot act and have no power, according to international law, to intervene." But America hadn't been hamstrung in its condemnation of Armenian persecution in Turkey or its full-blown war on Cuban soil, he noted.[93] Sulzer's reasoning here was disingenuous—Roosevelt and Root had consistently pointed to Russian disarray, not international law, as the basis for their quietude.

A Jewish outlet of Democratic persuasion, the *Hebrew Standard*, was also unsympathetic to Roosevelt but at least willing to engage the debate on TR's own terms. "It has been remarked with diplomatic regrets that the president cannot intercede in view of the fact that there is no responsible government at present in Russia," the *Hebrew Standard* acknowledged. Skeptical that Roosevelt's hands were tied quite so tightly, the paper mused, "It certainly seems strange that the man who was able to bring some sort of pressure to bear upon Japan to accept Russia's terms is powerless to stop the carnival of bloodshed." The *Hebrew Standard* suggested that the president was inadvertently culpable for the pogroms because the peacemaking in Portsmouth—which with Roosevelt was so closely associated—prevented the Japanese from delivering a "smashing defeat" to their Russian adversaries. Had the czarist regime crumbled at Japan's hands, then the ensuing pogrom wave wouldn't have come to pass. Naturally a Democratic paper like the *Hebrew Standard* would be disposed to critique TR. More telling, perhaps, was the relative silence from pro-Roosevelt quarters that would normally have defended him on Jewish issues.[94]

Still, disturbing developments in Russia could have only reinforced the president's inclination toward abstention. Ambassador Meyer reported to Roosevelt in late December that the czarist regime was making a fervent stand for its survival. "Reaction, during the last few days, has set in," wrote Meyer—the Russian government was shutting down the press, imprisoning editors, and unleashing armed forces on labor unions. But the troops weren't necessarily reliable. As Meyer disclosed, the army was plagued by "insubordination" in various cities throughout the empire, including the capital. His overall assessment was bleak: "Matters must soon come to a crisis."[95] Indeed, that very day, a strike commenced in Moscow that immobilized the city and quickly turned violent. As the Moscow uprising spurred similar revolts elsewhere in Russia, the government responded with brute force.[96]

Meyer spoke with a shockingly relaxed czar during a New Year's reception for diplomats at the imperial palace outside St. Petersburg. Czar Nicholas seemed obtuse to the turmoil upending his country. The American ambassador related the conversation in a cable to Roosevelt, scoffing at the czar's naïveté: "He has a sublime faith in God . . . not at all appreciating that God prefers to help those who try to help themselves."[97] In the face of deadly insurrection, Nicholas's nonchalance could not have inspired Roosevelt's confidence.

January, however, proved to be a good month for the czar. His government's strategy of ruthlessly repressing the Russian people finally led to the restoration of order. Witte's aspirations aside, it had not been liberal reform that earned the people's respect but rather state violence that demanded it. Pogroms largely ceased as the government reestablished control. The authorities wouldn't tolerate homicidal rioting of any kind, even when directed at a widely loathed target like Jews. Before the October Manifesto, pogroms were of real utility to the state; they deflected the people's anger toward a vulnerable minority and away from the czarist kleptocracy that should have elicited their indignation. But the past several months had demonstrated that mob violence against Russian Jewry could coincide with broader anarchy that the regime might struggle to contain.[98]

While Russia's strife was subsiding, the commencement of the Algeciras Conference presented an opportunity for the president to score a palpable win on Jewish rights. America's ambassador for the summit, Henry White, was under straightforward instructions: make the plight of Moroccan Jewry an actionable issue at the conference. In mid-January, delegates began descending on the amiable tourist town of Algeciras on Spain's southern coast. Nested in a bay across from her more famous neighbor Gibraltar, Algeciras boasted an enviable supply of fresh oranges and bright homes befitting the Mediterranean scenery.[99] Ambassador White found that the Hotel de Ville, playing host to the conference proceedings, had been "handsomely arranged for the sittings."[100]

In the conference's opening days, White communicated to Secretary Root that the Roosevelt administration had been given flawed intelligence with respect to Moroccan Jewry. Recall that Jacob Schiff had forwarded to Root a study from a French-Jewish charity—the *Alliance Israélite Universelle*—enumerating the civil disabilities imposed on Moroccan Jews. White, in turn, had dispatched a Jewish-American diplomat, Lewis Einstein, to conduct a fact-finding mission. Einstein journeyed to Morocco before the conference and interviewed various Western experts on Morocco who were on hand for the negotiations in Algeciras. The results were in, and they largely undermined the claims by the *Alliance*.[101]

White relayed as much to Root and appended the text of Einstein's report, which determined that anti-Jewish "restrictions have been abolished or else have fallen into abeyance." Einstein continued, "Almost unknown to the outside world, a peaceful humanitarian reform has silently been accomplished, and the Jews of Morocco are well-nigh emancipated from the oppression which formerly burdened their lot." His report proceeded to debunk many of the specific allegations that the *Alliance* had made. Still, Moroccan-Jewish life was perhaps not quite as "enlightened" as Einstein's rosy portrait would have it. He tried to trivialize ongoing civil disabilities, writing for example, "That a Jew may not testify in court is more oppressive in theory than practice." For all Einstein's soft-pedaling, the fact remained that the *Alliance* had overstated the discrimination endured by Moroccan Jewry, giving Ambassador White pause about a formal remonstrance in Algeciras.[102]

White shared with Root yet another factor weighing against a censure of Morocco: Moroccan Jews themselves thought it ill-advised. They feared that the Moroccan sultan would take offense, given his relatively broad-minded attitude toward his Jewish subjects. "Anything in the nature of a complaint, they deem not only unjustified but prejudicial to their best interests," explained White. However, Moroccan Jews still wanted America to issue some kind of statement at the conference praising the sultan's liberality toward Jews while also prodding him to direct his state officials to act alike.[103]

To that end, two distinguished Moroccan Jews each proposed language that the U.S. government might adopt, which White forwarded to Root. The first Jew, Mr. Pimienta, advised that any declaration from the Roosevelt administration ought to credit the sultan for his "equity and goodwill" toward Jews. It should further convey America's hope that the sultan "see to it that his Jewish subjects may never be denied justice nor suffer violence" at the hands of his subordinates.[104] Pimienta reached out to the grand rabbi of Tangier, who sent his own substantially similar statement to Ambassador White. That these Moroccan Jews wanted the United States to promulgate a statement at all—one designed to preempt their maltreatment and even bloodshed—underscores that their condition wasn't as benign as Einstein's report insisted. The grand rabbi closed his message to White with an expression of gratitude: "I pray Almighty God to bestow His blessings on President Roosevelt."[105]

Ambassador White turned his attention to other conference matters in the subsequent weeks. In late March, with the conference still ongoing, White informed Secretary Root that he planned to submit the Moroccan-Jewish question to his fellow delegates in short order. But he was conflicted about how to proceed; Moroccan Jews desired a statement in language that might be too moderate to pass muster with their coreligionists back in America. "I fear the form suggested by [the] grand rabbi and others will be inadequate and unsatisfactory to our Jewish fellow citizens," White confessed, "and yet it would be unwise to say anything likely to be prejudicial to Jews in Morocco."[106] If true, it is highly ironic that American Jews—in a bid to support fellow Jews in Morocco—would be displeased with language that Moroccan Jews themselves preferred, language designed to ensure their good standing with the sultan. The Roosevelt administration had already suspected (in the case of Russia) that Jewish-American activism on behalf of Jews abroad might be ill-advised. Here was a striking indication that those suspicions had some merit.

Secretary Root replied to Ambassador White that, in light of the Einstein report, it was not "necessary or desirable" for America to seek from the conference any sort of sharp-elbowed protest regarding Morocco's treatment of its Jews. Whether to pursue even a tempered statement along the lines recommended by the grand rabbi, Root left to White's discretion. Root didn't address White's concerns about the potential dissatisfaction of American Jews with the kind of measured phrasing favored by their Moroccan coreligionists.[107]

Five days later, White formally solicited the conference delegates for mutual assent to a statement on Moroccan Jewry. The draft language from White was somewhat more pointed than that offered by Mr. Pimienta and the grand rabbi. While it did applaud the "equity and kindness" that the sultan extended to his Jewish subjects, the statement nonetheless contended that Moroccan officials "in the parts of the country far removed from the central power are not always sufficiently inspired with the feelings of tolerance and justice that animate their sovereign." Employing a French term, the statement affirmed the conference's "voeu" that the sultan would direct these errant authorities to emulate his own enlightened approach.[108] (White later explained to Root that he chose "voeu" because it is "stronger than the English word 'hope.'"[109]) Every delegate in succession spoke approvingly of White's proposal—even Russia's Count Cassini, who had peddled antisemitic fictions to the American press during his former stint as an ambassador in Washington.[110] The Moroccan delegation in Algeciras declared that the delegates' collective sentiment would command the attention of the sultan, who could be counted upon to perpetuate his longstanding liberality.[111]

These developments garnered mainstream press coverage across the United States.[112] Ambassador White received a note of appreciation from the *Alliance Israélite Universelle*, whose semi-inaccurate report had catalyzed his monthslong initiative. And the grand rabbi of Tangiers, on behalf of Moroccan Jewry at large, wrote a missive requesting that White "convey to President Roosevelt and the American government the expression of our grateful feelings for their noble and generous intervention."[113] Both Jewish and mainstream papers throughout the United States published the grand rabbi's letter.[114] The Algeciras Conference thus gave Roosevelt a public win for Jews, albeit a minor one given his strained relationship with American Jewry amid the Russian bloodbath.

At the same time that White was raising the Jewish Question in Algeciras, the State Department learned that a fresh round of Russian pogroms might be in the offing. The prior two months had been relatively quiet ones for Russian Jewry after the devastation of last fall and early winter. But now Easter—a holiday that had coincided with anti-Jewish violence in the recent past—was imminent. American Jews with relatives in Russia were highly anxious that premeditated pogroms were afoot, and their fears came to the State Department's attention. The deputy secretary of state cabled Ambassador Meyer in St. Petersburg, asking him for details about how Russian authorities planned to forestall Jewish deaths. Meyer was also instructed to discuss the issue with Britain's ambassador to Russia; the British, compelled by their own

Jewish community, were themselves soliciting information from the Russian government about possible pogroms.[115]

Two days later, Ambassador Meyer wrote Secretary Root, "Witte appears to be very sanguine that there will be no Jewish troubles." Meyer relayed further that Russia's provincial governors had been directed to hold police accountable for the preservation of peace. Still, Meyer didn't expect an entirely nonviolent Easter. He warned Root, "I believe there is liability of some disturbances between Jews and subordinate authorities on account of the ill feeling which exists, but they should not be extensive if the governors of the various provinces act in good faith." By Russia's abysmal standards, this was promising news for Jewry.[116]

Meanwhile, Oscar Straus—apparently unaware of Meyer's inquiry—raised concerns with Roosevelt directly about imminent carnage in Russia. "I know you have so many things upon your mind," Straus began, "therefore pardon me if I take the liberty of reminding you of your intention to speak with Baron Rosen [i.e., the Russian ambassador in Washington] regarding the threatening Russian massacres on Easter." Straus also shared with Roosevelt the anxieties of a British Jew and former MP, Sir Samuel Montagu, who was anticipating bloodshed.[117]

The president informed Straus that he had actually already met with Baron Rosen, who made "the positive statement that Russia was fully alive to the situation and was taking every step to prevent any trouble to the Jews." TR divulged another detail from his meeting with the Russian ambassador: Rosen favorably remembered Straus's even-keeled comportment in Portsmouth, where Rosen had been party to Witte's conversation with the Jewish delegation the previous summer. But not everyone in New Hampshire had impressed Rosen. As the president now revealed, "I am bound to add that he stated that another prominent Jewish gentleman . . . had prejudiced Witte against the cause for which he was pleading, by his attitude"—a barely veiled reference to the outspoken Jacob Schiff.[118]

Between the inquiry that Ambassador Meyer made of Witte and the same that President Roosevelt made of Rosen, American diplomacy was once more at work for Russian Jewry. The Roosevelt administration had publicly announced throughout Russia's turbulent period months earlier that future entreaties to the Russian state about Jewish safety would hinge upon the return of law and order. With the tumult now subsided, Roosevelt and his State Department were making good on their word.

Still, Roosevelt hardly relished being pushed to intervene in other countries' affairs, especially since such requests were so common. In the foregoing letter to Straus, the president was candid about his frustration with frequent calls for him to speak out not just for Jews but also for the persecuted Armenians in Turkey and the innocent civilians of the Congo Free State, which was then under the brutal reign of the Belgian king. Roosevelt lamented, "It is a literal physical impossibility to interfere in any of these cases, save in the most guarded manner." Given that America would never levy war against Russia because of the pogroms, TR maintained that it would be "futile, undignified, and mischievous" to overplay his hand. He resented that some Jewish advocates were obtuse to such difficulties. "All of this it is needless to write as far as you are concerned," the president assured Straus, "but there are some of your friends who need to have these considerations ever clearly before their eyes."[119] Jacob Schiff was unquestionably on Roosevelt's mind with this latter comment. The president did not here specify what his professed reluctance meant for the future of his foreign policy vis-à-vis Jewish issues. Whether he would stay the course of periodically pressing Russia or retreat from that approach remained unclear.

Straus cabled his British counterpart, Montagu, relaying that Roosevelt had raised concerns about anti-Jewish violence with the Russian ambassador in Washington. Montagu, in turn, asked Straus for permission to publicize that information, an idea that Straus forwarded to the White House. But Straus caveated Montagu's message with his own recommendation—the Roosevelt administration should take the initiative of trumpeting its measures for Russian Jewry. The benefits of publicity, Straus believed, were twofold: it would prevent the president from being subjected to additional requests for action from those who were unaware of his current efforts, and if Easter pogroms did take place, the public would know that the American government had at least tried to take preemptive steps.[120]

Roosevelt felt some misgivings about irking Russia with publicity. "She might readily be made sensitive by having it published that we are bringing pressure upon her," the president explained to Straus. But TR ultimately put those worries aside, greenlighting Straus to disseminate a short statement about the recent American inquiry. Roosevelt provided Straus with language setting forth that the Russian government had offered the United States "the most positive assurances" that it was taking due care to avert anti-Jewish violence. The president's draft statement continued, "The strictest orders have been given to local officials, who understand that they will be held responsible for any disturbance."[121] American newspapers published that revelation a few days later just after Easter, which turned out to be a mercifully uneventful one for Russia's Jews.[122]

Perhaps the Russian directive that local authorities were to keep the peace reflected the czarist regime's own desire for law and order, regardless of Roosevelt's preferences. Or maybe Russia was indeed spurred by the knowledge that it was under American scrutiny. Both factors were likely implicated to some degree. In either case, the fear of an Easter slaughter remained unrealized, and Straus credited the president. "He prevented the massacres," Straus wrote matter-of-factly to a White House aide.[123] The aide replied the next day, "It is very gratifying to know that the president's action was effective."[124]

The absence of atrocities against Jews on Easter didn't signal a diminution in Russian antisemitism. One indication that Judeophobia still had traction was Witte's marginalization within the state apparatus. He found himself sidelined by Czar Nicholas in part because Witte didn't share the czar's inveterate hatred for Jews. Witte was still technically premier, but his title grew increasingly nominal. Nicholas told his mother that Witte was "absolutely discredited with everybody, except perhaps the Jews abroad." When Witte asked the czar to lift Jewish quotas at Russian universities, Nicholas bluntly replied, "The Jewish question should be considered in its entirety only when I consider it appropriate"—which was to say, never.¹²⁵ Shortly after Easter, Witte resigned his post. He was uninterested in serving as liberal cover for reactionaries any longer. Reflecting on his departure from office, Witte explained, "I did not wish to be a cat's-paw for General Trepov . . . and a shield for the Black Hundreds."¹²⁶ Russia's regime was now rid of its most prominent advocate for Jewish rights.

Although Witte no longer offered the czar a facade of reformism, Nicholas could begrudgingly rely upon the newly convened Duma to that end. Ambassador Meyer showed little confidence in this incremental step toward democracy. He reported to Roosevelt, "Russia is entering upon a great experiment, ill prepared and really uneducated." The tension between the czar and the legislature was palpable—and likely unsustainable. Meyer elaborated, "I do not mean to imply that a crash is coming at once, but that sooner or later a struggle . . . between the Crown and the Duma, unless all signs fail, is more than probable."¹²⁷ If Russian Jews thought that the establishment of the Duma was a hopeful harbinger for their future, they would be disabused of their illusions before long.

Situated near the Pale of Settlement's western edge, Bialystok was predominantly Jewish—fully three-fourths of the city's residents were Jews. They thought their majority status offered them a buffer against the kind of violence exacted upon their coreligionists elsewhere in the empire. But their sizable population only served to make the city a target-rich environment for pogromists. Two months after a calm Easter, the feast day of Corpus Christi in mid-June quickly turned into mass murder on the streets of Bialystok.¹²⁸

The three-day massacre entailed unconscionable cruelty. Jews were ruthlessly battered to death, with some assailants continuing to bludgeon the victims' bodies long after their final breaths. "The faces of the dead have lost all human semblance," observed a newspaper correspondent, "and the corpses simply are crushed masses of flesh and bone soaking in blood."¹²⁹ Even by Russian standards, the extent of government complicity was damning. Troops and police alike were active in the barbarity, firing at defenseless Jews and sometimes bayonetting them. When the governor was informed of the deadly havoc, he bogusly blamed the Jews for provoking it with their revolutionary violence.[130] Some Jews managed to flee the city, but no safe haven awaited them. As one journalist reported, "Jews who escaped from Bialystok are wandering, starving, in the fields and woods."[131] The final death count placed the loss of life at upwards of seventy Jews, with about as many injured, and large numbers of Jewish homes and stores were left ransacked.[132]

Bialystok's butchery made front-page headlines across the United States—in large cities with many Jews and small towns with very few. Jacob Schiff expressed to Roosevelt his concerns about "the devilish proceedings at Bialystok" and forwarded "heartrending cablegrams from Russia" in the hopes that TR might initiate some kind of intervention. Schiff fully appreciated that the president had grown weary of such diplomatic endeavors, but the atrocities in Bialystok prompted Schiff to spend whatever capital he might have left. "I do know in advance that unfortunately nothing can be done by our government," Schiff conceded, anticipating Roosevelt's resistance. Still he expressed "the faint hope" that the administration might press the "Russian government, such as it is, to abstain from instigating the low populace to bloodshed." Schiff confessed his displeasure at leaning on Roosevelt anew—"I feel mortified that I have again to address you on this depressing subject"—but asked TR to consider the recent carnage to be sufficient "excuse."[133] It is highly likely that Oscar Straus advised Schiff to proceed cautiously here given that the president had vented to Straus before Easter about certain "friends" in the Jewish community whose repeated solicitations were becoming nettlesome.[134]

Roosevelt's response to Schiff was restrained, indicating he would discuss the matter with his secretary of state but commit to nothing more. "You know how deeply we sympathize with your feelings and how shocked and horrified we are at what has occurred in Russia," he offered, "but you know also how well-nigh impossible it is to accomplish anything but harm by interference."[135] Two days later, Simon Wolf visited the White House to discuss Bialystok with the president. Wolf had been a dependable Roosevelt ally until the horrific events of the prior fall, when he publicly and unsuccessfully tried to prod the president into action. Now Wolf was attempting the same, this time in person. Although Russia was no longer in a state of mass upheaval, Roosevelt's answer remained unchanged: American involvement was untenable.[136]

There was some plausibility in the president's prediction that American interference might backfire. It would have come as little surprise to Roosevelt that his name had been invoked as a means of whipping up anti-Jewish sentiment just before the Bialystok pogrom. A circular distributed to troops in Bialystok falsely asserted that Russian Jewry was agitating against the motherland at the behest of President Roosevelt and King Edward of England. This Anglo-American duo had allegedly operated through Jews in an unsuccessful bid to coax Russian soldiers to break ranks in the late war against Japan. Then, the American president and English king purportedly turned their sights on sabotaging the czar's regime by abetting Jewish revolutionaries in Russia. The circular claimed that this "fierce foreign foe sets his snares through his friends, always the Jews" in a bid to "seize altogether the land of our fathers." The *Quarterly Review*, a British periodical, would later report that the Russian military had not merely consumed but actually printed this propaganda.[137] With the government having regained control of the country for several months now, apparently the authorities deemed it safe to once more permit and even promote mob violence against Jews without fear that broader chaos might ensue. And any public criticism that Roosevelt made of Russia could provide grist for antisemitic conspiracy theories fueling such violence.

Mourners gathered on the Lower East Side at the oldest Russian synagogue in America to grieve for Bialystok's fallen Jews. The crowd was so immense that it spilled out the building's doors onto Norfolk Street. Although the synagogue was Orthodox, the principal speaker was a reform rabbi, Joseph Silverman—an indication that Russian antisemitism was yet again uniting an American Jewish community that otherwise had numerous schisms. The rabbi read aloud the recent message from Roosevelt to Jacob Schiff about the hazards of intervention, and Silverman encouraged Jewry's deference to the president's discretion. "We must abide by the dictate of our own chief magistrate," insisted the rabbi. "If he thinks that the time is not ripe, then there shall be no diplomatic interference."[138]

But as it turned out, Roosevelt wasn't confining himself to diplomatic silence. Rather, he was maintaining the public illusion of nonintervention. TR wagered that covert solicitation, not overt censure, would elicit a more constructive reaction from the prideful Russians. He disclosed to Schiff, "I do not wish to say to anyone as yet what was done. The efficacy of anything that is done depends largely upon their being no symptom of offense to the Russian authorities." The president here intimated that a quiet appeal had already been made to St. Petersburg; in reality the administration was still finalizing how to proceed.[139]

Roosevelt then asked Schiff, if possible, to impress upon Jews in the United States that their conventional reliance on well-publicized clamor to support Russian Jewry would only undercut the administration's clandestine efforts to that same end. "Every public expression on their part looking to the interference of our government with Russia tends to defeat its own purpose and to make it more difficult for the [American] government to act," the president complained. "They simply hamper us in the effort to do whatever is possible and if they arouse antagonism in Russia, foredoom any such effort to failure." Roosevelt doubted that the leaders of American protests were even well-intentioned, contending, "There are demagogues engaged in these meetings whose purpose is not to do good to the poor sufferers in Russia, but to strengthen themselves with their people at home"—by this, he meant Democrats trying to gin up Jewish votes.[140]

Roosevelt's foregoing comment about "these meetings" wasn't an allusion to ongoing public demonstrations in America, as there simply hadn't been an eruption of mass meetings in the week since the Bialystok pogrom. Instead, it appears that Roosevelt was referencing the protests of the prior fall, and he anxiously anticipated that American Jewry might soon revive its public pressure campaign. The president warned Schiff that if his administration did push Russia publicly, it would inflict the dual harm of worsening Jewish life there and relegating the United States to an "undignified position" on the world stage.[141] Meanwhile, down the street from the White House, Congress was passing a joint resolution that expressed "hearty sympathy" for Bialystok's victims but notably avoided any criticism of the Russian government or any call for American intercession.[142]

The following day Secretary Root shared with Roosevelt draft language for a cable to St. Petersburg. That proposed cable directed Ambassador Meyer to "ascertain informally" from the Russians whether local officials in Bialystok were responsible for the pogroms, as was widely reported in the American press. Meyer was to convey the administration's belief that any local complicity surely ran counter to the central state's "true attitude," which Russia could reaffirm by holding "inculpated local officials" to account. Of course, the Roosevelt administration actually had little faith in the "true attitude" of the czar's regime; the State Department would be offering up a fiction and hoping that the Russian government might go along with it. Strikingly, the draft cable was candid that the administration's aim was to mollify popular uproar in the United States: Meyer was supposed to inquire whether the Russian government planned to "show its condemnation" and thereby "do away with the present unfortunate effect upon American public opinion."[143]

In forwarding this suggested language to the president, Root added his own ambivalent assessment of the draft cable. "I think it may do some good, though I do not feel sure of it," he confessed. "I do not know how it will be received. It may merely give offense. I am sure that to go further would do harm." And Root emphasized that even if Roosevelt did approve the cable for transmission to Meyer, it ought not be released to the press. After all, Russia wouldn't want to look like Roosevelt's puppet. An inquiry from Meyer to the Russian foreign minister—if kept discreet—might help induce Russia to bring local authorities in Bialystok to justice because Russia could prosecute them without appearing to have acted at America's behest. Roosevelt surely appreciated better than anyone that Root's insistence on "absolutely confidential communication" between America and Russia meant that the president wouldn't reap the political benefits at home of publicly stretching himself abroad. But Root was certain that staying sub rosa was necessary to avert further losses of Jewish life.[144] Roosevelt deferred to Root's discretion, agreeing to send the cable but keeping its existence from the newspapers.

The U.S. embassy in St. Petersburg received the cable the next morning. It was Ambassador Meyer's birthday, but he didn't take the day off. Instead, Meyer promptly requested a meeting with Count Izvolsky, the newly appointed Russian foreign minister, and was granted one for 4:30 that afternoon. Although the cable from Root to Meyer was written in cipher, the Russians had cracked the American code, so Izvolsky would have already seen Root's instructions prior to their conversation. Meyer himself was well aware that the Russians were in the habit of intercepting his cables from Washington. At their afternoon meeting, both statesmen partook in a bit of diplomatic fiction: Meyer told Izvolsky that he wanted to share with him a cable from Root, acting as if the cable would be unexpected news to the foreign minister; Izvolsky, in turn, pretended to be learning of the cable for the first time. Apparently, Izvolsky wasn't a very good performer. Meyer later wrote in his diary that Izvolsky's feigned ignorance was "unnatural."[145]

Having gotten through this rigmarole, Izvolsky informed Meyer of Russia's hard-line position: it would not entertain discussion of its internal affairs with a foreign power. Even though the cable from Washington was framed as merely a covert request for facts—and thus designed to avoid accusations that America was engaging in external interference—it was plainly a form of prodding. And the Russians saw it in exactly those terms, treating this bid at finesse as improper meddling. Izvolsky fell back on Russia's tried tactic of pointing out that the Roosevelt administration would not readily welcome Russian denunciation of American lynchings. As a modest concession, Izvolsky referred Meyer to a decree from the interior minister, promulgated after the Bialystok pogrom, declaring that "disorders of any kind, whether agrarian or anti-Jewish . . . must be suppressed in the most decisive manner." But the foreign minister would go no further. Ambassador Meyer found out the next day that his British counterpart in St. Petersburg, who had made similar inquiries of Izvolsky, met with comparable treatment. Meyer promptly communicated the whole of it to Root and later relayed the same in a letter to Roosevelt.[146]

TR aimed to placate Schiff, indicating that *something* had been done but withholding specific details. "I want to tell you that we have gone up to the very verge of receiving a rebuff that would put us in a very undignified and unpleasant position, in the effort to do what you suggested," the president divulged. "I do not wish to give you the particulars in writing, and I do not want you to quote what I am saying to you."[147] In turn, Schiff assured Roosevelt that this information would be held in "strict confidence." Still, Schiff was eager to learn more and shared that he would soon be visiting his son, whose new summer home was conveniently located in Oyster Bay near the president's own. "Perhaps you may then be willing to say something further to me," Schiff wrote nudgingly. For the time being, though, he promised not to "burden" the president anymore and closed his letter with a word of gratitude for the administration's recent effort.[148] Of course, Schiff stayed his hand for only so long before indulging the instinct to write Roosevelt again, this time to propose using American warships to ferry Russian Jews out of the czar's empire. TR replied with a token word of sympathy—"I quite appreciate the horror which all people must feel at what has gone on in Russia"—before giving his candid appraisal that Schiff's warship idea was "a spectacular bit of folly."[149]

Although Roosevelt's diplomatic play remained confidential, there was one public display of sympathy from the president: he signed the congressional resolution expressing condolences to Bialystok's Jews.[150] The English Jew Sir Samuel Montagu was optimistic that even this kind of exercise from the Americans, while not policymaking per se, had the potential to impact the Russian regime. He told the British press, "We are much gratified that President Roosevelt approved the resolution passed by Congress expressing horror over the massacres. Official declarations, such as this, have great influence in persuading the

St. Petersburg authorities to stop Jew-baiting."[151] The weight of foreign opinion would prompt a response from Russia, though not the kind that Montagu wanted.

Early July saw the Russian interior minister circulate his own report on the pogrom—riddled with antisemitic falsehoods—to various embassies in St. Petersburg for transmission to their home governments. It depicted the violence in Bialystok as effectively a pitched battle between local authorities and Jewish "terrorists" engaged in revolutionary assaults. Although the report did concede that there were blameless Jewish victims, it nevertheless insisted that their radical coreligionists had fomented conditions ripe for the loss of innocent life. Among the most egregious untruths was the denial of state culpability. In the report's words, "The government indignantly denies the rumors spread abroad that the anti-Jewish riots at Bialystok took place with the knowledge and connivance of the local administration and of the troops."[152] Of course, these were not rumors but facts, and they emanated not from foreign lands but from Bialystok itself.

That the Russian state took the extraordinary measure of disseminating a report at all to the international community was a concession of sorts—plainly, St. Petersburg felt compelled to respond amid the global revulsion at Russian barbarism. The *New York Times* noted that even though the report certainly did not countenance the propriety of foreign inquiries about internal affairs, still this "unprecedented action" amounted to a "distinct recognition of the power of public opinion abroad."[153] Public opinion abroad had power indeed: the power to elicit from Russia defensive posturing. The report reflected precisely the kind of reactionary impulse that Roosevelt had been wary of provoking.

But the czar's administrative apparatus was no longer the only voice of Russian governance. For the first time in the country's history, a pogrom had transpired with a legislative body, and not just the autocracy, exercising authority. And that body even included twelve Jews. The members of the Duma, known as "deputies," took decisive action when word of the atrocities reached St. Petersburg. A three-person committee set off for Bialystok to engage in an extensive investigation. When they returned, a dramatic session of the Duma convened to hear their findings at the very moment that the interior ministry was readying its sham report.[154]

A deputy representing the investigatory committee, M. P. Arakantzeff, took the floor before densely packed galleries. For two hours, he read aloud an unsanitized rendition of Bialystok's brutalities. Arakantzeff rejected the baseless allegation that Jewish revolutionaries were to blame and instead fingered local authorities for premeditating the attack. According to one account, the deputy spoke "in quiet, sober language and in a low voice, which only heightened the thrilling horror of the recital." Arakantzeff concluded his remarks by asking the Duma to pay its respects to Bialystok's dead. The entire body stood up in homage to those slain.[155]

Several days later, another deputy told the Associated Press that the central state itself was implicated in planning the pogrom.[156] In truth, it remains unclear even today whether the national government in St. Petersburg bore direct responsibility for the slaughter in Bialystok. That uncertainty holds for the pogroms at large—historians debate the extent to which the central authorities actively advanced pogroms versus passively tolerated them.[157] But the evidence is strong that at least some officials in high command relied on pogroms as a tool of statecraft. As Witte remarked of his rival, "Trepov did not love the art of pogrom-making for its own sake. He merely did not hesitate to resort to pogroms whenever he considered them necessary for the protection of the vital interests of the state." A number of Trepov's ilk were even more callous. Witte knew of "many other high officials to whom the bloody game of pogrom-making was a mere political amusement." Antisemitism had as much purchase on the upper echelons of the capital as it did the lower classes of the Pale.[158]

★ ★ ★

Back in the United States, Roosevelt grew annoyed when a Jewish paper called for more robust American intervention. In a letter to Nathan Bijur—a steadfast Jewish Republican ally—the president confessed his frustration: "We have gone to the very verge, perhaps beyond the very verge, of doing what as a government we could do in this matter, consistently with our own self-respect and with the advantage of the Russian Jews." He felt that pushing harder could only backfire so long as czarist Russia was hostile to American entreaties. An exasperated Roosevelt vented, "Surely it seems to me that the most foolish and hysterical person should realize that, under conditions as they actually are, it is impossible for us to do more than we have done in this matter." In what was becoming a recurring refrain in TR's correspondence, he grouped the cause of Jews in Russia together with Armenians in Turkey and Congolese under Belgian rule—this unholy trinity of humanitarian catastrophes elicited repeated requests for the president's intercession, but he maintained that America could not police the world.[159]

Roosevelt's letter to Bijur also reprised a cynical grievance that TR had shared with Schiff: those disposed to call on his administration for diplomatic protest were engaged in a self-serving ploy for political power. The president alleged to Bijur that public agitation "represents not an effective purpose to do good to those who are suffering in Russia, but to exploit, in the interest of entirely selfish individuals, the Jewish vote in America."[160] Roosevelt himself may not have been on the ballot, but 1906 was an election year for Congress and New York state alike; November clearly loomed large in his mind amid a difficult stretch with his Jewish constituents.

Of course, Democrats would prove eager in the fall campaign to condemn the pogroms and call for action by the U.S. government. But Roosevelt was too cynical by half. Most appeals for his intervention came not from politicians but from ordinary people, as testified by the one thousand Jewish immigrants, all from Bialystok, who came together in an anguished meeting at a Lower East Side synagogue. They mourned the dead, donated to the living, and petitioned the president. Their resolution called on TR to beseech the czar, pleading with Roosevelt, "In civilization and humanity's name, bring this universal protest, and the other powers will certainly follow." Many of those present still had family in Bialystok and feared that fresh outbreaks of violence might threaten the survivors.[161]

That gathering aside, Roosevelt was under less intense pressure to act than he had faced the prior fall. Bialystok, gruesome though it was, did not spark a tidal wave of antisemitic violence engulfing the whole Pale of Settlement, as happened eight months earlier. The scale of suffering was thus far more limited, and the response of American Jewry accordingly proportional. To be sure, June and July saw some Jewish demonstrations and donations in the United States, but nothing on par with the mass mobilization of the previous November and December. Schiff even suggested with striking optimism to a playwright that Bialystok "represented only the last outburst of impotent rage on the part of the old Russian governmental system in its final breakdown."[162] And Jews in America could take some comfort in knowing that Russia now had a Duma, one determined to surface the truth about Bialystok. "The Duma to the Rescue," read a headline in a Jewish weekly from California.[163]

Indeed, in the third week of July, the Duma's deputies passed a damning resolution. It pinned culpability for the massacre not just on local officials but on the central state as well, which purportedly approved "extensive propaganda for the organization of an attack." The resolution fulminated against the autocracy's "official reports [that] concealed the truth and clearly sought to justify the murder of peaceful citizens." Duma deputies also demanded in their resolution widespread punishment for all guilty parties, no matter how lofty their stations.[164] The next day, when Duma members arrived at their legislative hall, they found the doors bolted shut. On a nearby column hung a decree from the czar: the Duma was officially dissolved.[165] Nicholas would not stomach one day more of a legislature committed to justice for Jewish victims.[166]

With the threat of legislative oversight now vanquished, Russian troops instigated a pogrom in the town of Sedlits, some sixty miles from Warsaw, in early September. The American consul in Warsaw concisely captured the devastation in a five-word wire to the U.S. embassy in St. Petersburg: "Sedlits exact repetition of Bialystok."[167] And then quiet. Sedlits was the last pogrom of the appalling wave that had begun with

Kishinev in 1903. Survivors across the Pale were left to rebuild their lives amid the blood-stained rubble of three terrifying years. If there was now peace, Schiff remarked, "it is the peace of the graveyard."[168]

Theodore Roosevelt's relationship with American Jewry had suffered its greatest strains over the preceding ten months. His generic expressions of sympathy, decoupled from public pressure on Russia, left even his traditional supporters disappointed in his apparent inertia. Unlike his Jewish-American compatriots, TR believed that the widespread chaos following the October Manifesto precluded his solicitations of a Russian state that seemed to be careening toward collapse. Once the czar's government regained control, the president resumed his willingness—with some reluctance—to make use of diplomatic channels, first before Easter and again after Bialystok. Roosevelt was concerned, in part, about the embarrassment of a rebuff from Russia, which was always ready to invoke the principle of noninterference in domestic affairs and to remind Americans that the scourge of lynching made hypocrites of them. TR also worried that American overreach on the diplomatic front might actually worsen conditions for Russian Jews—indeed, there was plausible reason to think it could alienate the czar and incite popular resentment among Russian Gentiles.

Roosevelt therefore shielded his efforts from public view, lest the exposure undermine their efficacy. Unlike earlier episodes—the Romanian Note, the Kishinev Petition, the Passport Question—the past year left him bereft of any major win on Jewish causes that he, and his fellow Republicans, could trumpet. True, the Algeciras Conference allowed Roosevelt to score some points with the American Jewish community. But that was a trifling victory against the backdrop of mass murder in the Pale. Soon Jewish voters would head to the polls for the 1906 elections; their recent memory of seeming inaction by the president might well override their longer memory of prior instances when the Republican administration manifestly stood up for their coreligionists in Eastern Europe.

But Roosevelt wasn't going to passively watch Jews drift to the Democratic Party. He told a leading Republican official to consult with Jacob Schiff about the Jewish vote. The president then added, with deliberate ambiguity, "He knows of something which I am going to do."[169] For more than a year, Roosevelt had been quietly plotting a major move—whose significance to American Jewry would be unprecedented—and the opportune moment for his historic reveal was almost at hand.

7

APPOINTMENTS & IMMIGRANTS

Theodore Roosevelt's name may not have been on the ballot in the 1906 midterm elections, but Republicans well understood that the party's fate that fall would be inseparable from the president's stature. In places with large Jewish constituencies, Republicans wagered that Roosevelt's reputation was still favorable enough to bolster support for their candidates. A Yiddish daily in New York, the *Jewish Morning Journal*, published a letter in English from the RNC chairman insisting that "Theodore Roosevelt's personality must be a central figure and his achievements a central thought in the campaign."[1] The Republican calculus with Jewish voters would certainly not mean running away from the president and his record.

Still, the plight of Russian Jewry remained a vulnerability for Roosevelt and thus for the GOP. The Democratic *Hebrew Standard* suggested that his reticence to advocate for Russian Jewry was hypocritical. After all, the president had showed a strong willingness to insinuate himself into other nations' affairs in Latin America, especially when U.S. businesses stood to profit thereby. "If Russia were only a little nearer home and this country had some interest—financial if possible—in her affairs, how quickly President Roosevelt would intervene," the paper sneered.[2]

In New York state, which claimed more Jews than all other states combined, the local party conventions in late September betokened the importance of Russian Jewry to the campaign.³ The Democrats, gathering in Buffalo, included a platform plank calling on the national government to protect Russia's Jews from any further "atrocities" that have "shocked the conscience of civilization."⁴ Meanwhile, the Republicans adopted a platform in Saratoga that expressed "sincerest sympathy" for the pogrom's victims but notably made no comparable demand for action.⁵ Although both sides nodded to the state's considerable Jewish electorate, only Democrats had something to gain from pressuring the Roosevelt administration.

Among the most eager observers of New York's campaign season that fall was TR himself. He felt deeply attached to New York—both city and state—and was personally invested in ensuring Republican success there. Roosevelt's wide portfolio of international and domestic challenges as president did not preclude him from stressing about such granular details as the absence of a sufficiently religious Jewish candidate on a slate of nominees for the county bench covering Manhattan. In early October, a Republican congressman from New York City named Herbert Parsons, a non-Jew, brought the issue to Roosevelt's attention. Parsons argued that the GOP should not endorse a judicial ticket put forward by a group of self-styled nonpartisan lawyers and should instead furnish its own slate of judges. The reason: "There is not an Orthodox Jew on their ticket."⁶ He conveyed that the nonpartisan ticket did include a Jew, but that Jew wasn't traditionally devout. The ticket regrettably overlooked Otto Rosalsky, a young Orthodox judge who had received an interim vacancy appointment to the county bench and was now hoping for election to a full term. From the GOP perspective, the thirty-three-year-old Rosalsky was the ideal candidate: not only was he Orthodox and Republican, but he was so steeped in the Lower East Side that he still lived with his parents on Rivington Street.⁷ "There is nobody from the East Side," Parsons lamented.⁸

Roosevelt was incensed by the snub to the Orthodox community. "It was an outrage to leave off Rosalsky," the president fumed to Parsons. "You must have the East Side represented."⁹ TR also took up the matter with the Republican nominee for governor, Charles Evans Hughes. "They had no business to leave an excellent East Side Jew, Judge

Rosalsky, off of it," the president griped as he implored Hughes to throw his weight behind the Orthodox jurist.[10] Several days later, Rosalsky indeed earned a slot on the Republican judicial slate, no doubt thanks to Roosevelt's intervention.[11]

As a former resident of the governor's mansion, TR was particularly interested in Hughes's own race. Hughes was a lawyer (and future chief justice of the U.S. Supreme Court) who had earned a reputation for fighting corruption after undertaking state investigations into the utility and insurance industries. He was now facing off in the gubernatorial contest against William Randolph Hearst, a Democratic congressman who doubled as a newspaper tycoon. "The situation is certainly very serious in New York," Roosevelt cautioned Hughes. "Hearst will of course use money like water and with shameless corruption wherever he gets a chance." TR fully appreciated the importance of the state's Jewish vote, particularly in New York City, where one in five residents was Jewish. He advised Hughes to consult the state attorney general, himself a Jew who "ought to know the East Side." Roosevelt warned Hughes in a postscript, "I hear the Jews on the East Side are enthusiastic for Hearst."[12] Despite Republican victories in four consecutive governor's races, the president would take nothing for granted.

Roosevelt soon reached out to Timothy Woodruff—chairman of the state Republican committee—to share his worries about "the Jews, who I understand are inclined to go for Hearst in a mass."[13] Woodruff, however, was more sanguine about Hughes's Jewish prospects, informing Roosevelt, "The *Daily News* and the *Morning Journal* and the *Abend-Post*, all printed in Yiddish, which have an aggregate circulation of over a hundred thousand, are already supporting Hughes in their news columns." Lest the president wonder how an Anglo-Saxon blue blood like Woodruff kept abreast of the Yiddish papers, the state chairman explained, "I know because I have had the Yiddish translated for me."[14]

Roosevelt wasn't content to rest on this promising bit of intelligence, so he tapped his closest Jewish aide, Oscar Straus, for help. "See if there is not some way you could be of assistance in preventing the East Side vote—notably among the Jews—from going for Hearst," TR urged Straus. "He has completely misled those poor people over there.

I earnestly hope you can do this."[15] Straus tried to allay the president's concerns. "Bijur and I have our hands on the pulses on the East Side," he wrote, referring to the Jewish Republican and longtime Roosevelt confidant Nathan Bijur. "I think you need have no fear that Hearst will mislead your constituents over there." Straus encouraged TR to have faith in the Jewish electorate: "Our East Side friends, I am sure, will show a wise discrimination. There is much more wisdom over there than one would imagine." Oscar Straus also reiterated what Woodruff had already communicated to the president: the Jewish papers were standing behind Hughes. And Straus further assured TR that he was personally prepared to stump on the East Side.[16] The president's response was consummately Rooseveltian: "Bully for you!"[17]

Although Hearst may not have been as dominant with Jewish voters as Roosevelt fretted, the Democratic nominee for governor was nevertheless making considerable efforts to woo them. He pushed Tammany Hall to include the consummate East Sider Otto Rosalsky on the Democratic judicial slate, even though Rosalsky was a Republican (apparently, no rule prohibited both parties from putting the same nominee on their respective tickets).[18] Hearst also held a packed rally on the East Side where a surrogate touted the candidate as a longtime friend of the Jews.[19] A few days later, Hearst took a highly unusual step that only a press mogul would devise: he started his own Jewish newspaper for distribution on the Lower East Side to make his case to voters.[20] And then Hearst lined up an endorsement from a prominent Jewish philanthropist.[21]

But Roosevelt was the sitting president, and as such, there were tools at his disposal that even a newspaper magnate couldn't boast. Since at least the spring of 1905, TR had contemplated taking an unprecedented step forward for American Jewry.[22] The president disclosed his plan to a small circle but insisted on confidentiality; he wanted to maximize the impact of its publicity at the optimal moment. "Of course, see that under no circumstances any hint gets out, save from me," Roosevelt told Timothy Woodruff as the campaign season intensified in October. He added, "I wish to prevent its getting out until a week from today, Sunday, at the earliest, and then only with my authority."[23] Woodruff responded that he would, of course, defer to Roosevelt's discretion on timing but nonetheless felt "the quicker the better, from the standpoint of the best interests of the campaign."[24] Soon thereafter, with election day just two weeks away, voters learned of the president's seminal initiative: Oscar Straus would become the first Jew in American history to sit in the cabinet.[25]

★ ★ ★

Nine months earlier, Straus enjoyed an informal lunch at the White House with the president and a collection of guests. Roosevelt asked Straus to stay behind in the Red Room for a private discussion. "I don't know whether you know it or not, but I want you to become a member of my cabinet," TR divulged. Straus did indeed already know it; Jacob Schiff had tipped him off. Two earlier presidents—Ulysses S. Grant and Grover Cleveland—had offered a cabinet post to a Jew, but in both instances the prospective candidate declined the opportunity. Straus would be the first to accept. It was yet to be finalized which department Straus would head, but the president told him that "your character, your judgment, and your ability" all commended him to a cabinet appointment.[26]

The promotion wasn't just a reflection of Roosevelt's esteem for Straus; TR also considered it a move in global diplomacy. "I want to show Russia and some other countries what we think of the Jews in this country," the president informed Straus in their Red Room meeting. At that moment, in January of 1906, the spike in pogroms precipitated by the October Manifesto hadn't fully subsided. Roosevelt expressed to Straus his fear that denouncing Russian pogroms would play well at home but exacerbate Jewish conditions abroad. Far better to signal the United States' commitment to religious equality by example, TR reasoned. Jewish representation in the cabinet of the American president would offer a sharp contrast to the blood-drenched bigotry then prevailing in the Russian Empire.[27]

Over the summer, with the pending appointment still under wraps, Roosevelt indicated to Straus that his imminent placement and performance in the cabinet would offer a powerful rebuttal to antisemitic stereotypes in general. Straus had just given an interview to the *Cleveland Plain Dealer* in which he repudiated the pernicious myth that

Jews were materialistic, prompting Roosevelt to compliment Straus: "Your article in answer to the attacks upon the Jews was excellent." The president added, "I think the best answer, after all, my dear fellow, will be your appointment to the cabinet and the service you are certain to render thereunder."[28] Straus would later tell the president he understood that his promotion was intended to combat antisemitism within *and* beyond America's borders. "Your calling me to your cabinet ... I well know had a meaning which far transcended my personality," he recognized. "You desired to rebuke, not only in this country but also in others, that spirit of intolerance which is repugnant to the fundamental principles of our democratic institutions."[29]

The appointment was designed to send a message to Jews as well. As Roosevelt conveyed to the Christian theologian Lyman Abbott, Straus's elevation to the cabinet demonstrated to America's Jews that "they have in this country just the same rights and opportunities as everyone else." And it provided an exemplar for the upcoming generation of Jewish Americans. "I want the Jewish young man who is born in this country to feel that Straus stands for his ideal of the successful man rather than some crooked Jew money-maker," the president explained to Abbott.[30] We see once again Roosevelt's capacity for framing his defense of Jews in the trappings of prejudicial tropes.

In sum, Straus's identity as a *Jewish* cabinet member mattered. It showcased American inclusivity to audiences at home and abroad. It gave younger Jews in the United States a model to emulate. And it mattered electorally, too, or else TR wouldn't have waited until the eve of an election to reveal the nomination. Roosevelt unambiguously acknowledged to the social reformer and political ally Jacob Riis, "I did all I could to help out the campaign by announcing the selection of Oscar Straus for my cabinet."[31] Straus capitalized on that announcement by courting Jewish voters on behalf of Charles Evans Hughes, Republican nominee for the New York governorship.[32] For all the resources and reportage at his Democratic opponent's disposal, it was Hughes who emerged victorious on election day.

This is not to say that the Straus pick was purely about optics. To the contrary, the president had deeply valued Straus's advice for years, and not just on Jewish issues. Straus counseled Roosevelt on topics as varied as Indian affairs, labor conflicts, and Caribbean relations.³³ But Straus's unquestioned competence aside, the ascendance of a Jew to the presidential cabinet was of no small moment. Diplomatically, culturally, and politically, TR understood as keenly as anyone its significance.

Roosevelt had long been dogged by a philosophical tension in his hiring. He wanted to actively ensure that his recruits and appointees reflected America's heterogeneity while also resisting the idea that any factor beyond merit influenced his selection process. Whether as police commissioner, Rough Rider colonel, or chief executive of the nation, TR often championed religious diversity in employment. For instance, Roosevelt told Lyman Abbott that he had aimed to ensure that his cabinet—wherein Protestant, Jew, and Catholic served alongside one another—had "an absolutely representative character." But Roosevelt was also enamored of a countervailing concept: American civic life as an identity-neutral sphere where merit alone mattered.³⁴

The result was a Roosevelt divided against himself. He routinely stressed the importance of involving Jews in government *and* routinely denied that their Jewish backgrounds in any way informed his hiring or promotion decisions. In the very letter to Abbott where he acknowledged his conscious effort to make the cabinet reflect the nation's diversity, Roosevelt disavowed that self-same goal: "It is not considered whether any member of my cabinet is of English, or Scotch, or Dutch, or German, or Irish descent; whether he is Protestant, Catholic or Jew."³⁵ He could never bring himself to definitively choose between the identity-driven ideal of pluralism and the identity-free ideal of merit. In theory, Roosevelt might have reconciled the two by suggesting that true meritocracy would organically engender diversity. But he never made any such claim.

In fact, Roosevelt confessed in moments of candor that he appointed Jews in part *because* they were Jews. For example, he received word in 1904 that a Jewish federal marshal in New York City, William Henkel, had allegedly cultivated ties to Tammany Hall and ought to be relieved of his post. If Henkel were dispensed with, the president preferred that another Jew take his place. "We could substitute for him some first-class Jew," Roosevelt told a senator. "I would not want the Jews to feel that we had turned out one of their number when he is the only representative of the race at present holding a federal position in New York." The president also contemplated the possibility that the accusations against Henkel had been leveled "unjustly." In the end, Henkel retained his post.[36]

A similar episode arose the following year. Roosevelt received a letter from a congressman expressing concerns about a particular Jewish office-seeker whom the president planned to make the customs surveyor in Indianapolis. Despite the congressman's doubts, Roosevelt was determined to stay the course, admitting, "One reason, which I do not like to have spoken of much, is that I like when I can to appoint a Jew for the very reason that it is often so difficult to find just the right Jew to appoint."[37] It is unsurprising that Roosevelt did not like to speak much of it; he took pains to ensure religious diversity in the government workforce at the same time that he wanted to espouse merit as the only rightful qualification. The president neatly summed up these dueling imperatives when he put his hand on Straus's knee and remarked, "I don't appoint you because you are a Jew, but I am mighty glad you are one."[38]

For Straus to join the cabinet at all was consequential, but it became doubly so because he was tapped to lead the Department of Commerce and Labor, which housed the Bureau of Immigration. In other words, a foreign-born Jew would preside over American immigration policy. Some extended commentary here on the larger context of immigration is warranted because it throws into high relief the extraordinary nature of Straus's appointment.

The Rooseveltian age was a fraught one for immigrants, as a tidal wave of newcomers stoked nativist anxieties. Since the country's founding, American borders had been open to nearly anyone who sought to forge a life in the New World. Most of the immigrants for the first hundred years of the republic were Northern and Western European: British, Irish, French, German, Dutch, Swiss, and Scandinavian. But beginning in the late nineteenth century, these "old immigrants" were overtaken in number by "new immigrants" hailing from Southern and Eastern Europe: Italian, Greek, Slavic, Balkan, Turkish, and Jewish.[39] To be sure, there were immigrants from other continents, but more than 90 percent of foreign arrivals could claim European provenance.[40]

Russian Jews formed a sizable slice of the influx at American ports. Although some Jews fleeing the Russian Empire settled elsewhere—Western Europe, South America, Palestine—the bulk landed stateside. Jews constituted little more than 4 percent of the Russian population but almost 80 percent of Russia's emigrants. In fact, a Russian Jew was thirty times more likely than a Russian Gentile to expatriate. The horrific pogrom wave of 1903–1906 prompted an unprecedented Jewish exodus from Russia in those years, sevenfold the number who had left amid the pogroms of the 1880s. With the United States claiming more of these Russian-Jewish refugees than all other countries combined, Roosevelt's tenure at the White House aligned with a peak in Jewish immigration never before seen in American history.[41] It had previously taken more than two centuries for the Jewish-American population to reach its first million. TR's two terms in office saw that number almost double.[42]

And there were many more Jews yet to come. In 1906, the U.S. ambassador in St. Petersburg recounted to Roosevelt that he had recently inquired with a Russian official about a group of local Jews who were scheduled to embark for America, and the official "smiled and replied that they had seven million in Russia that we were welcome to."[43] The real number was closer to six million, but it was still the largest number of Jews in the world, even with the ever-quickening Jewish flight from czarist territory.[44] Other antisemitic countries, such as Romania and Austria-Hungary, also contributed to the Jewish migration stateside.[45]

Although the old immigrants in the United States hadn't always enjoyed the warmest welcome, the new immigrants—both Jew and Gentile—fomented particularly acute anxiety among the native-born. New immigrants spoke in strange tongues, practiced curious customs, and packed into ethnic enclaves in overcrowded cities. Many nativists feared that the essential character of the country was under siege.[46]

It had long been fashionable among some faction of Anglo-Saxon elites to imagine themselves as members of a superior race upon whose leadership rested the nation's fate. In response to the perceived threat posed by new immigrants, Anglo-Saxons became more accepting of old immigrants who had been previously marginalized. Anglo-Saxon nativists increasingly claimed a common "old stock" identity with others deriving from Northern and Western Europe. These nativists feared that American greatness could not withstand the unrelenting infusion of alien blood from Southern and Eastern Europeans.[47]

Madison Grant, the most prolific xenophobe of the day, fulminated against the "hordes of immigrants of inferior racial value" in his popular publication *The Passing of the Great Race*.[48] As a favor to a mutual friend, Roosevelt endorsed Grant's book, only to immediately rue that decision.[49] Grant's ilk hardly saw themselves as part of a shared white race that encompassed all European ancestries. For them, Jews ranked among those who fell outside the boundaries of whiteness.[50] Nativist angst reveals how antisemitism had ethnic, and not merely religious, dimensions. If the problem with Jews was solely their religion, conversion could remedy that much. But the nativists saw Jews as a congenitally flawed race; immigration restriction alone could protect the old stock.

Recall that in 1894 three young Harvard alumni of Anglo-Saxon lineage established the Immigration Restriction League, the most conspicuous organization seeking to reduce the inflow of Jews, Italians, and other stigmatized groups. The reactionary elitists who comprised the league formed an unlikely alliance with some portion of the laboring classes—blue collar workers who were concerned that impoverished immigrants, willing to toil for low wages in hazardous conditions, were jeopardizing their own earnings and job security.[51]

Even before the league's founding, anxieties about immigration had become sufficiently widespread by the early 1880s that Congress began implementing some novel regulations. In 1882, Congress passed a law refusing immigrants who were liable to become dependent on the state, and three years later, a new statute somewhat limited employers' ability to import labor. The following decade, another law created new categories of excludable immigrants, including polygamists, convicted felons, and the contagiously diseased. After William McKinley was felled by an anarchist's bullet, political extremism became another legally sanctioned reason for turning back fresh arrivals, as a 1903 statute barred anarchists and seditionists.[52]

Still, the borders remained relatively open. The emerging legal architecture of immigration didn't actually result in many deportations. What's more, not all Mayflower descendants or factory workers opposed the new immigrants. The nativist movement was underdeveloped and wouldn't achieve its restrictionist goals in earnest until the 1920s. Legislation before the xenophobic heyday of the 1920s didn't target immigrants on the basis of national origin or ethnicity (with the notable exception of the Chinese Exclusion Act of 1882). For Southern and Eastern Europeans in Roosevelt's age, cultural stigma more than legal prohibition presented the primary challenge to their belonging in American society.[53] That stigma was particularly severe for Jewish immigrants.[54]

The nationally renowned sociology professor Edward A. Ross gave voice to widely held misgivings about Jewish newcomers. In the popular periodical *Century Magazine*, he published a deeply antisemitic article entitled "The Hebrews of Eastern Europe in America." Ross's piece recycled well-worn stereotypes about Jewry as a plague on American society. He accused Jews of corrupting professional ethics—from law and medicine to newspapers and theaters—with their unscrupulous quest for wealth. From Ross's viewpoint, Jews had only themselves to blame for their exclusion from patrician social clubs and summer resorts. "Bigotry has little or nothing to do with it," Ross maintained. He explained that the Gentile doesn't want to fraternize with the Jew because "the Gentile resents being obliged to engage in a humiliating and undignified scramble in order to keep his trade or his clients against the Jewish invader." Drawing on yet another common trope about Jews, Ross alleged they were sexually unscrupulous. "Pleasure-loving Jewish businessmen spare Jewesses, but pursue Gentile girls," he warned Christian fathers.[55]

Jews not only degraded the marketplace and womanly virtue; according to Ross, they were outright lawbreakers. "The Eastern European

Hebrews feel no reverence for law as such," he reported, "and are willing to break any ordinance they find in their way." Although official statistics showed that Jews were substantially *underrepresented* among convicted criminals, Professor Ross was not so easily dissuaded by data. He contended that the comparatively low percentage of Jewish inmates was itself damning—it demonstrated the Jews' success at evading detection of their illicit schemes. "The fewness of the Hebrews in prison has been used to spread the impression that they are uncommonly law-abiding," he noted, but "it is harder to catch and convict criminals of cunning."[56] By arguing that the favorable crime statistics for Jews actually offered all the more evidence of Jewish illegality, Ross exemplified the kind of circular reasoning that so often shielded antisemitism from factual refutation. Antisemitic thought, unburdened by the demands of evidence and logic, contented itself with the unproven premise of Jewish degeneracy.

At times, Ross's article tempered its indictment of Jews with kinder observations. But even these compliments were in service of his broader criticisms. For example, he credited Jews for their "intellectuality" and recounted their considerable ability in a range of cognitively challenging endeavors. Yet that very same mental prowess was, purportedly, the most effective Jewish weapon against Gentiles. Ross depicted Jews as shrewd operators who relied on their "subtle Hebrew brains" to convince American Gentiles of "the blessings of immigration." He similarly groused that "keen-witted Hebrews" were taking over key positions in local and national government.[57] Toward the end of his piece, Ross warned in summation that "there will be trouble" if America continued to admit large numbers of Jewish immigrants.[58] That Ross enjoyed considerable stature suggests much about the resonance of his anti-Judaic biases among elites.

In response to contemporary antisemitism in America, the president of a B'nai B'rith local chapter expressed concern about "the low ebb of the public's favorable opinion of the Jew." He decried how "our petty vices have been magnified and our slightest errors exaggerated."[59] Although prejudicial stereotyping was the most common form of anti-Jewish bigotry, violence against American Jews was not unheard of. Sometimes assaults were perpetrated by other ethnic groups, other times by the police. And in one notorious case, a Jew named Leo Frank from New York met his mortal fate at the hands of a Georgia lynch mob after he was wrongly accused of murdering a Christian girl.⁶⁰

To be sure, America wasn't categorically antisemitic. Jews and Gentiles alike partook in mass protests against the Russian pogroms and donated fulsomely to the survivors. Then again, the public's condemnation of Russian oppression wasn't always an indication of unalloyed sympathy for Jews. Some American Gentiles resented the mass migration of Jews to the United States and hoped that liberalization in Russia would curb the impetus for Jews to flee the Pale.⁶¹ Conversely, a seemingly anti-Jewish position could obscure humanitarian motivations. Many Gentiles who were warmhearted toward immigrants counterintuitively favored immigration restriction, for example. They lamented the impoverished condition of immigrant life in American cities and—in a bid to improve the lot of those struggling souls—wanted to limit the influx of new arrivals, whose presence would further burden already congested urban slums.⁶²

American attitudes toward Jews, then, defy facile description. The voices of tolerance and those of nativism sometimes diverged and other times dovetailed. Jews in the United States had to navigate a complex social terrain indeed—and in Theodore Roosevelt, they found a president whose approach to immigration was just as conflicted as the country he led.

Historians debate the extent to which Roosevelt embraced immigrants throughout his career and the role that race played in his perspective on them. A comprehensive exploration of that topic could fill several books and lies beyond the scope of this one. However, a few key points merit consideration here. For one, minimal effort suffices to find Roosevelt contradicting himself in his thoughts on race. Even within a single paragraph he could endorse two distinct positions. His inconsistency goes some way toward explaining why scholars have differed when describing his appraisal of various racial groups. We ought not project coherence onto him, lest we paper over those contradictions. An honest accounting requires acknowledging Roosevelt's incongruity.

Complicating the issue further is that Roosevelt employed the term *race* to denote a number of discrete concepts. While he sometimes did use *race* to refer to ethnicity, frequently he meant *race* as a synonym of nationality. In Roosevelt's racial cosmology, therefore, Jews could constitute a "Jewish race" unto themselves in an ethnic sense and yet still be part of the "American race" based on a shared civic identity with American Gentiles. He also used *race* to indicate bonds that connected similar peoples across national boundaries, such as a "French race" that tied together France and French Canada. Finally, Roosevelt adopted *race* to signify geographic subdivisions of people within a given country, using terms like the "Texas race" or "Kentucky race."[63]

A failure to distinguish between Roosevelt's numerous meanings of *race* (and of synonyms like *stock*) has generated misunderstanding about his take on race and immigration. Many scholars, for instance, characterize Roosevelt's fear of "race suicide" as the principal example of his racism. They suggest that he defined "race suicide" as the declining birth rates among old-stock Americans, which would supposedly lead to societal decay.[64] His varying notions of race, however, complicate this conventional wisdom.

Undeniably, Roosevelt in the 1890s did express anxiety about population deflation among the traditional elite. "Most certainly there are evil forces at work among us in America," he fretted to a British friend. "The diminishing birth rate among the old native American stock, especially in the Northeast, with all that that implies, I should consider the worst."[65] Here, *stock* certainly does signify ethnicity, as Roosevelt revealed a xenophobic strain in his worldview. During his presidency, however, Roosevelt explicitly recast his concerns about race suicide in national, rather than ethnic, terms. He was troubled by the prospect of low birth rates among native-born and immigrant families alike. Roosevelt told the press that some other countries ought to be cautioned about the perils of population decline, but happily "the ordinary American, whether of the old native stock or the self-respecting son or daughter of immigrants, needs no such warning."[66] After his tenure at the White House, Roosevelt would continue to sound the alarm about race suicide among the "native stock" while defining that phrase in an ethnically inclusive manner. He took pains to clarify, "I use the term with elasticity to include all children of mothers and fathers who were born on this side of the water."[67] The ancestry of those mothers and fathers was immaterial.

As members of the "American race," Jews in the United States understood themselves to count among those whom Roosevelt wanted to procreate prolifically. A Jewish newspaper in San Francisco affirmed shortly after his tenure in office, "We are only too glad to commend and applaud our former president for his strenuous efforts against race suicide."[68] Another Jewish periodical reported that "the strenuous Colonel" had been invited to the Jewish Maternity Hospital on the Lower East Side "in order to convince him by the many triplets there that the fear of race suicide is considerably exaggerated, in our metropolitan ghetto at least."[69] Ultimately, Roosevelt's angst about race suicide demonstrates the importance of discerning his varied usages of both *race* and *stock*, and it also highlights the need to differentiate TR's changing positions across the decades of his career.[70]

Like many of his contemporaries, Roosevelt placed immigrant groups in a pecking order of desirability. Yet his hierarchies didn't map precisely onto popular nativist conceptions. American patricians, disproportionately of English ancestry, often saw Anglo-Saxons as the superior race. But Roosevelt did not. That he himself wasn't primarily Anglo-Saxon surely accounts, at least partially, for his immunity to that common belief.[71] "I have not got a drop of that kind of blood in me," he once remarked.[72] In fact, Roosevelt did have some English blood—as well as Scottish, French, and Irish—but the predominant strain was Dutch.[73] He was proud to descend from what he called "old Dutch knickerbocker stock."[74] In an indication that Roosevelt was untethered from Anglo-Saxon elitism, he ranked German immigrants above the vaunted Puritan settlers.[75] His departure from Anglo-Saxon supremacy notwithstanding, TR still thought old-stock immigrants on the whole were more desirable than Southern and Eastern Europeans.

Roosevelt's hierarchies sometimes came with caveats; a given group might rank high on one measure and low on another. Using the term

"American" in an ethnic sense to denote descendants of the old stock, Roosevelt once commented to a writer, "In the schools we find that the Jewish children are very much brighter than the American, or than any other foreigner, the American tending to come next and the Irish rather low down; yet in the Police Department in point of efficiency and usefulness, I should have said that on the average this was reversed." He then quickly hedged, "We must be very cautious about hasty generalization or dogmatization in this matter."[76] Even though Roosevelt had a penchant for group rankings, he routinely stressed the need to treat people according to their individual merits. As he once proclaimed in a speech, if a fellow citizen "has the right stuff in him, I care not a snap of my fingers whether he is Jew or Gentile."[77]

His views about ethnic hierarchies were deeply influenced by a particular variant of evolutionary theory known as Lamarckism. The French biologist Jean-Baptiste Lamarck had argued in the early nineteenth century that organisms acquire traits based on their environment and then pass on those traits to their offspring. During Roosevelt's lifetime, many American academics applied Lamarck's ideas to the comparative study of societies. They held that whole races could develop new characteristics because of their social context and then biologically bequeath those characteristics to the next generation. Lamarckians provoked plenty of criticism, but Roosevelt threw his lot in with them nonetheless. He believed that some races were at more advanced stages of development than others but that any race could—through Lamarckian evolution—better itself by cultivating traits favorable to its environment. Roosevelt's Lamarckian convictions undergirded his racially inflected imperialism, which saw "civilized" white nations as the proper custodians of "savage" non-white lands until the given indigenous population was, by his estimation, ready for self-government.[78]

But Roosevelt diverged somewhat from other Lamarckians because he didn't deem European and European-descended peoples to be necessarily of higher quality than those of other continents. Even as he held the Chinese, Filipinos, and Latin Americans in low regard, the Japanese regularly earned Roosevelt's praise.[79] He marveled at their success against the Russians in battle, writing to a friend, "What wonderful people the Japanese are!" They were on pace to become "a great civilized power."[80] But Japan wasn't merely better than benighted Russia—it rivaled even what Roosevelt considered the best countries of the West. As he maintained in his autobiography, "The Japanese are one of the great nations of the world, entitled to stand, and standing, on a footing of full equality with any nation of Europe or America." Far from inferior, "their civilization is in some respects higher than our own." However, his affinity for Japan did not mean that he encouraged immigration from there, warning, "It is eminently undesirable that Japanese and Americans should attempt to live together in masses. . . . But this is not because either nation is inferior to the other; it is because they are different."[81] Roosevelt thus saw the Japanese in a distinct light from the Jews, who may have emerged from inferior conditions but—he believed—were perfectly capable of thriving in an American context.

Roosevelt repeatedly promoted the notion of American identity as a melting pot.[82] The metaphor of the melting pot implies homogenization; differences dissolve into an unvariegated stew of national identity. Consistent with that conceit, Roosevelt called on newcomers to shed their past ways and adopt a universal Americanism. He espoused such views in 1894, for example, in a magazine called *The Forum*. There Roosevelt inveighed against "immigrants or the sons of immigrants [who] do not heartily and in good faith throw in their lot with us, but cling to the speech, the customs, the ways of life, and the habits of thought of the Old World." It was "necessary to Americanize the immigrants of foreign birth who settle among us." His melting pot had its egalitarian aspects. He rejected the nativist premise that the old stock ranked above the new in their authenticity as Americans, but only if the new immigrants' assimilation was absolute. In Roosevelt's words, "An immense number of them have become completely Americanized, and these stand on exactly the same plane as the descendants of any Puritan, Cavalier, or Knickerbocker among us"—here he was referring to the colonial settlers of, respectively, Massachusetts, Virginia, and New York.[83]

Roosevelt's embrace of an iconic play, *The Melting Pot*, offers the most pronounced example of his enthusiasm for a crucible where different ethnicities and nationalities merge into a superior phenotype: the American. Created by the famed British-Jewish playwright Israel Zangwill, *The Melting Pot* debuted in the latter days of Roosevelt's presidency. TR and his wife, Edith, were in attendance for the world premiere at the Columbia Theater, just a few blocks from the White House. Other luminaries on hand that evening included Oscar Straus and Zangwill himself.[84]

The play revolves around two young Russian immigrants in New York: David and Vera. David is a Jew who narrowly escaped the Kishinev pogrom even as the rest of his family was massacred; Vera is a Christian whose father served as an officer in the Russian military. Even the play's macabre twist—it turns out that Vera's father was responsible for the murder of David's family—does not derail their unlikely love story. In Zangwill's vision of the United States, the likes of David and Vera could cast off Old World antipathies and fuse their bloodlines into a purified American one.[85] The final scene features David gazing out into a sunset and musing, "There she lies, the great Melting Pot. . . . Celt and Latin, Slav and Teuton, Greek and Syrian, black and yellow." Vera affectionately leans into David, adding, "Jew and Gentile." He then continues, "Yes, East and West, and North and South, the palm and the pine, the pole and the equator, the crescent and the cross—how the great Alchemist melts and fuses them with his purging flame!"[86] Zangwill's sympathetic rendering of interfaith romance was probably informed by his own marriage five years earlier to a non-Jew.[87]

After its run in Washington, the play toured the American West and then headed to Broadway.[88] Jews nationwide condemned *The Melting Pot* for appearing to extol self-eradication via intermarriage. On the Upper West Side, immense crowds packed into the Free Synagogue to hear a visiting rabbi, Leon Harrison, deliver a repudiation of Zangwill's play.[89] The rabbi cautioned that if Zangwill's vision were to materialize, "the little Jewish race would be diluted to extinction." An impassioned Harrison further castigated Zangwill for "sacrificing the ancient sanctities of his people's faith on the altar of sentimental claptrap."[90]

Numerous Jewish papers throughout the country reported on Harrison's rousing sermon.[91]

On the other side of Central Park, at the iconic Temple Beth-El, Rabbi Judas Magnes delivered an equally scathing denunciation of Zangwill's "pernicious" production. "The melting process glorifies disloyalty to one's inheritance," Magnes warned. He glimpsed in *The Melting Pot* the specter of self-induced annihilation. Magnes scoffed, "We cannot be thankful to anyone for preaching suicide to us." Although Zangwill applied his assimilative logic to all ethnicities, Magnes pointed out that its threat was uniquely grave to Jews. Gentile newcomers originated in homelands where their people would continue to propagate, but for the stateless Jew, "America spells his great hope for the preservation of Judaism." Rabbi Magnes offered an alternative metaphor to the melting pot: the symphony. In the symphony, harmony results not from a "vast monotone" but rather from a "variety of distinct sounds blending into music under the artist's hand."[92] Each subgroup within the United States could contribute its individual note to the collective orchestra of American life.

The Jewish press joined in the repudiation of Zangwill's play. In New York, the *Hebrew Standard* deemed the melting pot a menace to Jewish perpetuity, no less than the pogroms themselves: "If others slay us, it is ruin ... but that we should thrust the knife within our very self is adding slaughter unto slaughter."[93] Meanwhile, a Jewish paper in Missouri addressed its defiant rebuke to Zangwill directly: "With a single stroke of the pen, you cannot obliterate an existence of four thousand years."[94] Jewish voices defending *The Melting Pot* were so rare that a Boston rabbi jokingly described himself as a "heathen" for endorsing the play.[95]

Unlike American Jewry at large, Roosevelt delighted in Zangwill's assimilative message. The president shouted down from his theater box to Zangwill, "A great play! A great play!" after the final scene on opening night.[96] TR may not have boasted credentials as a dramaturge, but that didn't stop him from proffering a suggestion to the playwright a couple days later. One character in *The Melting Pot* had a line making light of divorce's commonality in the United States, which sat poorly with a president for whom the decline of marriage and child-rearing was a foremost concern. Roosevelt hosted Zangwill for lunch at the White House so that TR could urge him to remove the offending dialogue.[97]

Soon thereafter Zangwill wrote Roosevelt, "I have changed the line to which you took exception." And Zangwill had a request of his own: the play's script would be printed as a book, and he wanted permission to dedicate it to TR.[98] The president responded that he would be "very much pleased" to have his name attached to *The Melting Pot*. "Let me again most heartily congratulate you upon your play," Roosevelt added. "I do not know when I have seen a play that stirred me as much."[99] Years later, Zangwill wrote him a letter making reference to "the play of mine ('The Melting Pot') which you have doubtless forgotten is dedicated to you."[100] Roosevelt responded effusively. "My dear sir, the idea of supposing that I have forgotten the 'Melting Pot,' and its dedication to me!" he exclaimed. "Now as a matter of fact, that particular play I shall always count among the very strong and real influences upon my thought and my life. It has been in my mind continually, and on my lips very often."[101] Although many Jewish people deemed Zangwill's purifying crucible an existential threat, Roosevelt saw in *The Melting Pot* the possibilities for American liberation from the Old World's stubborn hatreds. Indeed, TR was so enticed by the melting pot ideal that when an American humorist jokingly spelled his name in a seemingly Judaized way—*Tiddy Rosenfelt*—Roosevelt told him, "I wish I had a little Jew in me."[102]

Roosevelt's support for the notion of a melting pot serves to obscure the presence of a competing strain in his thought, one more inclusive than even the most expansive melting pot: pluralism. At times Roosevelt advanced a decidedly pluralistic vision of national life wherein members of different ethnicities need not choose between their particular group identity and a common civic one. Rather than abandon longstanding customs, they could harmonize their singular subcultures with a shared status as "Americans." Recall that a commemoration of the 250th anniversary of Jewish communal life—held in Carnegie Hall in 1905—featured the recitation of a letter from the president that applauded Jews for staying "loyal to their faith and their race traditions" while still becoming "indissolubly incorporated in the great army of American citizenship."[103]

Roosevelt sounded a similarly pluralistic note later in his presidency when he wrote to a group of Jewish children in advance of a Hannukah celebration at Jacob Riis's settlement house. "The fine loyalty and valiant achievements of the Maccabees have always made them favorite heroes of mine," he offered in a reprise of his days as police commissioner when he had routinely lauded American Jews who emulated their Maccabean forebearers. The president's letter continued, "It is a good thing that the Jewish boys and girls should keep their pride in and admiration for their own heroes of early days, and such pride and admiration, instead of hindering them, will help them to the friendliest and most brotherly relations with all their fellow Americans."[104] Jews could integrate into the United States by honoring, not disowning, their heritage.

Given Roosevelt's inconsistent views on immigrants, it unsurprising that his policy preferences reflected those inconsistencies. He felt torn throughout his career between his instinct to restrict immigration for the benefit of those already in the United States and his desire for America to serve as a refuge for the world's oppressed. Among Roosevelt's contemporaries who endorsed restriction, some did so out of a concern for protecting domestic labor from an influx of competition; others were driven by anxieties that foreign arrivals were racially incompatible with the native-born population. Roosevelt sometimes belonged to both camps simultaneously. In a magazine article published shortly before his appointment as police commissioner, he asserted, "It is urgently necessary to check and regulate our immigration, by much more drastic laws than now exist; and this should be done both to keep out laborers who tend to depress the labor market, and to keep out races which do not assimilate readily with our own." Yet Roosevelt decried xenophobia as "utterly un-American" in the very same article.[105] His position, in effect, was that immigrants deserved a warm welcome, but only if they posed no undue threat to laborers and were prepared to embrace American culture.

Roosevelt articulated a similarly conflicted attitude in another magazine, the *Review of Reviews*, three years later. That piece excoriated nativists for their self-perceived superiority. "I have no sympathy with mere dislike of immigrants," he announced. "There are classes and even nationalities of them which stand at least on an equality with the citizens of native birth." But in the next sentence, Roosevelt called for immigration restriction, fusing together concern for American labor with the prevailing racial biases of the day: "In the interest of our workingmen we must in the end keep out laborers who are ignorant, vicious, and with low standards of life and comfort, just as we have shut out the Chinese."[106] TR would carry these warring instincts about immigration into the White House.

During his presidency, Roosevelt's compassion for immigrants was evident in his oversight of William Williams, the commissioner of Ellis Island. Williams was a restrictionist with limited affinity for Southern and Eastern Europeans, and his stringent application of immigration laws reflected as much. Unsurprisingly, Jews weren't enamored of Williams.[107]

A group of Jewish leaders—headed by Roosevelt's old college classmate and congressional ally, Lucius Littauer—met with the president to voice their concerns that many Jewish immigrants were unfairly subjected to deportation. Afterward, TR told Williams about that visit, stressing that these Jewish leaders were "men of very high character" and "valued friends of mine." Roosevelt admonished Williams that it was "doubly incumbent scrupulously to avoid any appearance of unnecessary harshness" in deportation cases. The president conceded that immigrants who "tend to the physical or moral deterioration of our people" must be repatriated to their country of origin. But even so, Williams was to remain ever mindful in the case of any given candidate for deportation that "to send him back is often to inflict a punishment upon him only less severe than death itself, and in such cases we must be sure not merely that we are acting aright but that we are able to show to others that we are acting aright." Substance and optics both mattered. To those ends, the president instructed Williams to allow potential deportees of Jewish background to be accompanied by "a reputable representative of the United Hebrew Societies" to ensure the actuality of due process and its appearance. Roosevelt added that the same practice should hold for non-Jewish immigrants—like the Italians and

Irish—who would find comparable support from their own local aid societies as their deportation cases were adjudicated.[108]

In the same letter, TR pressed Williams to generally stay in "close touch" with charitable organizations that assisted immigrants. It behooved Williams to persuade them "that your aim is not to do anything to discriminate against the immigrant, especially the immigrant of any particular race or creed." To soften his message, Roosevelt assured Williams that the Jewish leaders who had conveyed their misgivings nevertheless praised the Ellis Island commissioner's integrity.[109] It is dubious that Williams actually believed they were terribly delighted with him.[110]

Later that year, TR made his first presidential visit to Ellis Island, and in Rooseveltian fashion, the whole affair was a string of sensational moments. He departed Oyster Bay on a government-owned yacht with an entourage that included his wife, his son Kermit, and America's most famous immigrant, Jacob Riis. The yacht forged its way through a tempest that roiled the Long Island Sound with ferocious winds and frightful waves. Officials back on Ellis Island were skeptical that Roosevelt would hazard the trip under such volatile conditions. But around two o'clock that afternoon, amid the fog and rain, the president's yacht improbably came into view. The party anchored some distance off Ellis Island, and a tug boat—due to deliver Roosevelt the final leg of the trip—defied the "howling gale" and attempted the "ticklish job" of aligning itself next to the president's yacht, as the *New York Times* detailed. He embarked on the tug and braved the last stretch of his journey on the deck, cheerfully waving his signature slouch hat as the precipitation drenched him. Once docked, Roosevelt raced across a wobbly plank onto the iconic isle where each day thousands of aspiring Americans first set foot.[111]

The president was then joined by a pair of U.S. senators and his longtime Jewish ally Nathan Bijur, among others. Roosevelt's first order of business: declaring the appointment of a special committee to uncover any discrimination on Ellis Island. The *New York Tribune* reported that the committee had been initiated at Williams's own request to investigate and debunk accusations of his malfeasance. Conversely, the *New York Times* contended that Williams had been deprived of "the slightest

FIGURE. 7.1. Immigrants at Ellis Island, with the Manhattan skyline in the distance. *Source*: Library of Congress, Prints and Photographs Division.

intimation" ahead of time about the committee and that this unexpected announcement "came like a thunderclap out of a clear sky." In either case, Williams was an unpopular figure with immigrant communities, and the creation of the special committee reflected Roosevelt's keen interest in cultivating a reputation for fair play. The remainder of the president's tour of the island, spanning nearly five hours, involved various gestures of courtesy to the foreign newcomers. He shook hands and exchanged words with those waiting to be processed. And in one remarkable instance, Roosevelt took it upon himself to personally adjudicate a detention case where he summarily decided to free a woman pleading for release.[112]

His diverse appointees for the investigatory committee nodded to the immigrant communities whose unease he hoped to assuage. An unsympathetic newspaperman chided the president for choosing "two Germans, two Irishmen and a Jew—not a single native American [i.e., Anglo-Saxon]." In turn, Roosevelt boasted to one of the committee members, "Evidently, that writer did not regard me as a 'nativist!'"[113] The committee's final report, while offering suggestions for improvement, exonerated Williams of any misconduct.[114] Still, it is notable that when Williams resigned his post toward the end of Roosevelt's first term, the president replaced him with a more moderate successor who was himself an immigrant.[115]

Notwithstanding a dramatic voyage to Ellis Island and his establishment of an investigatory committee, the president sided with the restrictionists on a key issue: the literacy test. In his second term, Congress considered making literacy in any language a prerequisite for admission into the country. The proposed law—although neutral on its face—would disproportionately exclude new-stock immigrants in practice. Illiteracy rates among them were high: one in four Jews, nearly two in five Russian Gentiles, and a majority of southern Italians. Conversely, immigrants from old-stock countries such as the England, Ireland, and Germany could boast literacy rates of 95 percent or better.[116] Like immigration restriction generally, the literacy test created some unlikely alliances. Proponents of the test included nativists, who were suspicious of alien blood, and laborers seeking to insulate themselves from competition. The opposition encompassed certain industrial interests, which wanted a steady influx of inexpensive workers, and people with genuine sympathy for new immigrants.

Back in 1896, Senator Henry Cabot Lodge successfully shepherded the literacy test through Congress, but President Grover Cleveland deemed it prejudicial and vetoed the bill. Roosevelt proved more sympathetic, endorsing the idea as early as 1901 in his first State of the Union message. By the spring of 1906, the Immigration Restriction League, working in tandem with the American Federation of Labor, made considerable headway in rallying lawmakers behind the literacy test. It looked as though Congress might well be poised to codify the measure, with the Senate approving it in late May. If the restrictionists could prevail in the House of Representatives as well and keep Roosevelt to his word to sign the bill, the literacy test would become the law of the land.[117]

The literacy test was distinct from passports and pogroms in that it wasn't a specifically Jewish issue. But Jewish interests were certainly implicated. Oscar Straus—still months away from his cabinet nomination at this point—fretted that a literacy requirement would preclude 10 percent of Jewish foreigners from entry into America, a number far too high for his comfort. Had he known that illiteracy among Jewish arrivals was actually 26 percent, Straus's angst would have been that much more acute. Still, he felt hesitant to lobby the president on the matter, telling a fellow Jewish leader, "We should not trouble him unless it becomes absolutely necessary."[118] Straus was understandably reticent to overspend his political capital with TR at that particular moment; only a month prior, he had solicited a wary Roosevelt to address Russia about the specter of renewed pogroms as the Easter holiday approached. However, Straus's misgivings about the literacy test soon outran his reluctance to pester the president. He pressed his case against the measure to TR with a letter in late May and then again in person in early June.[119] But Roosevelt was immovable, telling Straus that he felt bound by previous statements in which he publicly backed such a test.[120]

Fortunately for Oscar Straus, other forces joined him in opposing the restrictionists. He found a willing partner in America's most prominent Catholic, Cardinal James Gibbons, whose flock included many immigrants.[121] The cardinal took up the cause and beseeched Roosevelt to "prevent the passage of such an obnoxious bill."[122] Meanwhile, industries like shipping, railroad, and steel were all active in their resistance to the literacy test.[123] And there was public protest as well. At a mass meeting on the Lower East Side, the Federation of Jewish Organizations fulminated against the literacy test. Prominent attendees included a pair of New York congressmen—one a Democrat, the other a Republican. The meeting's chairman, Edward Lauterbach, addressed a packed throng of two thousand onlookers, proclaiming, "While the Russian government not long ago and even now is murdering and prosecuting the Jews . . . we should open our arms and say to them, 'Come to us. Come to our country, where you will have freedom, liberty, and work, even if you do not know how to read and write.'"[124] For thousands of Russia's Jews hoping to flee stateside, the stakes of the literacy test were existential.

Lauterbach organized a deputation to meet with Roosevelt the following week in the hopes of dislodging the president from his position on the bill. That group included leaders from various immigrant societies. Pro-immigration American Southerners were also present; they wanted to see new arrivals redirected from crowded coastal cities to the underdeveloped parts of their own region. Roosevelt expressed sympathy with his visitors' collective aims but made plain that his perspective remained unshaken.[125]

Although the test enjoyed widespread support among lawmakers, the domineering Speaker of the House—Joseph "Uncle Joe" Cannon—wouldn't necessarily throw his all-important weight behind the measure. Cannon maintained a studied silence, abstaining from any stance on the issue before debate opened on the House floor.[126] Roosevelt leaned on Cannon to pass the bill. In a letter, the president explained to the Speaker his own, somewhat begrudging, endorsement of the literacy test. TR admitted that he would prefer a more holistic approach to screening immigrants: in an ideal world, American consuls overseas would vet prospective newcomers to ensure they were "physically, morally, and intellectually of a good type." But that plan wasn't "at present practicable," and so Roosevelt was willing to settle for the literacy test—and he hoped Cannon would, too. The test would prevent "immense masses of cheap labor" from flooding the domestic marketplace. Roosevelt's letter also criticized certain business interests for fighting the literacy test in their self-serving bid to suppress wages for American workers, native-born and foreign-born alike.[127]

Two weeks later, the president sent another letter to Speaker Cannon, acknowledging that he was under pressure from Jews and Catholics. "I have had frank talks with very good and staunch friends of mine representing the Jewish and Italian elements in our population," Roosevelt informed Cannon. The president went on to recount the substance of those conversations: he had told those friends that he lacked "a particle of prejudice against any man because of creed or birthplace" and that his chief interest lay in protecting "manual laborers," a category that included countless recent immigrants. Whereas nativists were championing the literacy test because it promised to favor old-stock immigrants over the new, Roosevelt proceeded from a different logic: overcrowded tenements and meager earnings precluded new immigrants from achieving a better life. Those new immigrants stood only to benefit from an attenuated flow of human capital into the labor market, TR reasoned.[128]

In his foregoing letter to Cannon, the president expressly collapsed the distinction between old and new immigrants. "Like the Germans, the Scandinavians, the English, Irish, Dutch, French, and Swiss, so I believe that ultimately Jew and Italian, Mongol and Slav will, if given the chance, become, and see their children become, just as good citizens as anyone else," Roosevelt affirmed. "But I do not think that under the present laws they get this proper chance, and the effect is bad for them and bad for the rest of the country."[129] TR was surely genuine in his conviction that the literacy test would elevate rather than exacerbate conditions for new-stock immigrants. After all, he had shown a consistent willingness to embrace Southern and Eastern Europeans since his days as police commissioner, and his letter to Cannon reflects that long-standing commitment. The president's advocacy of the literacy test may have placed him on the same side of this policy debate as the nativists, but it wasn't because he shared their anxieties about Jews and other new-stock Europeans.

Roosevelt's appeals to Cannon fell on deaf ears. As the House members prepared to vote on the literacy test in late June, the Speaker announced his opposition and browbeat his caucus into defeating the provision. His imperious tactics on the House floor included seizing members by their collars and wrenching them from their chairs.[130] Despite his animosity to the test, Cannon didn't bother to disclose his motivations at the time. Years later he would clarify that he quashed the literacy test because relatively open immigration thus far had served the United States well and he saw no reason to change course.[131] Cannon was also undoubtedly informed by his laissez-faire economic philosophy, which saw immigration restriction as a form of government interference in the market that unduly boosted labor at the expense of capital.[132] And there were campaign considerations as well—his congressional district was home to a sizable immigrant vote.[133]

Although Cannon killed the literacy test at this juncture, its proponents hoped they might soon revive it in Congress. Roosevelt, however, became increasingly uninterested. He had never been as enthused about the test as were the xenophobic restrictionists. And Roosevelt grew concerned over the summer that Republican support for the literacy test might play poorly in the upcoming midterm elections. By October, he was voicing doubts about the test's efficacy to an advisor. The vice president of the Immigration Restriction League grumbled to one of the league's founders that TR was now taking a "more the merrier" approach to foreign transplants.[134]

Roosevelt's State of the Union that fall made a vigorous case for an inclusive nation. The president's earlier annual messages had hewed to a middle course that honored immigrants as valuable additions to American society while nonetheless objecting to their unfettered admission.[135] But now Roosevelt emphasized only the theme of acceptance. He maintained that the determination whether to admit a given immigrant must rest upon a principled blindness to both religious background and national origin. "Whether they are Catholic or Protestant, Jew or Gentile; whether they come from England or Germany, Russia, Japan, or Italy, matters nothing," stressed Roosevelt. "All we have a right to question is the man's conduct." The president declared that once immigrants secure entry into the country, they deserve respect. Drawing language from the Book of Exodus, he admonished his fellow citizens, "Especially do we need to remember our duty to the stranger within our gates." TR also confronted the xenophobic currents in American culture, asserting, "It is the sure mark of a low civilization, a low morality, to abuse or discriminate against or in any way humiliate such stranger who has come here lawfully and who is conducting himself properly."[136] On the very day that Roosevelt submitted this message to Congress, he sent his nomination of Oscar Straus to the Senate for confirmation as the cabinet secretary in charge of immigration. Entrusting a foreign-born Jew with the immigration portfolio was the most prominent indication yet that the president had abandoned his alliance with the restrictionists.

★ ★ ★

As the public learned that Oscar Straus would become the first Jew in the cabinet, contemporaries immediately recognized the multilayered significance of his appointment. The *Trenton Evening Times* marveled at the historic measure: "Never before in American history has a Jew held office in the president's cabinet."[137] Naturally, the Jewish press celebrated this milestone. The *Reform Advocate* gushed that the news "cannot fail to fill the heart of every American Jew with joy"—the Roosevelt administration was "epoch-making." That paper further suggested that Roosevelt's choice for the role was a clarion signal: surely, the president now opposed restrictionist legislation and preferred lenient interpretation of existing immigration statutes.[138]

Newspapers saw that the stakes were international. As the *Cleveland Plain Dealer* reported of Straus's nomination, "Abroad it is expected to give notice that this government is animated by the most friendly feelings toward the Jews."[139] Meanwhile, the *Reform Advocate* discerned a message to Jew-haters at home, contending that the appointment was intended as "a rebuke to possible antisemitic know-nothingism."[140] (The term "know-nothingism" derived from the "Know-Nothing Party," a xenophobic movement in America that had died out decades earlier but whose peculiar name endured in the national lexicon as a shorthand for nativism.) Some papers underscored the electoral consequences of Straus's ascendancy. Not only would Straus endear Jews all the more to the GOP, but he was also a Democrat whose willingness to break partisan ranks might well lure Gentile members of his party to do the same at the polls.[141]

As an undergraduate at Columbia in the 1860s, Straus had been denied membership in a campus literary society on account of his Jewish identity; now he was conferred membership in the cabinet of an American president.[142] Straus's gratitude to Roosevelt ran deep. "You have made me famous," he exclaimed, as congratulatory telegrams poured in from all corners of the globe. Straus knew that he carried the weight not just of the department he would lead but of the precedent he would set for American Jewry. As he told Roosevelt, "I appreciate the honor and its significance."[143] Straus further expressed the hope that he would live up to Roosevelt's expectations, prompting a warm reply from the president: "I only wish that I had as little cause for anxiety about the result of all my actions, great and small, as about the action in your case. Good luck to you!"[144]

★ ★ ★

Oscar Straus was a tireless cabinet member whose typical work week stretched seventy hours with no days off. Much of that time was spent advancing the cause of immigrants. Despite the department's diverse portfolio—which ranged from labor relations to lighthouses—Straus recalled that "no subject in the department occupied my daily attention to the extent that immigration did." He felt compassion for refugees fleeing persecution abroad, but this did not mean he saw the admission of foreigners as a mere act of charity by the United States. Rather, argued Straus, migration to America produced manifold benefits for the country. Immigrants spurred economic growth by furnishing fresh sources of human capital. And an inclusive immigration policy also strengthened American ties to other nations and thereby expanded trade opportunities. That the United States spanned a vast continent with space aplenty for settlement made the case all the stronger for a hearty embrace of aspiring citizens, Straus insisted.[145]

He personally visited immigration processing sites and directed officials to treat the recent arrivals with dignity. Straus even gave money from his own pocket to the Ellis Island commissioner for distribution to the neediest newcomers. Immigrants sometimes faced deportation on the grounds that they were prone to become a burden to the state, but they could appeal their pending expulsions; Straus took it upon himself to personally decide all such cases and showed great sensitivity to their plight. He was instinctively reluctant to condemn Russian Jews to a horrid fate back in the czar's empire. To be sure, Straus always operated within the confines of the law, but statutes could be applied with greater or lesser severity, and he unapologetically opted for a merciful approach. "I would be less than human if I failed to interpret the law as humanely as possible," he told his brother. Straus added, "I propose to remain on the side of the angels, come what will, and I shall defy hostile criticisms—to do less would be cowardly."[146] With a foreign-born Jew championing immigration, the criticism was destined to be hostile indeed.

The most conspicuous of objections to Straus came from the most predictable of sources: Prescott Hall, founding member of the Immigration Restriction League.[147] Hall's general xenophobia was of a piece with his particular antisemitism. Relying on well-worn stereotypes about Jewish connivery, he claimed that Jewish immigrants were "trying to gain some monetary advantage by craft and deceit."[148] Unsurprisingly, Hall did not thrill to Straus's appointment, deriding him as a "bitter opponent of immigration restriction."[149] Hall tried to persuade Roosevelt that the Jewish cabinet secretary was disregarding immigration laws in order to admit undesirable foreigners. The president was skeptical of Hall's accusations. "I have a very high regard for Secretary Straus," Roosevelt informed Hall, "and it is exceedingly difficult for me to believe that there has been the slightest conscious failure on his part to enforce the immigration law." His faith in Straus notwithstanding, TR was willing to submit the matter to the Immigration Commission—an investigatory body comprising three experts plus six lawmakers. Among the lawmakers was Henry Cabot Lodge, who had been the Senate's foremost proponent of the literacy test. Roosevelt assured Hall, "Lodge is very anxious that [immigration law] should be enforced with the utmost strictness."[150]

The commission simply could not find any evidence of malfeasance on Straus's part. Lodge reported to the president that Prescott Hall's allegations were left unsubstantiated: "[Hall] is extreme and does not understand that it is one thing to make general charges on hearsay and another to sustain them by proof." Senator Lodge had heartfelt sympathy for Hall and shared his restrictionist goals, but the commission's inquiry into Straus had been a fool's errand. "There was no escape from the facts," Lodge conceded.[151]

Still, Senator Lodge's letter to Roosevelt managed to convey doubts about Oscar Straus. Lodge speculated—without evidence, by his own admission—that Straus perhaps failed to adequately apply immigration laws when they disproportionately burdened indigent Jews. One such law excluded immigrants with "physical and mental defects" who would struggle to secure employment and were thus liable to become wards of the state. Pursuant to that statute, immigration officers employed a "poor physique" standard to assess new arrivals; many malnourished Jews who had just fled destitution were unlikely to fare well under such a precondition. Lodge told Roosevelt, "That Mr. Straus is adverse to the laws which affect the entry of poor Jews, and especially to the poor physique clause, I believe to be true, and if true it is unfortunate in the head of that Department. How far his influence is exerted to procure slackness in exclusions, I do not know. I can only say we found no proof." According to Lodge's antisemitic logic, even a complete lack of evidence that Straus had been malfeasant was insufficient to merit his exoneration.[152] Roosevelt, for his part, was unwilling to indulge Lodge's aspersions and instead deemed the commission's findings to be "conclusive" vindication of Straus.[153]

Given nativist anxieties around Jewish newcomers, the president must not have been terribly surprised that Straus's role irked the likes of the Immigration Restriction League. The elevation of Straus to the cabinet in any capacity would have been historic; the decision to place a Jew of foreign birth in charge of American immigration was arguably audacious. The president, after a tepid response to the 1905 pogrom surge, had reclaimed some goodwill with American Jewry thanks to the Straus appointment. But Roosevelt would soon find an unexpected threat to those warm relations. At the twilight of his presidency, a disturbing revelation surfaced, one that suggested his administration itself was becoming an active tool of Russian antisemitism.

8

ELECTION YEAR

As an election year dawned in 1908, a British-Jewish journalist named Maurice Low intimated in the London *Morning Post* that Theodore Roosevelt would break his promise not to seek a third term. The American president, in turn, sneered to an English friend, "Maurice Low is a circumcised skunk."[1] It was a rare, if not altogether unprecedented, antisemitic slur from Roosevelt. In any event, Low's reporting proved erroneous. TR was indeed determined to step down and bequeath the White House to his preferred heir-apparent: William Howard Taft, the secretary of war.[2]

Roosevelt was never one to take the Jewish vote for granted, and 1908 would prove no exception. He had always been keen—especially in election years—to solidify a favorable record on Jewish causes, one that fellow Republicans could tout in their own bids for office. But in the early weeks of 1908, the Passport Question suddenly reemerged as a major vulnerability for the Roosevelt administration, which found itself fending off accusations that it had become a willing accomplice in Russia's anti-Jewish agenda.

Recall that back in October 1904, Russia had given indication to the Roosevelt administration that it intended to repeal its passport restrictions on American Jews. The mere signal of reform had been a public win for the president, all the more valuable for its timing amid his reelection campaign. But in the years that followed, it became clear that passport revision was just another empty promise about Jewish rights that Russia had made for strategic reasons. Jews bearing American passports, with a handful of exceptions, continued to face exclusion from Russian borders.

For most of Roosevelt's second term, more urgent matters overshadowed the Passport Question. The scourge of pogroms abroad and the specter of a literacy test at home preoccupied American Jewry. But late in Roosevelt's presidency, Secretary of State Elihu Root promulgated a circular about passports that alarmed Jewish leaders. The circular announced that the State Department—consistent with Russia's own policy of excluding Jews—would decline to issue passports to U.S. citizens of Jewish faith who were intent on entering Russia.[3]

This circular diverged markedly from an earlier version in 1901, produced just before Roosevelt became president. The 1901 circular did warn American Jews about Russian restrictions on them, but the State Department at that time hardly shaped its own policies to accord with Russian prejudice. Jews with U.S. citizenship remained free to seek passports from their government. The State Department itself took no cognizance of any American's religious identity, even as Russian consulates on U.S. soil interrogated visa applicants to winnow out Jews. That status quo was now upended by the appearance of this new circular by Secretary Root, who appeared to be doing Russia's bidding. He officially divided Americans into two classes: Jews and Gentiles. The former were refused the right to a passport enjoyed by the latter—all to accommodate the bigotry of a foreign power, no less. Never before in the nation's history had its Jewish citizens been subject to a religious test by their government.[4]

The newly constituted American Jewish Committee (AJC) mobilized to combat this latest affront to Jewish dignity. The AJC had been formed just two years earlier, in 1906, in response to the mass violence visited on Russian Jewry. Before then, temporary Jewish committees had sprung up to collect donations and press the federal government for action as circumstances merited. But those ad hoc measures had their limitations—advocacy in Washington proved only as effective as the personal connections that Jewish grandees happened to share with political figures at a given moment. Jewry required a more institutionalized approach, a permanent body that could robustly address Jewish issues whenever they arose. The AJC promised to fill that need.[5]

True, there already *was* a longstanding institution with a history of lobbying American civic leaders on Jewish causes: B'nai B'rith. But B'nai B'rith principally emphasized humanitarian relief, not political persuasion. In theory, B'nai B'rith's top brass might have put ego aside and welcomed the creation of the AJC as a valuable complement to their own important role. In reality, they felt threatened by the idea of the AJC; the very prospect of the new organization felt like an indictment of B'nai B'rith's past efforts.[6] Proponents of the AJC pushed ahead, and their ranks included key German-American Jews such as Jacob Schiff and Oscar Straus (though Straus stepped aside after accepting his cabinet appointment). The AJC thus continued the custom whereby affluent Central European Jews served as the principal spokesmen for their impoverished Russian coreligionists.[7]

When the AJC learned of the State Department's prejudicial circular, a pair of AJC officials—Louis Marshall and Edward Lauterbach—took action. The two had much in common: both were Germans by descent, lawyers by profession, and New Yorkers by residence. They were also Republicans, so their criticism of the Roosevelt administration wasn't attributable to partisan politics. In a letter to Root sent in early February 1908, Marshall and Lauterbach inveighed against the State Department for conferring second-class citizenship on Jews. The right of American Jews to a passport had become conditional, whereas "all other citizens, of whatever race or creed, are assured an unlimited passport and are guaranteed the absolute protection of our flag." This kind of antisemitic discrimination was unprecedented in the annals of the republic, lamented Marshall and Lauterbach: "An American citizen applying to the State Department for a passport, who is suspected of being a Jew, is for the first time in our history obliged to disclose his faith." They referenced the Treaty of 1832, whereby Russian and American nationals were supposed to enjoy freedom of travel between the two countries. Root's circular was "practically justifying Russia in the violation of her treaty obligations and condoning her contemptuous disregard of the American passport." It had been degrading enough that Russian consulates in the United States interrogated visa applicants about their religion, but now—the AJC leaders fumed—America's own government "seeks to indulge in these inquisitorial practices and to apply an unconstitutional religious test." Marshall and Lauterbach closed their missive with a request that Root rescind the circular.[8]

As it turned out, Oscar Straus had already been working toward that end from within the administration. Straus brought the circular to Roosevelt's attention, and the president promptly ordered Root to eliminate the discriminatory language.[9] Unbeknownst to the AJC, Root had produced a new circular just days before he received the exasperated letter from Marshall and Lauterbach. This revised circular avoided any mention of Jews and forwent any provision for denying passports. It merely relayed that Russia considered it a crime for a Russian to assume citizenship in another country (unless the expatriate in question received the prior consent of the Russian authorities), and therefore Russian-born Americans who managed to return to their native land were liable to suffer imprisonment.[10]

But news of the amended circular did not fully insulate the administration from reproach. On the House floor, a Democratic congressman from New York, Francis Harrison, denounced the rescinded circular as a national embarrassment and a breach of the Treaty of 1832—a treaty in which the rights of American Jews weren't supposed to hinge "upon the whims and fancies of an unhappy autocrat," Harrison insisted. He endorsed a proposed resolution that would call on Secretary Root to provide the House with details about any efforts by the State Department to extract concessions from Russia on the Passport Question. Root had thus far been disinclined to divulge such details to Congress, probably because he had done very little. A Republican representative from Illinois who opposed the resolution came to Root's defense, declaring, "We have confidence enough in the secretary of state to believe that his judgment should be supreme on this question." To what was surely Root's relief, the resolution failed 118 to 97. Still, the prejudicial circular, even if no longer operative, had plainly created an opening for Democrats to agitate against the Roosevelt administration.[11]

That same day, Root submitted his revised circular to the AJC leaders and asked if they saw anything amiss with its phrasing. They did. Marshall and Lauterbach took issue with a specific line that read: "An

American citizen, formerly a subject of Russia, who returns to that country places himself within the jurisdiction of Russian law and cannot expect immunity from its operations." They argued that this language contravened a congressional statute requiring the president to defend the rights of Americans abroad. The State Department was effectively signaling to Russia that the U.S. government would not enforce its own statute, Marshall and Lauterbach cautioned. In their words, the circular was tantamount to "an implied invitation ... to violate the rights of American citizenship."[12] Root's deputy quickly informed the AJC that the State Department would dispense with the problematic wording.[13]

The State Department had now rectified its terminology twice, but the Passport Question continued to fester. Russia's longstanding ban on Jewish visitors showed no signs of abating, and Root's ill-advised circular inadvertently helped revive the Passport Question as a central concern for American Jewry. Rarely did Jews in the United States, whether Russian-born or not, harbor any desire to actually visit the czar's empire. But Jewish Americans on principle rejected the notion that a foreign nation could impose upon them a religious test on their own soil. And they were also alive to the implications of the Passport Question for Russia's Jews—observers in the United States had long believed that the admission of American Jews to Russia would create a chain reaction, culminating in the end of Russia's restrictions on her own Jewish subjects. This line of reasoning began with a provision in the Treaty of 1832 that afforded U.S. nationals in Russia the same rights as natives. Were Russia to open its gates to American Jews, then two classes of Jews would be found within the empire: domestic Jews, enduring a perilous struggle for life and livelihood; and foreign Jews, enjoying the very same liberties exercised by Russian Gentiles. Russia's regime of persecution would supposedly implode under the crushing weight of that contradiction.[14]

As early as 1881, the secretary of state conveyed to a State Department official that the sitting president, Chester Arthur, subscribed to this domino theory of Jewish emancipation. Arthur reportedly anticipated "that an amelioration of the treatment of the American Israelites in Russia could only result [in] a very decided betterment of the condition of the native Hebrews—that any steps taken toward the relief of one would necessarily react in favor of the other."[15] Recall that Jacob Schiff made a similar prediction in 1904. "When foreign Jews are equally entitled to cross the Russian border with other foreigners," he surmised, "then the Russian government will not long be able to insist on maintaining the scandalous restrictive laws against her own Jews."[16] Russia, too, recognized a necessary relationship between banning Jews from abroad and discriminating against Jews at home. In a letter to Roosevelt, Schiff recounted how a Russian official had candidly revealed to him that the czar's regime "would not grant to foreign Israelites the privilege to freely move about its domain, while its laws denied the same right to its own Jewish subjects."[17] American Jewry and the Russian government proved unyielding on the Passport Question precisely because each side understood its vast ramifications. The real stakes were not the very few Jews trying to enter Russia but the many millions of Jews with no means to escape it.

In May of 1908, the AJC decided to call for a radical move from the Roosevelt administration. This time the message came from AJC president Mayer Sulzberger, a state court judge in Pennsylvania, and it was addressed to Roosevelt directly. Sulzberger suggested that the United States should now force Russia's hand with "direct and emphatic" action: the unilateral withdrawal from the Treaty of 1832. Roosevelt could thereby coerce Russia to the bargaining table for a new treaty, one that would affirm the right to mutual travel while providing enforcement mechanisms to ensure Russia's fulfillment of its obligations. Drawing on his judicial background, Sulzberger argued that the U.S. Constitution guaranteed equal justice to all citizens, and therefore any treaties brokered under the Constitution's authority must accord with that paramount principle of equality. He acknowledged it was difficult to correct "wrongs encrusted with age" but nevertheless insisted that "the dignity of our own country" was on the line.[18]

Judge Sulzberger also encouraged Roosevelt to void another American treaty with Russia—an 1887 agreement providing for the reciprocal extradition of criminals. He explained that Russia, with its warped view of criminality, ruthlessly condemned political dissidents as lawbreakers. If such dissidents reached American shores, the treaty obliged the United States to forsake its rightful role as an asylum and ship these alleged "criminals" back to Russia's corrupt empire.[19] Extradition was something of a sidelight that American Jews hadn't previously emphasized in their lobbying of the administration. Even Sulzberger would have been surprised when unforeseeable events late in the campaign season would make extradition an explosive issue.

Roosevelt passed along the foregoing missive to Secretary Root, who in turn assured Judge Sulzberger, "The letter will receive attentive consideration."[20] But neither Roosevelt nor Root was inclined to take the drastic step of unilaterally dissolving Russo-American treaties. The administration let the matter rest, at least for the time being.[21]

Shortly thereafter, TR wrote Root, "The Jews always want to embroil us with Russia, and therefore feel very friendly with England" because England periodically launched its own diplomatic bids against Russian antisemitism. Roosevelt wasn't actually complaining here. Indeed, he saw American Jewry's aversion to Russia as beneficial to his foreign policy; it counterbalanced the Irish-American opposition to England. The president's letter ticked through a number of other immigrant communities—Poles, Danes, Norwegians, Swedes, Germans, French, Greeks, Armenians—each wanting him to adopt some particular position in global affairs, each offset by some other group. As Roosevelt mused, "It is a good thing from the standpoint of the Americans of this country that we have many different race elements coming, instead of simply one." Pluralism had created a diplomatic equilibrium that Anglo-Saxonism alone could not.[22]

As spring turned to summer, the campaign heated up along with the weather. Republicans were eager to court the Jewish vote and remained alive to the Passport Question. Their convention, as it had four years earlier, approved a platform calling for the protection of U.S. citizens abroad. The Democrats followed suit at their own convention two weeks later. But neither party went so far as to adopt AJC's hard-line position of unilateral treaty abrogation.[23]

With William Howard Taft poised to become the GOP standard-bearer, he came under pressure from the AJC to foreground the Passport Question. Judge Sulzberger urged Taft to address the issue in his speech accepting the Republican nomination. Taft obliged. Standing before a boisterous throng in his native Cincinnati, Taft decried as "repugnant" any foreign power that classified American citizens by religion. He pledged to advance Roosevelt's efforts by taking "every proper endeavor to secure the abolition of such distinctions." Yet Taft avoided specificity about what those endeavors would look like.[24]

The following month, Roosevelt was delighted by a flattering revelation from an improbable source—Russia's most esteemed sociologist. Professor Maksim Kovalevsky, from the University of St. Petersburg, had gained access to classified documents about the Portsmouth Peace Conference of 1905 and produced a report on the negotiations that proved highly laudatory of Roosevelt's contributions. Kovalevsky's study praised TR for keeping alive peace talks that might have easily unraveled. The professor also brought to light a previously unpublicized detail: in the days following the treaty signing, the American president had beseeched Count Witte to lift Russia's invidious ban on foreign Jews. This disclosure first appeared in a Russian outlet before reaching the American press; the New York Times dedicated nearly two full pages to its digest of the Kovalevsky report.[25]

The news came at an auspicious moment for Roosevelt. After the embarrassment of Root's discriminatory circular earlier that year, TR now scored a notable public relations win with Jewry just as the campaign season was ramping up. Leslie's Weekly, a well-regarded magazine, crowed in its coverage of the Kovalevsky report, "The Jewish people in the United States have every reason to entertain profound respect for the president."[26] Naturally, Roosevelt was "mighty interested" when the magazine's editor forwarded him a copy of that article. "I had never felt at liberty myself to speak of the fact that I interceded as strongly as I know how with Witte in the matter of passports for American citizens of Jewish faith," the president explained. "But I am very glad that someone has brought it out." He then recollected how he had "with the utmost emphasis" admonished Witte that as long as Russia persisted in its prejudice, so would the "constant bitterness" between their two countries.[27]

A month later, *Leslie's Weekly* continued to trumpet Roosevelt's advocacy for Jews, this time in a piece entitled, "What the Jew Owes to the Republican Party," by the partisan journalist Charles Harvey. His article was breathlessly loose in its fidelity to the facts. Harvey claimed about the Roosevelt-Witte meeting in 1905, "It is certain that the improvement in Russia's attitude toward the Jews dates from that affair, and Mr. Roosevelt had a decisive influence in bringing it about." Harvey's specific examples of such "improvement" were divorced from reality. He erroneously contended, "There have been no repetitions of the Kishinev massacre of the Jews." In reality, the bloodiest wave of pogroms began just *after* Roosevelt's meeting with Witte. The article also falsely asserted that the Passport Question was resolved: "In the attitude of Russia toward the American Jews who visit her, no line is drawn between them and the Christians." Harvey further credited Roosevelt with the establishment of "elections with the successive Dumas," neglecting to mention that the czar had dissolved the first two Dumas to preserve his autocratic agenda. Of course, the article's ultimate aim was to extend Roosevelt's popularity with Jews to Taft. "The Jews have known, too, that Secretary Taft was in hearty sympathy with the president," Harvey assured his vote-casting readers.[28]

That article's abundant inaccuracies aside, Roosevelt was pleased with the piece, alerting Taft to "an article by Harvey, which I think may help us among the Jews," and enclosing a copy for Taft's perusal. Roosevelt's missive also came with a cautionary note about campaign optics. "About your playing golf . . . I have received literally hundreds of letters from the West protesting about it," the president wrote. He advised Taft to delay his next eighteen holes until after election day.[29]

After the editor of *Leslie's Weekly* suggested to Roosevelt that Jewish support for the GOP was tepid, the president anxiously replied, "I am concerned at what you tell me as to the attitude of the Jews. My own information was that they were favorable." TR speculated that Harvey's "excellent" article had failed to reach a sufficient audience owing to a "lack of funds"—presumably from the Republican Party—that would have otherwise ensured its wide distribution.[30]

★ ★ ★

The battle for Jewish voters unexpectedly expanded to novel terrain in August: extradition. Previously, the topic hadn't preoccupied American Jewry; the AJC's request in May that Roosevelt void the extradition treaty with Russia was anomalous. Pogroms, passports, and literacy tests had been the focal points of Jewish activism. But in late summer 1908, extradition suddenly became a rallying cry.

The precipitating event was the extradition case of Jan Janoff Pouren. Hailing from the Latvian region of the Russian Empire, Pouren was a Gentile revolutionary who had agitated against the Russian authorities in 1906 before absconding to New York City. Russia requested his extradition in early 1908, and the State Department initiated the hearings that would decide Pouren's fate. According to Russia, Pouren was a criminal guilty of theft, arson, and homicide. According to Pouren's supporters, he was a humble peasant who had been forced to take up arms and defend his village against an unjust assault by Russian soldiers. His entire case turned on the distinction between these two perspectives. The governing treaty between Russia and America stipulated that criminals were subject to extradition but political refugees were not. If Pouren could demonstrate that his violent acts supported the revolutionary cause, then the U.S. government would have a legal basis to grant him asylum.[31]

Pouren's case had been obscure until mid-August, when an American extradition commissioner ruled against him. The commissioner found that Pouren failed to furnish evidence that his activities had been related to political upheaval in Latvia. That ruling was not akin to a majority opinion on the Supreme Court, which binds the executive branch. Rather, the Roosevelt administration had discretion to accept or annul the commissioner's decision.[32] As Pouren awaited an uncertain future, he remained locked up in a lower Manhattan prison nicknamed "The Tombs," where he had resided since the extradition proceedings began seven months earlier.[33]

Pouren's pending exile to Russia made national headlines. From Alaska to Alabama, newspapers decried Russia's bid to wield the extradition treaty as a weapon of counterrevolution. One journalist explained that the ramifications of Pouren's case were hardly limited to the "mild looking, fair-haired little peasant" facing the dismal prospect of czarist justice back home. The case instead raised the gravest of questions: "When fugitive militants ... reach our shores and seek refuge in our cities, shall we act as sleuth and police for the czar and chase down these unfortunates?" At stake was America's cherished status as a haven for political dissidents.[34]

Pouren wasn't Jewish, but the implications for Jews were immense. Even as most Russian Jews weren't revolutionaries, a number of Russian revolutionaries *were* Jews. Untold numbers of them who had fled Russian repression for American freedom might soon find themselves surrendered in shackles to their erstwhile oppressor. Unsurprisingly, then, American Jews were overrepresented in the movement to secure Pouren's release. A call for a petition quickly circulated throughout the Lower East Side, announcing, "Our only hope is in President Roosevelt."[35] Jews joined with Gentiles to form the Pouren Defense Conference, an ad hoc organization designed to orchestrate the campaign for his release. Its members hoped to exert pressure on the administration with a combination of grassroots activism and press coverage.[36]

Reputable outlets from the *New York Times* to *The Nation* proved eager to promote his cause. *The Outlook*—a popular weekly based in New York—asked pointedly, "Shall we return the fugitive to the torture chamber?"[37] That same day, Roosevelt alerted Secretary Root that the Pouren case was no ordinary matter. "*The Outlook* and all kinds of philanthropic bodies, not to speak of socialists and others, are very much interested," Roosevelt relayed to Root. By "socialists" he meant Jews, at least partly; many Russian-Jewish émigrés had seen socialism as an answer to czarism in the Old World, and they retained their socialist leanings after immigrating to America. The president's letter further stressed that Root himself should personally review the facts. "It is not a matter that should be handled... in a perfunctory way," warned Roosevelt. "You should go over it carefully yourself" rather than rely on underlings in the State Department. TR was keen to "forestall action being taken without you or me knowing anything about it." Roosevelt also divulged that a congressional ally, Herbert Parsons, had solicited him about the matter—not incidentally, as Parsons was serving as Pouren's lead counsel.[38]

The following week, a boisterous crowd descended on Cooper Union, the celebrated East Side venue, at the initiative of the Pouren Defense Conference. "The great hall was packed in every nook and corner," the *New York Times* observed, adding, "A good portion of those present were Jews." One speaker elicited a notable reaction when he suggested that the czar wanted to replace the Statue of Liberty with a statue of a Russian soldier. When Congressman Parsons took the stage, he spelled out the collective consequences of Pouren's individual fate: "The matter is of tremendous importance. It is a test case. If Pouren is extradited, there are thousands of men in this country who stand in Pouren's shoes. The question is, 'Are they safe here or not?' I have an abiding faith that they are safe, and that Pouren is safe." With this, the audience erupted into a proper frenzy.[39]

It took a few minutes for the crowd to calm itself before Rabbi David Blaustein, a Harvard-educated settlement house leader, could begin his remarks. Blaustein read aloud letters of support from preeminent Jews—like Jacob Schiff and Justice Greenbaum of the New York Supreme Court—and from an eclectic mix of Gentiles, including a trio of Christian clergymen, a socialist writer, and the president of City College. Resolutions against Pouren's extradition, for submission to Roosevelt and the State Department, were offered for the throng's approval. Well-nigh two thousand "ayes" rang out in unison. In one indicator of the robust Jewish presence that evening, two speeches were delivered in Yiddish.[40] Pouren, meanwhile, bided his time in a prison cell just a mile away.

Letters poured into the White House on his behalf, some signed by notable names of the era. The head of the American Federation of Labor, for instance, beseeched Roosevelt to intervene. So did the celebrated poet and octogenarian Julia Ward Howe, whose legendary lyrics "mine eyes have seen the glory" had been immortalized during the Civil War as an unofficial anthem by Union troops.[41] Roosevelt's old college friend Lucius Littauer—a recently retired Jewish congressman—also penned a note to the president about Pouren's cause.[42]

The celebrated Jewish reformer Lillian Wald was granted a personal audience with Roosevelt at the White House to discuss the matter. Recall that Wald had known Roosevelt since the 1890s, when he was the young police commissioner of New York and she the even younger founder of the Henry Street Settlement on the Lower East Side. Having dedicated her life to serving immigrants, Wald was a natural vessel for the anti-extradition message. She shared with Roosevelt a letter that she received from some of Pouren's fellow revolutionaries who had fought alongside him and themselves relocated to America. They begged, "Do not let him fall into the hands of the bloodthirsty vampire." To save Pouren's neck, these refugees were willing to risk their own—they offered to give affidavits in his defense even though that would risk alerting Russia to their own "crimes" against the czar's regime and thereby prompt extradition requests against them. Roosevelt assured Wald that any new affidavits would be duly considered.[43]

Happily for Pouren, his cause célèbre coincided with the height of a presidential campaign, a time when any administration is most likely to privilege electoral exigency over diplomatic delicacy.[44] A Republican paper in Massachusetts fretted about the party's prospects at the ballot box should the Roosevelt administration fail to spare Pouren. His extradition would "raise such a tempest among the Jews and Russians of New York and Chicago that the Republican Party in November would be crushed beyond recognition."[45] It required no great powers of prophecy to foresee the political blunder of permitting Russia to wage its reactionary war on American soil.

★ ★ ★

By late September, Roosevelt was pressing Root in his most vehement terms yet. TR wanted the commissioner's ruling against Pouren overturned—immediately and publicly. "My judgment is very strong that we ought to refuse to deliver this man and that we ought to make [an] announcement now," he implored Root. The president bemoaned that treaty obligations had put his administration in this difficult position, venting, "We never should have had an extradition treaty with Russia. Its conduct toward so-called political criminals is so inconceivably brutal and foolish." Given that Russia was inveterately "indifferent to the truth," Roosevelt felt that "we have no business to treat it as we do the average civilized nation." He also drew a connection between passports and extradition: since Russia wouldn't admit Jews, America shouldn't relinquish Pouren. In the president's words, Russia's "consistent attitude in the matter of the passports is such as to justify us on that ground alone in refusing to perform such an act of mere international comity."[46] The truth or falsehood of Russia's allegations against Pouren was immaterial by that reasoning.

Roosevelt's letter all but ordered Root to reverse the ruling. "Do go over the papers in this Pouren case carefully, and I will take it up with you," he wrote. "I feel that it would be a good thing from every standpoint if we could at once announce that we do not intend to permit the man to be extradited." Root surely understood that "every standpoint" included Taft's ongoing race for the presidency. Roosevelt closed his letter with an affirmation of his own authority over the State Department: "I am informed that under the uniform practice of the Department, the whole matter, both as to law and facts, as to extradition cases of this kind, is vested in the president." Root could not have missed the heavy-handed implication: if he failed to act, Roosevelt would.[47]

The argument against Pouren's extradition soon received a boost. New affidavits from other revolutionaries—probably the self-same whom Lillian Wald had discussed with Roosevelt—swore to the political character of Pouren's actions back in Latvia. His lawyers explained to Secretary Root that they had deliberately withheld testimony from these witnesses during their client's extradition hearing for fear of placing them in danger of their own extraditions.[48] The president seized upon this favorable development to pressure Root yet again. "I enclose herewith a number of affidavits in the Pouren case," Roosevelt wrote him in early October. "Unless controverted, these affidavits seem to establish clearly the fact that Pouren was a revolutionist and took an active part in the revolutionary troubles." Pouren's alleged acts were technically crimes, but they were in service of "the revolutionary proceedings and therefore political crimes," reasoned Roosevelt. Given the president's desire to rebuff Russia's extradition request even before this evidence had surfaced, Root could now scarcely have been surprised by Roosevelt's overdetermined conclusion: "Pouren's case is one that comes directly under the clause of the treaty which forbids the extradition of political offenders."[49]

Root forwarded the affidavits to the Russian embassy in Washington and invited a response.[50] As he waited, Jacob Schiff told Root that extradition would be a "terrible mistake." Schiff alluded to electoral considerations in positing, "Public opinion will never approve the surrender of Pouren to Russia, but to the contrary will condemn such an act most harshly." That same day, Roosevelt sent Root a trunk whose contents seemed to corroborate Schiff's take. Inside were some seventy-thousand signatures—"a monster petition," as the *New York Times* described it—that Congressman Parsons had passed along to the president.[51]

The Jewish community continued to call for the prisoner's release. Sounding much like Roosevelt, the *Hebrew Standard* insisted, "If Pouren committed a crime it was executed in the name and because of humanity. He is neither more or less than a political prisoner; as such his right to asylum here should not be invaded." The paper reflected the Jewish community at large in appreciating the broad stakes, acknowledging that Pouren's removal from U.S. soil would mean "no Russian immigrant of recent arrival here is safe." But the *Hebrew Standard* was optimistic: "America, we are sure, will not permit the czar's myrmidons [i.e., unscrupulous subordinates] to capture their unfortunate quarry in this land of freedom."[52] Notably, this vote of confidence came from a Democratic organ.

Two days later, Root heard from an official at the Russian embassy, Basile Kroupensky, who scoffed at the prospect of rebutting these new affidavits. "The embassy does not feel called upon to furnish any proof in addition to that already adduced before the [extradition] commissioner," Kroupensky related. He noted that the legal process culminating in the commissioner's ruling took eight months, more than enough time for Pouren's lawyers to have produced the testimony. Kroupensky further emphasized that the prisoner's legal team comprised "several experienced counsel" including a congressman; in other words, Pouren's attorneys were sufficiently versed in the law to know that these new witnesses should have testified *before* the ruling. That the affidavits were forthcoming only afterward—argued Kroupensky—not only violated established legal norms but also weighed heavily against their credibility. He asserted that "universally accepted principles of law" ought to preclude Root from considering the affidavits at all in his review of the case.[53]

Under intense pressure from the public and the president alike, Secretary Root disregarded Kroupensky's remonstrance and ordered the extradition commissioner to revisit the case in light of the new evidence. Root explained to the commissioner that although Pouren's lawyers had wrongly withheld witness testimony during the hearings, the prisoner shouldn't effectively "be punished for his counsel's mistake." The affidavits in question spoke directly to the potentially *political* nature of Pouren's actions, and so "the plain intent of the treaty would fail if this evidence were now altogether excluded from consideration," Root concluded.[54]

Roosevelt, meanwhile, searched for a means to free Pouren while the case was pending. "Why can't we admit Pouren to bail?" the president asked Root. "Is it possible to do this? It would help a great deal if this could be done." Indeed it would—the election was less than three weeks away. Apparently, Root proved unresponsive, as five days later Roosevelt wrote him again in emphatic terms, "Cannot we arrange at once to release Pouren on bail? Cannot this be done today or tomorrow? If he were an American citizen this would be done. Why discriminate against him because he is a political refugee from Russia?" An exasperated Roosevelt added for emphasis, "Oh, Lord!!"[55]

After several more days, Root finally acted. He superseded his earlier order for the extradition commissioner to reopen the case, announcing instead that the entire proceeding against Pouren was now dismissed "without prejudice"—meaning that Pouren's case was no longer active, but Russia remained free to submit a new extradition request, which would restart the hearing process from scratch.[56] Russia filed its new request immediately.[57] The practical consequence of these maneuvers was that, in late October, Pouren was released on the dismissal of his first case and rearrested moments later on the initiation of his second. "Free for a Minute," ran the headline in the *Grand Rapids Press*.[58] Contrary to Roosevelt's wishes, Pouren would remain confined to a prison cell. But Pouren did not face any immediate risk of being surrendered to the Russians, and he was poised to derive the benefit of exculpatory affidavits in the forthcoming proceedings. (Pouren's case would ultimately resolve shortly after Roosevelt's presidency, when the defendant was at last set free.[59])

If the provision of a new hearing for Pouren wasn't a *total* victory for the Republican administration, it was a victory nonetheless—and favorably situated on the calendar. The *Fort Worth Telegram* noted the auspicious timing: "On the eve of the presidential election, it is announced that Secretary Root has taken cognizance of the petition . . . to refuse the demand of Jan Janoff Pouren."[60] Meanwhile, the *Hebrew Standard* celebrated that Pouren thus far had evaded the vengeful claws of the bear. "We see signs which show that Russia's erstwhile dominance in this country is indeed a thing of the past," the paper remarked.[61] This reference to "signs" plural was well merited, for Pouren's chance at redemption was not the only recent indication of American resistance to Russian illiberalism.

In the latter half of October, as Pouren remained in legal limbo, Secretary Root curried favorable publicity on a different cause dear to Jewish voters. He sent a letter to Jacob Schiff—designed for circulation to the press and undoubtedly written at Roosevelt's behest—announcing a bolder stance from the administration on the Passport Question. Russia had long maintained that the Treaty of 1832 did not extend to Jews; America had long maintained that it did. Rather than endlessly recycle this decades-old dispute, the Roosevelt administration was now changing course. It had recently requested of the Russians "complete revision and amendment of the treaty," Root informed Schiff. The United States would insist upon treaty terms that left no ambiguity about the "reciprocal rights of residence and travel" for American passport holders—be they Jew or Gentile, native or naturalized. Granted, this approach did not go as far as the AJC suggested, wherein America would unilaterally void the existing treaty to jolt Russia into concessions. Root explained that the AJC's more aggressive tactic was ill-advised because it could result in a problematic interregnum between treaties during which all Americans and Russians lacked any rights whatsoever in the other nation. He closed the letter by assuring Schiff that "the administration is in full and sympathetic agreement with you" about passports.[62] After the letter's expeditious dissemination to the papers, the *Idaho Daily Statesman* gave the story front-page coverage. The *Dallas Morning News* trumpeted, "New Treaty Is Favored to Protect Americans." And the *New York Times* reprinted Root's missive to Schiff in full.[63]

William Howard Taft aimed to build on this momentum when he barnstormed through Brooklyn in the waning days of the campaign. At a packed rally in Saenger Hall, Taft's speech to a predominantly Jewish audience was preceded by an appearance from, of course, Oscar Straus. The first-ever Jewish cabinet member sparked an enthusiastic reception. With a portrait of Theodore Roosevelt in a Rough Riders hat hanging overhead, Straus lauded Taft as the man whom TR personally selected as his political heir. One journalist observed, "His first mention of the name of Roosevelt brought down the house." Straus cast the matter of succession in Biblical terms: just as Elijah ascended to Heaven in a chariot of fire and Elisha picked up Elijah's fallen mantle, so too would Taft carry on Roosevelt's mission. When Taft finally took the stage, he declared to the throng—in a voice hoarse from overuse—that he would labor diligently to protect the authority of the U.S. passport the world over. The Republican nominee also cautioned with candor that he couldn't promise results, but he vowed nonetheless "I shall give my very best energies" to the cause.[64]

Two days later, Taft was again courting New York Jewry, this time before a capacity crowd at the Thalia Theatre on Bowery Street in lower Manhattan. The venue housed a "typical East Side audience," in the words of one reporter. Taft told the assemblage, "I almost think that an audience made up of people newly come to this country is more patriotic than the descendants of the Puritans [who] take so much for granted."⁶⁵ He also reaffirmed his pledge to pressure Russia on passports. In Taft's words, "Our passports certifying our citizenship should secure to every man, without regard to creed or race, the same treatment, the same equality of opportunity, in every nation on the globe." And he once again demonstrated a keen awareness that his candidacy rested on Roosevelt's presidency, calling on voters to "commend the administration of Theodore Roosevelt" by choosing himself to perpetuate the passport fight.⁶⁶

This bid for the Jewish vote was hotly contested. The Democratic platform featured a plank on the Passport Question. Moreover, William Jennings Bryan—in his third stint as the Democratic nominee for the presidency—also earned good press by proposing that a rabbi serve among the chaplains at his party's convention.⁶⁷ And late in the campaign, Bryan submitted a letter for publication to Cleveland's *Jewish Independent* that insisted on the equal treatment of American citizens abroad. "I need hardly add that Russia is no exception," he wrote, "and that an American Jew ought to have as full protection as Americans of any other race or religion." That letter commanded attention beyond Ohio, eliciting coverage from St. Louis's *Jewish Voice* and prompting a favorable headline in the *New York Times*: "Bryan Would Protect Jews."⁶⁸

But Bryan had longstanding vulnerabilities with Jewish voters. His 1896 race for the presidency left him on the defensive over accusations of antisemitism. In that campaign, which was animated by economic populism, Bryan delivered a stemwinder from the floor of the Democratic National Convention in which he railed against the gold standard for the U.S. dollar. "You shall not press down upon the brow of labor this crown of thorns," he thundered. "You shall not crucify mankind upon a cross of gold." These two phenomena—the Crucifixion and the gold standard—were often blamed on Jews, and Bryan here managed to conflate them in a single memorable breath.⁶⁹

The *New York Sun* claimed that Bryan's followers crossed the line into overt antisemitism. They reportedly yelled at that 1896 convention,

"Down with gold! Down with the hook-nosed Shylocks of Wall Street! Down with the Christ-killing goldbugs!"[70] The *Sun* was a Republican paper and thus may have been exaggerating for political gain; either way, this news coverage could not have helped Bryan in Jewish precincts.[71]

Bryan's troubles in the 1896 cycle were exacerbated when he received—quite likely to his dismay—an enthusiastic endorsement from Hermann Ahlwardt, the invidious German Jew-hater whom Roosevelt as police commissioner had adroitly assigned thirty Jewish officers to protect in New York.[72] Bryan also found himself fending off accusations that his well-known criticism of the Rothschilds, a prominent Jewish banking family, meant that he harbored anti-Jewish bias.[73] There was, overall, much in his campaign that commended it to antisemites.

In his play for Jewish voters in 1908, Bryan could only do so much to reverse the damage of 1896. Moreover, his Christian fundamentalism surely held less appeal for many Jews than did Taft's liberal-minded Unitarianism. And Bryan lacked Taft's greatest asset: the incumbent president on his side. None of Bryan's backers were empowered to, say, coax the secretary of state to reverse an extradition ruling. Nor could any Bryan supporters initiate efforts to negotiate a new treaty with Russia that would honor Jewish-American rights. Roosevelt alone enjoyed the powers of the presidency, and in the waning weeks of the campaign he did not hesitate to wield them with Jewish voters in mind.

★ ★ ★

Election night for Taft—if not the once-in-a-century showing that Roosevelt had registered four years earlier—was a towering triumph in its own right. Taft won the popular vote by more than eight percentage points and racked up a nearly two-to-one margin in the Electoral College. His sweeping success across the North and West more than offset losses in Southern states, an echo of TR's own regional variations in 1904. Expressing "deep gratitude" to Roosevelt, the president-elect credited his nomination and victory to the current occupant of the Oval Office: "My selection and election are chiefly your work."[74]

Taft nearly matched Roosevelt's 1904 results for the Empire State at large, but he vastly underperformed TR on the traditionally Democratic Lower East Side. Whereas Roosevelt had narrowly won East Siders, Taft lost them by fourteen points. That neighborhood's sixteenth assembly district, which Roosevelt had carried by a handful of votes, now went to William Jennings Bryan by a twenty-five-point differential.[75] Comparing 1904 with 1908 demonstrates that Roosevelt's historic success with East Side Jews had not marked the beginning of an enduring shift by Jewish immigrants to the GOP. Instead, it underscores that TR's appeal on the Lower East Side was strikingly singular.

Roosevelt commenced the lame-duck stretch of his presidency with a public rebuke of religious bigotry. Large numbers of Americans, goaded by certain preachers and papers, had viewed Taft's Unitarianism with contempt during the campaign. Because Unitarians rejected the divinity of Jesus Christ, Taft was essentially a nonbeliever in many Christian eyes. Rumors also circulated that Taft was a Catholic, or at least in league with Catholics, and possibly even beholden to the Pope.[76] In August, Taft predicted that this line of attack from his adversaries might actually endear him to voters who abhorred religious prejudice. "It might prove to be a sword cutting both ways, especially among the Jews," he suggested to Roosevelt.[77] Taft was right. The Jewish paper *Emanu-El* exclaimed, "The whole matter is decidedly un-American, nay! It is positively anti-American."[78] Even the Democratic *Hebrew Standard* came to Taft's defense, reproaching hateful ministers for "sticking their clerical noses into politics." These clergymen were nothing more than "bigots."[79]

Roosevelt himself had been indignant about the infusion of religious intolerance into the race. In the campaign's closing weeks, TR vented to Taft, "The attacks upon you by a certain type of small Protestant bigot are so infamous as to make my blood boil."[80] But the president held his tongue and stayed his pen during the race—and advised Taft to do the same. After all, any defense of Taft's religious background would amount to a concession that a candidate's faith *should* be subjected to political scrutiny.[81] With election day now behind them, Roosevelt felt free to publicly voice his long-suppressed ire.

He trained his righteous anger on a piano dealer in Ohio named J. C. Martin. Like many Americans, Martin had sent a letter to the president amid the campaign season disparaging Taft's religious affiliation. The piano dealer predicted, erroneously, that Taft would prove unelectable because he is an "infidel (Unitarian) and his wife and brother [are] Roman Catholics." (In fact, neither Taft's wife nor his brothers were Catholic.) Roosevelt's post-election reply to Martin was scathing—and widely distributed to newspapers. "I received many such letters as yours," the president wrote him. "I did not answer any of these letters during the campaign because I regarded it as an outrage even to agitate such a question as a man's religious convictions, with the purpose of influencing an election." In response to Martin's insistence that Taft expose his religious beliefs for public examination, Roosevelt retorted, "It is a matter between him and his Maker, a matter for his own conscience; and to require it to be made public under penalty of political discrimination is to negative the first principles of our government, which guarantee complete religious liberty, and the right to each man to act in religious affairs as his own conscience dictates." This comment reflected not only the free exercise clause in the First Amendment but also the Constitution's explicit ban on religious tests for federal office.[82]

The president's letter to Martin venerated the religious variety in his administration, nodding to Oscar Straus's trailblazing role. "In my cabinet at the present moment there sit side-by-side Catholic and Protestant, Christian and Jew," he proudly boasted. Lest anyone think these appointees were tapped because of their identity rather than their merit, Roosevelt quickly added that all of them had been selected based on their fitness for office. Diversity of faith could also be found among elected officials, he noted. Whereas Martin had expressly doubted that Americans would vote for a Unitarian, TR highlighted the routine election of candidates who differed in creed from most of their constituents. "By their very existence in political life, they refute the slander you have uttered against your fellow Americans," he seethed. "I knew particularly well ... one man of Jewish faith who represented a district in which there were hardly any Jews at all"—this was an allusion to Roosevelt's college friend Lucius Littauer, whose rural district in upstate New York sent him to Congress five times. Roosevelt made a bold prediction about the liberality of America's electorate: "I believe that this Republic will endure for many centuries. If so, there will doubtless be among its presidents Protestants and Catholics, and, very probably at some time, Jews."[83] From Montana to Georgia, newspapers nationwide reprinted Roosevelt's letter on page 1.[84]

TR's frequent reference to Jewry in the letter is noteworthy. Plainly, he appreciated that if prejudice were to prevail against a Unitarian, all the more tenuous was the religious freedom of a Jew. American Jews understood this grim fact—and thus understood the significance of Roosevelt's letter for their own community. A Midwestern rabbi urged his congregants during a sermon, "If you have missed that letter, you should procure it and put it away among your most valuable family papers, to be bequeathed to your children."[85] An editorial in *Emanu-El* emphasized the letter's timing—that is, after the election—when Roosevelt's words could not be dismissed as a mere gambit for votes: "This expression of the president is no campaign document." It was, rather, a heartfelt pronouncement that rebutted "narrow-minded church bigots who would drag religion into politics."[86] Excited by Roosevelt's prediction of a Jewish head of state, Philadelphia's *Jewish Exponent* marveled at "the president's implied prophecy that Seder may be observed in the White House at some future day."[87] Notably, the Democratic-leaning *Hebrew Standard* printed a letter praising Roosevelt's response to Martin for its "undiluted Americanism."[88] Simon Wolf, the former president of B'nai B'rith, told Roosevelt, "Not a single act of yours will redound more to your glory and fame than the letter you have just written on religious liberty."[89]

Roosevelt spent his final morning as president hosting Taft for breakfast. The night before, a gentle snow had begun falling on Washington; by morning, blizzard-like conditions took hold. Armed with an umbrella and galoshes, Roosevelt emerged from the White House and boarded his horse-drawn carriage with his successor seated beside him. Some spectators trudged through three inches of slush on Pennsylvania Avenue to catch glimpses of the presidential pair en route to the Capitol.[90]

The ill-timed snowstorm brought Washington to a halt. Trains, trolleys, and telegraphs were all inoperable.[91] Taft's inauguration was forced to relocate from the publicly viewable Capitol steps to the seclusion of the Senate chamber, gravely disappointing the crowd on hand that had braved the weather.[92] Roosevelt enthusiasts had reason to cheer, however, once the inauguration concluded. He emerged from the Capitol to find an enthusiastic "marching club"—numbering nearly one thousand Republicans from New York—who had been patiently waiting to escort the former president's carriage to the train station. As Roosevelt and the marching club began the half-mile journey, a band played the somber tune "Auld Lang Syne," which seemed to capture the wistful mood in the air. The *New York Times* reported, "The whole mass of humanity that detached itself from the sea of faces around the Capitol to see the last of the retiring president moved on to the rise and fall of the song." Even the congenitally jovial Roosevelt grew pensive as the melancholic notes rang out. But spirits were soon lifted when the band transitioned to an upbeat number, "There'll Be a Hot Time in the Old Town Tonight." By the close of that second song, the procession reached the newly opened Union Station, an architectural wonder of its day. TR alighted from his carriage, and the marchers mobbed the ex-president in search of a handshake. Roosevelt managed to oblige a fortunate few in his immediate proximity before retiring to the station's waiting room to reunite with his family members. Finally, at 3:26 p.m., Roosevelt's train departed Washington and headed north to Oyster Bay. The man who had reshaped the presidency, and with it the nation, was once more a common citizen.[93]

The following day, the Jewish newspaper *Emanu-El* featured a retrospective on Roosevelt's tenure at the White House. "Even Roosevelt's severest critic must confess that he accomplished considerable [deeds] for the country and the world," *Emanu-El* remarked. The paper deemed him a "great leader" but acknowledged he wasn't quite a Lincoln or a Washington. Rehearsing Roosevelt's record on Jewish issues, *Emanu-El* found cause for celebration and frustration alike.[94]

That postpresidential assessment—upholding Roosevelt as worthy of admiration but still finding some fault—aptly epitomized the Jewish experience with him. With the Romanian Note and Kishinev Petition, he demonstrated a willingness to bend or even break diplomatic norms in defense of Jewry overseas. Roosevelt also repeatedly pressured Russia to respect the passports of his own Jewish constituents. Moreover, his administration extolled America as a political asylum for the world's persecuted, refusing to extradite a dissident refugee to the czar's clutches. Roosevelt consistently used the most visible means available—State of the Union messages, the GOP platform, his nomination acceptance—to champion Jewish causes. And he took an unprecedented measure in American history: the elevation of a Jew to the cabinet. For all these efforts, Jewish voters rewarded Roosevelt with historic support at the ballot box.

But Roosevelt's ties to Jewry sometimes frayed. During Russia's appalling bloodbath in 1905, the telegraph wires from Washington to St. Petersburg hardly hummed. Roosevelt defended his inaction, insisting that a diplomatic push for Jewish rights would be futile amid the anarchy. For many American Jews, however, Roosevelt's strategic inertia felt cruelly tepid in the face of mass slaughter. If that nonintervention marked a low point for Roosevelt-Jewish relations, it wasn't the only moment of strain. Roosevelt endorsed a literacy test for aspiring immigrants, to the chagrin of his Jewish allies. Limiting the influx of newcomers, he argued, would ease the burden on those already crammed into urban slums. Roosevelt's Jewish friends tried to dissuade him, but to no avail.

His complicated history with Jewry reflected the countervailing forces acting on him at any given time. Roosevelt often found himself caught between humanitarian crisis and diplomatic protocol, between philosemites and antisemites, between pluralism and assimilation. These tensions bespoke the complexities of the moment—and of the man. After all, Roosevelt was famously rife with incongruities. Here was the East Coast aristocrat who became a Dakota cowboy; the bookish intellectual who threw punches in the boxing ring; the combat-thirsty colonel who won a Nobel Peace Prize. There was perhaps no more fitting representative of a nation riddled with its own irresolvable contradictions.

EPILOGUE

Theodore Roosevelt remains the youngest person to claim the White House and the youngest to leave it. He emerged from office only fifty years old and brimming with energy. In the decade that followed, Roosevelt rarely took a beat. He ventured a treacherous exploration of the Amazon. He dined with royals in the palaces of Europe. He launched a third party—nicknamed the Bull Moose Party—in a bold bid to recapture the Oval Office. His legendary efforts in that race included delivering a stump speech after taking a bullet from a would-be assassin. Roosevelt lost that election but not his life. Even when TR wasn't on a ballot, Americans were seldom left to wonder what their former president thought of current events; he published editorials, essays, and books at an astounding rate. Roosevelt was still very much the man in the arena.

Amid this afterlife of his administration, he deepened his engagement with Jewish people and Jewish causes. The same issues that had preoccupied American Jewry during his presidency persisted thereafter: persecution abroad, immigration at home, and antisemitism on both sides of the Atlantic. Roosevelt was alive to these challenges. He weighed in on them routinely in public addresses and private correspondence. As with his presidential years, Roosevelt's standing with his Jewish fellow citizens depended on the moment. More often than not he earned their adoration; sometimes he elicited their consternation. The story of Roosevelt and the Jewish community in this postpresidential period is so rich that it merits a book all its own.[1] But suffice it to say that Jews

FIGURE 9.1. Theodore Roosevelt in his post-presidency. *Source*: Library of Congress, Prints and Photographs Division.

played a significant role in his journey until the very end—an end that came far sooner than the world expected.

On Christmas Eve, 1918, Roosevelt was discharged from the hospital after receiving treatment for inflammatory rheumatism. His prognosis was largely favorable, even if total recovery seemed unlikely. He plunged himself into writing after the new year, dictating pieces for *Metropolitan Magazine* and the *Kansas City Star*. But the first weekend of January had been a fitful one for Roosevelt. He told his wife that Sunday evening before bed that something felt amiss. The next day, Roosevelt's youngest son telegraphed his two older brothers: "The old lion is dead."[2]

As word spread from Sagamore Hill to the farthest reaches of the country, Americans were stunned by the sudden news of Roosevelt's demise.[3] Here was the Rough Rider who braved Spanish snipers unscathed, the Bull Mooser who campaigned with a bullet freshly lodged in his chest, the ex-president who improbably survived a perilous journey through the Brazilian jungle. And yet, for all Roosevelt's seeming invincibility, the life had quietly slipped from his body amid the calm slumber of a winter's night. "Death had to take Roosevelt sleeping, for if he had been awake there would have been a fight," the sitting vice president mused.[4]

At the spare funeral in Oyster Bay that could accommodate limited numbers, the exclusive guest list included the giants of American politics. There was Roosevelt's ally-turned-adversary William Howard Taft; his old confidant Senator Henry Cabot Lodge; and the imperious House Speaker "Uncle Joe" Cannon. Oscar Straus, besieged with grief, was of course in attendance. After a brief church service, the mourners adjourned to a nearby cemetery for the burial. Roosevelt had long ago chosen his resting place atop a hill that featured spectacular views and birdsong melodies. Six pallbearers labored mightily to lift the flag-draped coffin up a steep incline that was slick with snow.[5] That grueling final act was a fitting tribute to the man whose appetite for "the strenuous life" had been famously insatiable.[6]

For every individual on hand that day in Oyster Bay, millions more paid their respects from afar. Roosevelt's hometown of New York shut down to mark his passing—from schools and subways to firehouses and factories, a reverential stillness replaced the typical commotion. Further afield in the nation's capital, Congress and the Supreme Court suspended their proceedings. And in American military outposts the world over, the armed forces honored their former commander-in-chief by firing shots every thirty minutes from dawn until dusk. Nor were lamentations limited to Roosevelt's compatriots. Amid the capitals of war-torn Europe, orators gave homage to his legacy. Westminster Abbey even took the unprecedented measure of forgoing its evening service and holding a memorial ceremony.[7]

American Jews felt the loss deeply, especially those whose lives had been directly touched by Roosevelt. "He was the most encouraging person that ever breathed," remarked Edna Ferber, a Jewish novelist he had warmly buoyed.[8] Rabbi Joseph Krauskopf, who had once communed in Cuba with Roosevelt and his Jewish troops, arranged for his synagogue to install a stained-glass window commemorating the colonel.[9] Meanwhile, the Jewish Welfare Board—which Roosevelt had gifted a generous portion of his Nobel Prize cash award—organized a day of mourning for its constituent chapters throughout the country.[10]

Countless other Jewish Americans, who had never met the man, nursed hearts heavy with sadness. From synagogue pews, they heard sermons cataloguing Roosevelt's service to their people. Jewish newspapers published paeans to his conviction in religious equality. "Jewish immigrants had no better friend than Theodore Roosevelt," declared the *B'nai B'rith Messenger*. "He ever championed their cause." The *Hebrew Standard*, a Democratic organ that had often found fault with Roosevelt in his lifetime, now conceded after his passing that he was "the greatest of our fellow-citizens." Through these exercises in remembrance, Jews nationwide became reacquainted with the many chapters of Roosevelt's Jewish story: Police Commissioner Roosevelt's clever decision to guard an antisemite with thirty Jewish officers; Colonel Roosevelt's dogged fighting in Cuba alongside his Jewish volunteers; and above all President Roosevelt's defiant stands against Jewish suffering overseas.

As might be expected in the midst of mourning, Jewish commentators passed silently over Roosevelt's strained moments with their community. No rabbis reminded their congregants of his muted response when the pogrom wave crested in Russia. No Jewish editors prompted their readers to recall Roosevelt's support for a literacy test that would have barred a quarter of Jewish refugees. No Jewish memorial services recollected his enthusiasm for an assimilationist play that Jews themselves roundly condemned for seeming to promote Jewish self-extinction. Undoubtedly, Roosevelt *was* beloved by his Jewish constituents, but that love was never blind to his flaws, real or perceived.

Roosevelt ascended to the White House in the throes of a great national transformation. Once a fragile new republic committed to neutrality abroad, America was becoming a global player that projected its power well beyond its borders. Once a young country where Anglo-Saxons predominated, America increasingly saw its streets packed with strange newcomers speaking in alien tongues. In short, America was coming to the world, and the world was coming to America.

But the path to modernity wasn't smoothly paved. Roosevelt found himself navigating foreign resistance to American intervention and domestic anxiety about immigration. The Jewish challenges confronting him—from massacres to migration—assumed outsized importance in American political life because they threw into vivid relief just how rapidly the country had grown daring in its external engagement and diverse in its internal composition. His mixed approach to Jewish affairs aptly reflected a nation uncertain of its own destiny. Would the United States prove wary of crises abroad and suspicious of fresh arrivals to its shores? Or would the country embrace the forces of globalization that were collapsing vast distances between the Old World and the New?

Roosevelt's checkered answer was of no small moment. At stake for America was nothing less than its very self-conception; at stake for untold Jews was nothing less than their very survival.

The night before Roosevelt's funeral, his corpse lay in the trophy room of Sagamore Hill. He had asked a friend to design the room as an addition to the home, and Roosevelt thrilled to its completion halfway through his presidency. "You cannot imagine how delighted I am with the new room," he told the architect, adding, "Really, I like it better than any room in the White House which, as you know, is my standard of splendor!" Guests would descend from a raised platform down several steps into the trophy room, whose wood paneling and animal skins lent it the unmistakable air of a hunting lodge. The room was appropriately named—its various trophies, gifts, and mementos reflected Roosevelt's many sides. The buffalo head signified Roosevelt, the hunter. The Rough Rider saber represented Roosevelt, the soldier. And the golden eagle mounted between the windows symbolized Roosevelt, the patriot.[11]

A tradition common to Christianity and Judaism alike calls on the living to watch over the dead before burial. And as Roosevelt's corpse passed this final night in the trophy room, only one person was permitted to keep vigil over the body. That honor didn't fall to any of the famous personages who had populated his life, nor to the best man at his wedding, nor even to his eldest child. In these small hours, as the world slept, Roosevelt's sole companion was a Russian-Jewish immigrant: Otto Raphael.[12]

Recall that Roosevelt and Raphael met decades earlier, when Roosevelt had just taken over New York's police department and Raphael was a young man working at his family's failing meat market on the Lower East Side. Raphael was introduced to Roosevelt as the neighborhood hero who had rescued people from a burning building. With this, Roosevelt recruited him to the police force. The two became sparring partners in the boxing ring and ultimately developed a lifelong relationship. To be sure, the differences between them were striking—the one, a strictly kosher Russian Jew raised in the East Side slums; the other, a silver-spooned cowboy with Dutch blood and a Harvard diploma. But Roosevelt treated Raphael as an equal. It couldn't have been lost on Raphael that back in the czar's dominions he might have been savagely slaughtered, but in the United States he could keep company with an American president.

Theodore Roosevelt was an imperfect leader of an imperfect nation. Yet he fervently believed—when many others didn't—that the likes of Otto Raphael made America a better place. On that last evening in Sagamore Hill, amid a trophy room adorned with the tokens of feats and fame, there could be no finer symbol of the very best in Roosevelt than this final farewell between two faithful friends.

AUTHOR'S NOTE

Spelling, capitalization, italicization, and punctuation in quotations from primary sources have been modernized for readability.

ABBREVIATIONS

Archives

ERP Elihu Root Papers, Manuscript Division, Library of Congress, Washington, DC.

GCP George B. Cortelyou Papers, Manuscript Division, Library of Congress, Washington, DC.

GMP George von Lengerke Meyer Papers, Massachusetts Historical Society, Boston, MA.

JHP John Hay Papers, Manuscript Division, Library of Congress, Washington, DC.

OSP Oscar S. Straus Papers, Manuscript Division, Library of Congress, Washington, DC.

TRDL Theodore Roosevelt Digital Library, Dickinson State University.

TRP Theodore Roosevelt Papers, Library of Congress, Washington, DC.

USNA National Archives, College Park, MD.

Collected and Published Works

AJYB *American Jewish Year Book.*

Letters *The Letters of Theodore Roosevelt.* Edited by Elting Morris. 8 vols. Cambridge, MA: Harvard University Press, 1951–1954.

FRUS Foreign Relations of the United States Series.

NOTES

Introduction

1. Quotation appears in Elmer Ellis, *Mr. Dooley's America: A Life of Finley Peter Dunne* (New York: Knopf, 1941), 153–154. For Roosevelt's friendship with Dunne, see Barbara C. Schaaf, *Mr. Dooley's Chicago* (Garden City, NY: Anchor Press/Doubleday, 1977), 27. For Roosevelt's paternal and maternal lineage, see Kathleen Dalton, *Theodore Roosevelt: A Strenuous Life* (New York: Alfred A. Knopf, 2002), 15–16, 20.

2. For Roosevelt's speechifying on the Lower East Side, see Theodore Roosevelt speech, 1895, quoted in "New York's Greatest Son, a Friend of the Jews," in "Jews" folder, Theodore Roosevelt Subject Guide, Houghton Library, Harvard University, Cambridge, MA. For his recruitment of the "Maccabee type" to the police force, see TR to George Briggs Aiton, May 15, 1901, *Letters*, 3:78; Dalton, *Strenuous Life*, 152; and Theodore Roosevelt, *Theodore Roosevelt: An Autobiography* (New York: Macmillan, 1913), 192–193. For Roosevelt and Jewish brides, see TR to George Otto Trevelyan, October 1, 1911, *Letters*, 7:362.

3. For "Pork Chop," see Theodore Roosevelt, *The Rough Riders* (New York: P. F. Collier, 1899), 47. For Roosevelt's visit to the sweatshops and subsequent call for legislative reform, see Jacob A. Riis, *Theodore Roosevelt: The Citizen* (New York: Outlook, 1903), 217–220; and G. Wallace Chessman, *Governor Theodore Roosevelt: The Albany Apprenticeship, 1898–1900* (Cambridge, MA: Harvard University Press, 1965), 232–233.

4. Lawrence J. Epstein, *At the Edge of a Dream: The Story of Jewish Immigrants on New York's Lower East Side, 1880–1920* (San Francisco, CA: Jossey-Bass, 2007), 11.

5. Shlomo Lambroza, "The Pogroms of 1903–1906," in *Pogroms: Anti-Jewish Violence in Modern Russian History*, ed. John D. Klier and Shlomo Lambroza (Cambridge: Cambridge University Press, 1992), 195–247.

6. For Roosevelt's willingness to challenge Romania and Morocco, respectively, see TR to John Hay, July 18, 1902, TRP; and Elihu Root to Henry White, November 28, 1905, *AJYB* 8 (1906): 92–93.

7. For an example of American popular reaction to a notorious pogrom, see generally Cyrus Adler, ed., *The Voice of America on Kishineff* (Philadelphia: Jewish Publication Society of America, 1904). This finding—to wit, that Americans clamored for Roosevelt's diplomatic intervention—challenges the work of Lewis L. Gould, who argues, "Roosevelt knew . . . that the citizens of his country were reluctant to support the larger international role that he envisioned. . . . Americans wished to retain the gains of imperialism, but did not want to take on an expanded agenda overseas . . . or see their president engaged in international diplomacy" (*The

Presidency of Theodore Roosevelt [Lawrence: University Press of Kansas, 2011], 12). Moreover, my book proceeds in the vein of Charlie Laderman's excellent *Sharing the Burden: The Armenian Question, Humanitarian Intervention, and Anglo-American Visions of Global Order* (New York: Oxford University Press, 2019), which helps unearth Roosevelt's humanitarianism as "a significant but underexplored component" (50) of his foreign policy. It also builds on John M. Thompson's *Great Power Rising: Theodore Roosevelt and the Politics of U.S. Foreign Policy* (New York: Oxford University Press, 2019), which doesn't discuss much Jewish diplomacy but does rightly argue that Roosevelt had far more public backing for intervention abroad than scholars have conventionally assumed (3–5).

8. For concern among foreign diplomats and U.S. State Department officials, see "Roosevelt Has the Public Back of Him," *Salt Lake Telegram*, July 8, 1903, 4. For the secretary of state's possible resignation, see John Hay to Clara Hay, July 6, 1903, Reel 5, JHP.

9. For the possible disruption of American trade at Russian-controlled ports, see "Roosevelt Has the Public Back of Him," *Salt Lake Telegram*, July 8, 1903, 4. For the possible severance of diplomatic relations between America and Russia, see "President to Send Petition to Czar," *New York Times*, June 26, 1903, 1. For the prospect of criticism by Russia of American lynching and for Roosevelt's concerns about his public statements possibly worsening conditions for Russian Jews, see TR to John Hay, May 25, 1903, TRP. For Russian conspiracy theories about Roosevelt and Jewish revolutionaries, see "The Russian Government and the Massacres," *Quarterly Review* 205.409 (October 1906): 609.

10. For "manifest duty," see "The President's Annual Message," *New York Times*, December 7, 1904, 3, 4. For Roosevelt's "Big Stick" diplomacy in Latin America, see James R. Holmes, *Theodore Roosevelt and World Order: Police Power in International Relations* (Washington, DC: Potomac Books, 2007), 3; and Henry Kissinger, *Diplomacy* (New York: Simon & Schuster, 1994), 39.

11. For examples of newspaper criticism during Roosevelt's presidency, see David Francis Sadler, "Theodore Roosevelt: A Symbol to Americans, 1898–1912" (PhD diss., University of Minnesota, 1954), 168–169. For an example from a later generation, see U.S. Congress, Senate, Committee on Foreign Relations, Hearings on the Panama Canal Treaties, 95th Cong., 1st sess., 1977, 222.

12. This finding builds on the work of other scholars who have sought to add complexity to overly facile descriptions of Roosevelt as a brash imperialist—see, for instance, Richard H. Collin, *Theodore Roosevelt, Culture, Diplomacy, and Expansion: A New View of American Imperialism* (Baton Rouge: Louisiana State University Press, 1985), 7.

13. For an example of Roosevelt's reliance on Jewish allies instead of State Department officials, see Oscar S. Straus, *Under Four Administrations: From Cleveland to Taft* (Boston: Houghton Mifflin, 1922), 172–173. For an example of Roosevelt's secret support for his Jewish allies' shadow diplomacy, see TR to Oscar Straus, August 16, 1905, TRP.

14. For the distinctions between these two subsets of Jews, see Epstein, *At the Edge of a Dream*, 155–156; and Annie Polland and Daniel Soyer, *Emerging Metropolis: New York Jews in the Age of Immigration, 1840–1920* (New York: New York University Press, 2012), 46.

15. For genteel antisemitism, see Jonathan D. Sarna, *American Judaism: A History* (New Haven, CT: Yale University Press, 2004), 133; and John Higham, "Anti-Semitism in the Gilded Age: A Reinterpretation," *Mississippi Valley Historical Review* 43.4 (March 1957): 567. For an

example of TR's friendship with a genteel antisemite, see Edmund Morris, *Theodore Rex* (New York: Modern Library, 2001), 525.

16. Riis, *Citizen*, 65–66.

17. TR to James Andrew Drain, June 27, 1911, *Letters*, 7:299.

18. TR to Arthur Train, August 13, 1918, *Letters*, 8:1361. See also TR to Madison Grant, December 30, 1918, *Letters*, 8:1419; and TR to William Williams, January 23, 1903, *Letters*, 3:411.

19. For the popularity of champagne among the Newport elite, see Cecelia Tichi, *Gilded Age Cocktails: History, Lore, and Recipes from America's Golden Age* (New York: New York University Press, 2021), 89. For antisemitism among farmers and urban immigrants, see Leonard Dinnerstein, *Antisemitism in America* (New York: Oxford University Press, 1994), 48–50, 53; Higham, "Anti-Semitism in the Gilded Age," 574–577. For contemporary stereotypes about Jews, see, for example, Edward Alsworth Ross, "The Hebrews of Eastern Europe in America," *Century Magazine* 88.5 (September 1914): 785–792. For an example of Gentile philosemitism, see generally Madison C. Peters, *Justice to the Jew: The Story of What He Has Done for the World* (New York: F. Tennyson Neely, 1899).

20. TR to Arthur Hamilton Lee, February 2, 1908, *Letters*, 6:918; TR to Henry Cabot Lodge, September 18, 1896, Lodge-Roosevelt correspondence, Massachusetts Historical Society, Boston, MA; TR to Henry Cabot Lodge, September 18, 1896, in *Selections from the Correspondence of Theodore Roosevelt and Henry Cabot Lodge, 1884–1918*, ed. Henry Cabot Lodge and Charles F. Redmond (New York: Charles Scribner's, 1925), 1:235; TR to Arthur Hamilton Lee, March 25, 1918, *Letters*, 8:1304.

21. Francis E. Leupp, *The Man Roosevelt: A Portrait Sketch* (New York: D. Appleton, 1904), 285; TR to Lyman Abbott, May 29, 1908, TRP; TR to Robert Schauffler, February 2, 1912, TRP.

22. Higham, "Anti-Semitism in the Gilded Age," 563–564.

23. Jacob Schiff et al. to Sergius de Witte, August 18, 1905, TRP.

24. Jonathan D. Sarna, ed., *The American Jewish Experience* (New York: Holmes and Meier, 1986), 296.

25. For Roosevelt's celebration of Jewish immigrants' contributions, see TR to Jacob Schiff, November 16, 1905, TRP. For the Roosevelt administration's inclusive rhetoric on asylum-seekers, see John Hay to Charles W. Wilson, July 17, 1902, FRUS (1903), 913 [doc. 839]. For Roosevelt's chastisement of the Ellis Island commissioner, see TR to William Williams, January 23, 1903, *Letters*, 3:411–412. For Roosevelt's visit to Ellis Island, see "President Starts Ellis Island Inquiry," *New York Times*, September 17, 1903, 1. Roosevelt named Oscar S. Straus the head of the Department of Commerce and Labor, whose purview included immigration. For an example of "old stock" xenophobia, see Henry Adams, *The Education of Henry Adams: An Autobiography* (1907; Boston: Houghton Mifflin, 1918), 238.

26. Judith S. Goldstein, *The Politics of Ethnic Pressure: The American Jewish Committee Fight against Immigration Restriction, 1906–1917* (New York: Garland, 1990), 70, 73; TR to Joseph Cannon, May 27, 1906, *Letters*, 5:285; TR to Joseph Cannon, June 13, 1906, TRP.

27. "Oppose Restriction," *New-York Tribune*, June 5, 1906, 2; Goldstein, *Politics of Ethnic Pressure*, 79–80.

28. For an example of an East Side crowd rallying against the literacy test, see "Oppose Restriction," *New-York Tribune*, June 5, 1906, 2. For an example of a leading antisemitic nativist

hoping for liberal reforms in Russia, see Prescott F. Hall, *Immigration and Its Effects upon the United States* (New York: Henry Holt, 1906), 21.

29. Oscar Straus to Jacob Schiff, April 2, 1902, in *Jewish Disabilities in the Balkan States: American Contributions toward their Removal, with Particular Reference to the Congress of Berlin*, by Max J. Kohler and Simon Wolf (New York: The American Jewish Committee, 1916), 108–109.

30. John Hay to Charles L. Wilson, July 17, 1902, FRUS (1903), 912 [doc. 839]. For the number of Romanian-Jewish immigrants to America by year, see Samuel Joseph, *Jewish Immigration to the United States from 1881 to 1910* (New York: Columbia University, 1914), 167.

31. For Roosevelt's inclusion of Jewish issues in (1) the party platform, see William Nathan Cohen to TR, June 1, 1904, TRP; TR to Henry Cabot Lodge, June 2, 1904, *Letters*, 4:813; (2) his nomination acceptance, see TR to Jacob Schiff, August 5, 1904, TRP; (3) a surrogate speech, see TR to Elihu Root, June 2, 1904, *Letters*, 4:810. For the RNC chairman's involvement in declassification, see TR to Oscar Straus, September 13, 1904, TRP. For Roosevelt's pressure on his secretary of state over an extradition decision, see TR to Elihu Root, September 25, 1908, *Letters*, 6:1256. My findings here broadly dovetail with John M. Thompson's observation that "TR and his contemporaries were surprisingly frank about the political calculations that influenced their decision-making, at least in private correspondence and with trusted contacts in the media"— see Thompson, *Great Power Rising*, 7.

32. For the *Menorah* article and Roosevelt's reaction, see J. Lebowich, "Theodore Roosevelt and the Jews," *Menorah* 37 (October 1904): 189–194; and TR to Oscar Straus, October 15, 1904, TRP. For Roosevelt's outrage over and intervention in the judicial slate, see TR to Herbert Parsons, October 8, 1906, TRP; and TR to Charles Evans Hughes, October 5, 1906, *Letters*, 5:443.

33. TR to Oscar Straus, October 15, 1904, TRP. For Roosevelt's use of his pro-Jewish diplomatic positions during his reelection bid, see "Roosevelt's Letter Defends His Acts," *New York Times*, September 12, 1904, 5. For an example of Roosevelt's lining up a Jewish surrogate on the Lower East Side, see his reference to Meyer Isaacs in TR to Lemuel Ely Quigg, October 21, 1898, *Letters*, 2:887.

34. For an example of a single letter espousing both views, see TR to George Briggs Aiton, May 15, 1901, *Letters*, 3:78–79.

35. A published edition of the play, dedicated to Theodore Roosevelt, appeared the year after its theatrical debut: Israel Zangwill, *The Melting-Pot* (New York: Macmillan, 1909). For an example of Jewish criticism of the play, see "Dr. Harrison Preaches a Jewish Sermon before the Free Synagogue in New York," *Jewish Voice* (St. Louis), May 21, 1909, 39. For the play's influence on Roosevelt, see TR to Israel Zangwill November 27, 1912, TRP.

36. Quotation appears in TR to Jacob Schiff, November 16, 1905, TRP. For the Maccabees, see, for instance, TR to George Briggs Aiton, May 15, 1901, *Letters*, 3:78.

1. Ascent

1. Henry James, "The American Scene," in *The Jewish East Side, 1881–1924*, ed. Milton Hindus (1969; New Brunswick, NJ: Transaction Publishers, 1996), 72.

2. M. F. Sweetser and Simeon Ford, *How to Know New York City: A Serviceable and Trustworthy Guide, Having Its Starting Point at the Grand Union Hotel, Just across the Street from the Grand Central Depot*, rev. ed. (New York: J. J. Little, 1900), 7.

3. Jacob A. Riis, *How the Other Half Lives: Studies among the Tenements of New York* (New York: Charles Scribner's Sons, 1890), 104.

4. Riis, *How the Other Half Lives*, 105.

5. William Dean Howells, "Impressions and Experiences," in *The Jewish East Side, 1881–1924*, ed. Milton Hindus (1969; New Brunswick, NJ: Transaction Publishers, 1996), 57.

6. Richard Zacks, *Island of Vice: Theodore Roosevelt's Doomed Quest to Clean Up Sin-Loving New York* (New York: Doubleday, 2012), 2. This description held for New York City generally.

7. Scott D. Seligman, *The Great Kosher Meat War of 1902: Immigrant Housewives and the Riots That Shook New York City* (Lincoln: University of Nebraska Press, 2020), 6.

8. Lawrence J. Epstein, *At the Edge of a Dream: The Story of Jewish Immigrants on New York's Lower East Side, 1880–1920* (San Francisco, CA: Jossey-Bass, 2007), 62.

9. Riis, *How the Other Half Lives*, 115, 118. See also Zacks, *Island of Vice*, 40.

10. Epstein, *At the Edge of a Dream*, 86.

11. Zacks, *Island of Vice*, 40–41.

12. Riis, *How the Other Half Lives*, 132.

13. Epstein, *At the Edge of a Dream*, 198.

14. Hutchins Hapgood, "The Spirit of the Ghetto," in *The Jewish East Side, 1881–1924*, ed. Milton Hindus (1969; New Brunswick, NJ: Transaction Publishers, 1996), 162–163.

15. Epstein, *At the Edge of a Dream*, 190, 185, 193–194. For the Tenth Street Baths, see Annie Correal, "Shvitz or Spa? Depends on the Week," *New York Times*, January 31, 2016, MB1.

16. Price Collier, *America and the Americans, from a French Point of View* (New York: Charles Scribner's Sons, 1897), 21, 20, 22.

17. Riis, *How the Other Half Lives*, 124.

18. Seligman, *Kosher Meat War*, 5; Epstein, *At the Edge of a Dream*, 45.

19. Arnold Bennett, *Your United States: Impressions of a First Visit* (New York: Harper, 1912), 187.

20. Riis, *How the Other Half Lives*, 125, 108.

21. Epstein, *At the Edge of a Dream*, 65.

22. Riis, *How the Other Half Lives*, 123; Epstein, *At the Edge of a Dream*, 65–66.

23. Seligman, *Kosher Meat War*, 11.

24. Riis, *How the Other Half Lives*, 108.

25. Epstein, *At the Edge of a Dream*, 67.

26. Epstein, *At the Edge of a Dream*, 48, 56–58, 50; Seligman, *Kosher Meat War*, 5; Riis, *How the Other Half Lives*, 125.

27. Jacob Riis, "The Children of the Poor," in *The Jewish East Side, 1881–1924*, ed. Milton Hindus (1969; New Brunswick, NJ: Transaction Publishers, 1996), 111.

28. Riis, *How the Other Half Lives*, 134.

29. Epstein, *At the Edge of a Dream*, 58.

30. Riis, *How the Other Half Lives*, 109.

31. Epstein, *At the Edge of a Dream*, 71.

32. Riis, *How the Other Half Lives*, 134.

33. Riis, "Children of the Poor," 115–116.

34. Epstein, *At the Edge of a Dream*, 115, 110, 68; quotation appears on p. 113.

35. Howells, "Impressions and Experiences," 60.

36. Epstein, *At the Edge of a Dream*, 194–195, 73, 76.

37. Quotations appears in Seligman, *Kosher Meat War*, 9.

38. Epstein, *At the Edge of a Dream*, 46, 177.

39. Eric L. Goldstein, "The Great Wave: Eastern European Jewish Immigration to the United States, 1880–1924," in *The Columbia History of Jews and Judaism in America*, ed. Marc Lee Raphael (New York: Columbia University Press, 2008), 86.

40. Jacob Epstein, "Autobiography," in *The Jewish East Side, 1881–1924*, ed. Milton Hindus (1969; New Brunswick, NJ: Transaction Publishers, 1996), 8–9.

41. Irena Grosfeld, Alexander Rodnyansky, and Ekaterina Zhuravskaya, "Persistent Antimarket Culture: A Legacy of the Pale of Settlement after the Holocaust," *American Economic Journal: Economic Policy* 5.3 (August 2013): 195–196.

42. Epstein, *At the Edge of a Dream*, 8–9, 11–13.

43. Epstein, *At the Edge of a Dream*, 13–15.

44. Epstein, *At the Edge of a Dream*, 46.

45. Goldstein, "Great Wave," 71.

46. Epstein, *At the Edge of a Dream*, 16, 20, 15, 171.

47. Goldstein, "Great Wave," 73, 86; Epstein, *At the Edge of a Dream*, 173–174, 178; Seligman, *Kosher Meat War*, 2.

48. Riis, *How the Other Half Lives*, 112.

49. Zacks, *Island of Vice*, 5.

50. Jay Stuart Berman, *Police Administration and Progressive Reform: Theodore Roosevelt as Police Commissioner of New York* (Westport, CT: Greenwood Press, 1987), 2, 16–17; Epstein, *At the Edge of a Dream*, 124.

51. Berman, *Police Administration and Progressive Reform*, 27–32, 4–5.

52. Theodore Roosevelt, *New York* (New York: Longmans, Green, 1898), 224.

53. Zacks, *Island of Vice*, 4.

54. Berman, *Police Administration and Progressive Reform*, 5–8, 17.

55. Roosevelt, *New York*, 224.

56. Zacks, *Island of Vice*, 74, 77, 83.

57. Shelton Stromquist, *Reinventing 'The People': The Progressive Movement, the Class Problem, and the Origins of Modern Liberalism* (Urbana: University of Illinois Press, 2006), 3–7; Susan Strasser, "Customer to Consumer: The New Consumption in the Progressive Era," *OAH Magazine of History* 13.3 (Spring 1999): 12; Charles Hirschman and Elizabeth Mogford, "Immigration and the American Industrial Revolution from 1880 to 1920," *Social Science Research* 38 (2009): 897–898; Roger Daniels, "Immigration in the Gilded Age: Change or Continuity?," *OAH Magazine of History* 13.4 (Summer 1999): 23.

58. Theodore Roosevelt, "A Confession of Faith," August 6, 1912, in *The Works of Theodore Roosevelt* (New York: Charles Scribner's, 1926), 17:266. Although Roosevelt made this remark long after his tenure as police commissioner, it nonetheless reflects a pro-regulation sentiment on his part that dates back at least to his role as the youngest state legislator in Albany in the 1880s—see Theodore Roosevelt, *Theodore Roosevelt: An Autobiography* (New York: Macmillan, 1913), 88–89.

59. Berman, *Police Administration and Progressive Reform*, 8–11.

60. Edith Blumhofer, "Morality Writ Large: Theodore Roosevelt's Ecumenical Exceptionalism," *Review of Faith and International Affairs* 10.2 (Summer 2012): 23–24.

61. Benjamin J. Wetzel, *Theodore Roosevelt: Preaching from the Bully Pulpit* (New York: Oxford University Press, 2021), 15.

62. Zacks, *Island of Vice*, 5–6, 158, 169.

63. Zacks, *Island of Vice*, 86, 5; Edmund Morris, *The Rise of Theodore Roosevelt* (New York: Coward, McCann & Geoghegan, 1979), 482.

64. Theodore Roosevelt speech, 1895, quoted in "New York's Greatest Son, a Friend of the Jews," in "Jews" folder, Theodore Roosevelt Subject Guide, Houghton Library, Harvard University, Cambridge, MA.

65. TR to Henry Cabot Lodge, New York, August 27, 1895, *Letters*, 1:475.

66. For Murray, see Zacks, *Island of Vice*, 210. For Mayer, see "Mr. Mayer Succeeds Mr. Page," *New York Times*, July 24, 1895, 9.

67. TR to Henry Cabot Lodge, New York, August 27, 1895, *Letters*, 1:475.

68. Arthur Hertzberg, *The Jews in America: Four Centuries of an Uneasy Encounter: A History* (New York: Columbia University Press, 1997), 180–181.

69. Epstein, *At the Edge of a Dream*, 190.

70. Riis, "The Children of the Poor," 111.

71. Zacks, *Island of Vice*, 158, 109.

72. TR to Henry Cabot Lodge, New York, August 27, 1895, *Letters*, 1:476.

73. Zacks, *Island of Vice*, 179–181.

74. Theodore Roosevelt, "The Ethnology of the Police," *Munsey's Magazine* 17 (June 1897): 398.

75. Roosevelt, "Ethnology of the Police," 398, 397.

76. TR to Alphonse Major, January 29, 1896, *Letters*, 1:511.

77. Roosevelt, *Autobiography*, 204.

78. In at least one instance in Roosevelt's career, Jewish diversity and merit went hand-in-hand: Roosevelt as police commissioner took pains to ensure a robust Jewish presence on his force in part because he needed Yiddish-speaking officers who could understand Jewish residents, literally and culturally—see Kathleen Dalton, *Theodore Roosevelt: A Strenuous Life* (New York: Alfred A. Knopf, 2002), 152.

79. Nancy Schoenburg, "Officer Otto Raphael: A Jewish Friend of Theodore Roosevelt," *American Jewish Archives* 39.1 (April 1987): 71.

80. David Aberbach, *Realism, Caricature, and Bias: The Fiction of Mendele Mocher Sefarim* (Oxford, UK: Littman Library of Jewish Civilization, 1993), 56; Omeljan Pritsak, "The Pogroms of 1881," *Harvard Ukrainian Studies* 11 (June 1987): 12–13.

81. Schoenburg, "Officer Otto Raphael," 71–72; Stephen H. Norwood, "'American Jewish Muscle': Forging a New Masculinity in the Streets and in the Rings, 1890–1940," *Modern Judaism* 29.2 (May 2009): 167; Sarah Imhoff, *Masculinity and the Making of American Judaism* (Bloomington: Indiana University Press, 2017), 22. Quotations appear in Allan McLaughlin, "Hebrew, Magyar and Levantine Immigration," *Popular Science Monthly* 65 (September 1904): 435; and in Henry Brooks Adams to Elizabeth Cameron, June 11, 1896, in *The Letters of Henry Adams*, 4:388.

82. Morris, *Rise of Theodore Roosevelt*, 40, 60, 112.

83. Gail Bederman, *Manliness & Civilization: A Cultural History of Gender and Race in the United States, 1880–1917* (Chicago: The University of Chicago Press, 1995), 175–177.

84. Quotation appears in Simon Wolf, *The Presidents I Have Known from 1860–1918*, 2nd ed. (Washington, DC: Byron S. Adams, 1918), 195.

85. Josias Leslie Porter, *A Handbook for Travellers in Syria and Palestine* [. . .] (London: John Murray, 1868), 1:272–273.

86. TR to George Briggs Aiton, May 15, 1901, *Letters*, 3:78.

87. Zacks, *Island of Vice*, 183–184.

88. Roosevelt, *Autobiography*, 193.

89. Schoenburg, "Officer Otto Raphael," 69. For Raphael's age, see "Otto Raphael, 66, ex-Police Official," *New York Times*, September 3, 1937, 17.

90. Riis, *How the Other Half Lives*, 114.

91. Roosevelt, *Autobiography*, 192.

92. Schoenberg, "Officer Otto Raphael," 71.

93. Roosevelt, *Autobiography*, 193.

94. Schoenberg, "Officer Otto Raphael," 72–74, 77–78. One claim from Schoenberg—that Raphael escorted Roosevelt on inauguration day in 1905—should meet with skepticism. She cites no source to support the contention. Moreover, contemporary newspaper accounts, including those from Jewish papers, do not appear to have mentioned Raphael's attendance.

95. Roosevelt, *Autobiography*, 193.

96. Tom Buk-Swienty, *The Other Half: The Life of Jacob Riis and the World of Immigrant America*, trans. Annette Buk-Swienty (New York: W. W. Norton, 2008), 257; David Mark Chalmers, *The Social and Political Ideas of the Muckrakers* (New York: Citadel Press, 1964), 9, 105.

97. Zacks, *Island of Vice*, 96.

98. Dalton, *Strenuous Life*, 150; Buk-Swienty, *Other Half*, 250.

99. Dalton, *Strenuous Life*, 150.

100. Collier, *America and the Americans*, 61.

101. Jacob A. Riis, *Theodore Roosevelt: The Citizen* (New York: Outlook, 1903), 144.

102. Epstein, *Living at the Edge of a Dream*, 161, 188–189.

103. Epstein, *Living at the Edge of a Dream*, 158–161.

104. Dalton, *Strenuous Life*, 151; *Report of the Henry Street Settlement, 1893–1913* (New York: Henry Street Settlement, 1913), 34.

105. Arnaldo Testi, "The Gender of Reform Politics: Theodore Roosevelt and the Culture of Masculinity," *Journal of American History* 81.4 (March 1995): 1523–1524.

106. TR to Mrs. Bessie Van Vorst, October 18, 1902, *Letters*, 3:356.

107. Doris Groshen Daniels, "Theodore Roosevelt and Gender Roles," *Presidential Studies Quarterly* 26.3 (Summer 1996): 653.

108. The Jewish women in Roosevelt's orbit included the novelist Edna Ferber, the memoirist Mary Antin, and the suffragist Maud Nathan. See, for instance, TR to Edna Ferber, December 27, 1917, TRP; TR to Mary Antin Grabau, August 26, 1913, TRP; and Maud Nathan, *Once Upon a Time and Today* (New York: G. P. Putnam's, 1933), 129, 133, 139. Because Roosevelt's relationship with Jewish women came to full fruition in his post-presidency, the topic lies beyond the scope of this book. But it is a worthy subject that I am taking up in full in ongoing research.

109. Epstein, *At the Edge of a Dream*, 155–156; Annie Polland and Daniel Soyer, *Emerging Metropolis: New York Jews in the Age of Immigration, 1840–1920* (New York: New York University Press, 2012), 46. To be sure, some German Jews continued to populate the Lower East Side in the late nineteenth century, just as some Eastern European Jews—of varying economic status—moved uptown.

110. See, for instance, Gilbert Sandler, *Jewish Baltimore: A Family Album* (Baltimore: Johns Hopkins University Press, 2000), 45.

111. Hasia R. Diner, *A Time for Gathering: The Second Migration, 1820–1880* (Baltimore: Johns Hopkins University Press, 1992), 231–233; Epstein, *At the Edge of a Dream*, 46, 155; Polland and Soyer, *Emerging Metropolis*, 7, 13, 43; John Higham, "Anti-Semitism in the Gilded Age: A Reinterpretation," *Mississippi Valley Historical Review* 43.4 (March 1957): 567, 569; quotation appears in Epstein, *At the Edge of a Dream*, 155.

112. "Roosevelt's Political Adviser," *Boston Globe*, February 26, 1900, 6; Kurt F. Stone, *The Jews of Capitol Hill: A Compendium of Jewish Congressional Members* (Lanham, MD: Scarecrow Press, 2011), 58; Mary R. Cabot, ed., *Annals of Brattleboro, 1681–1895* (Brattleboro, VT: E. L. Hildreth, 1922), 2:592.

113. For his relationships with the Jewish Republicans Nathan Bijur and Jake Hess respectively, see Nathan Bijur to TR, November 9, 1881, Theodore Roosevelt scrapbook, 1:59, MS Am 1454.36, Houghton Library, Harvard University, Cambridge, MA; Dalton, *Strenuous Life*, 82.

114. Charles H. Crandall, ed., *The Season: An Annual Record of Society in New York, Brooklyn, and Vicinity* (New York: White, Stokes, & Allen, 1883), 289.

115. TR to George Otto Trevelyan, October 1, 1911, *Letters*, 7:362.

116. Lillian D. Wald, *Windows on Henry Street* (Boston: Little, Brown, 1934), 58–59.

117. TR to William Dean Howells, March 6, 1897, Howells Family Papers, 1850–1954, MS Am 1784 (411), Houghton Library, Harvard University, Cambridge, MA. "An East-Side Ramble" appeared in H. D. Howells, *Impressions and Experiences* (New York: Harper, 1896), 127–149.

118. TR to Anna Roosevelt Cowles, July 26, 1896, *Letters*, 1:550. The prospective donor was a sensible target, for she was not merely a lady of high society but a prolific author who valued female education—see Judith K. Major, *Mariana Griswold Van Rensselaer: A Landscape Critic in the Gilded Age* (Charlottesville: University of Virginia Press, 2013), 2, 3, 181.

119. TR to Henry Moskowitz, February 21, 1908, TRP.

120. Val Marie Johnson, "Protection, Virtue, and the 'Power to Detain': The Moral Citizenship of Jewish Women in New York City, 1890–1920," *Journal of Urban History* 31.5 (July 2005): 666.

121. TR to Myra Kelly, July 26, 1905, *Letters*, 4:1287.

122. TR to Raymond Robins, June 3, 1915, *Letters*, 8:934.

123. Higham, "Anti-Semitism in the Gilded Age," 567.

124. Henry Brooks Adams to Charles Milnes Gaskell, July 21, 1896, in *The Letters of Henry Adams*, ed. J. C. Levenson et al. (Cambridge, MA: Harvard University Press, 1988), 4:409.

125. Henry Brooks Adams to Elizabeth Cameron, September 15, 1893, in *Letters of Henry Adams*, 4:128.

126. Sarna, *American Judaism: A History* (New Haven, CT: Yale University Press, 2004), 133; Higham, "Anti-Semitism in the Gilded Age," 567.

127. Ernest Samuels, *Henry Adams* (Cambridge, MA: Harvard University Press, 1989), 284, 347; Riis, *Citizen*, 65–66.

128. Quotation appears in Naomi W. Cohen, "Antisemitism in the Gilded Age: The Jewish View," *Jewish Social Studies* 41.3/41.4 (Summer–Autumn 1979): 202.

129. The irony of the term "polite society" was contemporaneously addressed in Julia Ward Howe, *Is Polite Society Polite? And Other Essays* (Boston: Lamson, Wolffe, 1895).

130. Henry Adams, *The Education of Henry Adams: An Autobiography* (1907; Boston: Houghton Mifflin, 1918), 238.

131. Daniel Okrent, *The Guarded Gate: Bigotry, Eugenics, and the Law That Kept Two Generations of Jews, Italians, and Other European Immigrants Out of America* (New York: Scribner, 2019), 54–55; quotation appears on p. 58.

132. Leonard Dinnerstein, *Antisemitism in America* (New York: Oxford University Press, 1994), 48–50.

133. Hasia R. Diner, *The Jews of the United States, 1654 to 2000* (Berkeley: University of California Press, 2004), 170.

134. Quotation appears in "Are the Populists Anti-Semitic?," *Jewish Voice* (St. Louis), August 14, 1896, 4.

135. Higham, "Anti-Semitism in the Gilded Age," 572, 578.

136. Dinnerstein, *Antisemitism in America*, 53; Higham, "Anti-Semitism in the Gilded Age," 574–577.

137. See generally Yuri Slezkine, *The Jewish Century* (Princeton, NJ: Princeton University Press, 2004).

138. Marvin Perry and Frederick M. Schweitzer, *Antisemitism: Myth and Hate from Antiquity to the Present* (New York: Palgrave Macmillan, 2002), 18.

139. Quotation appears in Cohen, "Antisemitism in the Gilded Age," 201.

140. Matthew 21:12–13.

141. Quotation appears in Dinnerstein, *Antisemitism in America*, 42.

142. Cohen, "Antisemitism in the Gilded Age," 196.

143. Richard J. Evans, *The Coming of the Third Reich* (New York: Penguin, 2004), 22, 25–26.

144. Roosevelt, *Autobiography*, 205–206.

145. Francis E. Leupp, *The Man Roosevelt: A Portrait Sketch* (New York: D. Appleton, 1904), 285. Leupp served as a correspondent for the *Evening Post* before joining Roosevelt's presidential administration. His quotations of Roosevelt were from his own memory, which he submitted to Roosevelt for confirmation. For Roosevelt's blue eyes, see Zacks, *Island of Vice*, 69.

146. Quotations appear in Leupp, *The Man Roosevelt*, 285–286.

147. "Eggs for Herr Ahlwardt," *New York Times*, December 13, 1895, 2; "Ahlwardt Hit with a Bag Egg," *New York Herald*, December 13, 1895, 14. The accounts in the *Times* and *Herald* differ on whether Ahlwardt managed to dodge all three eggs or merely the first two.

148. Roosevelt, "Ethnology of the Police," 399.

149. Roosevelt, *Autobiography*, 206.

150. H. W. Brands, *T.R.: The Last Romantic* (New York: Basic Books, 1997), 291.

151. TR to Anna Roosevelt Cowles, November 13, 1896, *Letters*, 1:566.

152. TR to Henry Cabot Lodge, September 18, 1896, Lodge-Roosevelt correspondence, Massachusetts Historical Society, Boston, MA; Zacks, *Island of Vice*, 169, 309.

153. TR to Henry Cabot Lodge, September 18, 1896, in *Selections from the Correspondence of Theodore Roosevelt and Henry Cabot Lodge, 1884–1918*, ed. Henry Cabot Lodge and Charles F. Redmond (New York: Charles Scribner's, 1925), 1:235.

154. Roosevelt, *Autobiography*, 27.

155. Michael J. Crawford, "The Lasting Influence of Theodore Roosevelt's Naval War of 1812," *International Journal of Naval History* 1.1 (April 2002): 1.

156. Brands, *Last Romantic*, 311.

157. John Lawrence Tone, *War and Genocide in Cuba, 1895–1898* (Chapel Hill: University of North Carolina Press, 2006), 16–18, 193, 219; Brands, *Last Romantic*, 311.

158. Brands, *Last Romantic*, 311–312.

159. John R. Van Atta, *Charging Up San Juan Hill: Theodore Roosevelt and the Making of Imperial America* (Baltimore: Johns Hopkins University Press, 2018), 63.

160. Dalton, *Strenuous Life*, 166.

161. Theodore Roosevelt, "True Americanism," *The Forum* (April 1894), in Theodore Roosevelt, *American Ideals: And Other Essays, Social and Political* (London: G. P. Putnam's, 1897), 23, 22.

162. Van Atta, *Charging Up San Juan Hill*, 64.

163. Brands, *Last Romantic*, 315–316.

164. Van Atta, *Charging Up San Juan Hill*, 63, 12.

165. Brands, *Last Romantic*, 316.

166. Quotation appears in Stephen Kinzer, *The True Flag: Theodore Roosevelt, Mark Twain, and the Birth of the American Empire* (New York: Henry Holt, 2017), 34.

167. TR to French Ensor Chadwick, November 4, 1897, *Letters*, 1:707.

168. John L. Offner, "McKinley and the Spanish-American War," *Presidential Studies Quarterly* 34.1 (March 2004): 59.

169. Brands, *Last Romantic*, 322.

170. Van Atta, *Charging Up San Juan Hill*, 51–52.

171. Van Atta, *Charging Up San Juan Hill*, 53.

172. William R. Nester, *Power across the Pacific: A Diplomatic History of American Relations with Japan* (London: Palgrave Macmillan, 1996), 68.

173. H. G. Rickover, *How the Battleship* Maine *was Destroyed* (Washington, DC: Naval History Division, 1976), v, 127–128.

174. Van Atta, *Charging Up San Juan Hill*, 53.

175. Brands, *Last Romantic*, 328–329.

176. Kinzer, *True Flag*, 47–48.

177. Van Atta, *Charging Up San Juan Hill*, 3.

178. Quotation appears in Kinzer, *True Flag*, 48.

179. Kinzer, *True Flag*, 66.

180. Thomas G. Dyer, *Theodore Roosevelt and the Idea of Race* (Baton Rouge: Louisiana State University Press, 1980), 141.

181. Van Atta, *Charging Up San Juan Hill*, 89–90.

182. Brands, *Last Romantic*, 338–339.

183. Theodore Roosevelt, *The Rough Riders* (New York: P. F. Collier, 1899), 13, 22–23.

184. Quotation appears in Schoenburg, "Officer Otto Raphael," 74–75.

185. "The Jews at Santiago," *Jewish Voice* (St. Louis), August 19, 1898, 6. Regarding the Western origins of the Jewish Rough Riders, Sam Greenwald and Henry Weil hailed from Arizona, and Samuel Goldberg from New Mexico—see Roosevelt, *Rough Riders*, 237, 238, 255.

186. Mark J. Katz, "The Battleship 'Maine' and the Jews," *Hebrew Standard* (New York), March 12, 1909, 14.

187. Emil G. Hirsch, "Decoration Day Address," *Reform Advocate* (Chicago), June 4, 1898, 257.

188. Jeanne Abrams, "Remembering the Maine: The Jewish Attitude toward the Spanish-American War as Reflected in *the American Israelite*," *American Jewish History* 76.4 (June 1987): 443, 451.

189. Roosevelt, *Rough Riders*, 47.

190. Van Atta, *Charging Up San Juan Hill*, 91–95, 101.

191. Morris, *Rise of Theodore Roosevelt*, 615.

192. Van Atta, *Charging Up San Juan Hill*, 101–102; quotation appears on p. 106.

193. Letter reprinted in "Lieutenant Greenwald," *Emanu-El* (San Francisco), September 2, 1898, 12.

194. TR to George Briggs Aiton, May 15, 1901, *Letters*, 3:78; untitled, *The Jewish World* (London), November 4, 1898, 85.

195. "The Jews at Santiago," *Jewish Voice* (St. Louis), August 19, 1898, 6.

196. Van Atta, *Charging Up San Juan Hill*, 111–113.

197. For an example of the latter stereotype, see the excerpt from *The Monitor* reprinted in "Jews in the Army," *Emanu-El* (San Francisco), June 17, 1898, 3.

198. "Random Thoughts," *Emanu-El* (San Francisco), August 19, 1898, 1.

199. See, for instance, "The Jews at Santiago," *Jewish Voice* (St. Louis), August 19, 1898, 6; "Our Jewish Heroes," *Phoenix (AZ) Weekly Herald*, September 8, 1898, 2. For their prior meeting in 1896, see William W. Blood, *Apostle of Reason: A Biography of Joseph Krauskopf* (Philadelphia: Dorrance, 1973), 110.

200. "The Rough Riders Land at Montauk," *New York Times*, August 16, 1898, 1–2.

201. Van Atta, *Charging Up San Juan Hill*, 67, 108.

202. TR to Robert J. Fleming, May 21, 1900, *Letters*, 2:1305. See also Roosevelt, *Rough Riders*, 141; Van Atta, *Charging Up San Juan Hill*, 106.

203. Mary Stuckey, "Establishing the Rhetorical Presidency through Presidential Rhetoric: Theodore Roosevelt and the Brownsville Raid," *Quarterly Journal of Speech* 92.3 (August 2006): 287–288, 291–292.

204. TR to Lucius N. Littauer, October 24, 1901, TRP.

205. Dalton, *Strenuous Life*, 174, 179.

206. Morris, *Rise of Theodore Roosevelt*, 675; "Roosevelt an Easy Winner," *Columbus (GA) Enquirer-Sun*, September 28, 1898, 1.

207. "Roosevelt to Old Allies," *New York Times*, October 12, 1898, 2.

208. See, for instance, "The East Side Meeting," *New York Times*, October 21, 1898, 2.

209. A. L. Wolbarst to TR, October 3, 1898, *Letters*, 2:884n1. For Wolbarst's identity as a Jew, see "Jews of Prominence in the United States," *AJYB* 24 (1922): 215.

210. TR to Lemuel Ely Quigg, October 16, 1898, *Letters*, 2:884–885.

211. TR to Lemuel Ely Quigg, October 21, 1898, *Letters*, 2:887.

212. Abraham J. Karp, *To Give Life: The OJA in the Shaping of the American Jewish Community* (New York: Schocken, 1981), 23–24.

213. "Roosevelt in the Bowery," *New York Times*, November 6, 1898, 4.

214. "In the Jewish Quarter," *Boston Daily Advertiser*, November 7, 1898, 1, 5.

215. "Roosevelt in the Bowery," *New York Times*, November 6, 1898, 4.

216. Coolidge, "The Country," *Boston Evening Journal*, November 9, 1898, 3.

217. Riis, *Citizen*, 216–217.

218. Riis, *Citizen*, 217, 219.

219. Riis, *Citizen*, 220.

220. G. Wallace Chessman, *Governor Theodore Roosevelt: The Albany Apprenticeship, 1898–1900* (Cambridge, MA: Harvard University Press, 1965), 232–233. For an example of Jewish press coverage of the commission, see "Governor Roosevelt's Tenement Commission," *Reform Advocate* (Chicago), June 9, 1900, 492.

221. TR to George Briggs Aiton, May 15, 1901, *Letters*, 3:78–79.

222. "Jewish Woman Honored," וְעטעזאג עשידוי (New York), March 9, 1900, 6.

223. "Mrs. August Etta Elsner Falker," *Hebrew Standard* (New York), November 15, 1907, 3.

224. TR to George Briggs Aiton, May 15, 1901, *Letters*, 3:78–79.

225. TR to William McKinley, March 31, 1899, *Letters*, 2:975–976.

226. Egal Feldman, *The Dreyfus Affair and the American Conscience, 1895–1906* (Detroit: Wayne State University Press, 1981), 1–4; Louis Begley, *Why the Dreyfus Affair Matters* (New Haven, CT: Yale University Press, 2009), 6–9, 122–123.

227. Quotations appear in Kenton J. Clymer, "Anti-Semitism in the Late Nineteenth Century: The Case of John Hay," *American Jewish Historical Quarterly* 60.4 (June 1971): 347.

228. Feldman, *Dreyfus Affair*, 112–113, 116–117; Naomi W. Cohen, *Jacob H. Schiff: A Study in American Jewish Leadership* (Hanover, NH: Brandeis University Press, 1999), 125.

229. TR to Albert Joseph Seligman, Nathan Straus, and Madison Clinton Peters, June 10, 1899, *Letters*, 2:1020. For Picquart's role, see Feldman, *Dreyfus Affair*, 4.

230. Piers Paul Read, *The Dreyfus Affair: The Scandal That Tore France in Two* (New York: Bloomsbury, 2012), 306–312.

231. Untitled, *Idaho Daily Statesman* (Boise), October 1, 1898, 2.

232. Morris, *Rise of Theodore Roosevelt*, 709, 723.

233. Dalton, *Strenuous Life*, 196–197.

234. Morris, *Rise of Theodore Roosevelt*, 718, 721.

235. Corinne Roosevelt Robinson, *My Brother, Theodore Roosevelt* (New York: Charles Scribner's, 1926), 196.

236. Morris, *Rise of Theodore Roosevelt*, 729.

237. TR to William Woodville Rockhill, July 21, 1900, *Letters*, 2:1359.

238. Morris, *Rise of Theodore Roosevelt*, 729–730, 732.

239. Otto Raphael to TR, March 5, 1901, TRP.

240. TR to Otto Raphael, March 6, 1901, TRP.

241. Lucius N. Littauer to TR, November 6, 1900, TRP. For the Littauer-TR relationship, see "Roosevelt's Political Adviser," *Boston Globe*, February 26, 1900, 6.

242. Dalton, *Strenuous Life*, 200.

243. Morris, *Rise of Theodore Roosevelt*, 858n69; "Ex-Justice Cohen, Lawyer Here, Dies," *New York Times*, February 28, 1938, 15.

244. William Nathan Cohen to TR, September 11, 1901, TRP.

245. TR to William Nathan Cohen, September 14, 1901, TRP.

246. Dalton, *Strenuous Life*, 200.

247. Morris, *Rise of Theodore Roosevelt*, 740–741.

248. Morris, *Theodore Rex*, 3.

249. TR to William Nathan Cohen, September 14, 1901, TRP.

250. Dalton, *Strenuous Life*, 200.

2. Romanian Note

1. Howard M. Sachar, *The Course of Modern Jewish History* (Cleveland: World Publishing, 1958), 258–259; Oscar Straus to Jacob Schiff, April 2, 1902, in *Jewish Disabilities in the Balkan States: American Contributions toward their Removal, with Particular Reference to the Congress of Berlin*, by Max J. Kohler and Simon Wolf (New York: The American Jewish Committee, 1916), 108–110.

2. Cyrus Adler, *Jacob H. Schiff: His Life and Letters* (Garden City, NY: Doubleday, Doran, 1928), 2:152.

3. Naomi W. Cohen, *A Dual Heritage: The Public Career of Oscar S. Straus* (Philadelphia: Jewish Publication Society of America, 1969), 124.

4. Gary Dean Best, "The Jewish 'Center of Gravity' and Secretary Hay's Roumanian Notes," *American Jewish Archives* 32.1 (April 1980): 26, 28.

5. See generally Oscar S. Straus, *Under Four Administrations: From Cleveland to Taft* (Boston: Houghton Mifflin, 1922).

6. TR to Oscar Straus December 4, 1900, TRP.

7. Straus, *Under Four Administrations*, 165.

8. Cohen, *Dual Heritage*, 104.

9. Cohen, *Dual Heritage*, viii.

10. Cohen, *Dual Heritage*, 121–122.

11. Naomi W. Cohen, *Jacob H. Schiff: A Study in American Jewish Leadership* (Hanover, NH: Brandeis University Press, 1999), 1, xi, 62–63, 45; quotation appears on p. 46.

12. Cohen, *Dual Heritage*, 124.

13. Oscar Straus to Jacob Schiff, April 2, 1902, in Kohler and Wolf, *Jewish Disabilities*, 108–109.

14. Samuel Joseph, *Jewish Immigration to the United States from 1881 to 1910* (New York: Columbia University, 1914), 167 [583].

15. Oscar Straus to Jacob Schiff, April 2, 1902, in Kohler and Wolf, *Jewish Disabilities*, 110–111. Just after his short stint in the New York state legislature, Roosevelt had derided legislative

resolutions "assailing the czar for his conduct toward the Russian Jews" as political pandering by his fellow assemblymen to domestic constituencies—see Theodore Roosevelt, "Phases of State Legislation," in *Essays on Practical Politics* (New York: G. P. Putnam's, 1888), 43. This article was originally published in *The Century* in January 1885.

16. The meeting was recounted in Jacob Schiff to Adolph S. Ochs, May 14, 1902, reprinted in Adler, *Life and Letters*, 2:153.

17. Kenton J. Clymer, "Anti-Semitism in the Late Nineteenth Century: The Case of John Hay," *American Jewish Historical Quarterly* 60.4 (June 1971): 346–348.

18. Oscar Straus to TR, May 15, 1902, in Kohler and Wolf, *Jewish Disabilities*, 114, 111.

19. Oscar Straus to TR, May 15, 1902, in Kohler and Wolf, *Jewish Disabilities*, 111–114. Straus could have but did not mention that as early as 1840, an American president, Martin Van Buren, tapped diplomatic channels to convey American disapproval of antisemitism in Damascus—see Karine V. Walther, *Sacred Interests: The United States and the Islamic World, 1821–1921* (Chapel Hill: University of North Carolina Press, 2015), 108.

20. "12,000 Persecuted Jews," *Jackson (MI) Daily Citizen*, May 5, 1902, 1.

21. "Jews Leaving Roumania," *St. Albans (VT) Daily Messenger*, May 24, 1902, 4.

22. "Hebrews Answer Cry of Oppressed," *Philadelphia Inquirer*, May 12, 1902, 2.

23. Best, "Roumanian Notes," 29.

24. TR to Lucius N. Littauer, July 11, 1902, TRP.

25. Hay to TR, July 17, 1902, TRP.

26. John Hay to Charles L. Wilson, July 17, 1902, FRUS (1903), 912–913 [doc. 839].

27. John Hay to Charles L. Wilson, July 17, 1902, FRUS (1903), 913 [doc. 839].

28. John Hay to Charles L. Wilson, July 17, 1902, FRUS (1903), 914 [doc. 839].

29. Best, "Roumanian Notes," 29.

30. TR to John Hay, July 18, 1902, TRP.

31. John Hay to TR, July 21, 1902, TRP.

32. John Hay to Charles L. Wilson, July 17, 1902, FRUS (1903), 910–914 [doc. 839]. Although the initial note to Charles Wilson was confidential, word leaked to the *American Hebrew*, which reported on August 1 that Hay sent to Wilson a "most forcible remonstrance against the persecution practised by Roumania upon its defenseless Jewish inhabitants, which persecution is driving these unfortunate people into an unregulated emigration to this country," reprinted in "Secretary Hay Protests," *St. Albans (VT) Daily Messenger*, August 1, 1902, 1. Despite this coverage by the *American Hebrew* and *St. Albans Daily Messenger*, newspapers generally did not report on the matter until the second note to the signatories became public in September. The *American Hebrew*, at the request of the State Department, merely summarized and didn't reprint word-for-word the text of the note to Wilson—see Philip Cowen, *Memories of an American Jew* (New York: International Press, 1932), 263.

33. Jacob Schiff to Lucius Littauer, July 28, 1902, in Adler, *Life and Letters*, 2:153–154.

34. Hay to TR, July 28, 1902, TRP.

35. Charles S. Wilson to John Hay, August 8, 1902, FRUS (1903), 915 [doc. 840].

36. Best argues that "the subtleties of the note were apparently lost on" Wilson, and that "the real purpose of the communication, to criticize Roumanian treatment of its Jews, was apparently ignored by Wilson"—see Best, "Roumanian Notes," 30–31.

37. John Hay to Mr. McCormick, August 11, 1902, FRUS (1903), 42–45 [doc. 38].

38. "Editorial Notes," *American Hebrew* (New York), August 1, 1902, 291. See also Tyler Dennett, *John Hay: From Poetry to Politics* (New York: Dodd, Mead, 1934), 397, as well as Clymer, "Anti-Semitism," 350.

39. John Hay to Alvey Adee, August 30, 1902, Reel 4, JHP.

40. "United States Appeals to Save Jews," *Evening News* (San Jose, CA), September 18, 1902, 1.

41. "Hay Appeals to the Powers for Suffering Jews," *Salt Lake Telegram*, September 18, 1902, 7.

42. "The Nation's Protest against Oppression of Roumanian Jews," *Hebrew Standard* (New York), September 26, 1902, 8.

43. "Asks That Roumania Stop Oppressing Jews," *New York Times*, September 18, 1902, 8.

44. "Mr. Hay's Appeal to Europe," *Washington Post*, September 21, 18.

45. John M. Thompson, *Great Power Rising: Theodore Roosevelt and the Politics of U.S. Foreign Policy* (New York: Oxford University Press, 2019), 6.

46. Excerpt appears in "All Europe Discussing United States' Note," *New York Times*, September 20, 1902, 9.

47. Excerpt appears in "All Europe Discussing United States' Note," *New York Times*, September 20, 1902, 9.

48. Excerpt appears in "European Views of United States' Note," *New York Times*, September 19, 1902, 6.

49. Excerpt appears in "All Europe Discussing United States' Note," *New York Times*, September 20, 1902, 9.

50. Excerpt appears in "All Europe Discussing United States' Note," *New York Times*, September 20, 1902, 9.

51. Excerpt appears in "Little Hope for the Jews of Roumania," *New York Times*, September 24, 1902, 9.

52. Excerpt appears in "Little Hope for the Jews of Roumania," *New York Times*, September 24, 1902, 9.

53. "Germany Approves of Secretary Hay's Protest," September 21, 1902, 5; "Little Hope for the Jews of Roumania," *New York Times*, September 24, 1902, 9.

54. "Romania and the Powers," *New York Times*, September 20, 1902, 8; Charlie Laderman, *Sharing the Burden: The Armenian Question, Humanitarian Intervention, and Anglo-American Visions of Global Order* (New York: Oxford University Press, 2019), 58.

55. "All Europe Discussing United States' Note," *New York Times*, September 20, 1902, 9.

56. "Little Hope for the Jews of Roumania," *New York Times*, September 24, 1902, 9.

57. "Germany Will Not Aid in Coercing Roumania," *New York Times*, September 26, 1902, 9.

58. "Little Hope for the Jews of Roumania," *New York Times*, September 24, 1902, 9.

59. "Mr. Hay's Roumanian Note," *New York Times*, September 29, 1902, 2.

60. John Hay to Charles L. Wilson, July 17, 1902, FRUS (1903), 913 [doc. 839].

61. "British Snub for Roumania," *New York Times*, November 14, 1902, 9.

62. "Praise for Hay and Low," *New York Times*, September 22, 1902, 9.

63. "Thanks of Roumanian Jews," *New York Times*, October 5, 1902, 13.

64. "Grateful to Secretary Hay," *New York Times*, September 19, 1902, 6.
65. Cowen, *Memories of an American Jew*, 270–272.
66. "Simon Wolf," *Reform Advocate* (Chicago), June 16, 1923, 726–728, 731.
67. "Jews in World's Van," *Washington Post*, October 12, 1902, 5.
68. Quotation appears in Best, "Roumanian Notes," 33.
69. Jacob Schiff to TR, October 26, 1902, TRP. This letter isn't listed in the index of TRP, but it is designated part of TRP in the TRDL.
70. TR to Jacob Schiff, October 27, 1902, TRP.
71. Jacob Schiff to Narcisse Leven, October 28, 1902, in Adler, *Life and Letters*, 2:154.
72. Simon Wolf to TR, October 14, 1902, TRP.
73. Quotation appears in Clymer, "Anti-Semitism," 350.
74. "Lively Mixed Meeting at Cooper Union," *New York Times*, October 29, 1902, 1.
75. Clymer, "Anti-Semitism," 350.
76. "Rabbi Criticises Secretary Hay's Note," *New York Times*, November 10, 1902, 8.
77. John Hay to Oscar Straus, October 4, 1902, in Lara Rabinovitch, "'The Gravest Question': Romanian Jewish Migration to North America, 1900–1903" (PhD diss., New York University, 2011), 341.
78. Jacob Schiff to Charles Hallgarten, December 30, 1902, in Rabinovitch, "Gravest Question," 341.
79. Sachar, *Modern Jewish History*, 259. Inaccurate press reports in late 1902 suggested that the note had been effective. On New Year's Eve, the *Washington Post* reported that Romania would naturalize its Jews as citizens—see "Roumania Yields," *Washington Post*, December 31, 1902, 6—but in reality, citizenship would remain elusive for Romanian Jews until after Roosevelt's lifetime.
80. TR to John Hay, March 4, 1903, *Letters*, 3:438.
81. John Hay to John Jackson ["envoy in Balkans"], March 8, 1903, in Rabinovitch, "Gravest Question," 344–345.
82. John Jackson to Hay, April 18, 1903, FRUS (1904), 704 [doc. 665].

3. Kishinev Petition

1. Michael Davitt, *Within the Pale* (New York: A. S. Barnes, 1903), 99, 157–159.
2. Steven J. Zipperstein, *Pogrom: Kishinev and the Tilt of History* (New York: Liveright, 2018), xvii.
3. Davitt, *Within the Pale*, 155–156, 163–164.
4. Davitt, *Within the Pale*, 122, 99.
5. Cyrus Adler, ed., *The Voice of America on Kishineff* (Philadelphia: Jewish Publication Society of America, 1904), ix; Zipperstein, *Pogrom*, 57.
6. Robert Weinberg, "The Blood Libel in Eastern Europe," *Jewish History* 26.3/4 (December 2012): 275.
7. Davitt, *Within the Pale*, 123–124.
8. Zipperstein, *Pogrom*, 63–64.
9. Davitt, *Within the Pale*, 127–128, 193–194; quotation appears on p. 128.

10. Zipperstein, *Pogrom*, 81.

11. Davitt, *Within the Pale*, 166–167.

12. Zipperstein, *Pogrom*, 69, 73–74.

13. Zipperstein, *Pogrom*, 66.

14. Zipperstein, *Pogrom*, 66, 80, 86–88.

15. Zipperstein, *Pogrom*, 90, 81.

16. Adler, *Voice of America*, x; Zipperstein, *Pogrom*, 72. Adler listed 92 as "severely injured" and another 345 as "slightly injured" while untold numbers received medical treatment outside hospitals. Adler placed the death toll at 47, but that number was subsequently updated to 49—see Zipperstein, *Pogrom*, xiv.

17. See, for instance, "Twenty-Five Jews Killed," *St. Albans (VT) Daily Messenger*, April 23, 1903, 1.

18. See, for instance, "Russians Killed Many Jews," *Evening News* (San Jose, CA), April 25, 1903, 1.

19. Simon Wolf to John Hay, April 29, 1903, in Simon Wolf, *The Presidents I Have Known from 1860–1918*, 2nd ed. (Washington, DC: Byron S. Adams, 1918), 187–188.

20. Francis B. Loomis to Simon Wolf, May 9, 1903, in Wolf, *Presidents*, 189–190.

21. "Horrible Atrocities," *Fort Worth Telegram*, May 10, 1903, 1.

22. Adler, *Voice of America*, xviii–xix.

23. Philip Ernest Schoenberg, "The American Reaction to the Kishinev Pogrom of 1903," *American Jewish Historical Quarterly* 63.3 (March 1974): 264.

24. "Chinese Help for Jews," *New York Times*, May 12, 1903, 3.

25. "To Aid Kishineff Sufferers," *New York Times*, May 8, 1903, 7.

26. Schoenberg, "American Reaction," 264.

27. "Chinese Help for Jews," *New York Times*, May 12, 1903, 3; Zipperstein, *Pogrom*, 101.

28. See, for instance, "More Details of the Kishineff Massacre," *New York Times*, May 16, 1903, 1.

29. Adler, *Voice of America*, 112–113.

30. "Flood of Requests," *St. Albans (VT) Daily Messenger*, May 16, 1903, 2.

31. Adler, *Voice of America*, xix.

32. "Denounce Anti-Jewish Outrage," *Idaho Daily Statesman* (Boise), May 18, 1903, 1.

33. Adler, *Voice of America*, 57–58.

34. Adler, *Voice of America*, xii–xiii.

35. "Kishineff Assassins Escaping Scot Free," *New York Times*, May 22, 1903, 1.

36. Quotation appears in Taylor Stults, "Roosevelt, Russian Persecution of Jews, and American Public Opinion," *Jewish Social Studies* 33.1 (January 1971): 17.

37. TR to John Hay, May 21, 1903, *Letters*, 3:477.

38. Stephen S. Wise to TR, May 22, 1903, TRP. For Wise, see Rafael Medoff, *The Jews Should Keep Quiet: Franklin D. Roosevelt, Rabbi Stephen S. Wise, and the Holocaust* (Philadelphia: Jewish Publication Society, 2019), 1–3.

39. TR to John Hay, May 25, 1903, TRP.

40. Zipperstein, *Pogrom*, 194, 200.

41. "All Shocked at the Kishineff Horror," *Philadelphia Inquirer*, May 24, 1903, 8.

42. Stults, "Roosevelt," 15.

43. See, for instance, Adler, *Voice of America*, 94, 346–347.

44. "Jews Denounce Russia," *Jackson (MI) Daily Citizen*, June 22, 1903, 1; "French Denounce Russia," *New York Times*, June 27, 1903, 1; Monty Noam Penkower, "The Kishinev Pogrom of 1903: A Turning Point in Jewish History," *Modern Judaism* 24.3 (October 2004): 190.

45. Joseph Jacobs, "Statistics," in *The Jewish Encyclopedia*, ed. Isidore Singer (New York: Funk and Wagnalls, 1905), 11:531–532.

46. For instance, the British Parliament passed the "Jew Bill" in 1753, which modestly removed some economic constraints on Jewish foreigners. But even these limited reforms were beyond the pale for the public, which successfully clamored for the Jew Bill's repeal. See Dana Rabin, "The Jew Bill of 1753: Masculinity, Virility, and the Nation," *Eighteenth-Century Studies* 39 (Winter 2006): 157, 159. For the relatively restrained response of British Jewry to the Kishinev pogrom, see Sam Johnson, *Pogroms, Peasants, Jews: Britain and Eastern Europe's 'Jewish Question,' 1867–1925* (Basingstoke, UK: Palgrave Macmillan, 2011), 89–91.

47. Adler, *Voice of America*, 117–118, 125, 128.

48. "Christians Protest in Behalf of Jews," *New York Times*, May 28, 1903, 1.

49. Adler, *Voice of America*, 124–125.

50. Adler, *Voice of America*, 339.

51. The most prominent English-language correspondent on the ground in Kishinev was Michael Davitt; see Schoenberg, "American Reaction," 272. Davitt didn't reach Kishinev until five weeks after the pogrom; see Zipperstein, *Pogrom*, 123. Davitt's reporting on details about the events of April 19 and 20 appears to have first reached American papers nearly seven weeks after the pogrom; see, for instance, "Terrible Scenes in Desolate Kishineff," *Fort Worth Telegram*, June 7, 1903, 1.

52. Adler, *Voice of America*, xx.

53. "To Explain Kishineff Status," *New York Times*, June 3, 1903, 3.

54. "Russia's Attitude on the Kishineff Massacre," *New York Times*, June 11, 1903, 9.

55. Adler, *Voice of America*, 468.

56. "Russia's Attitude on the Kishineff Massacre," *New York Times*, June 11, 1903, 9.

57. "Count Cassini Confers with the President," *New York Times*, June 13, 1903, 9; Wolf, *Presidents*, 197.

58. Marguerite Cassini, *Never a Dull Moment: The Memoirs of Countess Marguerite Cassini* (New York: Harper, 1956), 188–189, 193–194; quotations appear on p. 188. See also Marc Peyser and Timothy Dwyer, *Hissing Cousins: The Untold Story of Eleanor Roosevelt and Alice Roosevelt Longworth* (New York: Doubleday, 2015), 48–49, 55.

59. Wolf, *Presidents*, 190.

60. James M. Goode, *Capital Losses: A Cultural History of Washington's Destroyed Buildings* (Washington, DC: Smithsonian Institution Press, 1979), 176–178.

61. Wolf, *Presidents*, 190–191.

62. "President Hears the Case of the Jews," *New York Times*, June 16, 1903, 1.

63. Wolf, *Presidents*, 191; "President Hears the Case of the Jews," *New York Times*, June 16, 1903, 1.

64. Adler, *Voice of America*, 469–471.

65. Quotations appears in Wolf, *Presidents*, 191–192.

66. Quotations appears in Wolf, *Presidents*, 192.

67. It would go too far to suggest that Hay's reticence stemmed from prejudice toward Jews; after all, he donated $200 ($7,000 today) from his own pocket to a Kishinev relief fund—see "Secretary Hay Helps Kichinef [sic] Sufferers," *Anaconda (MT) Standard*, May 21, 1903, 14.

68. Wolf, *Presidents*, 193, 206.

69. Quotations appear in Wolf, *Presidents*, 206.

70. Wolf, *Presidents*, 193–194, 198.

71. Wolf, *Presidents*, 194–196; quotation appears on p. 196.

72. Wolf, *Presidents*, 197.

73. Wolf, *Presidents*, 198–199.

74. See, for instance, "President Hears the Case of the Jews," *New York Times*, June 16, 1903, 1; "The Kishineff Case," *Dallas Morning News*, June 16, 1903, 1.

75. Untitled, *Jewish American* (Detroit), June 19, 1903, 4.

76. Quotations appear in Adler, *Voice of America*, 384–385, 376.

77. "Count Cassini Much Pleased," *Worcester (MA) Spy*, June 20, 1903, 7.

78. "American Jew Warns Russian Ambassador," *New York Times*, June 25, 1903, 3.

79. John Hay to Simon Wolf, June 24, 1903, in Wolf, *Presidents*, 199. For press coverage of Hay's letter to Wolf, see, for instance, "Send It to Russia," *Evening Press* (Grand Rapids, MI), June 25, 1903, 1.

80. "Receives Jewish Petition to Russia," *New York Times*, June 26, 1903, 1.

81. "President to Send Petition to Czar," *New York Times*, June 26, 1903, 1.

82. "Russia Walks Chesty," *Emporia (KS) Gazette*, June 30, 1903, 1.

83. "Cassini May Go," *Los Angeles Times*, June 28, 1903, 1.

84. Quotation appears in Edmund Morris, *Theodore Rex* (New York: Modern Library, 2001), 658n17.

85. Francis Butler Loomis to TR, July 1, 1903, TRP; Loomis wrote partly in shorthand and with spelling errors. For the actual phrasing from the Associated Press, see "Russia Stands on Its Dignity and Will Not Be Lectured by Foreign Powers," *Tucson Citizen*, July 1, 1903, 1. For Hay's visit to Newport, see Tyler Dennett, *John Hay: From Poetry to Politics* (New York: Dodd, Mead, 1934), 399.

86. TR to Henry Cabot Lodge, June 16, 1905, *Letters*, 4:1232.

87. TR to John Hay, July 1, 1903, *Letters*, 3:509.

88. TR to Francis Butler Loomis, July 1, 1903, *Letters*, 3:508.

89. See, for instance, "No Official Explanation," *Idaho Daily Statesman* (Boise), July 2, 1903, 2; "Russia Has Made No 'Explanation,'" *Augusta (GA) Chronicle*, July 2, 1903, 1; "Denied by the Russians," *Baltimore American*, July 2, 1903, 3; "Jewish Petition Held Up for an Address," *Boston Journal*, July 2, 1903, 4; "The B'nai B'rith Petition," *Charlotte Daily Observer*, July 2, 1903, 1.

90. "Kishineff Petition Will Be Forwarded," *New York Times*, July 2, 1903, 1.

91. "Think Petition Unwise," *New York Times*, July 4, 1903, 7.

92. John Hay to Clara Hay, July 6, 1903, Reel 5, JHP.

93. Simon Wolf to TR, July 2, 1903, in Wolf, *Presidents*, 201–202. For Wolf's "embarrassment," see p. 200.

94. Simon Wolf to TR, July 3, 1903, TRP.

95. For instance, see "President Upheld—Cassini a Fizzle," *Boston Journal*, July 7, 1903, 5.
96. Wolf, *Presidents*, 202.
97. William Loeb to Simon Wolf, July 10, 1903, TRP.
98. Wolf, *Presidents*, 202.
99. "Conference on Tuesday," *Idaho Daily Statesman* (Boise), July 12, 1903, 2.
100. J. N. Westwood, *Russia against Japan, 1904–05: A New Look at the Russo-Japanese War* (Albany: State University of New York Press, 1986), 12–17.
101. "Roosevelt and Russia," *Irish World and American Industrial Liberator* (New York), July 11, 1903, 4.
102. "Roosevelt Has the Public Back of Him," *Salt Lake Telegram*, July 8, 1903, 4.
103. John Hay to TR, July 9, 1903, Reel 4, JHP.
104. John Hay to Clara Hay, July 6, 1903, Reel 5, JHP.
105. "Conference over Jewish Petition," *The Patriot* (Harrisburg, PA), July 9, 1903, 1.
106. Dennett, *John Hay*, 347.
107. Roosevelt, *Autobiography*, 342.
108. Bill Bleyer, *Sagamore Hill: Theodore Roosevelt's Summer White House* (Charleston, SC: History Press, 2016), 42.
109. Morris, *Theodore Rex*, 254.
110. Bleyer, *Sagamore Hill*, 11, 32. For elite summering in Newport, see Cecelia Tichi, *Gilded Age Cocktails: History, Lore, and Recipes from America's Golden Age* (New York: New York University Press, 2021), 88–89.
111. In some scholarly renditions of the July 8 meeting, historians describe the details of the conversation between Hay and Roosevelt and cite primary sources. However, these sources do not actually furnish the details described—see Morris, *Theodore Rex*, 658n25; John Taliaferro, *All the Great Prizes: The Life of John Hay, from Lincoln to Roosevelt* (New York: Simon and Schuster, 2013), 602. Morris and Taliaferro each relies on a letter written *before* the July 8 meeting (July 4 and July 3, respectively).
112. John Hay to Clara Hay, July 8, 1903, Reel 5, JHP.
113. John Hay to TR, July 9, 1903, Reel 4, JHP.
114. TR to John Hay, July 11, 1903, TRP.
115. John Hay to TR, July 13, 1903, TRP.
116. John Hay to TR, July 11, 1903, Reel 4, JHP. Hay spent much of the first two weeks of July scrambling to dissuade Roosevelt from sending the petition. On July 1, he suggested that the administration consider Russia's statement in the press indicating it would refuse the petition as a de facto rejection. Rather than irk the Russians by sending it anyway, Hay advised "print[ing] the petition as an American document—in a message to Congress, or in reply to a question from either House, with a statement that the Russian government in a *communiqué* addressed to the American press refused in advance to allow it to come to the knowledge of the emperor"—quotation appears in Dennett, *John Hay*, 399. Two days later, Hay reasoned in a letter to Roosevelt that the State Department could ask the Russians to confirm through diplomatic channels what they were already telling the press—to wit, that they would refuse the petition. Hay felt that such an inquiry, sans the petition, was sufficient to "have complied with our engagement to the Jews in this country"—see John Hay to TR, July 3, 1903, Reel 4, JHP. Hay

reiterated those sentiments on July 11, three days before Roosevelt was scheduled to meet with Jewish leaders, suggesting to Roosevelt, "I rather hope you will conclude after seeing our friends to make the inquiry by cable, which will put a speedy end to the international incident"—see John Hay to TR, July 11, 1903, Reel 4, JHP. The July 11 letter cited at the beginning of this note is distinct from the July 11 letter cited at the end; Hay wrote TR at least two letters on that date.

117. "Roosevelt Has the Public Back of Him," *Salt Lake Telegram*, July 8, 1903, 4.

118. Wolf, *Presidents*, 205.

119. Wolf, *Presidents*, 202–203; Oscar S. Straus, *Under Four Administrations: From Cleveland to Taft* (Boston: Houghton Mifflin, 1922), 172. Wolf suggested that a member of the "English Parliament" was in attendance, but Oscar Straus identified the Brit in question as "Morris Sheldon Amos," undoubtedly a reference to Sir Percy Maurice Maclardie Sheldon Amos.

120. Wolf, *Presidents*, 203–204.

121. Adler, *Voice of America*, xvii–xviii, 468.

122. Historians have depicted Roosevelt's decision to send the petition as motivated purely by self-interest and a reaction to overwhelming public pressure. Stuart E. Knee insists, "It is neither accurate nor justified to portray their [i.e., Roosevelt and Hay's] actions in any other than the light of personal preferences, national considerations and pragmatic self-interest" ("The Diplomacy of Neutrality: Theodore Roosevelt and the Russian Pogroms of 1903–1906," *Presidential Studies Quarterly* 19.1 [Winter 1989]: 73). In the same vein, Stults writes, "Public opinion, primarily Jewish in origin, forced the administration's response" ("Roosevelt," 22). To be sure, there was popular domestic pressure bearing on Roosevelt, and he did stand to accrue some political benefit from sending the petition. But these scholars overlook the countervailing forces that could have easily pushed Roosevelt in another direction. That so many considerations of national interest and even self-interest actually weighed *against* sending the petition suggests that, for Roosevelt, matters of principle and a genuine philosemitism were also factors.

123. Straus, *Under Four Administrations*, 172–173; Wolf, *Presidents*, 205.

124. "President Receives Kishineff Petition," *New York Times*, July 15, 1903, 3.

125. TR via B. F. Barnes to John Hay, July 14, 1903, TRP.

126. Edward Everett Hale to TR, July 12, 1903, TRP.

127. TR to Edward Everett Hale, July 14, 1903, TRP.

128. "Leo N. Levi, on Behalf of Jewish Kishineff Committee, Issues a Statement as to Oyster Bay Conference," *New York Times*, July 16, 1903, 1.

129. Straus, *Under Four Administrations*, 172–173.

130. Wolf, *Presidents*, 208.

131. Schoenberg, "American Reaction," 279; Straus, *Under Four Administrations*, 172.

132. John Hay to TR, July 16, 1903, TRP. Note that this telegram from Hay contained the verbatim cable from Riddle.

133. John Hay to TR, July 16, 1903, TRP. Note that these quotations are Riddle's paraphrasing of the Russian minister's comments.

134. John Hay to TR, July 16, 1903, TRP.

135. John Hay to TR, July 16, 1903, TRP.

136. TR to John Hay, July 16, 1903, *Letters*, 3:518. See also John Hay to Simon Wolf, July 17, 1903, in Wolf, *Presidents*, 209.

137. "Text of Petition Reached Russians," *Philadelphia Inquirer*, July 18, 1903, 1.

138. "Not in Vain," *New York Times*, July 18, 1903, 6.

139. "Russia Explains," *St. Albans (VT) Daily Messenger*, July 18, 1903, 1.

140. "Desired Effect Produced," *New York Times*, July 18, 1903, 7.

141. Quotation appears in Schoenberg, "American Reaction," 282.

142. TR to John Hay, July 18, 1903, TRP.

143. Simon Wolf to TR, July 18, 1903, TRP.

144. TR to Simon Wolf, July 20, 1903, TRP.

145. "Commends the President," *New York Times*, July 21, 1903, 5; "Hebrew Praise for Roosevelt," *Philadelphia Inquirer*, July 21, 1903, 1; "Straus Thanks President," *Trenton Times*, July 21, 1903, 7.

146. TR to Lucius Nathan Littauer, July 22, 1903, *Letters*, 3:524–526.

147. Jacob Schiff to TR, August 6, 1903, TRP. Schiff's criticism of the petition is curious because some two weeks prior, he had expressed his approval of the same in a letter to a founder of the *Alliance Israélite Universelle*; see Cyrus Adler, *Jacob H. Schiff: His Life and Letters* (Garden City, NY: Doubleday, Doran, 1928), 2:118–119.

148. TR to Jacob Schiff, August 13, 1903, TRP.

149. "Literary," *Hebrew Standard* (New York), July 31, 1903, 2.

150. "The Non-Delivery of the Protest," *Jewish American* (Detroit), July 24, 1903, 2.

151. Wolf, *Presidents*, 211, 212, 215.

152. Zipperstein, *Pogrom*, 146.

153. Penkower, "Kishinev Pogrom of 1903," 200–201; Adler, *Voice of America*, xxvi.

154. George Kennan to TR, January 6, 1904, TRP.

155. Shlomo Lambroza, "The Czarist Government and the Pogroms of 1903–06," *Modern Judaism* 7.3 (October 1987): 287.

156. Zipperstein, *Pogrom*, 205–206.

157. Schoenberg, "American Reaction," 263.

158. Westwood, *Russia against Japan*, 17.

159. TR to John Hay, July 18, 1903, TRP.

160. TR to John Hay, July 29, 1903, *Letters*, 3:532.

161. Mina Muraoka, "Jews and the Russo-Japanese War: The Triangular Relationship between Jewish POWs, Japan, and Jacob H. Schiff" (PhD diss., Brandeis University, 2014), 179–180.

162. John Albert White, *Transition to Global Rivalry: Alliance Diplomacy and the Quadruple Entente, 1895–1907* (Cambridge: Cambridge University Press, 1995), 78–79.

163. Charlie Laderman, *Sharing the Burden: The Armenian Question, Humanitarian Intervention, and Anglo-American Visions of Global Order* (New York: Oxford University Press, 2019), 61–63.

164. "Mind Your Own Kishineffs," *Springfield (MA) Daily Republican*, May 20, 1903, 6.

165. "The United States' Roll of Shame," *Salt Lake Telegram*, July 14, 1903, 4.

166. "The American Protest against Jewish Massacres," *Evening Post* (Louisville, KY), July 21, 1903, quoted in Adler, *Voice of America*, 320. For other examples of commentators who downplayed the similarities between pogroms and lynchings, see Adler, *Voice of America*, 10, 373, 392, 410.

167. TR to John Hay, May 25, 1903, TRP.

168. Between the end of the American Civil War and the date of Roosevelt's letter to Hay (1865–1903), the total number of Jewish deaths from pogroms was almost certainly less than the *annual* death count of American Blacks from lynching between 1889 and 1898. For pogrom death tolls prior to Kishinev, see "Persecution of the Jews in Odessa," *Jewish Chronicle* (London), July 28, 1871, 10; Antony Polonsky, *The Jews in Poland and Russia* (Portland, OR: Littman Library of Jewish Civilization, 2010), 2:5; and Mark W. Kiel, *The Jews of Częstochowa: The Life and Death of a Community, a Concise History* (Berlin: De Gruyter Oldenbourg, 2023), 47. For the annual Black lynching victims between 1889 and 1898, see Leroy G. Dorsey, *We Are All Americans, Pure and Simple: Theodore Roosevelt and the Myth of Americanism* (Tuscaloosa: University of Alabama Press, 2007), 98.

169. TR to Lucius Nathan Littauer, July 22, 1903, *Letters*, 3:526.

170. Zipperstein, *Pogrom*, 193.

171. Adler, *Voice of America*, 96.

172. Zipperstein, *Pogrom*, 199–202.

173. TR to Lucius Nathan Littauer, July 22, 1903, *Letters*, 3:526.

4. Passport Question

1. Cyrus Adler, "Jews in the Diplomatic Correspondence of the United States," *Publications of the American Jewish Historical Society* 15 (1906): 76–77.

2. Adler, "Diplomatic Correspondence," 84–85.

3. Quotation appears in *AJYB* 6 (1904): 284.

4. Adler, "Diplomatic Correspondence," 86.

5. Adler, "Diplomatic Correspondence," 86–87; *AJYB* 6 (1904): 291.

6. Shlomo Lambroza, "The Pogroms of 1903–1906," in *Pogroms: Anti-Jewish Violence in Modern Russian History*, ed. John D. Klier and Shlomo Lambroza (Cambridge: Cambridge University Press, 1992), 212, 220–221.

7. *AJYB* 6 (1904): 294–299.

8. Quotation appears in *AJYB* 6 (1904): 285–286.

9. *AJYB* 6 (1904): 300.

10. "Russia's Exclusion of Jews," *New York Times*, March 29, 1902, 3; "Goldfogle Resolution Adopted," *New York Times*, May 1, 1902, 3.

11. "Treatment of American Citizens of the Jewish Religious Faith: Letter from the Secretary of State, Responding to the Inquiry of the House Relating to Treatment of American Citizens of the Jewish Religious Faith," *United States Congressional Serial Set*, vol. 4377, doc. no. 590, May 5, 1902, 1–2.

12. "Rights of American Citizens in Russia," *New York Times*, June 2, 1902, 12.

13. "May Treat with Russia," *New York Times*, November 20, 1903, 1.

14. *AJYB* 6 (1904): 303–304.

15. "Russia's Exclusion of Jews," *New York Times*, February 19, 1904, 2; "Russia's Exclusion of Jews," *New York Times*, April 22, 1904, 1.

16. "Russian and American Jews," *New York Times*, April 30, 1904, 9.

17. TR to Elihu Root, June 2, 1904, *Letters*, 4:810.

18. Oscar S. Straus, *Under Four Administrations: From Cleveland to Taft* (Boston: Houghton Mifflin, 1922), 180.

19. *AJYB* 13 (1911): 42.

20. TR to William Nathan Cohen, May 21, 1904, TRP.

21. TR to William Nathan Cohen, March 16, 1901, TRP; William Nathan Cohen to TR, March 19, 1901, TRP.

22. William Nathan Cohen to TR, June 1, 1904, TRP. Some uncertainty exists over the precise scope of Cohen's contribution to the platform. Cohen told Roosevelt in the above letter that his enclosed slip provided commentary on the Kishinev Petition, but Cohen also conveyed that, with respect to the passport issue, he did "not have the affrontery to put it in words." It appears that Cohen meant he did not have the affrontery to include a platform plank on the Passport Question specifically, but he was seemingly willing to offer some abstract language about the rights of Americans overseas. Evidence in support of that assumption can be found in Roosevelt's June 2 letter to Henry Cabot Lodge, cited below, which suggests that Cohen provided language that alluded indirectly to Kishinev *and* passports. Moreover, an editorial note in *Letters*, 4:813n1 credits Cohen for the platform plank, "Protection of Citizens Abroad," which was a reference to the Passport Question.

23. TR to Henry Cabot Lodge, June 2, 1904, *Letters*, 4:813.

24. "An Immense Coliseum," *Cleveland Plain Dealer*, August 21, 1900, 2.

25. "Root Makes Powerful Address," *Aberdeen (SD) Daily News*, June 22, 1904, 1.

26. "Root Makes Powerful Address," *Aberdeen (SD) Daily News*, June 22, 1904, 1.

27. John Hay and Elihu Root, *The Republican Party: "A Party Fit to Govern"* (New York: Privately Printed, 1904), 50.

28. Quotations appear in Alan J. Ward, "Immigrant Minority 'Diplomacy': American Jews and Russia, 1901–1912," *Bulletin (British Association for American Studies)* 9 (December 1964): 10; and *AJYB* 6 (1904): 283.

29. John Hay to Robert McCormick, July 1, 1904, FRUS (1905), 790–791 [doc. 805].

30. "Name of Grover Cleveland Evokes Volleys of Applause," *Augusta (GA) Chronicle*, July 7, 1904, 3.

31. William Nathan Cohen to TR, June 1, 1904, TRP.

32. "Platform Makers Ride over Bryan," *New York Times*, July 7, 1904, 2.

33. Jacob Schiff to TR, July 31, 1904, TRP.

34. The latter quotations appear in Republican National Committee, *Republican Campaign Text-Book, 1904* (Milwaukee: Evening Wisconsin Company, 1904), 526. Hay recalled Roosevelt's "drunken skunk" comment in John Hay to TR, July 7, 1904, TRP.

35. "Name of Grover Cleveland Evokes Volleys of Applause," *Augusta (GA) Chronicle*, July 7, 1904, 3.

36. TR to Cornelius Newton Bliss, July 14, 1904, TRP.

37. Oscar Straus to TR, July 18, 1904, Box 4, OSP.

38. TR to Oscar Straus, July 19, 1904, TRP.

39. "Oscar Straus Favors Roosevelt," *Baltimore American*, July 21, 1904, 2.

40. Untitled, *Jewish Voice* (St. Louis), August 5, 1904, 4. This article was summarizing a piece that had appeared in another paper, in Hancock, MI.

41. Simon Wolf to William Loeb, July 21, 1904, TRP.
42. Untitled, *Jewish Voice* (St. Louis), May 13, 1904, 4.
43. TR to Cornelius Newton Bliss, July 14, 1904, TRP.
44. Oscar Straus to TR, July 21, 1904, TRP; Jacob Schiff to William Loeb, July 18, 1904, TRP; James Speyer to William Loeb, July 18, 1904, TRP.
45. "The Nomination Was Accepted," *Columbus (GA) Enquirer*, July 28, 1904, 1.
46. "President Formally Opens the Campaign," *Anaconda (MT) Standard*, July 28, 1904, 1.
47. Gil Troy, *See How They Ran: The Changing Role of the Presidential Candidate*, rev. ed. (Cambridge, MA: Harvard University Press, 1996), 118–119.
48. Quotations appear in Richard J. Ellis and Mark Dedrick, "The Presidential Candidate, Then and Now," *Perspectives on Political Science* 26.4 (Fall 1997): 213.
49. Jacob Schiff to TR, July 31, 1904, TRP.
50. Jacob Schiff to Paul Nathan, August 12, 1904, quoted in Naomi W. Cohen, "The Abrogation of the Russo-American Treaty of 1832," *Jewish Social Studies* 25.1 (January 1963): 7–8.
51. Jacob Schiff to TR, July 31, 1904, TRP.
52. Cohen, "Russo-American Treaty," 7–8.
53. TR to Jacob Schiff, August 2, 1904, TRP.
54. TR to Jacob Schiff, August 5, 1904, TRP.
55. TR to Oscar Straus, August 5, 1904, TRP; TR to Nathan Bijur, August 5, 1904, TRP.
56. Jacob Schiff to TR, August 7, 1904, TRP; Oscar Straus to TR, August 9, 1904, TRP; Nathan Bijur to TR, August 8, 1904, TRP.
57. Oscar Straus to TR, August 9, 1904, TRP.
58. Robert McCormick to Count Lamsdorff, August 22, 1904, FRUS (1905), 791–793 [doc. 806].
59. "Our Request to Russia," *New York Times*, August 22, 1904, 2.
60. "Russia Will Refuse," *New York Times*, August 30, 1904, 6.
61. "Roosevelt Takes Up the Challenge," *Baltimore American*, September 12, 1904, 1, 3, 4; "Mr. Roosevelt Defends His Big-Stick Administration," *Anaconda (MT) Standard*, September 12, 1904, 2.
62. "Roosevelt's Letter Defends His Acts," *New York Times*, September 12, 1904, 5.
63. Oscar Straus to TR, September 12, 1904, TRP.
64. TR to Oscar Straus, September 13, 1904, TRP.
65. See Philip Cowen to Simon Wolf, September 2, 1904, TRP; and item #9 in the accompanying memo. Alvey Adee, the second assistant secretary at the State Department, warned Hay in early September, "Goldfogle has written asking for copies of your Jew Passport instruction. He is probably setting a springe to catch a woodcock," a Shakespearean reference suggesting trickery on Goldfogle's part. See Alvey Adee to John Hay, September 1, 1904, Reel 6, JHP. By all appearances, Goldfogle was not granted privileged access to Hay's instructions.
66. Oscar Straus to Nathan Bijur, September 21, 1904, Box 24, GCP.
67. Nathan Bijur to John Hay, September 21, 1904, Reel 20, JHP.
68. Nathan Bijur to George Cortelyou, September 24, 1904, Box 24, GCP.
69. John Hay to TR, September 22, 1904, TRP.
70. TR to John Hay, September 24, 1904, *Letters*, 4:952.

71. TR to George Bruce Cortelyou, September 29, 1904, *Letters*, 4:960.

72. George Bruce Cortelyou to TR, September 30, 1904, TRP.

73. TR to Nathan Bijur, October 6, 1904, TRP. For a reference to Goldfogle's speech, see *AJYB* 6 (1904): 304.

74. Count Lamsdorff to Robert McCormick, October 4, 1904, FRUS (1905), 794 [doc. 807].

75. Richard Connaughton, *Rising Sun and Tumbling Bear: Russia's War with Japan* (London: Cassell, 2003), 23–24.

76. "Japanese Strike by Night," *New York Times*, February 10, 1904, 1.

77. Quotation appears in Cyrus Adler, *Jacob H. Schiff: His Life and Letters* (Garden City, NY: Doubleday, Doran, 1928), 1:217. See pp. 213–215 for details concerning the dinner.

78. Gary Dean Best, "Financing a Foreign War: Jacob H. Schiff and Japan, 1904–05," *American Jewish Historical Quarterly* 61.4 (June 1972): 314–315.

79. Von Plehve and Schiff communicated through an intermediary, Dr. Katzenelsohn, to whom Schiff explained, "The unwillingness of American money markets to take up Russian financing, and the antipathy which has recently been revealed by the American people toward Russia, are due purely to the disgust that is felt here against a system of government which permits such things as the recent Kishineff episodes and the legal discrimination which is the order of the day in Russia"—see Adler, *Life and Letters*, 2:124.

80. Jacob Schiff to TR, July 31, 1904, TRP.

81. Konni Zilliacus, *The Russian Revolutionary Movement*, trans. (New York: E. P. Dutton, 1905), 339, 344.

82. Connaughton, *Rising Sun and Tumbling Bear*, 214–223.

83. For skepticism in the American press about the intentions behind Russia's gesture, see "Russia and American Jews," *Cleveland Plain Dealer*, November 8, 1904, 4.

84. "Jews May Get a Better Deal," *Duluth (MN) News-Tribune*, October 7, 1904, 5.

85. "Plea Not in Vain—America Wins Victory at Russian Court," *Morning Oregonian* (Portland), October 7, 1904, 1.

86. "May Modify Laws," *Washington Post*, October 7, 1904, 1.

87. Best, "Financing a Foreign War," 315–316, 317, 319.

88. Robert McCormick to John Hay, September 27/[October] 9, 1904, Reel 20, JHP.

89. Robert McCormick to John Hay, September 27/[October] 9, 1904, Reel 20, JHP.

90. Robert McCormick to John Hay, September 27/[October] 9, 1904, Reel 20, JHP.

91. Edmund Morris, *The Rise of Theodore Roosevelt* (New York: Coward, McCann & Geoghegan, 1979), 358–359.

92. Robert McCormick to John Hay, September 27/[October] 9, 1904, Reel 20, JHP.

93. Robert McCormick to John Hay, September 27/[October] 9, 1904, Reel 20, JHP.

94. "President Roosevelt and the Jews," *Reform Advocate* (Chicago), October 15, 1904, 179.

95. J. Lebowich, "Theodore Roosevelt and the Jews," *Menorah* 37 (October 1904): 189–194.

96. TR to Oscar Straus, October 15, 1904, TRP.

97. TR to Oscar Straus, October 15, 1904, TRP.

98. Oscar Straus to TR, October 17, 1904, TRP.

99. Louis Wiley, "Shall American Passports Be Respected?" *Hebrew Standard* (New York), October 28, 1904, 11, 6.

100. "Parker on the East Side; Cheered and Idolized," *Hebrew Standard* (New York), October 28, 1904, 5. That rabbi, David Blaustein, tallied among a very small group of Jewish leaders whom the Roosevelt administration had consulted about whether and when to release the diplomatic correspondence. In all likelihood, Blaustein's dinner with Parker was a hedge rather than a symbolic break from Roosevelt. For Blaustein's biographical details, see Jesse Isidor Straus, "David Blaustein," *Publications of the American Jewish Historical Society* 22 (1914): 206–211.

101. "To Admit American Jews," *Springfield (MA) Daily Republican*, November 3, 1904, p. 12; "Will Recognize Passports," *Anaconda (MT) Standard*, November 3, 1904, 3; "Grant Wish of United States," *Cleveland Plain Dealer*, November 3, 1904, 4; "Will Recognize Passports," *Morning World-Herald* (Omaha), November 3, 1904, 2; "Will Recognize the Passports," *Baltimore American*, November 3, 1904, 4; "Russia Will Recognize American Jews," *Bellingham (WA) Herald*, November 3, 1904, 1.

102. "Russia Will Favor Jews," *Morning Oregonian* (Portland), November 3, 1904, 6; "American Jews to Be Protected," November 3, 1904, *Augusta (GA) Chronicle*, 5.

103. This book evaluated Roosevelt's performance with Lower East Side Jews in the 1904 election by aggregating vote counts in overwhelmingly Jewish election districts (EDs) on the Lower East Side. To avoid confounding factors, this analysis excluded Lower East Side EDs that had meaningful numbers of non-Jews even when those EDs were majority Jewish. Overwhelmingly Jewish EDs were determined by cross-referencing a 1910 map of residents (found in Gergely Baics, Wright Kennedy, Rebecca Kobrin, Laura Kurgan, Leah Meisterlin, Dan Miller, and Mae Ngai, *Mapping Historical New York: A Digital Atlas* [New York: Columbia University, 2021], https://mappinghny.com) with the ED boundaries and corresponding vote counts found in *The City Record: Official Journal for the City of New York*—see October 20, 1904, for ED boundaries and January 21, 1905, for vote counts. The 1910 map shows residents by national origin rather than religion, but Russian immigrants on the Lower East Side were Jewish to such an extent that Russian birth serves as an effective marker of Jewish identity. For McKinley's performance in the sixteenth assembly district, see *The Tribune Almanac and Political Register, 1901* (New York: Tribune Association, 1901), 355. Note that assembly districts comprised election districts.

104. Michael J. Dubin, *United States Congressional Elections, 1788–1997: The Official Results of the Elections of the 1st through 105th Congresses* (Jefferson, NC: McFarland, 1998), 334, 343, 352, 361, 370, 379.

105. Moses Rischin, *The Promised City: New York's Jews, 1870–1914* (Cambridge, MA: Harvard University Press, 1962), 229.

106. TR to Jacob Schiff, November 9, 1904, TRP. See also TR to Nathan Bijur, November 9, 1904, TRP.

107. Oscar Straus to TR, November 10, 1904, TRP.

108. "Theodore Roosevelt's Triumph," *Hebrew Standard* (New York), November 11, 1904, 9.

109. Untitled, *B'nai B'rith Messenger* (Los Angeles), November 16, 1904, 6. For an anti-Roosevelt voice, see reprint from the *Press-Post* in "Russia and the Jew," *B'nai B'rith Messenger* (Los Angeles), October 15, 1904, 3.

110. Straus, *Under Four Administrations*, 183–185.

111. "The President's Annual Message," *New York Times*, December 7, 1904, 4.

112. "The President's Annual Message," *New York Times*, December 7, 1904, 4.

113. "Chronic Marranoism," *Reform Advocate* (Chicago), December 17, 1904, 392.

114. Simon Wolf, "Simon Wolf on Nissim Behar," *Hebrew Standard* (New York), December 30, 1904, 3.

115. "President's Criticism May Offend Russia," *New York Times*, December 7, 1904, 1.

116. "Three Slaps at Russia," *Dallas Morning News*, December 8, 1904, 1.

117. "Russian Paper Rubbing It In over Lynching," *Wilkes-Barre (PA) Times*, December 8, 1904, 11.

118. "Russia and American Jews," *Cleveland Plain Dealer*, November 8, 1904, 4.

5. Peace At Portsmouth

1. "Roosevelt Takes the Oath in Midst of Grandest Splendor and Most Magnificent Pomp Most Spectacular," *Augusta (GA) Chronicle*, March 5, 1905, 1. For the weather, see David M. Ludlum, *The Weather Factor* (Boston: Houghton Mifflin, 1984), 133–135.

2. "Roosevelt Takes the Oath in Midst of Grandest Splendor and Most Magnificent Pomp Most Spectacular," *Augusta (GA) Chronicle*, March 5, 1905, 1, 4.

3. Kathleen Dalton, *Theodore Roosevelt: A Strenuous Life* (New York: Alfred A. Knopf, 2002), 200.

4. "Peace of Justice Roosevelt's Ideal," *New York Times*, March 5, 1905, 4.

5. Eugene P. Trani, *The Treaty of Portsmouth: An Adventure in American Diplomacy* (Lexington: University of Kentucky Press, 1969), 29, 32–33.

6. Oscar Straus to TR, February 11, 1904, TRP.

7. Abraham Ascher, *The Revolution of 1905: Russia in Disarray* (Stanford, CA: Stanford University Press, 1988), 46, 51.

8. TR to Cecil Spring Rice, December 27, 1904, TRP.

9. Trani, *Treaty of Portsmouth*, 36.

10. Theodore Roosevelt, *Theodore Roosevelt: An Autobiography* (New York: Macmillan, 1913), 583.

11. Edmund Morris, *Theodore Rex* (New York: Modern Library, 2001), 377–379.

12. TR to John Hay, April 2, 1905, *Letters*, 4:1157–1158.

13. Morris, *Theodore Rex*, 380, 382.

14. Trani, *Treaty of Portsmouth*, 102–103.

15. Ascher, *Revolution of 1905*, 3, 157, 112, 133, 170, 1.

16. Ascher, *Revolution of 1905*, 43, 53.

17. Morris, *Theodore Rex*, 387–391.

18. Oscar Straus to TR, June 14, 1905, TRP.

19. TR to Oscar Straus, June 15, 1905, TRP.

20. Trani, *Treaty of Portsmouth*, 65–66.

21. Tyler Dennett, *John Hay: From Poetry to Politics* (New York: Dodd, Mead, 1934), 436–439.

22. "Honor Memory of Hay at Synagogue Service," *New York Times*, July 10, 1905, 7; "The Weather," *New York Times*, July 10, 1905, 7.

23. "Honor Memory of Hay at Synagogue Service," *New York Times*, July 10, 1905, 7.

24. "Roumanian Jews Mourn for Hay," *New York Times*, July 10, 1905, 7.

25. "Honor Memory of Hay at Synagogue Service," *New York Times*, July 10, 1905, 7.

26. Richard Allen Morton, *Roger C. Sullivan and the Making of the Chicago Democratic Machine, 1881–1908* (Jefferson, NC: McFarland, 2016), 34.

27. Oscar S. Straus, *Under Four Administrations: From Cleveland to Taft* (Boston: Houghton Mifflin, 1922), 189; Mikhail Agursky, "Conversions of Jews to Christianity in Russia," *Soviet Jewish Affairs* 20.2–3 (1990): 80.

28. Adolf Kraus, *Reminiscences and Comments: The Immigrant, the Citizen, a Public Office, the Jew* (Chicago: Toby Rubovits, 1925), 156.

29. Sergei Witte, *The Memoirs of Counte Witte*, trans. Abraham Yarmolinsky (Garden City, NY: Doubleday, Page, 1921), 140, 154; "Witte Speaks Frankly," *Boston Globe*, August 14, 1905, 12.

30. Jacob Schiff to Philip Cowen, August 7, 1905, in Philip Cowen, *Memories of an American Jew* (New York: International Press, 1932), 328.

31. "Adolph Lewisohn Dies at Age of 89," *New York Times*, August 18, 1938, 1.

32. As governor, Roosevelt had reappointed Isaac Newton Seligman as a trustee of a state hospital—Mitchell C. Harrison, *Prominent and Progressive Americans: An Encyclopedia of Contemporaneous Biography* ([New York]: New York Tribune, 1902), 1:308. Roosevelt's papers reveal that he maintained correspondence with many members of the Seligman family.

33. Isaac Newton Seligman to TR, August 17, 1905, TRP; Straus, *Under Four Administrations*, 190. Straus would keep Roosevelt abreast of both the Jewish causes raised with Witte and the peace negotiations more broadly, as per the president's request.

34. Witte, *Memoirs of Counte Witte*, 140–144. For Witte's height, see Robert B. Zoellick, *America in the World: A History of U.S. Diplomacy and Foreign Policy* (New York: Twelve, 2020), 121.

35. Witte, *Memoirs of Counte Witte*, 144–145.

36. For a brief description of Portsmouth in that era, see Karl Baedeker, *The United States with an Excursion into Mexico: Handbook for Travellers*, 3rd ed. (Leipzig: Karl Baedeker, 1904), 125.

37. Trani, *Treaty of Portsmouth*, 123–125; "Peace Envoys Ready for Work," *Baltimore American*, August 9, 1905, 1.

38. Trani, *Treaty of Portsmouth*, 66–67, 125–126.

39. Witte, *Memoirs of Counte Witte*, 151.

40. Trani, *Treaty of Portsmouth*, 126.

41. Trani, *Treaty of Portsmouth*, 124.

42. "Witte Speaks Frankly," *Boston Globe*, August 14, 1905, 12.

43. "Witte Speaks Frankly," *Boston Globe*, August 14, 1905, 12.

44. "Is It the Jewish Question?," *Kansas City (MO) Star*, August 14, 1905, 1.

45. "The Jews of Russia," *New York Times*, August 16, 1905, 6. For Roosevelt's "square deal" line, see "Rights of Each," *Evening Press* (Grand Rapids, MI), September 8, 1903, 10.

46. "Asked Witte to Aid Jews in Russia," *Philadelphia Inquirer*, August 15, 1905, 1.

47. "Witte Receives Jews in Appeal for Race," *New York Times*, August 15, 1905, 2.

48. Schiff et al. to Sergius de Witte, August 18, 1905, TRP.

49. Schiff et al. to Sergius de Witte, August 18, 1905, TRP.

50. Witte, *Memoirs of Counte Witte*, 164.

51. Isaac Newton Seligman to TR, August 17, 1905, TRP.

52. Sidney Harcave, *Count Sergei Witte and the Twilight of Imperial Russia: A Biography* (Armonk, NY: M. E. Sharpe, 2004), 139.

53. Kraus, *Reminiscences and Comments*, 156.

54. Witte, *Memoirs of Counte Witte*, 164.

55. Schiff et al. to Sergius de Witte, August 18, 1905, TRP.

56. Kraus, *Reminiscences and Comments*, 157. Regarding Schiff's edge, see Witte's comment about Schiff's "sharp retort" in Witte, *Memoirs of Counte Witte*, 164. For the small proportion of Jews involved in revolutionary activity, see Shlomo Lambroza, "The Pogroms of 1903–1906," in *Pogroms: Anti-Jewish Violence in Modern Russian History*, ed. John D. Klier and Shlomo Lambroza (Cambridge: Cambridge University Press, 1992), 212, 220–221.

57. Naomi W. Cohen, *Jacob H. Schiff: A Study in American Jewish Leadership* (Hanover, NH: Brandeis University Press, 1999), 138.

58. Witte, *Memoirs of Counte Witte*, 164.

59. Isaac Newton Seligman to TR, August 17, 1905, TRP.

60. "Witte Receives Jews in Appeal for Race," *New York Times*, August 15, 1905, 2. On the expectation that the meeting would last only one hour, see "Leading Hebrews Confer with Peace Commissioner," *Wilkes-Barre (PA) Times*, August 15, 1905, 5.

61. Jacob Schiff to TR, August 18, 1905, TRP.

62. Isaac Newton Seligman to TR, August 17, 1905, TRP.

63. Oscar Straus to TR, August 15, 1905, TRP.

64. TR to Oscar Straus, August 16, 1905, TRP.

65. Morris, *Theodore Rex*, 411–413.

66. "Condition and Treatment of the Jews in Russia Discussed," *Colorado Springs Gazette*, August 15, 1905, 1; "Condition of Russian Jews," *Dallas Morning News*, August 15, 1905, 1; "Asks Rights for Russian Jews," *Duluth (MN) News Tribune*, August 15, 1905, 1; "Jews of America Appeal to Witte," *Augusta (GA) Chronicle*, August 15, 1905, 1. See also "Treatment of Jews in Russia," *Daily Picayune* (New Orleans), August 15, 1905, 1.

67. "Witte Talked with Bankers," *Cleveland Plain Dealer*, August 15, 1905, 1.

68. "In the Balance," *Jewish Voice* (St. Louis), August 18, 1905, 4.

69. "Russia's Jewish Question," *Idaho Daily Statesman* (Boise), August 17, 1905, 4.

70. "M. Witte and the Jewish Bankers," *Cleveland Plain Dealer*, August 16, 1905, 4.

71. "Jews Like M. Witte," *Salt Lake Telegram*, August 17, 1905, 1.

72. "Impressed by Witte," *Fort-Worth Star Telegram*, August 18, 1905, 1.

73. "Witte Discusses Jewish Question," *Hebrew Standard* (New York), August 18, 1905, 4.

74. "Witte's Triple Mission," *New York Times*, August 17, 1905, 2.

75. For an alternative discussion of Jewish reactions to the meeting, see Cohen, *Jacob H. Schiff*, 139.

76. "May Get Loan," *Aberdeen (SD) Daily News*, August 15, 1905, 1; "Would Loan Russia Money," *Morning World-Herald* (Omaha), August 15, 1905, 3.

77. Untitled, *Aberdeen (SD) Daily News*, August 17, 1905, 2.

78. Oscar Straus to TR, August 15, 1905, TRP.

79. Isaac Newton Seligman to TR, August 17, 1905, TRP.

80. "Progress of Peace Matters," *Dallas Morning News*, August 16, 1905, 2; "Jews Like M. Witte," *Salt Lake Telegram*, August 17, 1905, 1.

81. "Witte Talked with Bankers," *Cleveland Plain Dealer*, August 15, 1905, 1.

82. "An Open Letter to His Excellency, Sergius de Witte," *Reform Advocate* (Chicago), August 26, 1905, 17–19. This letter first appeared in the *American Hebrew*.

83. Morris, *Theodore Rex*, 411–414; Trani, *Treaty of Portsmouth*, 156–157.

84. Quoted in Morris, *Theodore Rex*, 414.

85. Morris, *Theodore Rex*, 415.

86. See, for instance, "The Suppressed Panama Message," *Literary Digest* 27.22, November 28, 1903, 272.

87. Oscar Straus to TR, September 12, 1905, TRP.

88. Roosevelt, *Autobiography*, 587. That endeavor did not, in the end, materialize.

89. "Ends in Peace and Sunshine," *Baltimore American*, September 6, 1905, 1–2.

90. "Treaty of Portsmouth an Accomplished Fact," *Augusta (GA) Chronicle*, September 6, 1905, 1.

91. "Ends in Peace and Sunshine," *Baltimore American*, September 6, 1905, 1–2.

92. Witte, *Memoirs of Counte Witte*, 160; "Treaty Signed; The War Ended," *New York Times*, September 6, 1905, 1, 2.

93. TR to George Otto Trevelyan, September 12, 1905, *Letters*, 5:22–23.

94. Zoellick describes Witte as "gruff" and "blunt" in *America in the World*, 121.

95. TR to George Otto Trevelyan, September 12, 1905, *Letters*, 5:23. Straus recounted in his memoirs, in an apparent reference to Roosevelt's September meeting with Witte, that "when the Portsmouth Conference was over, the president further took a deep interest in bringing about the amelioration of the condition of the Jews in Russia," in *Under Four Administrations*, 191.

96. TR to Sergius Witte, September 10, 1905, in Straus, *Under Four Administrations*, 191.

97. Witte, *Memoirs of Counte Witte*, 174–175.

98. Charles M. Harvey, "What the Jew Owes to the Republican Party," *Leslie's Weekly*, September 24, 1908, 302.

99. "Witte Sails for Home; Will Return, He Says," *New York Times*, September 13, 1905, 4. Schiff telegrammed Witte to express his regrets at not being available for this second meeting and, striking a different tone than he had in Portsmouth, offered gratitude for Witte's ear in Portsmouth—see Jacob Schiff to Sergei Witte, September 11, 1905, in Cyrus Adler, *Jacob H. Schiff: His Life and Letters* (Garden City, NY: Doubleday, Doran, 1928), 2:132–133.

100. "M. Witte as Described by Mr. Adolf Kraus," *Jewish Voice* (St. Louis), September 22, 1905, 4.

101. "Witte Sails for Home; Will Return, He Says," *New York Times*, September 13, 1905, 4.

102. "Witte Gives Assurance," *Hebrew Standard* (New York), September 15, 1905, 4. For his lunch at the Union Club, see "Witte Sails for Home; Will Return, He Says," *New York Times*, September 13, 1905, 4.

103. Harcave, *Count Sergei Witte*, 167–170, 173, 175; Zvi Gitelman, *A Century of Ambivalence: The Jews of Russia and the Soviet Union, 1881 to the Present*, 2nd ed. (Bloomington: Indiana University Press, 2001), 23. Quotations appear in Harcave, *Count Sergei Witte*, 175.

6. Pogroms

1. Shlomo Lambroza, "The Pogroms of 1903–1906," in *Pogroms: Anti-Jewish Violence in Modern Russian History*, ed. John D. Klier and Shlomo Lambroza (Cambridge: Cambridge University Press, 1992), 232; Sidney Harcave, *Count Sergei Witte and the Twilight of Imperial Russia: A Biography* (Armonk, NY: M. E. Sharpe, 2004), 179; Rebecca Kobrin, "The 1905 Revolution Abroad: Mass Migration, Russian Jewish Liberalism, and American Jewry, 1903–1914," in *The Revolution of 1905 and Russia's Jews*, ed. Stefani Hoffman and Ezra Mendelsohn (Philadelphia: University of Pennsylvania Press, 2008), 227.

2. Quotation appears in Gerald D. Surh, "Russia's 1905 Era Pogroms Reexamined," *Canadian–American Slavic Studies* 44 (2010): 295.

3. Lambroza, "Pogroms of 1903–1906," 225.

4. Quotation appears in Victoria Khiterer, "The October 1905 Pogroms and the Russian Authorities," *Nationalities Papers* 43.5 (2015): 789.

5. Lambroza, "Pogroms of 1903–1906," 231.

6. Khiterer, "October 1905 Pogroms," 789.

7. "Took Merely a Word to Stop Massacres," *New York Times*, December 1, 1905, 5.

8. "Latest Account of Deeds at Odessa Add Horror," *Macon (GA) Telegraph*, November 6, 1905, 1. See also "Blood Flows Freely in Russian Empire," *The State* (Columbia, SC), November 2, 1905, 1.

9. Khiterer, "October 1905 Pogroms," 788; Lambroza, "Pogroms of 1903–1906," 227, 231; Hannan Hever, "Rebellion in Writing: Yosef Haim Brenner and the 1905 Revolution," in *The Revolution of 1905 and Russia's Jews*, ed. Stefani Hoffman and Ezra Mendelsohn (Philadelphia: University of Pennsylvania Press, 2008), 153. Khiterer and Lambroza place the death toll around 3,100, whereas Hever places it at 1,000.

10. Surh, "Russia's 1905 Era Pogroms Reexamined," 294. For the flags and singing, see "Took Merely a Word to Stop Massacres," *New York Times*, December 1, 1905, 5.

11. Quotation appears in Khiterer, "October 1905 Pogroms," 797.

12. Lambroza, "Pogroms of 1903–1906," 234.

13. Surh, "Russia's 1905 Era Pogroms Reexamined," 294; Khiterer, "October 1905 Pogroms," 792.

14. Quotation appears in Khiterer, "October 1905 Pogroms," 796.

15. Richard Wortman, "Nicholas II and the Revolution," in *The Revolution of 1905 and Russia's Jews*, ed. Stefani Hoffman and Ezra Mendelsohn (Philadelphia: University of Pennsylvania Press, 2008), 37.

16. Khiterer, "October 1905 Pogroms," 797.

17. Quotation appears in Harcave, *Count Sergei Witte*, 180.

18. Sergei Witte, *The Memoirs of Counte Witte*, trans. Abraham Yarmolinsky (Garden City, NY: Doubleday, Page, 1921), 190.

19. Harcave, *Count Sergei Witte*, 178, 203–205.

20. H. Custis Vezey to George von Lengerke Meyer, November 11, 1905, Box 6, GMP.

21. Lambroza, "Pogroms of 1903–1906," 208, 213, 231.

22. For newspaper coverage, see, for instance, "Aided by Military," *Los Angeles Times*, September 24, 1903, 4; "Many Jews Slain in West Russia," *Chicago Sunday Tribune*, July 16, 1905, 1

[Part III Editorial]. For the concerns of Schiff and others about the pogroms, see Jacob Schiff to TR, December 31, 1903, TRP; TR to Jacob Schiff, January 1, 1904, TRP; Jacob Schiff to TR, January 4, 1904, TRP; Oscar Straus to TR, March 31, 1904, TRP.

23. "Odessa Looted; Jews Massacred," *New York Times*, November 2, 1905, 1; "Hundreds Slain in Odessa; Mobs Rule," *Philadelphia Inquirer*, November 2, 1905, 1.

24. See, for instance, "Wild Rioting and Bloodshed in Many Cities Follow Liberty," *Olympia (WA) Daily Recorder*, November 1, 1905, 1; "Great Disorder in Russia," *St. Albans (VT) Daily Messenger*, November 2, 1905, 1; "Russia Gone Mad over Peace Plan," *Evening Press* (Grand Rapids, MI), November 2, 1905, 1, 8; "Police Join the Rioters," *Montgomery (AL) Advertiser*, November 1, 1905, 1; "Rivers of Blood Flow in Russia," *Morning Oregonian* (Portland), November 2, 1905, 1.

25. "Wholesale Plunder of Jews," *St. Albans (VT) Daily Messenger*, November 4, 1905, 1.

26. "5,000 Dead and Wounded," *Montgomery (AL) Advertiser*, November 3, 1905, 1.

27. "Great Massacre of the Jews," *Evening World-Herald* (Omaha), November 2, 1905, 1.

28. Jacob Schiff to Sergei Witte, November 3, 1905, in Cyrus Adler, *Jacob H. Schiff: His Life and Letters* (Garden City, NY: Doubleday, Doran, 1928), 2:134.

29. Sergei Witte to Jacob Schiff, November 5, 1905, in Adolf Kraus, *Reminiscences and Comments: The Immigrant, the Citizen, a Public Office, the Jew* (Chicago: Toby Rubovits, 1925), 162.

30. Khiterer, "October 1905 Pogroms," 797.

31. Harcave, *Count Sergei Witte*, 203.

32. Quotation appears in Thomas G. Barnes and Gerald D. Feldman, eds., *Nationalism, Industrialization, and Democracy, 1815–1914* (1972; Lanham, MD: University Press of America, 1980), 3:248.

33. Quotation appears in "Mr. Roosevelt Unable to Aid Russian Jews," *New York Times*, November 7, 1905, 2.

34. TR to George von Lengerke Meyer, November 6, 1905, Box 6, GMP.

35. George von Lengerke Meyer to TR, November 7, 1905, TRP.

36. TR to George von Lengerke Meyer, November 9, 1905, Box 6, GMP.

37. "American Jews to Aid Sufferers in Russia," *New York Times*, November 8, 1905, 12.

38. "American Jews to Aid Sufferers in Russia," *New York Times*, November 8, 1905, 12.

39. Wolf's message was reprinted in "Begs President to Act," *New York Times*, November 10, 1905, 2; "Appeals to Roosevelt," *Dallas Morning News*, November 10, 1905, 2; "Asks Roosevelt to Save the Jews," *Duluth (MN) News-Tribune*, November 10, 1905, 1; "Jews Appeal to Roosevelt," *Lexington (KY) Herald*, November 10, 1905, 1; "Another Appeal Made," *Montgomery (AL) Advertiser*, November 10, 1905, 1; "Roosevelt Invoked to Stop Slaughter," *Philadelphia Inquirer*, November 10, 1905, 2.

40. Wolf soon clarified for the press that he was appealing to Roosevelt to act as an individual, not as head of state. This nicety was probably designed to allow Wolf to stand by his initial entreaty to Roosevelt without being seen as pressuring the *government* to interfere in Russia in the wake of Roosevelt's insistence that his administration would not—see "President's Power to Act," *New York Times*, November 11, 1905, 2.

41. "The Horrors of Hell," *Hebrew Standard* (New York), November 10, 1905, 8.

42. For an example of a first-hand account appearing in the American press, see "Writes of the Odessa Horror," *Baltimore American*, November 21, 1905, 18.

43. "Jewish Relief Fund Passes $500,000 Mark," *New York Times*, November 20, 1905, 6.

44. "Carnegie Gives $10,000 for Russian Relief," *New York Times*, November 13, 1905, 1.

45. Jacob Schiff to Samuel Rea, November 14, 1905, in Adler, *Life and Letters*, 2:133–134.

46. "America's Heart Throbs with Sympathy," *Jewish Voice* (St. Louis), November 17, 1905, 4.

47. "Pittsburgh, Penn.," *Emanu-El* (San Francisco), November 17, 1905, 11.

48. "Hebrew Veterans Call on Roosevelt to Act," *Hebrew Standard* (New York), November 24, 1905, 5.

49. "Says President Can Act," *New York Times*, November 20, 1905, 4.

50. "Carnegie Gives $10,000 for Russian Relief," *New York Times*, November 13, 1905, 1.

51. "United States Should Speak, Says Dr. Abbott," *New York Times*, November 27, 1905, 6.

52. For Abbott's relationship with Roosevelt, see Ira V. Brown, *Lyman Abbott, Christian Evolutionist: A Study in Religious Liberalism* (Cambridge, MA: Harvard University Press, 1953), 178–179.

53. "St. Louis to the Front," *Jewish Voice* (St. Louis), November 17, 1905, 3.

54. "To Relieve the Suffering Jews," *Baltimore American*, November 25, 1905, 18.

55. "Atlantic City," *Hebrew Standard* (New York), November 24, 1905, 5.

56. M. A. De Wolfe Howe, *George Von Lengerke Meyer: His Life and Public Services* (New York: Dodd, Mead, 1919), 222.

57. Cecil Spring Rice to Edith Kermit Carow Roosevelt, November 27, 1905, TRP. Root's track record on Jews wasn't uniformly negative. In 1893, Root supported Theodore Seligman's admission to the Union League Club, in opposition to the overtly antisemitic majority that rejected Seligman's application for membership—see "Mr. Seligman Blackballed," *New York Times*, April 15, 1893, 1.

58. "Jewish Relief Fund Nears Million Mark," *New York Times*, November 26, 1905, 12.

59. Elihu Root to U.S. Embassy in St. Petersburg, November 22, 1905, RG 59, M77-Diplomatic Instructions of the Department of State, 1801–1906, Roll 140 [image 385], USNA.

60. Spencer Eddy to Elihu Root, November 25, 1905, RG 59, M35-Despatches from U.S. Ministers to Russia, 1808–1906, Reel 64 [image 614], USNA. See also Spencer Eddy to Elihu Root, November 26, 1905, RG 59, M35-Despatches from U.S. Ministers to Russia, 1808–1906, Reel 64 [image 616], NA; Spencer Eddy to Elihu Root, November 29, 1905, RG 59, M35-Despatches from U.S. Ministers to Russia, 1808–1906, Reel 64 [image 621], USNA.

61. See figure 1 in Lambroza, "The Pogroms of 1903–1906," 227.

62. Karine V. Walther, *Sacred Interests: The United States and the Islamic World, 1821–1921* (Chapel Hill: University of North Carolina Press, 2015), 356n101; see also p. 144 for the causes of the Algeciras Conference.

63. Jacob H. Schiff to Elihu Root, November 21, 1905, subinclosure, *AJYB* 8 (1906): 94–98.

64. See Henry White to Elihu Root, January 30, 1906, FRUS (1909), 1471–1476 [doc. 555].

65. Elihu Root to Henry White, November 28, 1905, *AJYB* 8 (1906): 92–93.

66. Elihu Root to Henry White, November 28, 1905, Box 187 (Part I, November 1905), ERP.

67. Jacob Schiff to Sergei Witte, circa late November 1905, in Adler, *Life and Letters*, 2:135–136.

68. "Jewish Celebration Full of Enthusiasm," *New York Times*, December 1, 1905, 1. While conventionally historians have pointed to the arrival of Jews to New Amsterdam in the 1650s as

the founding moment for communal Jewish life in North America, Leo Hershkowitz argues otherwise in "By Chance or Choice: Jews in New Amsterdam 1654," *American Jewish Archives Journal* 57 (2005): 10.

69. "Jewish Celebration Full of Enthusiasm," *New York Times*, December 1, 1905, 1.

70. "Jewish Celebration Full of Enthusiasm," *New York Times*, December 1, 1905, 4.

71. TR to Jacob Schiff, November 16, 1905, TRP.

72. TR to Jacob Schiff, November 16, 1905, TRP. Roosevelt's willingness to rebut antisemitic tropes calls into question scholar Walter Laqueur's depiction of him. Laqueur ranks Roosevelt among the "supporters" of Houston Stewart Chamberlain, a British-German writer whose antisemitic publications inspired Adolph Hitler—see Walter Laqueur, *The Changing Face of Anti-Semitism: From Ancient Times to the Present Day* (New York: Oxford University Press, 2006), 94. Roosevelt, in truth, explicitly and publicly rejected Chamberlain's antisemitism. In a review of a book by Chamberlain, Roosevelt derided him as "an extremist whose doctrines are based upon foolish hatred. . . . Mr. Chamberlain's hatreds cover a wide gamut. They include Jews"—see Theodore Roosevelt and Lyman Abbott, review of *The Foundations of the Nineteenth Century*, by Houston Stewart Chamberlain, *The Outlook* (New York), July 29, 1911, 729.

73. TR to Jacob Schiff, November 16, 1905, TRP.

74. "Can't Bar Tenant Because of Creed," *Emanu-El* (San Francisco), November 29, 1907, 16.

75. "Jews, in Huge Parade, Mourn Dead in Russia," *New York Times*, December 5, 1905, 6. The *New York Times* tallied the parade's participants at 125,000; *The American Jewish Year Book* placed the number at just below 100,000—see *AJYB* 8 (1906): 241.

76. "Fund Exceeds $1,000,000, Still More to Come," *New York Times*, December 3, 1905, 8.

77. Quotations appear in "Root Says We Cannot Intervene in Russia," *New York Times*, December 6, 1905, 6.

78. H. Custis Vezey to George von Lengerke Meyer, December 2, 1905, Box 6, GMP.

79. George von Lengerke Meyer to Henry Cabot Lodge, December 12, 1905, Box 6, GMP.

80. Schiff to TR, December 8, 1905, in Adler, *Life and Letters*, 2:137–138.

81. TR to Jacob Schiff, December 14, 1905, TRP.

82. TR to Jacob Schiff, December 14, 1905, TRP.

83. TR to Oscar Straus, December 14, 1905, TRP.

84. Oscar Straus to TR, December 15, 1905, TRP.

85. Oscar Straus to TR, December 15, 1905, TRP.

86. Harcave, *Count Sergei Witte*, 205–206.

87. "The Daily Telegraph," December 12, 1905, Box 6, GMP.

88. "Random Thoughts," *Emanu-El* (San Francisco), December 15, 1905, 5.

89. "Mark Twain Speaks after Bernhardt Acts," *New York Times*, December 19, 1905, 9.

90. Mark Twain, *Mark Twain's Autobiography* (1913; New York: Harper & Brothers, 1924), 2:293–294.

91. "Time May Raise Station of Jew," *Cleveland Plain Dealer*, August 26, 1906, 4.

92. "Asks House to Act for Jews," *New York Times*, December 6, 1905, 6.

93. "A Call to American Humanity," *Hebrew Standard* (New York), December 29, 1905, 1. Sulzer submitted his own resolution that fulminated against Russia but made no ask of the Roosevelt administration, surprisingly so given Sulzer's floor speech.

94. "Is American Humanity Dead?," *Hebrew Standard* (New York), December 29, 1905, 8.

95. George Meyer to TR, December 20, 1905, Box 6, GMP.

96. Harcave, *Count Sergei Witte*, 209–211.

97. George Meyer to TR, January 15, 1906, TRP.

98. Lambroza, "Pogroms of 1903–1906," 229, 238.

99. "Algeciras," *Sunday Star* (Washington, DC), January 21, 1906, 16.

100. Henry White and Samuel R. Gummeré to Elihu Root, January 25, 1906, FRUS (1909), 1470 [doc. 554].

101. Henry White to Elihu Root, January 30, 1906, FRUS (1909), 1471–1472 [doc. 555].

102. "A Report on the Restrictions Suffered by the Jews in Morocco," [Inclosure 1], FRUS (1909), 1472–1476 [doc. 555]; quotations appear on pp. 1472, 1474.

103. Henry White to Elihu Root, January 30, 1906, FRUS (1909), 1472 [doc. 555].

104. "Mr. A. Pimienta's Suggestion as to the Form of Our Intervention in Behalf of the Jews," [Inclosure 2–Translation], FRUS (1909), 1476 [doc. 555].

105. Mardochée Bengio to Lewis Einstein, [Inclosure], January 31, 1906, FRUS (1909), 1477 [doc. 556].

106. Henry White to Elihu Root, March 28, 1906, M37-Despatches from Special Agents of the Department of State, 1794–1906, Roll 22 [image 449], USNA.

107. Elihu Root to Henry White, March 28, 1906, FRUS (1909), 1487 [doc. 562]. It is unclear whether Root even consulted Roosevelt before sending this latest cable to White, who had expressly asked Root for the president's input about how best to proceed. On January 30, 1906, White had written to Root, "I beg to request that you will be so good as to inform me what course of action the president would wish me to pursue" regarding the "Moroccan Hebrews"—see FRUS (1909), 1472 [doc. 555].

108. "Motion of the American Delegation," [Inclosure.–Translation], April 8, 1906, FRUS (1909), 1493–1494 [doc. 566].

109. Henry White to Elihu Root, April 8, 1906, FRUS (1909), 1493 [doc. 566].

110. Henry White and Samuel R. Gummeré to Elihu Root, April 8, 1906, FRUS (1909), 1490 [doc. 563].

111. Henry White to Elihu Root, April 8, 1906, FRUS (1909), 1493 [doc. 566].

112. See, for instance, "Equality for Jews in Morocco," *Morning Oregonian* (Portland), April 4, 1906, 11.

113. Mardochée Bengio to Henry White, April 23, 1906, in "Moroccan Jews Return Thanks to America," *Idaho Daily Statesman* (Boise), June 10, 1906, 9.

114. "Thanks of Hebrews Sent to President," *Philadelphia Inquirer*, June 10, 1906, 2; "Jews in Morocco," *Daily Picayune* (New Orleans), June 10, 1906, 1, 2; "Jews of Morocco Thank America for Good Offices," *Sunday World-Herald* (Omaha), June 10, 1906, 3; "Domestic Happenings," *Emanu-El* (San Francisco), June 15, 1906, 11; "Interesting Items," *Jewish Voice* (St. Louis), June 29, 1906, 8.

115. Robert Bacon to George Meyer, April 7, 1906, RG 59, M77-Diplomatic Instructions of the Department of State, 1801–1906, Reel 140 [image 400], USNA. For British-Jewish advocacy, see Gary Dean Best, *To Free a People: American Jewish Leaders and the Jewish Problem in Eastern Europe, 1890–1914* (Westport, CT: Greenwood Press, 1982), 124–125.

116. George Meyer to Elihu Root, April 9, 1906, RG 59, Despatches from Diplomatic Officers, 1789–1906, M35-Despatches from U.S. Ministers to Russia, 1808–1906, Reel 66 [image 35], USNA.

117. Oscar Straus to TR, April 9, 1906, TRP.

118. TR to Oscar Straus, April 10, 1906, TRP.

119. TR to Oscar Straus, April 10, 1906, TRP.

120. Oscar Straus to William Loeb, April 10, 1906, TRP.

121. TR to Oscar Straus, April 13, 1906, TRP.

122. See, for instance, "Jews Considered Safe," *Boston Evening Transcript*, April 17, 1906, 9; "No Repetition of Kishineff," *Duluth (MN) News-Tribune*, April 17, 1906, 1.

123. Oscar Straus to William Loeb, May 7, 1906, TRP.

124. William Loeb to Oscar Straus, May 8, 1906, Box 4, OSP.

125. Quotations appear in Harcave, *Count Sergei Witte*, 221, 225.

126. Witte, *Memoirs of Counte Witte*, 315.

127. George Meyer to TR, May 21, 1906, TRP.

128. Rebecca Kobrin, *Jewish Bialystok and Its Diaspora* (Bloomington: Indiana University Press, 2010), 58–59; Official Communication on the Disorders at Bielostock, [Inclosure], FRUS (1909), 1297 [doc. 408]. For the population of Bialystok—total and Jewish—see *AJYB* 8 (1906): 64.

129. "Bialystok Horror," *Washington Post*, June 19, 1906, 1.

130. "Report of the Duma Commission on the Bialystok Massacre," *AJYB* 8 (1906): 76–78.

131. "Bialystok in Flames; Massacre Continues," *New York Times*, June 17, 1906, 2.

132. Sara Bender, *The Jews of Bialystok during World War II and the Holocaust* (Waltham, MA: Brandeis University Press, 2008), 15.

133. Jacob Schiff to TR, June 18, 1906, in Adler, *Life and Letters*, 2:138–139.

134. Naomi W. Cohen, *A Dual Heritage: The Public Career of Oscar S. Straus* (Philadelphia: Jewish Publication Society of America, 1969), 135.

135. TR to Jacob Schiff, June 18, 1906, TRP.

136. "Blood Orgy in Bialystok," *Idaho Daily Statesman* (Boise), June 21, 1906, 2.

137. "The Russian Government and the Massacres," *Quarterly Review* 205.409 (October 1906): 609.

138. "New York Jews Lament," *New York Times*, June 21, 1906, 2.

139. TR to Jacob Schiff, June 22, 1906, TRP.

140. TR to Jacob Schiff, June 22, 1906, TRP.

141. TR to Jacob Schiff, June 22, 1906, TRP.

142. "Congress Expresses Horror," *New York Times*, June 23, 1906, 5.

143. Elihu Root to George Meyer, June 23, 1906, RG 59, M77-Diplomatic Instructions of the Department of State, 1801–1906, Roll 140 [Image 411], USNA.

144. Elihu Root to TR, June 23, 1906, TRP.

145. Howe, *George Von Lengerke Meyer*, 292–293.

146. George Meyer to Elihu Root, June 27, 1906, RG 59, M35-Despatches from U.S. Ministers to Russia, 1808–1906, Reel 66 [Images 397–398], USNA; George Meyer to TR, July 11, 1906, TRP.

147. TR to Jacob Schiff, June 26, 1906, TRP.

148. Jacob Schiff to TR, June 27, 1906, TRP.

149. TR to Jacob Schiff, July 26, 1906, *Letters*, 5:336–337.

150. "President Acts on Russia," *New York Times*, June 28, 1906, 1.

151. "World's Outcry against Jewish Massacres Has Had Its Effect Russian Officials Warned," *Wilkes-Barre (PA) Times*, June 29, 1906, 7.

152. Official Communication on the Disorders at Bielostock, [Inclosure], FRUS (1909), 1297–1300 [doc. 408].

153. "Roused against the Duma," *New York Times*, July 10, 1906, 5.

154. Sidney S. Harcave, "The Jewish Question in the First Russian Duma," *Jewish Social Studies* 6.2 (April 1944): 164, 166, 168.

155. *AJYB* 8 (1906): 70–86; quotation appears on p. 86.

156. "General and Prince Accuse One Another," *Aberdeen (SD) Daily American*, July 10, 1906, 1.

157. See, for instance, Khiterer, "October 1905 Pogroms," 797–798, 800; Lambroza, "Pogroms of 1903–1906," 241–242.

158. Witte, *Memoirs of Counte Witte*, 327; see also p. 190.

159. TR to Nathan Bijur, July 11, 1906, TRP. For examples of Roosevelt grouping together Russian Jewry, Armenians, and the Congo Free State, see TR to Andrew Carnegie, August 6, 1906, *Letters*, 5:345; and TR to Lyman Abbott, January 3, 1907, *Letters*, 5:536.

160. TR to Nathan Bijur, July 11, 1906, TRP.

161. "New York," *Emanu-El* (San Francisco), July 20, 1906, 8–9.

162. Jacob Schiff to Israel Zangwill, July 5, 1906, in Adler, *Life and Letters*, 2:140.

163. "The Douma to the Rescue," *Emanu-El* (San Francisco), June 22, 1906, 2.

164. *AJYB* 8 (1906): 89.

165. Khiterer, "October 1905 Pogroms," 800–801.

166. "The End and a Beginning," *Hebrew Standard* (New York), July 27, 1906, 8.

167. Vice-Consul Fuchs to Chargé Eddy, [Inclosure 1], September 14, 1906, FRUS (1909), 1311 [doc. 410].

168. Jacob Schiff to Ernest Cassel, January 17, 1907, in Adler, *Life and Letters*, 2:141.

169. TR to Timothy Woodruff, October 5, 1906, TRP.

7. Appointments & Immigrants

1. "To Republicans," זשורנאל מארגען דער (*Jewish Morning Journal*) (New York), August 3, 1906, 8.

2. Untitled, *Hebrew Standard* (New York), September 21, 1906, 8.

3. For statistics on the Jewish population, see Charles M. Harvey, "What the Jew Owes to the Republican Party," *Leslie's Weekly*, September 24, 1908, 302. Half of America's Jews lived in New York City alone.

4. "Buffalo Platform Not on Hearst Lines," *New York Times*, September 27, 1906, 3.

5. "Hughes Is Choice," *Dallas Morning News*, September 27, 1906, 1.

6. Herbert Parsons to TR, October 3, 1906, TRP.

7. "Otto A. Rosalsky, Jurist, Dies at 63," *New York Times*, May 12, 1936, 23.
8. Herbert Parsons to TR, October 3, 1906, TRP.
9. TR to Herbert Parsons, October 8, 1906, TRP.
10. TR to Charles Evans Hughes, October 5, 1906, *Letters*, 5:443.
11. Herbert Parsons to TR, October 11, 1906, TRP.
12. TR to Charles Evans Hughes, October 2, 1906, *Letters*, 5:439.
13. TR to Timothy Woodruff, October 5, 1906, TRP.
14. Timothy Woodruff to TR, October 8, 1906, TRP.
15. TR to Oscar Solomon Straus, October 9, 1906, TRP.
16. Oscar Straus to TR, October 12, 1906, TRP.
17. TR to Oscar Straus, October 13, 1906, TRP.
18. "Hearst Starts Up New Hebrew Paper," *Kalamazoo (MI) Gazette*, October 20, 1906, 3.
19. "New York's Hot Campaign," *Kansas City Star*, October 11, 1906, 3.
20. "Jewish Voters Do Not Need Hearst's Help," *New York Times*, October 22, 1906, 6.
21. "Both Hearst and Hughes Ready for Whirlwind Finish," *Trenton Evening Times*, November 1, 1906, 1.
22. Naomi W. Cohen, *A Dual Heritage: The Public Career of Oscar S. Straus* (Philadelphia: Jewish Publication Society of America, 1969), 146.
23. TR to Timothy Woodruff, October 21, 1906, *Letters*, 5:461.
24. Timothy Woodruff to TR, October 22, 1906, TRP.
25. In some sense, Alexander Hamilton was likely the first Jew to sit in the cabinet in that he was probably born Jewish, and even though he did not identify as Jewish in adulthood, under Jewish law, Jewish identity is permanent—see Andrew Porwancher, *The Jewish World of Alexander Hamilton* (Princeton, NJ: Princeton University Press, 2021). Straus was undoubtedly the first professing Jew in the cabinet.
26. Oscar S. Straus, *Under Four Administrations: From Cleveland to Taft* (Boston: Houghton Mifflin, 1922), 209–211. For Straus's foreknowledge of the cabinet appointment, see Cohen, *Dual Heritage*, 146; and Oscar Straus to TR, January 4, 1912, TRP. For earlier cabinet position offers made to Jews, see "Jews in Public Life," *Washington (DC) Herald*, November 11, 1906, 6.
27. Straus, *Under Four Administrations*, 210–211.
28. TR to Oscar Straus, September 6, 1906, TRP. For Straus's interview, see "Time May Raise Station of Jew," *Cleveland Plain Dealer*, August 26, 1906, 1, 4.
29. Oscar Straus to TR, March 3, 1909, TRP.
30. TR to Lyman Abbott, May 29, 1908, TRP.
31. TR to Jacob Riis, October 28, 1906, TRP.
32. "Bright for Hughes," *Colorado Springs Gazette*, November 3, 1906, 1.
33. For Indian affairs, see TR to Oscar Straus, December 4, 1900, TRP. For labor conflicts, see Oscar Straus to TR, June 28, 1904, TRP; TR to Oscar Straus, June 30, 1904, TRP. For Caribbean relations, see Oscar Straus to TR, March 30, 1905, TRP.
34. TR to Lyman Abbott, May 29, 1908, TRP.
35. TR to Lyman Abbott, May 29, 1908, TRP. For another example of Roosevelt insisting that his hiring and promotion of Jews were unrelated to their identities, see TR to George Briggs Aiton, May 15, 1901, *Letters*, 3:78–79.

36. TR to Thomas C. Platt, December 22, 1904, *Letters*, 4:1075. For Henkel's retention of his post, see *Letters*, 4:1075n1.

37. TR to Lucius Burrie Swift, December 26, 1905, *Letters*, 5:123.

38. Oscar Straus to TR, July 8, 1918, TRP.

39. Leroy G. Dorsey and Rachel M. Harlow, "'We Want Americans Pure and Simple': Theodore Roosevelt and the Myth of Americanism," *Rhetoric and Public Affairs* 6.1 (Spring 2003): 59–60.

40. Cynthia Bansak, Nicole B. Simpson, and Madeline Zavodny, *The Economics of Immigration* (New York: Routledge, 2015), 285.

41. Rebecca Kobrin, "The 1905 Revolution Abroad: Mass Migration, Russian Jewish Liberalism, and American Jewry, 1903–1914," in *The Revolution of 1905 and Russia's Jews*, ed. Stefani Hoffman and Ezra Mendelsohn (Philadelphia: University of Pennsylvania Press, 2008), 228; Eli Lederhendler, "Democracy and Assimilation: The Jews, America, and the Russian Crisis from Kishinev to the End of World War I," in *The Revolution of 1905 and Russia's Jews*, ed. Stefani Hoffman and Ezra Mendelsohn (Philadelphia: University of Pennsylvania Press, 2008), 245; Jonathan D. Sarna, *American Judaism: A History* (New Haven, CT: Yale University Press, 2004), 153.

42. *AJYB* 3 (1901): 159; *AJYB* 12 (1910): 277.

43. George Meyer to TR, October 28, 1906, TRP.

44. *AJYB* 16 (1914): 337.

45. Sarna, *American Judaism*, 151–152.

46. Dorsey and Harlow, "'We Want Americans Pure and Simple,'" 60, 62.

47. Russell A. Kazal, *Becoming Old Stock: The Paradox of German-American Identity* (Princeton, NJ: Princeton University Press, 2004), 121; Dag Blanck, "'A Mixture of People with Different Roots': Swedish Immigrants in the American Ethno-Racial Hierarchies," *Journal of American Ethnic History* 33.3 (Spring 2014): 45, 50–51.

48. Madison Grant, *The Passing of the Great Race: or the Racial Basis of European History* (New York: Charles Scribner's, 1916), 77.

49. Edmund Morris, *Colonel Roosevelt* (New York: Random House, 2010), 705–706.

50. Eric L. Goldstein, *The Price of Whiteness: Jews, Race, and American Identity* (2006; Princeton, NJ: Princeton University Press, 2008), 42–44.

51. Judith S. Goldstein, *The Politics of Ethnic Pressure: The American Jewish Committee Fight against Immigration Restriction, 1906–1917* (New York: Garland, 1990), 77–80.

52. Roger Daniels, "Two Cheers for Immigration," in *Debating American Immigration, 1882–Present*, ed. Roger Daniels and Otis L. Graham (Lanham, MD: Rowman & Littlefield, 2001), 13–16.

53. Daniels, "Two Cheers for Immigration," 13–16.

54. Leonard Dinnerstein, *Antisemitism in America* (New York: Oxford University Press, 1994), 68.

55. Edward Alsworth Ross, "The Hebrews of Eastern Europe in America," *Century Magazine* 88.5 (September 1914): 791, 787–788.

56. Ross, "Hebrews of Eastern Europe," 787–788. For Jewish crime statistics, see Dinnerstein, *Antisemitism in America*, 72.

57. Ross, "Hebrews of Eastern Europe," 789, 786, 787.

58. Ross, "Hebrews of Eastern Europe," 791.

59. Quotation appears in Dinnerstein, *Antisemitism in America*, 74.

60. Dinnerstein, *Antisemitism in America*, 70, 71, 74.

61. See, for instance, Prescott F. Hall, *Immigration and Its Effects upon the United States* (New York: Henry Holt, 1906), 21. Another example appears to be Joseph Lee, a committed restrictionist who joined forces with the Friends of Russian Freedom organization, which supported the liberalization of Russia and whose ranks included Jewish allies of Roosevelt's such as Jacob Schiff, Lillian Wald, and Nathan Bijur—see Joseph Lee to Mr. Kennaday, February 27, 1917, Joseph Lee Papers, Massachusetts Historical Society, Boston, MA; John Higham, *Strangers in the Land: Patterns of American Nativism, 1860–1925* (New Brunswick, NJ: Rutgers University Press, 1994), 102; Frederick F. Travis, *George Kennan and the American-Russian Relationship, 1865–1924* (Athens: Ohio University Press, 1990), 205–206.

62. Goldstein, *Politics of Ethnic Pressure*, 83–84.

63. Thomas G. Dyer, *Theodore Roosevelt and the Idea of Race* (Baton Rouge: Louisiana State University Press, 1980), 28–30.

64. See, for instance, Christopher N. Matthews, "Gilded Ages and Gilded Archaeologies of American Exceptionalism," *International Journal of Historical Archaeology* 16.4 (December 2012): 720–721.

65. TR to Cecil Spring Rice, August 11, 1899, *Letters*, 2:1053.

66. TR to Albert Shaw, April 3, 1907, *Letters*, 5:638.

67. Theodore Roosevelt, *The Foes of Our Own Household* (New York: George H. Doran, 1917), 256.

68. "The Melting Pot," *Emanu-El* (San Francisco), October 29, 1909, 2.

69. Geo. Selikowitsch, "Flats and Sharps," *Reform Advocate* (Chicago), June 18, 1910, 919–920. See also William Rosenau, "The Blessing of Children," *Jewish Voice* (St. Louis), November 24, 1911, 4–5.

70. Eugenics was another reproductive matter that prompted comment from Roosevelt. Like many mainstream progressives, he supported eugenics. But any discussion of his brand of eugenics requires two caveats: first, it did not have a racial cast; second, he supported in the abstract sterilization of criminals and the "feeble-minded" but thought there was no way to implement such a program, and so Roosevelt instead stressed "getting desirable people to breed"—see Theodore Roosevelt, "Twisted Eugenics," *The Outlook* (New York), January 3, 1914, in *The Works of Theodore Roosevelt: Literary Essays* (New York: Charles Scribner's, 1924), 14:172. In Roosevelt's age, eugenics wasn't yet synonymous with antisemitism; some Jews notably promoted eugenics during the Progressive Era—see Christine Rosen, *Preaching Eugenics: Religious Leaders and the American Eugenics Movement* (New York: Oxford University Press, 2004), 107–109.

71. Gary Gerstle, *American Crucible: Race and Nation in the Twentieth Century* (Princeton, NJ: Princeton University Press, 2017), 21.

72. TR to Carl Schurz, July 13, 1895, *Letters*, 1:466.

73. William Montgomery Clemens, *The Ancestry of Theodore Roosevelt* (New York: William M. Clemens, 1914), 3.

74. TR to unidentified reporter, May 1, 1884, *Letters*, 1:67. See also Kathleen Dalton, *Theodore Roosevelt: A Strenuous Life* (New York: Alfred A. Knopf, 2002), 15.

75. Dyer, *Idea of Race*, 129.

76. TR to Robert Schauffler, February 2, 1912, TRP.

77. Theodore Roosevelt, "America for Americans," May 31, 1916, in *The Progressive Party: Its Record, from January to July, 1916* (New York: Mail and Express, [1916]), 77.

78. Dyer, *Idea of Race*, 6, 37–44.

79. Dyer, *Idea of Race*, 140, 136–137.

80. TR to Cecil Spring Rice, June 16, 1905, *Letters*, 4:1233.

81. Theodore Roosevelt, *Theodore Roosevelt: An Autobiography* (New York: Macmillan, 1913), 414–415.

82. Scholars entertain significant disagreement about the degree of diversity within his preferred melting pot. Some suggest it was limited to Northern and Western Europeans while others contend that Southern and Eastern Europeans were also welcome. Still others insist that Roosevelt's melting pot included people with no European ancestry, such as Native Americans and Blacks. In fact, TR variously supported each of those positions. For a discussion of scholars arguing that Roosevelt limited his melting pot to old immigrants, see Gerstle, *American Crucible*, 50. For a proponent of the pan-European interpretation of Roosevelt's melting pot, see Dyer, *Idea of Race*, 132. For the view that the Rooseveltian melting pot was multiracial, see Leroy G. Dorsey, *We Are All Americans, Pure and Simple: Theodore Roosevelt and the Myth of Americanism* (Tuscaloosa: University of Alabama Press, 2007), 6.

83. Theodore Roosevelt, "True Americanism," *The Forum* (April 1894), in *American Ideals: And Other Essays, Social and Political*, by Theodore Roosevelt (London: G. P. Putnam's, 1897), 26, 20, 26.

84. "President Roosevelt at the Premier Production of Zangwill's 'The Melting Pot,' " *Jewish Voice* (St. Louis), October 16, 1908, 8; "President Sees New Play," *New York Times*, October 6, 1908, 9.

85. Lederhendler, "Democracy and Assimilation," 249; Gerstle, *American Crucible*, 50–51.

86. Israel Zangwill, *The Melting-Pot* (New York: Macmillan, 1909), 198–199.

87. Barbara Cantalupo, introduction to *Other Things Being Equal*, by Emma Wolf (Detroit: Wayne State University Press, 2002), 31. Zangwill publicly insisted that his wife, while not a "racial" Jew, still had Jewish bona fides in the sense that she embodied "Jewish ideals" and had been raised in part by her Jewish stepmother—see "Zangwill Explains His Intermarriage," *Jewish Telegraphic Agency* (New York), January 29, 1924, 3.

88. Joe Kraus, "How *The Melting Pot* Stirred America: The Reception of Zangwill's Play and Theater's Role in the American Assimilation Experience," *MELUS* 24.3 (Fall 1999): 3.

89. "Our New York Weekly Bulletin," *Reform Advocate* (Chicago), May 22, 1909, 422.

90. "Dr. Harrison Preaches a Jewish Sermon before the Free Synagogue in New York," *Jewish Voice* (St. Louis), May 21, 1909, 39.

91. In addition to the above-cited *Reform Advocate* and *Jewish Voice*, Philadelphia's *Jewish Exponent* also reported on Harrison's sermon.

92. Judah L. Magnes, "The Melting Pot," October 9, 1909, in *Dissenter in Zion: From the Writings of Judah L. Magnes*, ed. Arthur A. Goren (Cambridge, MA: Harvard University Press, 1982), 101–106.

93. Harry Weiss, "The Maccabean Spirit Contrasted with That of Zangwill's Melting Pot," *Hebrew Standard* (New York), December 30, 1910, 3.

94. "The Melting Pot," *Jewish Voice* (St. Louis), April 2, 1909, 3.

95. "More Truth Than Poetry," *Hebrew Standard* (New York), November 20, 1908, 8.

96. "President Shouts Praise for Play," *Trenton Evening Times*, October 7, 1908, 2.

97. "Roosevelt Criticises Play," *New York Times*, October 10, 1908, 9; "Objects to a Zangwill Line," *Kansas City Star*, October 9, 1908, 1.

98. Israel Zangwill to TR, October 14, 1908, TRP.

99. TR to Israel Zangwill, October 15, 1908, TRP.

100. Israel Zangwill to TR, November 14, 1912, TRP.

101. TR to Israel Zangwill, November 27, 1912, TRP.

102. Elmer Ellis, *Mr. Dooley's America: A Life of Finley Peter Dunne* (New York: Knopf, 1941), 153–154.

103. TR to Jacob Schiff, November 16, 1905, TRP.

104. TR to Stephen Wise, December 17, 1908, TRP.

105. Roosevelt, "True Americanism," 27, 30.

106. Theodore Roosevelt, "How Not to Better Social Conditions," *Review of Reviews* 15.1 (January 1897): 39.

107. Naomi W. Cohen, "Commissioner Williams and the Jews," *American Jewish Archives Journal* 61.2 (2009): 99–100.

108. TR to William Williams, January 23, 1903, *Letters*, 3:411.

109. TR to William Williams, January 23, 1903, *Letters*, 3:411–412.

110. Williams responded defensively to Roosevelt, suggesting that the criticisms leveled against him were without merit and reflected ulterior motives—see Cohen, "Commissioner Williams and the Jews," 100.

111. "President Starts Ellis Island Inquiry," *New York Times*, September 17, 1903, 1.

112. "President Starts Ellis Island Inquiry," *New York Times*, September 17, 1903, 1; "Roosevelt in Peril," *New-York Tribune*, September 17, 1903, 1, 3.

113. TR to Ralph Trautmann, November 28, 1903, TRP. Note that Roosevelt quoted the newspaper article in the postscript of the foregoing letter.

114. "Ellis Island Report In," *New-York Tribune*, February 29, 1904, 3.

115. Hans P. Vought, *The Bully Pulpit and the Melting Pot: American Presidents and the Immigrant, 1897–1933* (Macon, GA: Mercer University Press, 2004), 44.

116. Goldstein, *Politics of Ethnic Pressure*, 70, 73.

117. Goldstein, *Politics of Ethnic Pressure*, 69, 79–80, 88, 92, 95.

118. Goldstein, *Politics of Ethnic Pressure*, 102–103, 125; quotation appears on p. 103.

119. Straus's written plea to the president was passed via TR's private secretary—see William Loeb to Oscar Straus, May 29, 1906, Box 4, OSP.

120. Oscar Straus to Cyrus Sulzberger, June 14, 1906, Box 4, OSP.

121. Oscar Straus to James Gibbons, June 4, 1906, Box 4, OSP.

122. James Gibbons to TR, June 7, 1906, TRP.

123. Goldstein, *Politics of Ethnic Pressure*, 105.

124. "Oppose Restriction," *New-York Tribune*, June 5, 1906, 2.

125. "The Immigration Bill," *Hebrew Standard* (New York), June 15, 1906, 4.
126. Goldstein, *Politics of Ethnic Pressure*, 93–94.
127. TR to Joseph Cannon, May 27, 1906, *Letters*, 5:285.
128. TR to Joseph Cannon, June 13, 1906, TRP.
129. TR to Joseph Cannon, June 13, 1906, TRP.
130. Robert F. Zeidel, "Hayseed Immigration Policy: 'Uncle Joe' Cannon and the Immigration Question," *Illinois Historical Journal* 88.3 (Autumn 1995): 173–174.
131. Goldstein, *Politics of Ethnic Pressure*, 94.
132. Vought, *Bully Pulpit and the Melting Pot*, 55.
133. Zeidel, "Hayseed Immigration Policy," 183.
134. Zeidel, "Hayseed Immigration Policy," 183–184.
135. See, for instance, "Message of the President," December 3, 1901, FRUS (1902), xx–xxi; "Message of the President," December 7, 1903, FRUS (1904), xii; "Message of the President," December 5, 1905, FRUS (1906), xlvi–xlvii.
136. "Annual," December 3, 1906, FRUS (1909), xl–xli.
137. "Naming of Straus for the Cabinet Causes a Howl," *Trenton Evening Times*, October 24, 1906, 1.
138. "Editorial Notes," *Reform Advocate* (Chicago), October 27, 1906, 301. For other favorable commentary in the Jewish press on Straus's appointment, see "The City," *Jewish Voice* (St. Louis), October 26, 1906, 3.
139. "Warning to Russia," *Cleveland Plain Dealer*, October 25, 1906, 4.
140. "Editorial Notes," *Reform Advocate* (Chicago), October 27, 1906, 302.
141. For the electoral benefits with Jewish voters, see "Predictions Now in Order," *Daily Picayune* (New Orleans), October 25, 1906, 1. For the electoral benefits with Democrats, see "Naming of Straus for the Cabinet Causes a Howl," *Trenton Evening Times*, October 24, 1906, 1.
142. Naomi W. Cohen, "Antisemitism in the Gilded Age: The Jewish View," *Jewish Social Studies* 41.3/41.4 (Summer–Autumn 1979): 188.
143. Oscar Straus to TR, October 25, 1906, TRP.
144. TR to Oscar Straus, October 26, 1906, TRP.
145. Cohen, *Dual Heritage*, 151, 154; Straus, *Under Four Administrations*, 213; quotation appears in latter source on p. 216.
146. Cohen, *Dual Heritage*, 154–155; Straus, *Under Four Administrations*, 216–217; quotations appear in the former source.
147. Erika Lee, *America for Americans: A History of Xenophobia in the United States* (New York: Basic Books, 2019), 118–120.
148. Hall, *Immigration and Its Effects*, 51.
149. Prescott F. Hall, "The Recent History of Immigration Restriction," *Journal of Political Economy* 21.8 (October 1913): 737.
150. TR to Prescott Farnsworth Hall, June 24, 1908, *Letters*, 6:1096–1097.
151. Henry Cabot Lodge to TR, July 26, 1908, in *Selections from the Correspondence of Theodore Roosevelt and Henry Cabot Lodge, 1884–1918* (New York: Charles Scribner's Sons, 1925), 2:306.

152. Henry Cabot Lodge to TR, July 26, 1908, in *Selections*, 2:306. For details on the "poor physique" standard, see Douglas C. Baynton, "Defectives in the Land: Disability and American Immigration Policy, 1882–1924," *Journal of American Ethnic History* 24.3 (Spring 2005): 35.

153. TR to Henry Cabot Lodge, August 8, 1908, *Letters*, 6:1160.

8. Election Year

1. TR to Arthur Hamilton Lee, February 2, 1908, *Letters*, 6:918; see 918n for context.

2. Doris Kearns Goodwin, *The Bully Pulpit: Theodore Roosevelt, William Howard Taft, and the Golden Age of Journalism* (New York: Simon & Schuster, 2013), 535–536. For most of Roosevelt's second term, it was widely and correctly understood that Taft was Roosevelt's preferred successor—see Edmund Morris, *Theodore Rex* (New York: Modern Library, 2001), 379, 458.

3. Cyrus Adler and Aaron M. Margalith, *With Firmness in the Right: American Diplomatic Action Affecting Jews, 1840–1945* (New York: American Jewish Committee, 1946), 278–279. The circular was promulgated on May 28, 1907, but didn't come to the attention of Jewish leaders for many months. The State Department prohibition on issuing passports would not apply to those rare instances when Russia consented in advance to an American Jew's admission.

4. Adler and Margalith, *With Firmness in the Right*, 279.

5. Naomi W. Cohen, *A Dual Heritage: The Public Career of Oscar S. Straus* (Philadelphia: Jewish Publication Society of America, 1969), 137–139.

6. Deborah Dash Moore, *B'nai B'rith and the Challenge of Ethnic Leadership* (Albany: State University of New York Press, 1981), 90–93.

7. Judith S. Goldstein, *The Politics of Ethnic Pressure: The American Jewish Committee Fight against Immigration Restriction, 1906–1917* (New York: Garland, 1990), 53, 57.

8. Louis Marshall and Edward Lauterbach to Elihu Root, February 1, 1908, *AJYB* 13 (1911): 24.

9. Cohen, *Dual Heritage*, 172–173.

10. *AJYB* 13 (1911): 25.

11. "Czar's Duplicity in U.S. Passports," *Augusta (GA) Chronicle*, February 12, 1908, 2.

12. Louis Marshall and Edward Lauterbach to Elihu Root, February 13, 1908, *AJYB* 13 (1911): 25–27.

13. *AJYB* 10 (1908): 254.

14. Naomi W. Cohen, "The Abrogation of the Russo-American Treaty of 1832," *Jewish Social Studies* 25.1 (January 1963): 7.

15. James G. Blaine to James Russell Lowell, November 22, 1881, in Adler and Margalith, *With Firmness in the Right*, 206.

16. Jacob Schiff to Paul Nathan, August 12, 1904, quoted in Cohen, "Russo-American Treaty," 7–8.

17. Jacob Schiff to TR, July 31, 1904, TRP.

18. Mayer Sulzberger to TR, May 18, 1908, *AJYB* 13 (1911): 28–33.

19. Mayer Sulzberger to TR, May 18, 1908, *AJYB* 13 (1911): 31.

20. Elihu Root to Mayer Sulzberger, June 4, 1908, *AJYB* 13 (1911): 33.

21. Besides Root's foregoing letter, "no further response was received from the Department of State or President Roosevelt to indicate that the matter was receiving due and proper consideration"—see *AJYB* 13 (1911): 37.

22. TR to Elihu Root, July 2, 1908, *Letters*, 6:1104.

23. *AJYB* 13 (1911): 37–38. The Democratic platform did expressly signal amenability to treaty revision but didn't endorse one-sided abrogation. Meanwhile, the Republican platform opted not to mention treaty revision at all, instead pledging in broad language that the party would undertake "all proper efforts" to secure American rights abroad.

24. *AJYB* 13 (1911): 82. See also "Taft Is Notified; Cincinnati Joyful," *New York Times*, July 29, 1908, 1, 3; "Taft Will Advance on Roosevelt Lines," *New York Times*, July 29, 1908, 4.

25. Herman Bernstein, "The Part Played by Roosevelt in the Portsmouth Treaty of Peace," *New York Times*, August 23, 1908, SM1–SM2. For additional coverage in America, see "Russian View of Portsmouth Treaty," *Springfield (MA) Daily Republican*, August 25, 1908, 6. For the initial appearance of the report in a Russian magazine, see Charles M. Harvey, "What the Jew Owes to the Republican Party," *Leslie's Weekly*, September 24, 1908, 302.

26. "The Plain Truth," *Leslie's Weekly*, August 13, 1908, 146.

27. TR to John A. Sleicher, August 8, 1908, TRP. Note that the article in question appeared in *Leslie's Weekly* five days after Roosevelt sent this letter; either Sleicher gave Roosevelt an advance copy or the publication date on the masthead of that issue is not a precise indication of its contemporaneous public availability.

28. Harvey, "What the Jew Owes to the Republican Party," 302.

29. TR to William Howard Taft, September 14, 1908, TRP.

30. TR to John Sleicher, October 12, 1908, TRP.

31. Frederick C. Giffin, "The Pouren Extradition Case," *Social Science* 56.2 (Spring 1981): 88; "Audience Goes Wild in Patriot's Defense," *New York Times*, September 12, 1908, 7.

32. "Jan Pouren's Case," *Augusta (GA) Chronicle*, October 4, 1908, 18.

33. "A Prisoner for Russia," *The Sun* (New York), August 15, 1908, 3; "Head of Red Hand Caught in New York," *Meriden (CT) Daily Journal*, January 9, 1908, 2.

34. "Jan Pouren's Case," *Augusta (GA) Chronicle*, October 4, 1908, 18. See also "Ask Mercy for Russian," *Alaska Daily Record* (Juneau), August 26, 1908, 3; "Treaty with Russia," *Montgomery (AL) Advertiser*, October 22, 1908, 13.

35. "Revolutionist Is Ordered Deported," *Fort Worth Star-Telegram*, August 24, 1908, 7.

36. Giffin, "Pouren Extradition Case," 89.

37. "Shall We Return the Fugitive to the Torture Chamber?" *The Outlook* (New York), September 5, 1908, 2.

38. TR to Elihu Root, September 5, 1908, *Letters*, 6:1207. On the migration of "Russian revolutionary socialism" to America, see Eli Lederhendler, "Democracy and Assimilation: The Jews, America, and the Russian Crisis from Kishinev to the End of World War I," in *The Revolution of 1905 and Russia's Jews*, ed. Stefani Hoffman and Ezra Mendelsohn (Philadelphia: University of Pennsylvania Press, 2008), 246.

39. "Audience Goes Wild in Patriot's Defense," *New York Times*, September 12, 1908, 7.

40. "Audience Goes Wild in Patriot's Defense," *New York Times*, September 12, 1908, 7.

41. Giffin, "Pouren Extradition Case," 89.

42. Although Littauer's letter isn't extant, two other surviving letters from Roosevelt, taken in tandem, demonstrate that Littauer wrote the president about Pouren—see TR to Lucius N. Littauer, September 25, 1908, TRP; and TR to Elihu Root, September 25, 1908, *Letters*, 6:1256.

43. Lillian D. Wald, *The House on Henry Street* (New York: Henry Holt, 1915), 236–237. For Roosevelt's early acquaintance with Wald, see Kathleen Dalton, *Theodore Roosevelt: A Strenuous Life* (New York: Alfred A. Knopf, 2002), 151.

44. Katherine Unterman, *Uncle Sam's Policemen: The Pursuit of Fugitives across Borders* (Cambridge, MA: Harvard University Press, 2015), 175–176.

45. *Springfield (MA) Daily Republican* reprinted in "Political Dynamite in This," *Pawtucket (RI) Times*, September 26, 1908, 6.

46. TR to Elihu Root, September 25, 1908, *Letters*, 6:1256.

47. TR to Elihu Root, September 25, 1908, *Letters*, 6:1256.

48. Giffin, "Pouren Extradition Case," 90.

49. TR to Elihu Root, October 6, 1908, *Letters*, 6:1276.

50. Elihu Root to B. Kroupensky, October 7, 1908, FRUS (1914), 515 [doc. 481].

51. Schiff quotations appear in Giffin, "Pouren Extradition Case," 90. For the petitions, see "Jan Pouren's Case Reopened by Root," *New York Times*, October 22, 1908, 5; Giffin, "Pouren Extradition Case," 93n8.

52. Untitled, *Hebrew Standard* (New York), October 9, 1908, 8.

53. Memorandum, [Inclosure], October 11, 1908, FRUS (1914), 516 [doc. 482].

54. Quotation appears in Giffin, "Pouren Extradition Case," 90.

55. TR to Elihu Root, October 14, 1908, TRP; TR to Elihu Root, October 19, 1908, TRP.

56. Elihu Root to B. Kroupensky, October 23, 1908, FRUS (1914), 517–518 [doc. 484].

57. B. Kroupensky to Elihu Root, October 24, 1908, FRUS (1914), 518 [doc. 485].

58. "Free for a Minute," *Grand Rapids (MI) Press*, October 27, 1908, 2.

59. Giffin, "Pouren Extradition Case," 92.

60. "70,000 Protest against Giving Victim to Russia," *Fort Worth Telegram*, October 25, 1908, 3.

61. Untitled, *Hebrew Standard* (New York), October 30, 1908, 8.

62. Elihu Root to Jacob Schiff, October 18, 1908, *AJYB* 13 (1911): 40–41.

63. "Root Outlines Attitude," *Idaho Daily Statesman* (Boise), October 22, 1908, 1; "New Treaty Is Favored to Protect Americans," *Dallas Morning News*, October 22, 1908, 2; "For New Treaty with Russia," *New York Times*, October 22, 1908, 5.

64. "Taft in Brooklyn Tackles Gompers," *New York Times*, October 27, 1908, 3. Other sources have Taft's wording different in form, albeit it the same in substance—see *AJYB* 13 (1911): 41; Louis Marshall, "Russia and the American Passport," *The Maccabean* 20.2 (February 1911): 63.

65. "Taft on Hurry-Up Tour of the City," *New York Times*, October 29, 1908, 2.

66. *AJYB* 13 (1911): 41.

67. "Happenings in the Jewish World," *Hebrew Standard* (New York), June 19, 1908, 4. Although this paper reported that Bryan recommended Nathan Krass as a chaplain, in fact a different rabbi, Samuel Koch, served in that capacity. The RNC also had a Jewish chaplain, but it doesn't appear that Taft was personally credited for the presence of that rabbi—see reference to Tobias Schanfarber in "National Committee Nearly Completed," *Philadelphia Inquirer*, June 16, 1908, 4.

68. "Our Exchanges," *Jewish Voice* (St. Louis), October 23, 1908, 4; "Bryan Would Protect Jews," *New York Times*, October 17, 1908, 3.

69. Edward Berenson, *The Accusation: Blood Libel in an American Town* (New York: W. W. Norton, 2019), 122.

70. "Jewbaiter Is for Bryan," *The Sun* (New York), September 16, 1896, 3.

71. For a defense of Bryan, see James Ledbetter, "Has the Famous Populist 'Cross of Gold' Speech Been Unfairly Tarred by Anti-Semitism?," *JSTOR Daily*, July 6, 2016.

72. "Jewbaiter Is for Bryan," *The Sun* (New York), September 16, 1896, 3.

73. William J. Bryan, *The First Battle: A Story of the Campaign of 1896* (Chicago: W. B. Conkey, 1896), 581.

74. William Howard Taft to TR, November 7, 1908, TRP.

75. This book evaluated Taft's performance with Lower East Side Jews in the 1908 election by aggregating vote counts in overwhelmingly Jewish election districts (EDs) on the Lower East Side. To avoid confounding factors, this analysis excluded Lower East Side EDs that had meaningful numbers of non-Jews even when those EDs were majority Jewish. Overwhelmingly Jewish EDs were determined by cross-referencing a 1910 map of residents (found in Gergely Baics, Wright Kennedy, Rebecca Kobrin, Laura Kurgan, Leah Meisterlin, Dan Miller, and Mae Ngai, *Mapping Historical New York: A Digital Atlas* [New York, NY: Columbia University, 2021], https://mappinghny.com) with the ED boundaries and corresponding vote counts found in *The City Record: Official Journal for the City of New York*—see November 2, 1908, for ED boundaries and December 31, 1908, for vote counts. The 1910 map shows residents by national origin rather than religion, but Russian immigrants on the Lower East Side were Jewish to such an extent that Russian birth serves as an effective marker of Jewish identity. Note that assembly districts comprised election districts. The claim about Taft's twenty-five-point loss in the sixteenth assembly district refers only to the share among voters who cast ballots for either major party.

76. See, for instance, "Mr. Taft's Religion," *Charlotte Observer*, July 28, 1908, 10.

77. William Howard Taft to TR, August 16, 1908, TRP.

78. "The National Election," *Emanu-El* (San Francisco), September 11, 1908, 3–4.

79. Untitled, *Hebrew Standard* (New York), September 11, 1908, 8.

80. TR to William Howard Taft, October 12, 1908, TRP.

81. Edgar Albert Hornig, "The Religious Issue in the Taft-Bryan Duel of 1908," *Proceedings of the American Philosophical Society* 105.6 (December 15, 1961): 532.

82. TR to J. C. Martin, November 6, 1908, *Letters*, 6:1333–1334. Note that the quotations from Martin's letter appear in Roosevelt's reply.

83. TR to J. C. Martin, November 6, 1908, *Letters*, 6:1335.

84. "Religion of Taft Text for Remarks by the President," *Anaconda (MT) Standard*, November 9, 1908, 1; "Mr. Taft's Religious Belief Is Purely His Own Concern," *Augusta (GA) Chronicle*, November 9, 1908, 1.

85. "The City," *Jewish Voice* (St. Louis), November 20, 1908, 3.

86. Montague N. A. Cohen, "Editorial Comment," *Emanu-El* (San Francisco), November 27, 1908, 3.

87. Reprinted in "Our Exchanges," *Jewish Voice* (St. Louis), December 18, 1908, 4.

88. "Jewish Sabbath Association to President Roosevelt," *Hebrew Standard* (New York), December 4, 1908, 3.

89. Simon Wolf to TR, November 9, 1908, in Simon Wolf, *The Presidents I Have Known from 1860–1918*, 2nd ed. (Washington, DC: Byron S. Adams, 1918), 284.

90. "Ride to the Capitol," *New York Times*, March 5, 1909, 1.

91. "Ride to the Capitol," *New York Times*, March 5, 1909, 1.

92. "Taft Is Sworn in Senate Hall," *New York Times*, March 5, 1909, 1.

93. "Roosevelt Says Good-Bye," *New York Times*, March 5, 1909, 3.

94. Montague N. A. Cohen, "Editorial Comment," *Emanu-El* (San Francisco), March 5, 1909, 4.

Epilogue

1. I am at work on such a book.

2. Edmund Morris, *Colonel Roosevelt* (New York: Random House, 2010), 551–552; H. W. Brands, *T. R.: The Last Romantic* (New York: Basic Books, 1997), 810–811; quotation appears in latter source.

3. Morris, *Colonel Roosevelt*, 553.

4. Quotation appears in Daniel Okrent, *The Guarded Gate: Bigotry, Eugenics, and the Law That Kept Two Generations of Jews, Italians, and Other European Immigrants Out of America* (New York: Scribner, 2019), 231.

5. Oscar S. Straus, *Under Four Administrations: From Cleveland to Taft* (Boston: Houghton Mifflin, 1922), 394; Morris, *Colonel Roosevelt*, 553, 556, 555, 557.

6. TR gave a speech entitled "The Strenuous Life" in Chicago in 1899—see Theodore Roosevelt, *The Strenuous Life: Essays and Addresses* (New York: Century, 1902), 1–21.

7. Morris, *Colonel Roosevelt*, 556, 553, 559.

8. Quotation appears in Frederick S. Wood, *Roosevelt as We Knew Him: The Personal Recollections of One Hundred and Fifty of His Friends and Associates* (Philadelphia: John C. Winston, 1927), 380.

9. William W. Blood, *Apostle of Reason: A Biography of Joseph Krauskopf* (Philadelphia: Dorrance, 1973), 243.

10. "J. W. B. Roosevelt Memorial Services," *The Sentinel* (Chicago), January 31, 1919, 10.

11. Bill Bleyer, *Sagamore Hill: Theodore Roosevelt's Summer White House* (Charleston, SC: History Press, 2016), 129, 70–71; quotation appears on p. 71. See also David H. Wallace, *Sagamore Hill: Sagamore Hill National Historic Site, Oyster Bay, New York* (Harpers Ferry, WV: Harpers Ferry Center, National Park Service, U.S. Department of Interior, 1989), 1:51–52.

12. Charles Hanson Towne and Daniel Henderson, "The Fighting Roosevelts," *Pittsburgh Press*, January 28, 1919, 18; *Roosevelt Night, Middlesex Club, Boston, October 27, 1921* ([Boston]: Middlesex Club, 1922), 5.

INDEX

Abbott, Lyman, 189, 227
Abend-Post, 224
Aberdeen Daily News, 172
Adams, Brooks, 46
Adams, Henry, 40–41, 46, 62, 63, 72
Addams, Jane, 93
Ahlwardt, Hermann, 43–46, 66, 274
Aleichem, Sholem, 37, 179–180
Alexander II, Czar, 23
Algeciras Conference, 190–192, 202–205, 220
Alliance Israélite Universelle, 67, 75, 191, 202–203, 205
American Baptist Missionary Union, 98
American Civil War, 48, 49, 124, 267
American Federation of Labor, 246, 266
American Hebrew, 78–79
American Hero Club, 37
American Jewish Committee (AJC), 256–261, 272
anarchism, 24
antisemitism, 2; Hermann Ahlwardt and, 43–46, 274; American, 7–8, 40–43; Christian teachings and, 42–43; Dreyfus affair and, 61–63; expressed by Roosevelt in private, 46, 48–49, 255; among farmers, 41–42; Gentile, 40–43; industrial capitalism and, 42; in Kishinev, 89–90; old vs. new immigrants and, 230–232; among other urban immigrants, 42; in Romania, 10–11, 67–84; Edward A. Ross and, 232–233; in Russia (*see* Russia)
Arakantzeff, M. P., 217

Arthur, Chester, 153, 259–260
Augusta Chronicle, 170

bathhouses, 18–19
Bernhardt, Sarah, 199
Bessarabetz, 90, 121
Bialystok pogrom, 209–220; American reaction to, 210–216
Bijur, Nathan, 139, 141–143, 218, 225, 244
Black Americans, lynchings of, 50, 96, 123–125, 152, 153, 154, 165, 214
Black Hundreds, 179–180, 182, 209
Black servicemen, 55
Blaine Club, 57
Blaustein, David, 266
B'nai B'rith, 142, 233, 257; Kishinev and, 98–108, 113–121
B'nai B'rith Messenger, 151, 284
Boston Evening Journal, 58
Boston Globe, 165
Boston Herald, 41
Brownsville affair, 55
Bryan, William Jennings, 64, 273–274, 275
Buffalo Soldiers, 55
Bull Moose Party, 281

Cannon, Joseph, 248–250, 283
Carnegie, Andrew, 187
Cassini, Arthur, 93, 98–99, 103–108, 145–146, 205
Cassini, Marguerite, 99
Century Magazine, 232
Chatham Square Library, 22

Chinese Exclusion Act of 1882, 232
Civil Service Commission, 25
Cleveland, Grover, 97, 127, 153, 193, 226, 246
Cleveland Plain Dealer, 155, 170, 171, 173, 226, 251
Cohen, William, 65, 131, 135
Collier, Price, 19
Colorado Springs Gazette, 170
conspicuous gallantry, 31
Cooper Union, 45, 266
Cortelyou, George, 141, 142–143
cowboy diplomacy, 5–6, 174
Cuba, 47–50; Rough Riders in, 52–55

Daily News, 224
Dallas Morning News, 153, 272
Darrow, Clarence, 93
Democratic Party: condemnation of pogroms and Roosevelt's actions, 218–219; Passport Question and, 135–136; Romanian Note and, 84–85
Destruction of Kishinev, The, 93
Dreyfus, Alfred, 61–63
Dreyfus Affair, 61–63
Duluth News-Tribune, 145

Educational Alliance, 37, 128
Einstein, Lewis, 202–203, 204
Ellis Island, 9, 10, 243–246, 252
Emanu-El, 54, 198–199, 275, 277, 278–279
Emanu-El fundraiser, 185–186
epidemics, 21
Evening News, 79
Evening Sun, 35
Evening World-Herald, 183
extradition issue, 260–261, 264 271

Falker, Etta, 60
Federation of Jewish Organizations, 247
Ferber, Edna, 284
First Volunteer Cavalry. *See* Rough Riders
Fischer, Israel, 61
Fleischer, Charles, 188
Fort Worth Telegram, 271

Forum, The, 238
France, 48, 61–63, 72, 167, 191, 235
Frank, Leo, 234

Germany, 38, 43, 72, 81–82, 167, 191, 246, 250
Gibbons, James, 247
Goldberg, Sam, 53
Goldfogle, Henry, 128–130, 136, 141, 143, 149, 150, 153, 159–160, 200
governor of New York, Roosevelt as, 58–65; appointment of Jews under, 60–61; sweatshops during Roosevelt's tenure as, 58–60
Grant, Madison, 231
Grant, Ulysses S., 226
Greenschopin, Mordecai, 91
Greenwald, Sam, 52–53, 56, 66

Hall, Prescott, 253
Harper's Weekly, 55
Harrison, Leon, 239
Harvard Club, 7
Harvey, Charles, 263–264
Hay, John, 62, 72–73, 87, 139, 145, 146; death of, 159–160; Kishinev Jews and, 92, 94, 96, 98–99, 101–108, 110–119, 121, 122; Passport Question and, 128, 129, 134, 141–142, 143; Romanian Note and, 75–78, 83, 84, 86; Russo-Japanese War and, 157
health and disease among Lower East Side Jews, 21
Hearst, William Randolph, 224–225
Hebrew Standard, 60, 79, 120, 151, 171, 187, 222, 275, 277; on death of Roosevelt, 284; Democratic-leaning column in, 148–149; on *The Melting Pot*, 240; on the Pouren case, 269, 271; viewpoint on Roosevelt's alleged culpability for pogroms, 200–201
Henkel, William, 228–229
Henry Street Settlement, 37, 39
Hirschberg, Judge, 61
Howe, Julia Ward, 267
Howells, William Dean, 39

How the Other Half Lives, 16, 17, 35
Hughes, Charles Evans, 223–224, 225, 227

Idaho Daily Statesman, 63, 171, 272
identity politics, 12–13, 139, 147–148
Immigration Restriction League, 41, 231, 246, 250, 253, 254
industrial capitalism and antisemitism, 40, 42
Isaacs, Meyer, 57
Izvolsky, Count, 214–215

Jackson, John, 87–88
James, Henry, 16
Japan, 110, 122–123, 143–145, 154, 163, 211, 237–238, 250; Roosevelt's efforts at peacemaking between Russia and, 156–159, 170, 173–174, 186, 200. *See also* Witte, Sergei
Jewish American, 104, 120
Jewish Americans: in administrations of Roosevelt, 60–61, 226–229 (*see also* Straus, Oscar); assimilation by, 41; celebration of 250th anniversary of life in America, 193–194; concern over 1905 pogroms of Russian Jews, 183, 185–190, 194–201; contributions to Roosevelt's foreign policy, 6; education of, 22; elite, Gentile paranoia about, 40–43; extradition issue and, 264–271; health of, 21; housing conditions of, 19–21; identity politics and, 12–13, 139, 147–148; integration into American life, 13–14; literacy test for immigrants and, 10, 246–250; living in the Lower East Side, 16–25; newspaper coverage of Roosevelt during reelection campaign and, 147–149; Orthodox community of, 223–224; Passport Question and (*see* Passport Question); religious lives of, 24–25; response to the Romanian Note, 82–84; from Romania, 76–78; Roosevelt's deep history with, 2–3; Roosevelt's nomination for reelection and, 136–139, 140–143; Roosevelt's views on race and, 234–238; Elihu Root's concern with protests by, 189–190; in the Rough Riders, 51–54, 66; settlement house movement and, 36–38, 39; strained relationship with Roosevelt due to noninterference, 220; support for Roosevelt's response to Russia, 5; voting for Roosevelt, 11, 150; working in the New York Police Department, 31–34
Jewish Exponent, 277
Jewish Independent, 273
Jewish Messenger, 42–43
Jewish Morning Journal, 222, 224
Jewish Voice, 136, 273
Josephus, 64

Kansas City Star, 283
Kennan, George, 121
Kishinev Jews, 89–90; American public pressure regarding, 96–98; B'nai B'rith and, 98–105, 108, 118, 120–121; consequences of violence against, 121–125; Kishinev Petition regarding, 99, 101–102, 105–111, 113–121, 125, 130, 132, 152, 159, 166, 279; Manchuria and, 110; meeting at Oyster Bay to discuss, 113–117; Passport Question and, 129; pogrom against, 90–92, 121–122, 180, 183; press reports of violence against, 92–94, 97; Roosevelt's diplomatic actions regarding, 104–117; Russian response to violence against, 93, 98–99, 103–105, 107–117
Know-Nothing Party, 251
Korea, 110, 143
Kovalevsky, Maksim, 262–263
Kraus, Adolf, 160–161, 171, 177
Krauskopf, Joseph, 54, 85–86, 284
Kroupensky, Basile, 269–270

Lamarck, Jean-Baptiste, 237
Lamsdorff, Count, 145
Lauterbach, Edward, 247–248, 257–259
Lebowich, Joseph, 147–148
Leslie's Weekly, 262–263
Levi, Leo, 99, 101, 102, 105, 109, 113–116, 118, 121
Lewisohn, Adolph, 161

literacy test for immigrants, 10, 246–250
Littauer, Lucius, 75, 77, 84, 120, 124, 125, 243, 277; Pouren case and, 267; in Roosevelt's Jewish kitchen cabinet, 86; support for Roosevelt, 64–65
Lodge, Henry Cabot, 29–30, 31, 46, 195–196, 246, 253–254, 283
Loomis, Francis, 106–108
Los Angeles Times, 106
Low, Maurice, 255
Low, Seth, 97
Lower East Side, 16–23, 24–25; bathhouses of, 18–19; education in, 22; elevated train through, 19; fundraising for Jews overseas in, 97; health and disease in, 21; Pig Market in, 17–18; religious life in, 18, 24–25; restaurants of, 18; settlement house movement and, 36–38; sweatshops of, 20, 58–60; tenements of, 19–21
lynchings, American, 50, 96, 123–125, 152, 153, 154, 165, 214

Maccabees, the: historical account of, 33; Jewish children and, 242; Jewish policemen described as, 33–34
Magnes, Judas, 240
Manchuria, 110–111, 122–123, 143–144
Marshall, Louis, 257–259
Martin, J. C., 276
Mayer, Julius, 30
May Laws, 23
McCormick, Robert, 92, 134, 139–140, 143, 145–147, 151, 154
McKinley, William, 1, 9, 46–49, 57, 61, 63–65, 128, 150, 232
Melting Pot, The, 13, 239–241
melting pot identity of Americans, 238–242
Menorah, 12, 147
Metropolitan Magazine, 283
Meyer, George, 185, 189, 201, 205, 206, 209; Bialystok pogrom and, 213–215; skepticism about Russian situation, 195–196
Mocatta, F. D., 68

Monroe, James, 80
Monroe Doctrine, 80–81
Montagu, Samuel, 206–207, 215
Montgomery Advertiser, 183
Morning Oregonian, 145
Morning Post, 255
Morocco, 190–192, 202–205
muckraking, 35
Munsey Magazine, 31
Murray, Joe, 30

Nation, The, 265
nativism, 85, 231–232, 251, 254; Roosevelt and, 10, 103, 122, 194, 229, 236, 238, 242–243, 246, 249
Naval War of 1812, The, 47
newspapers, Yiddish, 92, 224
New York News, 104
New York Police Department: Jewish representation in, 31–34; Roosevelt's ascension to head of, 25–28; Roosevelt's work with, 28–31
New York Press, 104
New York Sun, 273–274
New York Times, 45, 58, 68, 149, 199, 216, 244; coverage of 1905 pogroms, 183; on the Kishinev Jews, 97, 106, 108, 117–118; on the Kovalevsky report, 262; on the Passport Question, 129–130, 140, 272, 273; on the Pouren case, 265, 266, 269; on the Romanian Jews, 79, 82, 85; on Roosevelt's final day as president, 278; on Roosevelt's State of the Union message, 153; on Russian treatment of American Jews, 140; on William Williams and Ellis Island, 244–245; on Sergei Witte, 166
New York Tribune, 244
Nicholas II, Czar, 3, 5, 102, 109–110, 116, 152, 160, 171, 184, 196, 201, 209, 219, 220; lack of compassion for Jews, 180, 182, 208; October Manifesto and, 177–180; Russo-Japanese War and, 157–158, 167–169
Norton, Charles Eliot, 50
Novoe Vreyma, 154

October Manifesto, 178, 179, 180, 182–185, 198, 220, 226
Orthodox community, 223–224
Outlook, The, 265

Pale of Settlement, 23–24, 89, 165, 102, 125, 180, 209, 219
Parker, Alton, 134, 137, 149
Parsons, Herbert, 223, 266, 269
Passing of the Great Race, The, 231
Passport Question, 126–128, 137–145, 147, 149, 183, 255–262, 271–273; addressed in Roosevelt's State of the Union message, 151–154; Henry Goldfogle and, 128–130; Kovalevsky report and, 262–263, party conventions in 1904 and, 130–134, 135
Philadelphia Inquirer, 96, 117, 183
Pinkos, Henry, 126–127
pogroms, 3–4, 96, 125; American media coverage of, 183, 187; Bialystok, 209–211; fundraising and advocacy for victims of, 184–190, 199–201; government responses in Russia to, 180–182; interfaith support for victims of, 187–189; in Kishinev, 90–92, 121–122, 180, 183; in response to the October Manifesto, 179–182; Russian state reports on, 216–217; Sedlits, 219–220; threat of new round of, 205–208
Popular Science, 32
Populist Party, 41–42, 46
Pouren, Jan Janoff, 264–271
Progressive Era, 26–28, 37
Protocols of the Elders of Zion, The, 121

Quarterly Review, 211
Quigg, Lemuel, 57

race, Roosevelt's views on, 234–238
Raphael, Otto, 34–35, 51, 64, 66, 286–287
Reform Advocate, 147, 153, 251
Republican Party, 11–12, 26, 28, 30–31, 46; elections of 1906 and, 222–225; Passport Question and, 130–134; Romanian Note and, 84–85; Roosevelt's campaign for governor and, 56–58
Review of Reviews, 242–243
Reynolds, James Bronson, 39
Riddle, John, 116–117
Riis, Jacob, 30, 57, 242, 244; as advisor to Governor Roosevelt, 59; on life of Jewish immigrants, 16–18, 20–21, 25, 34, 35–36
Romanian Jews, 10–11, 67–88; American press on, 78–80; American public awareness and attitudes toward, 74–75, 85–86; European press on, 80–81; migration to the United States, 76–78; response of American Jews to the Romanian Note and, 82–84; Romanian Note and, 75–87, 159
Roosevelt, Alice, 99, *100*, 113
Roosevelt, Bamie, 46
Roosevelt, Corinne, 64
Roosevelt, Theodore: Hermann Ahlwardt and, 43–46; on American identity as a melting pot, 238–242; attitudes toward Blacks, 55; becomes president in 1901, 1–2, 65, 155–156; cowboy diplomacy of, 5–6, 174; Cuba and, 47–54; death and funeral of, 283–285; Alfred Dreyfus and, 61–63; early interactions with Jews, 39–40; entry into gubernatorial politics, 56–58; extradition issue and, 264–271; final morning as president, 277–278; frustration with a Jewish newspaper, 218; as governor of New York, 58–65; as head of New York Police Department, 25–31; identity politics and, 12–13, 139, 147–148; inauguration in 1905, 155–156; inconsistent immigration policies of, 242–251; Jews appointed by, 60–61, 68, 226–229; Kishinev Jews and (*see* Kishinev Jews); lame-duck period of, 275–278; literacy test for immigrants and, 10, 246–251; lynchings addressed by, 96, 124, 152, 153; medical issues during childhood, 32–33; newspaper coverage of reelection campaign of, 147–149; 1906 elections and,

Roosevelt, Theodore (*continued*) 222–226; Nobel Peace Prize awarded to, 174; nomination for reelection, 136–139, 140–141; Passport Question and (*see* Passport Question); postpresidential assessment of, 278–279; private antisemitic remarks of, 46, 255; privileged upbringing in Gramercy Park, 35–36; progressive views of, 26–28; Protestant family history of, 1; reelection of, 150–151; repudiation of antisemitism by, 7–8; Romanian Jews and (*see* Romanian Jews); Rough Riders and (*see* Rough Riders, the); strained relationship with American Jewry during second term, 220; succeeded by William Howard Taft, 274–278; support for Jewish immigration to America, 9, 194; viewpoint on attacks on Russian Jews, 3–6; views on Jewish immigration, 9–11; views on race, 234–238

Root, Elihu, 130, 132, 184–185, 191–192, 195, 202–205, 206, 261; American Jewish Committee and, 256–259; Bialystok pogrom and, 213–215; concerns about Jewish protests, 189–190; Pouren case and, 265–271

Rosalsky, Otto, 223–224, 225

Rosen, Baron, 161, 206

Ross, Edward A., 232–233

Rough Riders, the, 2, 57; in Cuba, 50–55; Jewish Americans in, 51–54, 56, 103, 148, 286–287; Jewish press coverage of, 54; Roosevelt's fame and popularity after, 55–56; segregation of Black servicemen and, 55

Russia: addressed in Roosevelt's State of the Union message, 151–153; antisemitism in, 3–6, 10, 23–24, 89–90, 144; extradition and, 260–261, 264–271; growing insurrection in, 157–158, 182, 201–202; Manchuria and, 110–111, 122–123, 143–144; migration of Jews from, 9–10, 24; October Manifesto in, 178, 179, 180, 182–185, 198, 202, 220, 226; Pale of Settlement in, 23–24, 89, 102, 125, 165, 180, 209, 219; pogroms in (*see* pogroms); response to the Romanian Note, 81–82; Roosevelt's efforts as peacemaking between Japan and, 156–159, 173–174; treatment of American Jews visiting or living in, 126–128, 139–140, 144–145, 255–259. *See also* Kishinev Jews; Witte, Sergei

Russo-Japanese War, 143–144, 156–159; signing of peace treaty ending, 174–175; Sergei Witte and negotiations over, 160–161, 173–174

Salt Lake Telegram, 79, 110, 124

Schiff, Jacob, 70–71, 150–151, 226, 257, 271–272; communications with Sergei Witte, 183–184, 206; consulted about the Jewish vote, 221; Kishinev Jews and, 94, 120; on Moroccan Jews, 191, 202; nomination of Roosevelt for reelection and, 136–138; Passport Question and, 135, 138–139; Pouren case and, 266, 269; Romanian Jews and, 71–72, 77, 84, 86; Russo-Japanese War and, 144, 145, 161; settlement house movement and, 38, 39; on treatment of Jews in Russia, 168–169, 170, 183, 184, 186, 187, 192, 196–197, 207, 210, 212–213, 215, 219, 220, 260; 250th anniversary celebration of Jewish life in America and, 193

Schiff, Rivka, 91

Sedlits pogrom, 219–220

Seligman, Isaac Newton, 161–162, 169, 170, 171, 173, 177

settlement house movement, 36–38

Silverman, Joseph, 212

Silverman, Louis, 45

Singer, Isidor, 173

Social Gospel, 27

socialism, 24, 146, 265

Spain, 47–49, 51–53, 57–58, 102, 190, 202

Speyer, James, 137

Springfield Daily Republican, 123–124

Spring Rice, Cecil, 146, 190

St. Albans Daily Messenger, 183

Story of Kishinev: A Tragedy in Five Acts, The, 96
Straus, Oscar, 68–70, 125, 135–136, 148, 151, 200, 239, 257, 272, 276, 283; advising on and participation in the Witte summit, 161–162, 166–170, 172–173, 177; advising on the State of the Union message, 152; appointment to Roosevelt's cabinet, 226–229, 250–252; Bialystok pogrom and, 210; concern about new pogroms, 206–208; elections of 1906 and, 224–226; Kishinev Jews and, 109, 113–116, 119–120; on the literacy test for immigrants, 247; nomination of Roosevelt for reelection and, 136–137, 139, 141; Passport Question and, 130, 135–136, 139, 141–142, 258; Romanian Jews and, 68, 71–74, 77, 86; Russo-Japanese War and, 156, 158, 174; on treatment of Jews in Russia, 176, 184, 186, 197–198; work as Secretary of Commerce and Labor, 252–254
Strunsky, Anna, 124–125
Sulzberger, Mayer, 260–262
Sulzer, William, 200
sweatshops, 20, 22, 38, 58–60

Taft, William Howard, 255, 262, 263, 268, 272–278, 283
Tammany Hall, 25–27, 30–31, 149, 225, 229
Tenement House Act, 60
tenements, 19–21, 34, 38, 58–60, 249
Treat, Charles, 84
Treaty of Berlin, 67–68, 72, 74, 77
Treaty of 1832, 127, 257–260, 271
Trenton Evening Times, 251
Trepov, Dmitri, 182, 184, 209, 217
Twain, Mark, 37, 199–200

United Hebrew Societies, 243

Van Rensselaer family, 39
Vezey, H. Custis, 182, 195

Wald, Lillian, 37–39, 267, 268
Washington, Booker T., 55
Washington Post, 79, 145
Weissman, Meyer, 91
White, Henry, 191, 202–205
Wiley, Louis, 149
Williams, John Sharp, 135–136
Williams, William, 243–246
Wilson, Charles, 75, 77–78
Windsor Theater, 93
Wise, Stephen, 94–96
Witte, Sergei, 160, 165, 189, 195–196, 198, 206, 208–209, 217, 262, 263; arrival in New York, 162–163; communications with Jacob Schiff about 1905 pogroms, 183–184, 192; conclusion of activities in the U.S., 175–177; delegation from Japan meets with, 163–165; Jewish contingent meets with, 166–169; October Manifesto and, 178, 182, 198; peace negotiations led by, 169–170; press coverage of Jewish summit with, 170–173; recruited to negotiate with Russia and Japan, 160–162; return to Russia, 177–178; Roosevelt's efforts to support negotiations by, 173–174; at signing of peace treaty, 175
Wolbarst, Abraham, 56–57
Wolf, Simon, 83, 86, 195, 277; Bialystok pogrom and, 210–211; Kishinev Jews and, 92, 98, 99, 101–104, 105, 108–109, 113–115, 119–121; Passport Question and, 136, 142–143; public appeal to Roosevelt, 186; Romanian Jews and, 83–84; on the State of the Union message, 153
Wood, Leonard, 50, 52
Woodruff, Timothy, 224, 225–226

xenophobia, 74, 231–232, 235, 242, 250, 251, 253

Zangwill, Israel, 239–241
Zeitung, 81